WELLINGTON IN THE PENINSULA

WELLINGTON IN THE PENINSULA

by Jac Weller

By the same author

Wellington at Waterloo
Wellington in India
On Wellington

Greenhill Books, London
Stackpole Books, Pennsylvania

Greenhill Books

This edition of *Wellington in the Peninsula*
first published 1999 by Greenhill Books, Lionel Leventhal Limited,
Park House, 1 Russell Gardens, London NW11 9NN
and
Stackpole Books, 5067 Ritter Road, Mechanicsburg, PA 17055, USA

British Library Cataloguing in Publication Data
Weller, Jac
Wellington in the peninsula
1. Peninsular War, 1807–1814
I. Title
940.2'7

ISBN 1-85367-381-1

Library of Congress Cataloging-in-Publication Data available

Publishing History
Wellington in the Peninsula was first published in 1967 (Nicholas Vane,
London) and reprinted in 1992 by Greenhill Books exactly as the
original edition, with a new Introduction by the author. It is
reproduced now in paperback exactly as the first Greenhill edition.

Printed in Great Britain

CONTENTS

ILLUSTRATIONS

MAPS

Author's Note: These simplified battle and campaign diagrams cannot take the place of the superb maps contained in Fortescue and Oman. Those included herein are intentionally distorted and show only the topographical features of real importance in the actions of the contending armies. If they are simple and easy to comprehend, they will have served their entire purpose.

To
PROFESSOR SIR CHARLES OMAN
AND SIR JOHN FORTESCUE
*In humble acknowledgment of debt
and in appreciation of
their great talents*

INTRODUCTION

FORTY-FOUR YEARS LATER

How many men have the privilege of writing a new foreword for a book forty years old? I'm lucky and am humbly thankful. *Wellington in the Peninsula* was a relatively young man's book. My Little Wife and I have reread it carefully and know we couldn't do as well today. Sure there are mistakes. We acknowledge and apologize for these, especially to the memory of the last Colonel of the Connaught Rangers whose letter was the most flattering I ever received. He joined the Regiment during the First Zulu War and was one of its commanders during the 1914–1918 conflict. In his nineties, he wrote clear and strong, 'You didn't give the Connaughts sufficient praise for their fight at Fuentes d'Onoro.'

We have just reread what I said about the battle. 'The Wild Irishmen of the Connaught Rangers used their bayonets with considerable effect. A party of over 100 French grenadiers were cut off in a cul-de-sac and killed almost to a man by the 1/88th.' If I didn't say enough, I'm sorry. But it's near impossible to be as 'fair' to all those wonderful British regiments who fought so well. We are just glad that men like they were once lived in Britain, and maybe still do! They did well in the Falkland Islands.

My second bad mistake has been called to my attention by several learned Englishmen as well as British soldiers. In praising Wellington, I neglected the fact that 'Marlborough didn't ever lose a battle either!' Frankly, we didn't know enough about John Churchill, First Duke of Marlborough, in 1960. We had studied and walked over the site of Ramallies and Malplaquet, and tried to see Oudenarde, but had not been close to Blenheim (Blindheim), due to customs regulations and a car rented in London in 1953. But the Wellers followed the route of the Scarlet Caterpillar to the Danube and saw Blenheim exhaustively in October and November 1990. John Churchill was old for top field command in 1704 (fifty-four) and lacked many advantages that accrue to men who have unified commands and proper logistics support, but he was truly an able captain and never lost. If the battle of Blenheim could be slipped into Marlborough's record at the end, rather than at almost its beginning, the comparison of the two great English commanders would be closer. Those Prussians had little to do with Wellington winning Waterloo, but they sure came in handy in making the Duke's victory total.

Early on, I played and coached American football. Coaches on their blackboards always attack from the south against a defence in the north. This is especially true if you were born in Georgia. The finished battle diagrams in *Wellington in the Peninsula* are not entirely mine, but the sketches from which the diagrams were made are. Sorry, but you must get used to fighting south-to-north.

Lionel Leventhal has asked us – My Little Wife and me since we now write jointly in name as well as fact – to explain how we came to write *Wellington in the Peninsula* before *Wellington at Waterloo* and *Wellington in India*. Simple! My NATO and Smallarms writing took us to Spain and Portugal. We carried with us Oman and Fortescue and wrote an article 'In Wellington's Peninsular Footstep'. A publisher saw it and offered a contract for a book, so there was a book.

We did enjoy those two countries and the people of the countryside. We were young and vigorous ourselves then, but our Spanish was spoken mostly without verbs. Flamencos in Madrid are fine even today, but polished. We spent one night in a Spanish village below Maya where the pipers of the 92nd Highlanders played before the Argylls marched into immortality against a whole French corps. Spaniards cry at their flamencos, but so do some Americans. By the time d'Erlon was pushed into France only one piper and one field officer were left.

JAC WELLER

Princeton, New Jersey
15 December 1991

PREFACE

Another book on Wellington and the Peninsular War may require some explanation, for there have been many. In the nineteenth century, an unprecedented number of histories and biographies appeared, together with journals, memoirs, and collections of letters. The most well known was Napier's *History of the War in the Peninsula*; the author took part in many of the actions he described.

The first quarter of the twentieth century saw the publication, spread over a number of years, of Professor Oman's brilliant *Peninsular War*, and Sir John Fortescue's authoritative *History of the British Army*, of which eight of the twenty volumes deal with the war in the Peninsula. *The Duke*, by Guedalla, published in 1931, is a biography worthy of the man.

Previously unpublished memoirs and journals even now find their way into print, often carefully edited. Modern studies of Wellington and the Peninsula also continue to be published, but usually are limited in scope, and in some instances are influenced unduly by modern political or sociological thought. Napier, Oman, and the Peninsular period in Fortescue total twenty-one volumes; all have long been out of print, and are not likely to be republished. There is room perhaps for a one-volume account of one of the greatest sustained military efforts of all time. It produced the only undefeated first-rank general in history and precipitated the first downfall of Napoleon. Wellington was to accomplish the second and final defeat of his only contemporary rival at Waterloo, fourteen months after the fall of Toulouse.

One book of moderate length cannot give details included in the average seven thick volumes of Napier, Fortescue or Oman. I have eliminated, except for occasional brief references, British, Portuguese and Spanish politics, actions fought by Spanish and Portuguese alone against the French, and the general history of the times. I have usually given only brief descriptions of actions in which Wellington was not in general command and have occasionally ignored minor combats neither important strategically nor tactically. I have endeavoured, however, to give a full account of the war strategically and to describe the important battles in detail, especially in regard to tactics, and I have tried to explain

Wellington's military success in terms of his pre-eminence in organizing his army, planning for its most profitable use in the field, and then carrying out those plans in actual battles and campaigns.

I have spent many months in Spain, Portugal and Southwestern France and have first-hand knowledge of the battlefields and campaign territory there. Such topographical research was necessary for me to appreciate Wellington's unusual abilities. The Peninsular battlefields and besieged towns have changed little in 150 years, except for San Sebastian and Toulouse.

Military history has often been written to give the reader full information as to what was taking place in both armies. Oman and Fortescue always follow this procedure; no general in the field, regardless of his system of intelligence, ever knows so much. Douglas Freeman in his studies of Lee and Washington rejected this all-knowing approach which tends to produce in the minds of readers a false feeling of superiority to both commanders. Any competent field officer, given the full intelligence possessed by military historians, could evolve manoeuvres to defeat all the great commanders of history. In order to appreciate fully a general's capacities, the reader should not know more at any point than the commander himself knew at that time.

Some of the more recent British writers on the Peninsula and Wellington concern themselves with things that to me seem trivial, at least from a military standpoint. My approach to the subject has ignored, excepting in one brief passage in Chapter XX, the literary whispering campaigns, and cruel personal attacks on the Duke by reputable men of letters in regard to his morals, politics, and private opinions.

It may be of interest to point out that this study of the Peninsular War is written after much personal experimentation with the Brown Bess musket, the Baker rifle and similar European weapons. I know their capabilities, not only from written records, but also from much actual firing under simulated combat conditions; much military history has been written by men without first-hand knowledge of the ordnance and weapons used.

Some gifted military writers have been confused as to tactics; their accounts of battles are full in regard to what happened before and after, but do not state clearly how the actual fighting took place. The British line, which almost always won against the French column, is regarded as a kind of minor miracle; there was nothing miraculous, nor even mysterious about Peninsular tactics. Lines have been used in warfare ntermittently for hundreds of years. So have columns. Missile arms have an advantage in lines; columns deliver more shock. It was not the formation alone, but the constitution of that formation, and Wellington's methods of employing it, that caused it to be victorious. I have tried to clear up some of this old confusion and have drawn heavily on my several investigations of infantry tactics elsewhere.

My indebtednesses are many and varied, extending from a nameless Spanish Government Gamekeeper at the Arapiles to the Honourable A. N. Kennard, Supervisor of Arms at the Tower of London. The British, Portuguese and Spanish Governments have kindly given me modern military maps of all campaign areas. The Princeton University Library and its affiliates have provided me with books, photostats and micro-films where the originals were not available.

Many people have contributed far more than they realize, especially Professor E. H. Dudley Johnson of Princeton who showed early confidence in this project and shaped the final result, and Professor Gordon Craig, now at Leland-Stamford, who has given me professional assistance and encouragement. Captain Basil H. Liddell Hart provided a vital spark and much valuable advice. I am particularly appreciative of the help given to me by Major MacDonald Harbord in the Oporto and Cavado region.

My staff, headed by my wife, have worked indefatigably; without their aid in research, secretarial assistance, and optimism, I could not possibly have finished the job.

JAC WELLER

Princeton, New Jersey
1 December 1961

CHRONOLOGY OF THE PENINSULAR WAR

1807,	18 October	French troops cross Franco-Spanish border
	30 November	Lisbon occupied by the French
1808,	23 March	Madrid occupied by the French
	May–June	Insurrections against the French throughout Spain and Portugal
	1–8 August	The British army under Sir Arthur Wellesley lands at the mouth of the Mondego River, Portugal
	17 August	Battle of Rolica
	21 August	Battle of Vimiero
	10 December	The British army under Sir John Moore advances from Salamanca
	24 December	Moore retreats from Sahagun
1809,	16 January	Battle of Corunna
	22 April	Wellesley again in command of British forces in Portugal
	12 May	Wellesley takes Oporto
	3 July	The British army under Wellesley enters Spain
	28 July	Battle of Talavera
	20 October	Work commences on the Lines of Torres Vedras
1810,	10 July	The French army under Massena takes Ciudad Rodrigo
	27 September	Battle of Busaco
1811,	3 March	Massena retreats from Santarem
	3–5 May	Battle of Fuentes de Onoro
	16 May	Battle of Albuera
	23–25 June	Wellington offers battle on the Caia
	28–30 September	Wellington offers battle near the upper Coa
1812,	19 January	Wellington takes Ciudad Rodrigo
	6 April	Wellington takes Badajoz
	22 July	Battle of Salamanca

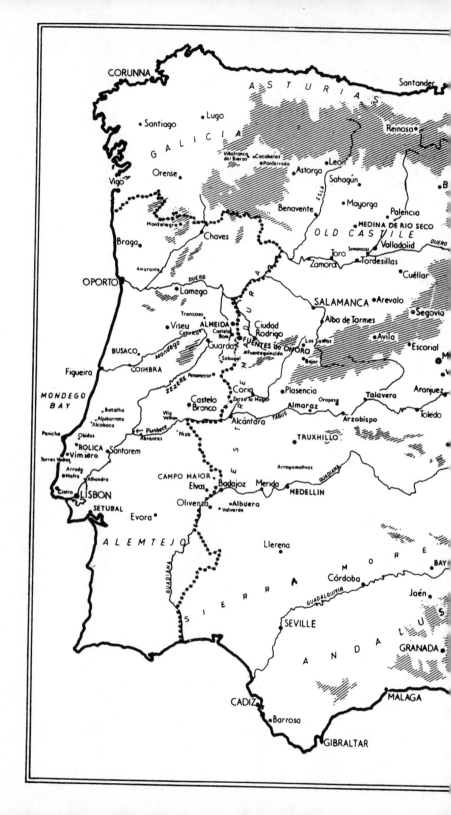

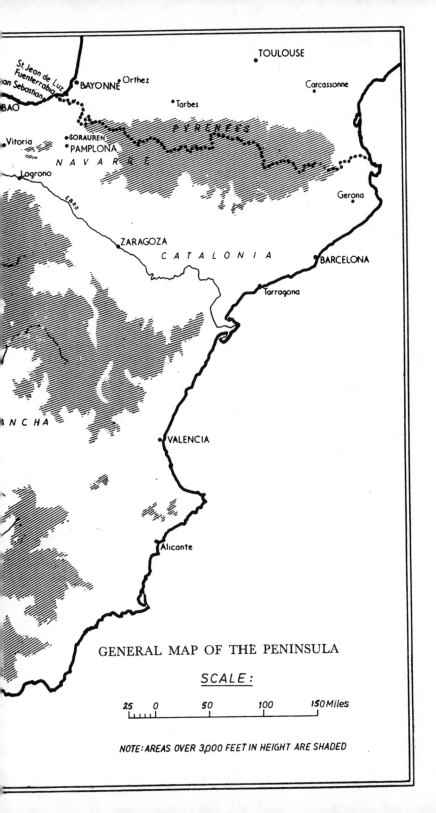

GENERAL MAP OF THE PENINSULA

SCALE:

25 0   50   100   150 Miles

NOTE: AREAS OVER 3,000 FEET IN HEIGHT ARE SHADED

I

PROLOGUE

THIS book concerns Wellington and his long struggle against Napoleon's forces in Portugal, Spain and Southwestern France between 1808 and 1814. In order to present a comprehensive picture, some paragraphs must be devoted to outlining events preceding this period. It is also necessary to describe briefly the military characteristics of the two contending powers.

FRANCE, NAPOLEON, AND SPAIN

The French Revolution proper began in 1789, but Louis XVI was not executed until 21st January 1793. The First Coalition of European Monarchies against Republican France led to fighting favourable to the French. The Spirit of the Revolution so well expressed in the Marseillaise inspired forces guided by a few professional soldiers of the old regime to victory over the smaller but better trained Coalition armies.

One of these professional officers from the old army was Napoleon Bonaparte, only twenty-six years of age when he defended on 4th October 1795 one of several French governments, which succeeded each other at short intervals, with his 'whiff of grape' from field pieces in the centre of Paris. In March of the following year, he took command of the French army which invaded Northern Italy and began an unbroken fourteen months of military success there.

Upon Napoleon's return to Paris, he was 'included in the government', if not yet entirely in their confidence. A mutually acceptable plan for sending Napoleon and a powerful expedition to the Middle East in the summer of 1798 was formulated. The French navy was crushed by Nelson at the Battle of the Nile (1st August 1798). The French army was victorious in Egypt, but failed in Syria where Sir

Sydney Smith successfully defended Acre. Napoleon returned to France in the autumn of 1799, the military saviour of all who opposed a restoration of the Bourbons, and seized power with two fellow consuls on 9th November. After much political manoeuvring, Napoleon crowned himself Emperor on 18th May 1804.

During this period, Napoleon greatly strengthened France, and was well on his way to defeating the rest of Europe. After the Peace of Tilsit in 1807, he found himself unopposed on the Continent. He was dissatisfied, however, with Spain, his ally in the recent naval war with Britain which Nelson won so completely at Trafalgar (21st October 1805), and decided to replace the Bourbon king of Spain, Charles IV, by his own brother, Joseph Bonaparte.

Conditions in Spain were propitious for such a *coup*. Charles IV was in theory an absolute ruler, but was dominated by the Queen and her favourite, Manuel Godoy; the government was hopelessly inefficient. By means of a secret treaty with Godoy, Napoleon secured the help of Spain in putting pressure on Portugal. The latter nation and Sweden were Britain's last continental allies. On 12th August 1807, the representatives of Spain and France in Lisbon delivered to the Prince Regent, John of Portugal—acting on behalf of his insane mother—identical notes demanding not only that the Portuguese abandon their alliance and declare war on Britain, but also seize all British ships in their ports and imprison all British subjects. Before Napoleon received an answer, he dispatched an army of 30,000 men under General Junot across Spain; it reached Lisbon on 30th November. The Prince Regent, his mother, and most of the Portuguese nobility had sailed for Brazil the previous day.

Napoleon continued to feed French troops into Northern Spain on the pretext of supporting his army in Portugal. These forces treacherously took over the fortress cities of Pamplona, Barcelona, San Sebastian and Figueras (Catalonia). Marshal Murat, Napoleon's brother-in-law, crossed the Bidassoa at the head of 100,000 troops and marched on Madrid.

So far there had been no fighting; the Spanish army still considered the French their allies. Before Murat reached Madrid a mob rose against Godoy and Charles IV demanding that the minister be removed and stand trial, and that the king abdicate in favour of his son. After a turbulent two and a half days, Ferdinand VII assumed the throne; Godoy narrowly escaped with his life. The new monarch, ironically, placed his confidence in Murat. During April 1808 Ferdinand was lured to Bayonne by Napoleon, together with the deposed Charles IV, the Queen, and Godoy. They were all treated as prisoners, and were forced to acknowledge Joseph Bonaparte as King of Spain.

The Spanish people were hostile. On 2nd May a pro-Bourbon mob in Madrid was suppressed ruthlessly by the French, but other sections of the nation rose in revolt. Later Murat was forced to leave Spain on account of ill-health.

Delegations were sent to Britain from Galicia and the Asturias demanding money and arms. Sir Hew Dalrymple, commander at Gibraltar, was soon involved in Andalusian schemes to resist the French. Spanish armies sprang into being overnight. In numbers, these forces were impressive; the French were understandably cautious.

The Portuguese resented deeply Napoleon's invasion and the high-handed attitude of Junot and his soldiers. The rebellion in Spain provoked a similar and even more violent reaction in Portugal. The natives were neither organized nor equipped to fight veteran French armies in the field, but they were willing to risk their lives freely. Junot and his army soon found that they controlled only a few fortified towns and the ground on which they themselves stood. Early in the summer of 1808, the entire Peninsula was preparing for a sanguinary conflict.

WELLINGTON

Arthur Wellesley was born in Dublin on 29th April 1769, the fourth son of the Earl of Mornington and Ann Hill, eldest daughter of Viscount Dungannon.[1] He was educated at Eton, and the Military Academy at Angers, in France. He did not distinguish himself scholastically. He appeared to have a weak constitution, some musical talent, and a remarkable facility for mental arithmetic.

On 7th March 1787, a commission was purchased for him in the 73rd, a regiment then in India. He never joined this regiment, but did some duty at its depot in England. During the next six years, he was on the rosters of three other foot regiments and two cavalry regiments, but served actively only for short periods. He was from November 1787 until March 1793 A.D.C. to two Lord Lieutenants of Ireland, the Marquis of Buckingham, and then the Earl of Westmorland. He sat in the Irish Parliament from April 1790.

---

[1] The family name had been Wesley for two generations, until 1798, when it was changed to Wellesley; it was originally Colley or Cowley.

On 30th April 1793, Arthur Wellesley was gazetted a major in the 33rd; five months later he was in command with the rank of lieutenant colonel.[1] He now devoted himself exclusively to his regimental duties. In June the following year, he embarked at Cork for Ostend and took part in the Duke of York's unsuccessful invasion of the Low Countries.

Wellesley was for the first time under fire on 14th July 1794. The main British force had suffered a check, and was retreating in disorder. Wellesley had his battalion deployed in line; he opened out by companies to allow the retiring troops to pass through, and then closed again. The 33rd delivered unhurried volleys and stopped the enemy in their tracks; the action then ended. Later in the campaign, Wellesley was in command of an infantry brigade; he happened to be senior to the other battalion commanders present. He remarked some years later that at least he learned something of the way things ought not to be done.

On 17th February 1797, Wellesley reached India with the 33rd. He had given up the violin and cards, but brought with him, and studied regularly, as fine a military library as could be acquired at that time. Wellesley reported to Lord Cornwallis, the titular colonel of the 33rd and also Governor General of India, a position soon to be filled by Mornington, Arthur's eldest brother. This increased Colonel Wellesley's opportunities for demonstrating his abilities, although the 33rd was already remarkable for its efficiency, organization, discipline and internal economy. General Harris, writing in February 1799, praised the colonel highly for his 'judicious and masterly arrangements in respect to supplies.'

After a period of semi-active military but important political service, Wellesley carried out two rapid campaigns in March–April and August–December 1803 and completely vanquished far larger French-trained Mahratta armies. In this fighting, he manoeuvred at speed, and used surprise more than force. He once covered sixty miles in thirty hours with all his cavalry, three battalions of infantry, and four guns. He won the battles of Assaye (23rd September) and Argaum (29th November), and stormed the extremely strong fortification of Gawilghur (15th December). At Assaye, with an Anglo–Indian army of 4,500, of whom no more than 1,500 were Europeans, he crushed a force of over 40,000, including 10,000 European-trained infantry, supported by 100 guns.

Even though Wellesley had received the permanent rank of major general on his thirty-third birthday, he resigned his command on 24th

[1] Titular colonels of regiments rarely served with them.

February 1804 and was back in England on 10th September. Eight years in India had made him wealthy, but British generals with reputations won in the East were not uncommon at that time.[1] He was given command of a brigade in Kent, took a minor part in the ill-fated Hanover expedition, and later was placed in command of another brigade at Hastings.

Wellesley recommenced his political activities without giving up his military status. He sat in Parliament and was appointed Chief Secretary for Ireland under the Duke of Richmond, the Lord Lieutenant. He stipulated in his acceptance of this office that it should not keep him from active military service. During the summer of 1807, he commanded the only British force actually engaged during the Danish expedition, and gained a victory at the Battle of Kioge in which 1,500 Danes were taken prisoners. The total killed and wounded on both sides was under 400. Wellesley received the permanent rank of lieutenant general on 25th April 1808, less than three months before he landed in the Peninsula.

FRENCH ARMY ORGANIZATION AND TACTICS

The French army was raised under laws requiring universal military service. The whole nation furnished soldiers; promotions were frequently from the ranks. The army, under Napoleon, was pampered; soldiering was a respected profession.

France beat the armies of the First Coalition by massing poorly trained and disciplined but enthusiastic recruits in deep columns which moved forward irresistibly. They won, but the price in casualties was great. Before Napoleon's rise to power, this system had been modified to ensure that the whole front was covered by an irregular swarm of skirmishers, called *tirailleurs*. This light infantry shielded the columns behind them and disorganized the main line of the enemy ahead by their accurate but irregular fire.

---

[1] Wellesley to his brother, William, 13th September 1809, *Wellington At War*, 169, 'When I came from India I had 42 or 43,000 Pounds which I made as follows. I got 5,000 Prize money at Seringapatam; 25,000 Pounds Prize money in the Mahratta War; the Court of Directors gave me 4,000 Pounds for having been a Comr. in Mysore; & the Govt. paid me about 2,000 Pounds in one Sum the arrears of an Allowance as Cmg. Officer at Seringapatam; & the remainder was Interest upon these Sums Saving &c during the time I was in India.'
Refer to the Bibliography, page 378, for details of Short Titles given in footnotes.

Napoleon added field artillery to the *tirailleur*-column offensive concept. The guns would go forward beside, or even in front of, the infantry columns and open fire at effective canister range, roughly 200 to 300 yards. Napoleon preferred to have five field pieces to 1,000 infantry, a very high ratio for any period. A gunner himself, he realized the value of concentrated fire on a single point from several angles. He and his commanders used their artillery effectively in both offence and defence.

French cavalry had been excellent prior to the Revolution, but the Republican armies were deficient in horsemen. Napoleon soon rectified this shortcoming. During the Empire, the cavalry was numerous, well equipped, well mounted, and professionally efficient. It had two major functions; the light cavalry carried out reconnaissance and undertook shielding missions, and kept open lines of communication, while the heavy cavalry was often held in reserve for shock attacks at critical moments in battle. The medium cavalry, the dragoons, were suited to some extent for both purposes; dragoons far outnumbered the combined heavy and light cavalry in the Peninsula.[1]

A French infantry regiment in Spain usually consisted of three or four battalions. Two or three regiments formed a brigade, and two or three brigades constituted a division. A corps was an autonomous unit of divisions. Tactically, the basic unit was the battalion which after 1808 consisted of six companies of about 140 men each when at full strength.[2] The normal company formation was 40 files three ranks deep with some 20 additional personnel consisting of officers, sergeants, drummers, and colour guards. One company of each battalion was always designated light infantry, or *voltigeurs*; these men, together with those from similar companies in other battalions, formed the line of *tirailleurs*, and were often slighter physically. Theoretically, a second company of each battalion was designated the grenadier company and was composed of taller and stronger men.[3]

French infantry columns were formed in various ways. An entire brigade might advance on a single company front, 40 men wide by about 135 men deep. It was even possible to attack with a front of only half a company and twice the depth. A battalion could also form an

[1] A superb monograph on Napoleon's cavalry forms a part of *Oman's Studies*.

[2] Junot's army which left France in 1807 retained the nine company organization until its surrender after Vimiero.

[3] Grenades had not been used in the field for half a century; the designation is a survival from earlier times when the taller and stronger men threw explosive grenades in action.

offensive column on a front of two companies in line.[1] Sometimes a brigade would advance with its battalions one behind the other, but could also be formed with the individual battalion columns moving parallel to each other. The strength of the musket-armed columns was psychological rather than physical; only the first three ranks could fire their weapons. If the head of a column could be brought to a halt, the ranks behind could exert little pressure. Bayonets were rarely used in actions during this period.

Napoleonic armies were expert at living off the country. Soldiers were taught to cut, thrash, and mill grain, and were adept at discovering hidden food and wine. Veterans could live well anywhere in central Europe without receiving supplies from France. They could take care of themselves, and required only replacement arms and ammunition.

BRITISH ORGANIZATION AND TACTICS

All British soldiers were volunteers; the result not being always fortunate. They came mainly from two dissimilar socio-economic classes. The officers were almost entirely from the landed gentry, and bought their commissions. Enlisted men joined because they were in trouble at home, unable to earn a living in any civilian capacity, or lured by the cash bounties offered for enlistment, which they often spent on drink. This distinction between officers and enlisted men was, however, the most important single factor in the remarkable battalion combat effectiveness of the army. Aristocratic officers could lead; only an exceptional man who rose from the ranks could gain the same respect and confidence.

The British army had done little fighting on the Continent during the previous fifty years; it had not been particularly successful there since Marlborough's time. In a long series of little wars, mostly outside Europe, a continuity of tradition and unit morale of a high order had been evolved, together with distinctive infantry tactics. When fighting other infantry, a two deep line was used which could be transformed quickly to a square for receiving cavalry attacks.[2] The discipline, training, and courage of British infantry was of a high order.

[1] I have been unable to discover how a six-company French infantry battalion without its *voltigeurs* formed a column of double companies. Logically, half the column would be nine ranks deep and the other half six. Such an irregularity would probably not have been tolerated.

[2] This change appears to have been made first in India. *Dundas*, the drill book current in 1808, still calls for three ranks, but two appear to have been usual, even for parades.

Its most remarkable asset was its weapons effectiveness. They had excellent small arms, both smoothbore and rifled.[1] They perfected their use by actual practice.[2] Due to bad luck and bad management, British expeditionary forces for fifteen years prior to 1808 had usually been unsuccessful, but the troops sent out had been good fighters. British infantry in line had won against superior French columns at Maida in southern Italy in 1806 and had fought creditably in Egypt in 1802.

An infantry battalion consisted of ten companies, but varied in strength from 1,200 to as few as 400 men. The big, powerful men were normally in the grenadier company, while the smaller, more nimble fellows were placed in the light company. These two companies were considered the *élite* of the battalion, and were often uniformed differently from the eight battalion or line companies.[3] The light companies and all riflemen were trained as skirmishers; these adopted in part the tactics of American rangers and relied on accurate individual fire rather than volleys. The real power of British infantry lay in its 'thin red line'; since it was but two ranks deep, every musket could be fired effectively.

By using the 'Nineteen Movements', a battalion commander and his subordinates could take a battalion practically anywhere in any required formation.[4] These movements were similar to modern close-order drill, except that the basis of each movement was usually an entire company

---

[1] The smoothbore musket was the Brown Bess. It was made in enormous quantities in both Birmingham and London during the Napoleonic Wars, was similar to that used in the British army since the 1720's, but modified in accordance with recent field requirements. See *Blackmore, passim*, for details. The ammunition for one shot was contained in a paper cartridge, sixty of which were normally carried in a weatherproof pouch by each soldier. The weapon was the best of its type and could be fired four times a minute by trained men. It took a bayonet which was fixed only in emergencies; when mounted on the muzzle, it interfered greatly with the quick loading of the musket. The Baker rifle was chosen from among many different rifled weapons proposed for use in the British army in 1800 and was issued to various battalions of the 60th and 95th Foot. For details, see Ezekiel Baker, *Remarks on Rifle Guns*, London, 1835, *passim*. The rifle was more accurate than the musket, but would not give such a high rate of fire.

[2] Incredible as it may seem, the French infantry did not practice 'live' firing. *Marbot*, 423, says in this connexion, 'Up to this time the English were the only troops who were perfectly practiced in the use of small arms, whence their firing was far more accurate than that of any other infantry.'

[3] The physical qualifications for these two flank companies—they took both ends of the line when the whole battalion formed one—appear to have been secondary to soldierly excellence. The best men were chosen and then divided between the two according to size, although big men were occasionally found in the light company.

[4] See both *Nineteen Movements, passim*, and *Dundas, passim*, which explain in great detail proper procedures.

rather than a small squad. Much practice and great speed on the company flank must have been necessary to make some of these look well.

British cavalry regiments were normally composed of four squadrons of approximately 200 troopers each when at full strength. British horses were superior to the French, but both officers and men lacked campaign and combat experience. The socio-economic distinction between officers and men appears to have been greatest in this arm, perhaps because cavalry regiments were far more likely to remain at home than infantry battalions.[1] Cavalry officers often put personal pleasure and appearance before military efficiency.

The British artillery was separate from the infantry and cavalry; it was not even controlled initially by the C-in-C of the Army, but by the Master General of Ordnance. Field and horse artillery batteries, then called brigades, usually consisted of five 6-pounder guns and one 5·5-inch howitzer.[2] The proportion of guns to infantry was traditionally low, about two per 1,000 bayonets. Even though the 'regiment' lacked experience in concentrations of fire defensively, and in attacking together with other arms in co-ordinated field movements, they were extremely well drilled within each battery and had superior *matériel*. The gunners had always done their full share of fighting and were noted for their size and prowess.[3] They were capable of manhandling their pieces into inaccessible positions and across rough terrain, and would fight to the last man.[4]

The British army at this time contained an auxiliary force known as the King's German Legion; George III was also Elector of Hanover. This army within an army was professional throughout, and included infantry, cavalry, and artillery. Its organization was similar to the British. Both line and light infantry battalions included riflemen. The experience and efficiency of the K.G.L. officers and NCO's was high; the K.G.L. cavalry was particularly effective.

[1] During the American War of 1775–83, two of 24 cavalry regiments saw active service, while 52 of 70 infantry battalions were involved; Edward E. Curtis, *The Organization of the British Army in the American Revolution*, New Haven, 1926, 4.

[2] Both 3- and 9-pounders were also used.

[3] Since gunners had to manhandle field pieces in action, they were chosen for their size and strength. The Royal Artillery was particularly impressive in this respect in the American Revolution; see *Journal of Captain Pausch* edited by William L. Stone, Albany, New York, 1886. This German officer states, 95, '. . . the English artillerists are the tallest, strongest and handsomest men in the world.' See also 140.

[4] Guns were dragged up Mount Defiance in a single day, which forced the surrender of Ticonderoga in 1777. The behaviour of Tarleton's gunners at Cowpens deserves mention; every one of them was killed, or incapacitated by wounds, at their pieces.

The staff which Wellesley was to command could be broken down theoretically into nine separate parts; these varied widely in importance.[1] The chief of artillery as the senior ordnance officer was also responsible for supplying the infantry and cavalry with ammunition, replacement weapons, and spare parts. The commissariat was a civilian department responsible to the Treasury. The quartermaster general (QMG) provided quarters and routes for the army, but not supplies; in actual fact, this post was comparable to a modern Chief of Staff. The adjutant general (AG) was responsible for personnel, training, reports as to numbers, and sometimes intelligence. The surgeon general, apothecary general, paymaster general, and chief engineer had obvious functions. The military secretary did much more than handle correspondence.

The great weakness of the British staff organization was that the C-in-C of an expeditionary force was not in complete command of his own staff. Eight of his nine senior staff officers were primarily responsible to their superiors at home. A commissary general might differ violently with a local C-in-C and be upheld by the Treasury in London. The power of a C-in-C abroad to reward and punish was drastically curtailed. He could not choose subordinate officers nor get rid of those who proved incapable.

[1] See *Ward*, 7, for an organization chart. Its extreme complication cannot be easily simplified.

II

ROLICA

O N 14th June 1808, Sir Arthur Wellesley was formally appointed to command a force assembled at Cork originally intended for an attack on the Spanish colonies in America. Even though Wellesley had commanded more men in the field than any other British officer, and had the finest record in combat, he was still the most junior lieutenant general and was only thirty-nine years old. As Chief Secretary for Ireland, he was a member of the Cabinet and temporarily more a politician than a soldier. He received this command largely because of Castlereagh's reliance on his judgment in military matters. He certainly did not have the backing of the Duke of York, C-in-C of the Army, and his associates at the Horse Guards.[1]

Wellesley began to reorganize his army immediately, realizing that it would probably be used in the Peninsula. He looked to every detail himself, but was careful to train his subordinates at the same time. The infantry was first-rate; the officers were in general acceptable. His most serious problems were in connexion with transportation and supply. There were no horses for the artillery nor any wagon train.

Two small wagon companies, with officers, men, and horses were eventually transferred from the Irish establishment to this Expeditionary Force. A few additional mounts were secured, but even if there had been more time, it was then impossible to carry sufficient animals to be independent of local civilian transport once ashore. Even on a relatively short voyage such as to the Peninsula, only a few animals could be taken on the small transports normally used.[2]

---

[1] The Duke of York was attacked by some of his contemporaries, and maligned by *Oman*, I, 225. See also a defence of him, *Fortescue* VI, 190. The Horse Guards' Barracks in London was at that time the headquarters of the army. All orders bore this address which accounts for the popular expression, 'Straight from the horse's mouth'.

[2] A total of 564 horses eventually arrived safely in Portugal.

As the month progressed, Portugal became the most probable area for a significant blow against the French. But Wellesley's final official instructions made sufficient mention of Northern Spain for him to have landed there, if he thought proper. He was to report directly to Castlereagh and not through the Duke of York. He was to command not only his own force of 10,000, but also 5,000 more under General Spencer already co-operating with the Spanish in Andalusia.

Wellesley sailed aboard the frigate *Crocodile* on 20th July and soon reached Corunna. He went ashore immediately to confer with the Galician Junta. This organization had sent representatives to Britain earlier. They were voluble in regard to their hatred of the French and had what was to prove unwarranted confidence in their own combat effectiveness. They desired British gold and arms, but not a British army. They certainly did not wish Wellesley to land his force. They suggested instead that Sir Arthur should sail on to Portugal and fight the French army there while the Galicians took care of themselves. They admitted a defeat on 14th July at Medina de Rio Seco, but minimized their losses while magnifying those of the French. They had some absolutely false good news.[1]

Leaving Corunna, Wellesley proceeded to Oporto, arriving there on the 24th. The Junta of Oporto was accepted as the Supreme Junta by all Portugal not under French control. Old Don Antonio de Castro, Bishop of Oporto, was all-powerful in this organization. He was both popular and patriotic, but no statesman and no administrator. Wellesley received everything that he could desire in the way of promises, and more accurate information than at Corunna. The battle at Rio Seco had been a disaster for the Galicians; the French army under Marshal Bessieres had suffered only moderate casualties.

The French in Portugal under General Junot had abandoned seven-eighths of the country; they still occupied an area around Lisbon bounded by the Atlantic, the Tagus, and a line running east from Peniche on the seacoast to Abrantes on the river. They also held a fortified camp at Setubal, across the Tagus from the capital, and the fortress cities of Almeida and Elvas on the Spanish border. Outside these areas, French columns moved at will and inflicted severe losses on

---

[1] The Galicians reported the surrender of a French army under General Dupont which was said to have occurred on 26th June 1808 under circumstances remarkably similar to the surrender of that army at Baylen on 20th July. The actual capitulation did not take place until the day Wellesley reached Corunna, and could not have been known to the Galicians for a considerable period thereafter.

any Portuguese forces which tried to resist them, as well as barbarous cruelties on the people. A force under General Loison had been particularly active; only the rugged country to the north around Oporto was safe from these incursions.[1]

Sir Arthur left Oporto on 25th July and sailed for the mouth of the Tagus to consult with Admiral Sir Charles Cotton, senior naval officer in the area. The entire British force was going to be landed in Portugal; Wellesley's transports were ordered to proceed south from Vigo, while Spencer was to sail north from near Gibraltar.

The mouth of the Tagus was unsuitable as a landing place. The British navy was in complete control of the open sea, but the river near its mouth had two channels only, one close to the north bank and the other near the south. A number of French-manned reconditioned Portuguese men-of-war lay in the Tagus estuary. There was also a Russian fleet in port which had to be considered unfriendly to Britain.[2]

Even if a landing in the Tagus could have been effected, Wellesley's force would have come ashore cramped from a long sea voyage and lacking both proper land transport and space to manoeuvre. Sir Arthur would have had to fight Junot's entire veteran army before his own was shaken down. The only harbour between the Tagus and Oporto suitable for transports was Peniche, but French-occupied fortifications, with effective cannon, dominated this anchorage.[3]

Cotton and Wellesley agreed on the mouth of the Mondego for the coming debarkation. A small fortress, originally held by the French, had been taken by students from Coimbra University on 27th June and turned over to Cotton, who sent ashore marines to hold it. A landing here would not be easy; open boats would have to brave the heavy surf in crossing the bar, but it was the best place available.

---

[1] Loison had attempted to march from Almeida towards Oporto, but had found himself surrounded by belligerent Portuguese peasants in their mountain fastnesses. These not only fired at his soldiers from the steep, rugged hillside, but rolled down boulders, exterminated stragglers, and cut the throats of sentries at night. After three days of this, Loison moved back into open country.

[2] Admiral Siniavin was willing to fight the British fleet if it tried to force the entrance of the Tagus. He would take no part, however, in French operations ashore, since Russia had not declared war on Portugal and had not acknowledged annexation of that country by Napoleon. Perhaps Siniavin was of the party in Russia which opposed Napoleon: *Oman*, I, 209.

[3] The only manufacturing arsenal in Portugal was at Lisbon where Junot had 10,000 Portuguese hard at work casting cannon, making military equipment, and repairing ships-of-war. There were plenty of guns of the most modern type for the extensive fortifications garrisoned by the French.

Sir Arthur joined his transports off the fortress of Figueira and ordered a landing there on 1st August. He was ashore himself early in the day. The landing progressed slowly; boats, men, and equipment were lost in the surf. But Wellesley's force was on shore by the evening of the 5th. Spencer arrived off the Mondego that afternoon; his men were landed during the next three days.

It was necessary to feed the army without recourse to plundering, placate a civilian population, and deal amicably with the local authorities. Wellesley had to teach a large number of officers and men their jobs; sometimes a caustic mentor, his patience was inexhaustible.

The two companies of the Irish wagon train, procured with so much difficulty, were particularly valuable as a nucleus around which to build a transportation system. Wellesley had experience of bullocks and carts even if the commissariat had not; he set about supplementing his few wagons with these and pack animals. British armies in the past had relied on civilian transport under contract, even for artillery teams and drivers.[1] Wellesley soon realized that he could not do this in Portugal. Animals, carts, and civilian drivers would have to be hired, and then controlled rigidly by the commissary general's department. The efficient system of supply and transport, which was eventually to give Wellesley such an advantage over the French, was started at the mouth of the Mondego. The shriek of solid wooden wheels revolving in ungreased ox-cart journals would be heard beyond the Pyrenees (Plate 1). All services and supplies obtained from civilians were paid for immediately; this practice was to prove equally valuable.

But Wellesley still lacked horses for the cavalry and artillery. After buying all available, he had only enough to mount 240 of his 390 light dragoons and to draw three batteries. Spencer's artillery and the unmounted dragoons would have to be left behind.

Wellesley visited Bernadino Freire, the commander of the local Portuguese army, at Montemor Velho, just north of the Mondego, on 7th August. After inspecting Freire's force, Sir Arthur ordered 5,000 British muskets, bayonets, and sets of infantry equipment to be issued

[1] Field artillery had been dependent on horses for strategic mobility throughout the eighteenth century. The Driver Corps was not formed until 1794; it replaced civilian drivers and hired horses. A. W. Wilson, *The Story of the Gun*, Woolwich, 1944, says, 45, the 1794 Driver Corps '. . . was rechristened the Corps of Royal Artillery Drivers in 1806, but did not actually become a part of the Royal Artillery until after Waterloo.' There were many instances in the American Revolution, however, of British artillerymen using government owned horses to pull their pieces. The Horse Artillery began as all mounted batteries in 1793.

to them. Freire promised to meet the British army at Leiria on the Lisbon road where, according to the Portuguese general, a magazine of supplies had been collected for the use of the British army.

Early in the morning of the 10th, Wellesley's force marched south along the coast road. It numbered about 14,000 and had been divided into six small brigades with three field pieces attached to each.[1] The infantry had left their heavy packs aboard ship and were marching light, but each man was carrying rations for four days. The roads were deep in sand; a pitiless August sun soon blistered fair British skins. The army was more exhausted by their twelve mile march to Lugar than it would be later by twice that distance. It reached Leiria on the 11th to find the Portuguese army waiting.

Wellesley soon found cause to be dissatisfied with Freire and his command. Even though the Portuguese had received 5,000 stands of British arms, only 6,000 men were present at Leiria in any semblance of order. Freire was not willing to advance in company with the British in the open country near the sea. The Portuguese, in spite of their bombastic manifestoes and the courage of the individual peasants, still considered the French to be invincible. Freire wanted Wellesley to march with him towards Lisbon by an interior route where the terrain was such that a total defeat was almost impossible.

Even if Sir Arthur had been willing to plunge into the hills, the whole scheme was impractical. The British army was dependent upon their transports for food. Freire had taken everything accumulated at Leiria for his own forces, even though he personally had promised it to Wellesley. He insisted that the Portuguese army should draw food and equipment from the British transports, if it accompanied Wellesley along the coast road. Freire finally agreed to remain in the vicinity of Leiria and await the result of Wellesley's clash with Junot. He was shamed into lending Sir Arthur some 1,600 light troops commanded by a British officer in the Portuguese service, Colonel Nicholas Trant.[2]

[1] See the Appendix to this chapter for the constitution of these brigades. *Fortescue*, VI, 204, goes into considerable detail in connexion with the artillery assignment, but falls into an arithmetical absurdity. This distribution of guns to brigades was not permanent; a battery of 9-pounders at least remained under Colonel Robe, Chief of Artillery.

[2] This Irishman is a controversial figure. Born in 1769, he entered the British army as a lieutenant of the 84th Foot in May 1794. In 1799, he appears to have assisted in the organization of the Minorcan Regiment in which he held the rank of major. He entered the Royal Staff Corps in 1803, but as an ensign. He was sent to Portugal as a military agent in 1808 and rose to the rank of brigadier general in the Portuguese army. He was successful in independent command of Portuguese militia, but was seriously wounded in 1812. Beresford, the Portuguese C-in-C, did not appreciate him, and he received scant reward for his services, dying in comparative poverty in 1839.

Wellesley had received conflicting reports of the strength of Junot's army. Originally it had consisted of 30,000 men; sufficient replacements had arrived to make up all losses sustained. In June, the British had been informed that there were no more than 4,000 French in Lisbon. Sir Arthur was now advised that at least 12,000 were in and around the capital, with other forces nearer Leiria. On 12th August, Delaborde's army, estimated at 6,000 men, lay across the Lisbon road at Obidos, two days' march south of Leiria. Loison's army of approximately 9,000 lay at Abrantes, or at Tomar further east, resting after winning several 'battles' in central Portugal. In the wake of these one-sided combats, the French had pillaged, burned, tortured and raped.[1] Loison's army was still a strong mobile force, and might attack the British left flank, or join Delaborde.

Wellesley could do little formal scouting on account of his weakness in cavalry, but two or three well-mounted officers confirmed this intelligence. There was no doubt that both French armies were in the approximate positions reported, although their strength was probably exaggerated. Even if Delaborde and Loison did unite and had every man credited to them, they would barely outnumber the British army as it now stood. More French troops might come up from Lisbon, but Wellesley also was expecting reinforcements. He gave orders to continue the march south and entered Alcobaca on the 14th. The first engagement of the Peninsular War took place next day near a windmill at Brilos. Three companies of the 95th Rifles routed a French outpost, which was pursued three miles to Obidos. In their enthusiasm, they followed too far and ran into difficulties, but Spencer soon extricated them.[3]

The French gave up Obidos and retreated to a strong position before the village of Rolica on the 16th. The countryside between the Mondego and Leiria had been flat and sandy. South of Alcobaca, low rolling hills appeared; near Obidos, these grew rugged and militarily formidable. Rolica lay in the centre of a horseshoe of hills with the open section facing Obidos (Plate 2). The terrain within this horseshoe

---

[1] That before Evora on 29th July 1808 was perhaps the most important. A force of 1,500 organized Portuguese troops and a Spanish contingent of the same size supported by indifferently armed peasants and townspeople, were annihilated. The French inflicted perhaps as many as 8,000 casualties while suffering only 290 of their own. The town was practically destroyed; few inhabitants survived.

[3] Total British casualties were an officer and 26 men.

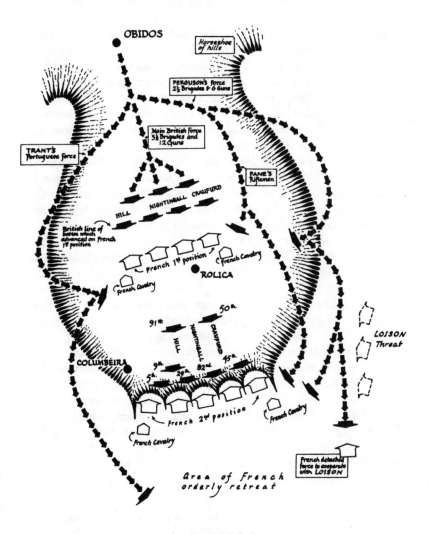

OBIDOS

Horseshoe of hills

FERGUSON'S force 2½ Brigades & 6 Guns

Main British force 3½ Brigades and 12 Guns

TRANT'S Portuguese force

FANE'S Riflemen

HILL NIGHTINGALL CRAWFURD

British line of battns which advanced on French 1st position

French 1st position

ROLICA

French Cavalry

French Cavalry

50th.

91st.

HILL NIGHTINGALL CRAWFURD

COLUMBEIRA

9th. 82nd. 45th.

5th. 29th.

French 2nd position

French Cavalry

LOISON Threat

French Cavalry

French detached force to cooperate with LOISON

Area of French orderly retreat

1. ROLICA

is broken and irregular; there are several natural rock towers rising in an irregular line north and south, and a number of minor ridges, but the entire valley is much lower than the surrounding hills.

The British army spent the night of the 16th at Obidos. A report was received at headquarters that Loison's army had passed Rio Maior at noon; this town was only half a day's march to the east. Nevertheless, Wellesley at daybreak pushed on towards Rolica; he was determined to fight whether or not the two French armies had united. As was his invariable custom, he had his entire force under arms an hour before dawn. He saw nothing of his opponents from the towers of Obidos, but was more fortunate on reaching one of the unusual rock outcrops further south. Delaborde's army could be discerned still in front of Rolica, but Loison's was not visible.[1]

The British advance continued; Wellesley had divided his force into three columns. The most powerful of these under his direct command moved down the centre of the valley towards the French position north of Rolica; it consisted of three and a half brigades of British infantry, a weak battalion of Portuguese *Cacadores* (light infantry), some British and Portuguese cavalry, and 12 guns, in all about 9,000 men. When still two miles from the French, this force opened out into battle array. Catlin Craufurd's Brigade was on the left, the brigades of Nightingall and Hill comprised the centre and right respectively. The Frenchmen, who wrote down their impressions soon after the battle, agree that the display was magnificent. Scarlet lines moved forward, corrected their alignment as if on parade, and then pressed on again.

Wellesley seldom made a show without some practical reason. If the French had concentrated on the spectacle in front of them, they would have fallen into a trap. Far in advance of the main British force, to the right and west, a flanking column of 1,350 Portuguese under Colonel Trant hastened through the hills as one half of a pincer to encircle the French before Rolica. The other half of this same movement was a far more powerful column to the left and east. It was commanded by Major General Ferguson and consisted of his and Bowes's Brigades, half of Fane's Brigade (the rifle battalions), a detachment of 40 cavalry, and

---

[1] These early morning observations have been stated by various writers to have taken place at Obidos, either on the old walls or from the church tower. I found the distance from Obidos to Rolica to be too great, even with modern 10 × 50 binoculars. The rock hill in the centre of the valley further south may very well have been his observation site. Wellesley was a superb horseman and could have ridden to the summit; from here, the whole valley is perfectly visible.

six guns.[1] The strength of the eastern column, about 4,500 British bayonets and sabres, was necessary to protect that flank should Loison attack.

As Wellesley's column approached the French position, the British artillery unlimbered and opened fire ineffectively at long range. If the French could be coaxed to stay where they were for a few more minutes, all would be well. But Delaborde was watching from a windmill just behind the French right; he was a veteran commander not easily tricked. He also had a detached force to the east awaiting Loison, which was also observing Ferguson's advance and was reporting on it periodically. The French line of *tirailleurs* was soon engaged both with the light companies of Wellesley's central column and riflemen from Ferguson's force. Delaborde's five guns opened fire with solid shot and grape; his cavalry manoeuvred on his flanks.

The main force of French infantry was never fully engaged in front of Rolica. Delaborde waited until Wellesley showed his hand and then withdrew behind a cavalry screen to a second position two miles further south which he had chosen some days earlier. This was actually part of the horseshoe of hills; the French occupied a section about three-quarters of a mile wide. Each flank rested on deep breaches in the hills worn by winter streams. The front of the position appeared too steep to climb, except where four boulder-choked gullies reached back into the ridge. A weathered igneous dike could be seen in places along the summit and gave the French what amounted to a fine breastwork. Their cannon from the top of the ridge could sweep the valley through which the British had to advance (Plates 3 and 4).

Although Wellesley had been unable to cut off the French in his initial manoeuvres, he had forced their retirement. He now repeated the same strategic move. It would be more difficult for his flanking forces to attack the French flanks because of the defiles protecting them, but they still might encircle Delaborde even further to the south. During this manoeuvring, as in the fighting before Rolica, Ferguson's force was mainly concerned with Delaborde's detached force awaiting the arrival of Loison's army. Fane's riflemen operated more to the west and were

---

[1] There is a discrepancy in regard to Fane's Brigade and its constitution in the battle at Rolica. Both Oman and Fortescue follow *Supplementary Dispatches*, I, 101, and say that it contained only four companies of the 2/95th and the 5/60th. *Leach*, 49, says, 'About this time, the 50th Regiment was appointed to our brigade (Fane's), in place of the 45th, which was moved to General Catlin Craufurd's.' The assignment of battalions to brigades was perhaps not so definite in 1808 as it was later. Both the 1/45th and the 1/50th stayed with the central column.

almost continuously engaged.[1] They acted as a connecting link between Wellesley and Ferguson. Apparently Trant's Portuguese never took an active part in the fighting.

Wellesley's main column advanced within artillery range of the second French position and deployed into line of battle. The brigades of Craufurd, Nightingall, and Hill were still ranged from left to right.[2] Spirited skirmishing between the light companies and the French *tirailleurs* at the foot of the slope commenced almost immediately, but Sir Arthur did not intend to press his attack until his flanking forces were sufficiently far advanced to aid the main attack. Meanwhile, he was keeping up sufficient pressure with his skirmishers and Robe's artillery to make Delaborde's withdrawal difficult.

One of those courageous blunders which occur frequently in the history of the British army now took place. Colonel Lake commanded the 1/29th which was third from the left of the four battalions in the first line.[3] Instead of skirmishing with his light company against the French *tirailleurs*, he led four of his line companies up one of the boulder-strewn gullies which ran deep into the French position. This ravine narrowed and turned to the east while rising steeply. Before Lake realized what he was doing, he was 200 yards behind the French front line with a relatively small force and in a cramped position.

The disordered British column received a murderous fire from both flanks to which it could make no effective reply. Heroically, Lake led his men out of the cleft and tried to form, but the entire French left-centre came down on him. British casualties were severe; four officers and about 30 unwounded men were taken prisoner. A few managed to retire to safety. The noise of this unsuccessful thrust appears to have caused it to seem larger than it was. Hill brought forward the 1/9th from the second line to support Lake, who was killed.

Wellesley realized that severe fighting was inevitable and ordered an immediate general attack. The whole British line moved forward not only into the four gullies, but up the steep slopes between them. They were unable to take advantage of their numerical superiority, nor could they use any definite formation. The assault was made at first by isolated small units of company size which suffered heavy casualties considering the number of men actually exposed.

[1] *Leach*, 46–9.

[2] The battalion array was 1/45th, 1/82nd, 1/29th, 1/9th (in reserve at first), and 1/5th. The 1/50th and 1/91st were in close support.

[3] Lake and the 29th had been a part of Wellesley's army for twelve days or less; they had arrived off the Mondego with Spencer on the evening of 5th August.

The tide of battle turned quickly, however, when certain units found ways which enabled them to reach the summit without serious opposition. Soon there was a continuous line of British infantry formed along the western half of the ridge itself. The fighting was now even and bloody; the French were resisting stubbornly, particularly near their eastern flank, as if they still expected Loison's army to come to their rescue.

Once the French position was carried, Delaborde accepted defeat, but minimized it by skilfully withdrawing his four infantry battalions alternately, two at a time. His superior cavalry covered these movements with short, controlled charges. The horsemen inflicted few casualties for they did not press home their attacks, but were able to stem any rapid advance by the British infantry. After an orderly retreat of about a mile, the French reached a shallow defile to the south of the hamlet of Zambugeira. A combination of pressure from the rear and the constricting of the flanks caused Delaborde's army to disintegrate suddenly. The French left three of their five guns here, together with a number of prisoners. But once they gained the far side of the defile, they were safe. The French cavalry was still strong and able to hold back any pursuit in open country. Wellesley did not press his advantage for he received intelligence that Loison's force was only five miles away. That night the victorious army bivouacked facing south and east.

Rolica was the first battle of the Peninsular War. When compared with some fought later, it was inconsiderable. Wellesley's army was three times as strong as Delaborde's, even though the numbers actually engaged were about equal. The Loison threat never materialized, but was nevertheless a considerable advantage to Delaborde. Many commanders in Wellesley's position would not have advanced at all.

The French casualties were about 700 compared to 485 British.[1] Delaborde was driven from two positions, one very strong, and lost three fifths of his artillery. The retreat through the defile of Zambugeira approached a rout.

---

[1] I have assumed that the French prisoners taken at Rolica amounted to approximately 100; there were 600 French killed and wounded. After the Convention of Cintra, all French troops in Portugal became prisoners of war; the separate totals of battlefield captures at Rolica and Vimiero is not available. The figure given for the British casualties however, includes not only killed and wounded, but also prisoners, all taken when Lake met his unfortunate end.

In order to appreciate the full significance of this battle, we must realize the background. For a period of sixteen years, the French were seldom defeated in the field regardless of the relative size of the contending armies. Delaborde's veterans had fought to win, stubbornly and well.[1] The victory of Rolica was proportionately greater when contrasted with the many recent failures of British expeditions which landed, fought inconclusively or were actually defeated, and sailed home having accomplished nothing.[2]

Rolica showed little that was tactically significant other than a more successful than usual employment of British skirmishers, including riflemen. Strategically, Wellesley planned his attack, marshalled his forces, and co-ordinated his manoeuvres with complete success. Lake's blunder precipitated a change of plan which was carried out well. Throughout the day, Sir Arthur was on his guard against a surprise attack from the east, but did not allow Loison's possible flank attack to interfere with his operations against Delaborde. The French would have done well to remember Rolica some years later when, before Salamanca, they admitted that Wellington was magnificent in defence but said he was incapable of fighting an offensive battle.

[1] Delaborde definitely wanted to fight, *Oman*, I, 235. The French commander had examined the advantageous position at Batalha near Alcobaca where John I of Portugal had beaten the Spaniards at the decisive Battle of Aljubarotta in 1385. He found this position choked by trees in 1808.

[2] The British public must have been particularly conscious of Steward's abortive invasion of Calabria in 1806 and the Buenos Aires fiasco under Whitelock in 1807. An invasion of Egypt failed in 1807, as did Duckworth's attack on Constantinople in the same year. Britain had done well in the East and in the West Indies, but her efforts nearer home had frequently been dramatically unsuccessful.

THE BRITISH ARMY UNDER WELLESLEY   TOTAL = 14,000

Six Infantry Brigades, 14½ Battalions   = 13,500

1st Brigade, Rowland Hill

1/5th, 1/9th and 1/38th

2nd Brigade, R. Ferguson

1/36th, 1/40th and 1/71st

3rd Brigade, M. Nightingall

1/29th and 1/82nd

4th Brigade, B. F. Bowes

1/6th and 1/32nd

5th Brigade, Catlin Craufurd

1/45th and 1/91st

6th Brigade, H. Fane

1/50th, 5/60th, 4 Cos. 2/95th

Part of the 20th L. D., Charles D. Taylor   = 240

Three Artillery Batteries, William Robe   = 226

(Probably five 9-pounders, ten 6-pounders, and three 5·5-inch howitzers)

Portuguese auxiliaries (none actually engaged)   Approximately 2,000

THE FRENCH ARMY UNDER DELABORDE   TOTAL = 4,400

INFANTRY, Five Battalions   = 4,000

CAVALRY, Three Squadrons   = 300

ARTILLERY, One Battery (probably 5 guns)   = 100

TOPOGRAPHICAL OBSERVATIONS

The small fort at the mouth of the Mondego is still in existence. The sandy road through Lugar is now paved, and can be followed without difficulty. The village of Obidos, still surrounded by its Moorish wall, lies slightly north of the Rolica valley. The first French positions at Rolica are not well defined, but their second line southeast of the village of Columbeira is obvious; one can walk up the rugged gulley into which Lake led half the 29th.

III

VIMIERO

WELLESLEY had his force under arms an hour before dawn on the morning of 18th August. Because of his weakness in cavalry, an effective picket line was impossible, but the army had bivouacked in line of battle. An attack by Delaborde's defeated force alone was extremely unlikely, but if Loison had joined Delaborde during the night, a combined attack might easily have been attempted.

Daybreak revealed no French in the immediate neighbourhood. Wellesley allowed his men to pile arms and cook their breakfast. At headquarters, however, all was bustle. Portuguese civilians were coming in with a variety of reports; scouts from Wellesley's staff and small cavalry patrols were returning with news. A dispatch was received from a fleet of British transports with reinforcements aboard which had just arrived off the coast. Wellesley calmly assimilated each piece of information.

The position of the enemy soon became clear. Delaborde and Loison had both marched to the southeast; presumably, they had joined forces. Obviously, they were not planning a counter-attack until reinforced from Lisbon, and no French column was reported moving north from there. Wellesley estimated Junot's force in Portugal at less than 25,000, but some units of the actual 30,000 were as far away as Elvas and Almeida. Sir Arthur had only 13,000 men under arms at this time, but the transports contained 4,000 additional infantry which had to be got ashore as soon as possible.

Peniche, the only safe harbour between the Mondego and Lisbon, was still in French hands; to sail back to the Mondego was impractical. Wellesley heard of a crescent-shaped beach at the mouth of the Maceira river, some fifteen miles southwest of Rolica (Plate 5). The river is, and was, hardly deep enough to float a canoe, but the headlands at either end of the beach offered some protection from the heavy Portuguese surf.[1]

Wellesley sent off orders for the transports to proceed to the mouth of the Maceira and had the entire army marching in that direction before noon. Both were there before dark; the landing would begin at dawn, weather permitting, while the army took up a position to cover the disembarkation. Anstruther's Brigade was brought ashore on the 19th; Acland's followed on the 20th. Wellesley was briefly in command of nearly 17,000 British soldiers, but they were not to remain his for long.

Early on the afternoon of 20th August, Sir Harry Burrard, a lieu-tenant general senior to Wellesley, arrived off Maceira. This was no surprise to Wellesley; the Secretary of War, Castlereagh, had advised him of his coming loss of command even before the Mondego landings.[2] The Tory Ministry had been unable to retain Wellesley as C-in-C in Portugal in the face of pressure from the Duke of York and the King himself. To make matters worse, Sir Arthur would soon be outranked not only by Burrard, but also by Sir Hew Dalrymple and Sir John Moore, both now on their way to Portugal. Wellesley resolved to con-tinue to do his job to the limit of his ability, neither increasing nor decreasing the speed of his operations on account of impending re-placement.[3]

He had himself rowed out to Burrard's ship. After a long conference, Wellesley was ordered not to move from his present position. Burrard decided correctly that Wellesley was underestimating the enemy's strength. An additional force under Sir John Moore would soon come ashore at the mouth of the Mondego and march south. Burrard's plan was to wait before advancing on Lisbon until he had his total force concentrated, even though this might cause a delay of two weeks.

[1] There is a graphic description of the difficulties of landing at Maceira Bay even in good weather in *Schaumann*, 1–3 and 8. Many soldiers were drowned here on 2nd September.

[2] The C-in-C of the British army, either the Duke of York or Sir David Dundas during the Peninsular War, 'placed the troops in the hands of the ministers': he exercised only the loosest control over their use: *Napier*, II, 146–7. Ultimate authority for an expedition came from the Secretary of State: *Ward*, 32. Orders as to objectives and move-ments were issued by Castlereagh, then known as 'Secretary of State': *Dispatches*, IV, throughout. This same position was later called 'Secretary of War': *National Biography*, VIII, 1,232.

[3] Wellington to Castlereagh, 1st August, *Dispatches*, IV, 55, 'All that I can say upon that subject is, that whether I am to command the army or not, or am to quit it, I shall do my best to insure its success; and you may depend upon it that I shall not hurry the operations, or commence them one moment sooner than they ought to be commenced in order that I may acquire the credit of the success.'

After Burrard had given Wellesley instructions which would prevent the latter from taking any chances with the army, the senior general decided to stay on board ship another night. He had some letters to write. Wellesley returned at nightfall to the mouth of the Maceira with only a few hours of independent command left; there appeared to be no chance that he would distinguish himself further. Little did he realize that before Burrard came ashore next morning a great battle would be in process.

North of Vimiero two long hills lie end to end at right angles to the coastline. The Maceira river flows north through a defile between them, and then turns abruptly west before entering the sea. South of this gap lies the village of Vimiero and Vimiero hill, a round, flat-topped eminence considerably lower than the two ridges. The Maceira receives a tributary from the east immediately south of the eastern ridge. The country was, and is, picturesque and rugged, but infantry and even guns could move almost anywhere except on certain slopes of the ridges which were particularly precipitous.[1]

Wellesley had originally posted his army mainly on the western ridge, to defend the bay against an attack from the south. On the night of 20th August, five and two-thirds of his eight brigades were there; two more lay on Vimiero hill. A single battalion was posted on the eastern ridge as a flank guard; the Portuguese auxiliaries were further north. There were six guns on Vimiero hill, eight on the western ridge, and four in reserve near the defile between the ridges.[2] Wellesley had placed his transport and baggage between Vimiero and this cleft. The cavalry bivouacked nearby.

Soon after midnight on the 21st, Wellesley received intelligence that a French army was advancing in his direction from Torres Vedras. He sent out additional patrols and had his entire command under arms in line of battle long before dawn. Sir Arthur in person was on the western ridge at daybreak, surveying the territory to the south. But there were

[1] The terrain in the gorge of the Maceira required climbing technique, but there was a road practical for artillery at the southeast corner of the western ridge.

[2] Authorities do not agree as to where the British field pieces were on 20th and 21st August. *Fortescue*, VI, 222–3, implies that three 9-pounders were brought down the rugged road (mentioned in the previous note) during the *night* before the battle. I doubt whether this was possible.

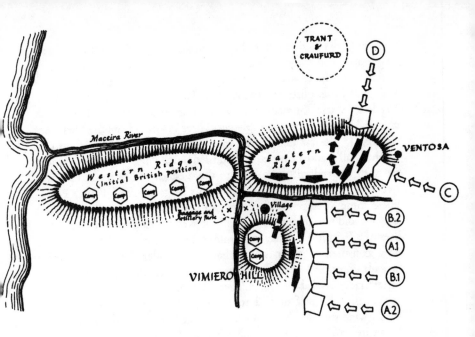

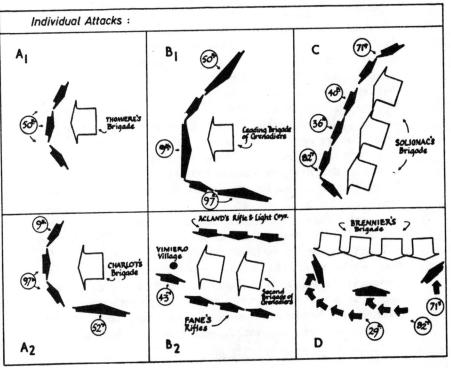

II. VIMIERO

no signs of the French, either there or to the east. The army was ordered to pile arms and cook breakfast.

About 9 a.m., clouds of dust were seen to rise far to the east; bayonets and gunbarrels glittered in the sun. The French army was turning Wellesley's left. Immediately Sir Arthur issued brief orders which changed his battle array completely. Three brigades from the west were ordered to the far end of the eastern ridge; these were Ferguson's, Nightingall's, and Bowes's. Acland's Brigade, which was slightly under strength, moved with two guns to the western end of the same ridge, overlooking Vimiero village. Craufurd's Brigade joined Trant's Portuguese some distance north of the gap between the ridges. Only Hill's Brigade and two guns remained on the western ridge. Vimiero hill had been the British left flank; it was now the right centre. The left centre now consisted of seven strong battalions under Ferguson as senior brigade commander; it was formed in two lines facing east where the eastern ridge rises above the village of Ventosa.

Wellesley himself moved to the eastern ridge. His right and left flanks were guarded by Hill on the western ridge, and Craufurd and Trant in broken country to the north of the eastern ridge; they were practically unassailable. His centre consisted of two brigades on Vimiero hill, three on the extremity of the eastern ridge, and one connecting them; all were strongly placed. Soon unmistakable signs of an attack in three columns could be made out. One was continuing to march north; another appeared to be heading northwest and would collide with Ferguson. The last, and apparently the heaviest, was approaching Vimiero hill from just south of east. These observations were approximate only; the country through which the French were advancing was neither flat nor open, but hillocky and partly wooded. Their line of march was more easily followed by watching the clouds of dust which they raised than from any continuous view of their ranks. It was soon evident that the column nearing Vimiero hill would strike some time before the other two.

Wellesley disposed the brigades of Fane and Anstruther to protect this hill in a fashion often repeated as the war progressed. More than half of Fane's Brigade was deployed about 800 yards in front of the hill itself in what amounted to a heavy skirmish line. It consisted of four companies of 2/95th, all of that battalion present, and the entire 5/60th; both these units were armed with rifles. The hill proper was held by the remaining five battalions of these two brigades; three were at the crest, or slightly to the rear of it, with the other two further back in support.

From north to south, the front line battalions were the 1/50th, the 2/97th and the 2/52nd; the 2/9th and the 2/43rd were behind them. There were twelve guns on the flat hilltop.[1]

Suddenly, the French attack on Vimiero hill took definite shape in the form of two columns about 400 yards apart, one moving along a road directly towards the hill and the other against its southeastern face. Both these powerful infantry columns were shielded by *tirailleurs* and supported by field artillery moving forward with them. Cavalry was protecting their flanks, although the ground was not particularly favourable for mounted men. The French here were following precisely the all-conquering offensive tactics proved on so many fields by Napoleon.

The *tirailleurs* were unable to subdue Fane's riflemen. The French light infantry were supposed to shield the French columns and unsettle the British main line with accurate individual fire, but exactly the reverse occurred. The *tirailleurs* required the help of their columns to force back the riflemen. So long and stubbornly did the Rifles keep up the fight that they masked the British guns until the last moment. Colonel Robe's pieces had time for only one murderous discharge before the French infantry met the British in line.

Each of the two French columns was composed of two battalions, one behind the other; the mass was about 30 men broad and extended back 42 ranks in depth.[2] The northern column was slightly in the lead; it came into contact with the 1/50th which was in a two-deep line some minutes before the southern column attacked.

The first volley from the 1/50th was fired at a range slightly over 100 yards; others followed regularly at 15-second intervals as the range gradually shortened. Slowly, the flanks of the 50th wrapped around the column. The British line was using every one of its 900 muskets; the French could reply with no more than 200 of their 1,200 firearms. General Thomieres, who commanded the French brigade, endeavoured to deploy from column into line under fire, but found this impossible. The French recoiled at each volley; they finally broke and fled to the rear with the riflemen in hot pursuit.

[1] I have followed, in the main, *Fortescue*, VI, 225, which is confirmed by *Oman*, I, 248 and 254. Napier's account of Vimiero is questionable; he and those who followed him have Anstruther's Brigade and Fane's 50th reversed, I, plate 4 facing 134. *Wyld's Atlas* is not of great value for Vimiero.

[2] Junot's army, having left France before the infantry structure was reorganized in February 1808, still had powerful battalions of approximately 1,100 men. There were seven line companies, one grenadier company, and one *voltigeur* company in each. Junot had concentrated his grenadier companies into a separate organization. Each line company formed three ranks deep, but varied in width according to its strength.

The second column further south was more protected by the terrain; it came to within 300 yards of the Vimiero hill before suffering from British skirmishers. Anstruther's Brigade, posted by Wellesley, had only a small part of its force showing. The left battalion, the 2/97th, was protected by a fold in the hill, but lay directly in the path of the French column.

As the mounted officers saw the French approach, they brought the 2/97th forward in line two deep to the military crest. Initially, the French had an advantage in numbers, about 1,200 to 695, but their formation was against them. The entire head of the column appeared to melt away at the first British volley; rolling fire by half companies followed in a steady roar. The 2/52nd wheeled in on the French left flank; Anstruther had the 2/9th advancing from the second line to wheel against their right. The French brigade dissolved into a mass of panic-stricken soldiers heading for the rear. Again the riflemen pursued but did not press their advantage far.

Both these French brigades had been accompanied by supporting artillery; the French gunners had been so harassed by Fane's riflemen that their fire had been light and ineffective. Men and horses were shot at long range; when the infantry columns broke, the artillery was stranded. All seven guns were captured.

Sir Harry Burrard joined the army at about this time, but sensibly and magnanimously refused to take immediate command. Wellesley was to finish the battle he had begun. The British skirmish line in front of Vimiero hill had scarcely been re-established when the French advanced again with fresh troops. A swarm of *tirailleurs* preceded two more close-order columns, each composed of two battalions, one behind the other, but with an appreciable interval between them.

Robe's artillery was better placed than previously and could clear the British riflemen. Howitzers firing the new Shrapnel shell were particularly effective.[1] They had a pattern at 1,000 yards like canister at close range; when the fuse worked properly, pieces of shell casing and several dozen musket balls came down in a cone on the target. Round shot from Robe's guns were, of course, capable of inflicting serious damage on a column at long range, but required more precise directing.

---

[1] British batteries, then called brigades, usually consisted of five field guns, at Vimiero either 6- or 9-pounders, and one 5·5-inch howitzer, also known as a 24-pounder howitzer. Shrapnel shells were used for the first time during this campaign and were effective only in the larger howitzer size. Guns normally fired solid shot or case (canister); howitzers fired shrapnel shell or case. Oman uses the word 'shell' to apply to all artillery fire; only howitzers fired explosive projectiles in either the British or French field artillery.

This second attack was again accompanied by artillery, probably four pieces. During the advance, they unlimbered and replied to the British pieces on Vimiero hill, but were handicapped because of their lower positions and were frequently masked by *tirailleurs*.

The French column, now identified as grenadiers, could not be stopped by artillery fire and riflemen alone, no matter how effective.[1] Fane's men disengaged without embarrassing the British line as they had before. The leading French column was directed at the 2/9th which was placed in line between the two areas the previous columns had struck. The 1/50th wheeled round from the north and the 2/97th from the south; all three battalions opened a converging fire on the French grenadiers at long range, about 200 yards. The volleys were not so effective as when fired at closer quarters, but the 2,000 muskets brought the French to a halt. The British battalions advanced slowly, firing as they came. In less than two minutes, the first grenadier brigade disintegrated; four guns which accompanied their advance were taken within 300 yards of the crest of Vimiero hill.

In the confusion attending this repulse, the second grenadier brigade veered off to the right towards Vimiero village, keeping to the lower protected ground which may have contained a sunken road. They were now north of the 1/50th and had nothing between them and the sprawling stone dwellings. But they were exposed to an attack from the eastern ridge. Wellesley ordered forward two guns which took them in flank at comparatively long range. He also sent down to close range Acland's two companies of the 1/95th and his two light companies.

The French grenadiers were slowed up and suffered considerable loss; just as they reached the village, the 2/43rd which Anstruther had ordered north from his second line behind Vimiero hill met them. The grenadiers and the 2/43rd were soon fighting in the narrow, stone-walled streets, partly with bayonets. The British had no formation advantage and were outnumbered by about nine to seven. The French were worried about being cut off. After some confused and bloody fighting, they gave up that part of the village they held briefly and retreated, running the gauntlet between Acland's and Fane's riflemen; many were killed, wounded, or captured.

---

[1] Junot, following a custom common in European armies, but never used by Wellesley, had taken the grenadier company from each of his eighteen infantry battalions and organized them into semi-permanent battalions and brigades: *Oman*, I, 244–5.

Four French attacks had now been shattered; the plain east and south of Vimiero hill was covered with stragglers and groups helping wounded to the rear. Every gun that had been brought forward had been taken. Wellesley now ordered his small cavalry force to advance, for there was a good opportunity of a counter-stroke. Some 240 men of the 20th L. D., and about the same number of Portuguese, all under the command of Colonel Taylor, rode forward gallantly, breaking up a quickly formed square of French grenadiers. The Portuguese horsemen soon lost heart and rode to the rear amid the jeers of British infantry, but Taylor and his 20th charged through a regiment of French dragoons and galloped on, completely out of control. They swept past more infantry, but inflicted few casualties and took no prisoners. They were far beyond the support of their own artillery, and were badly beaten by horsemen more numerous and more skilful than themselves. Taylor fell mortally hurt; half his men were killed, wounded, or captured.[1] It is remarkable that any managed to escape. Going out of control at full gallop, which made both manoeuvre and response to orders impossible, was to be the curse of British cavalry during the war.

The fighting in front of Vimiero itself, and the cavalry charge, was over by 11 a.m., although severe fighting had already commenced on the eastern ridge above Ventosa some time previously. The two columns which had been seen earlier, advanced into this area shortly after 9 a.m. The first moved to the north beyond the ridge; Wellesley allowed it to pass on, for it would have to negotiate much broken country before meeting Craufurd and Trant. The second column turned west at Ventosa towards Ferguson's position on the ridge. This French force consisted of about 3,000 infantry with some cavalry and three guns; a line of *tirailleurs* preceded three battalions columns abreast, each column one company, approximately 30 men, wide.

Ferguson's three brigades contained seven battalions totalling 5,782 men; he also may have had three guns.[2] Wellesley posted this force himself, or at least checked personally their dispositions. They were in three lines, the first composed of seven light companies deployed in skirmish order on the military crest. The second or main line lay behind on the summit and consisted of (from north to south) the 1/71st, 1/40th,

[1] *Fortescue*, VI, 229, differs from Oman, whose completed work the former had available to him at this stage of their great, but separate labours in the same field. Neither contradicts the other except when supported by conclusive evidence! *Oman*, I 357, suggests a considerably smaller loss.

[2] The distribution of British field pieces is impossible to determine precisely; see note 2 p. 44. I base this on *Oman*, I 253, '. . . Bowes, Nightingall, and Acland . . . taking with them six guns. . . .' We know Acland retained two.

1/36th, and 1/82nd. The third, or supporting line, still further back, contained the 1/32nd, 1/6th, and 1/29th. Only the light companies were exposed to view, for the main line was lying down.

The French commander, General Solignac, thought himself at least equal in number, and superior in quality, to his opponent. But his *tirailleurs* were at a disadvantage numerically and tactically; they were trying to drive in the British skirmishers who were higher up the hill and settled behind isolated rocks and in depressions from which they were firing. The French columns had to help their line of *tirailleurs* to clear the military crest. Their three battalions were somewhat disordered in the process, but reformed and came on with lateral intervals of about 300 yards between them. Solignac may have mistaken the British skirmishers for a main line; if so he was soon disillusioned.

When the French columns were only 100 yards from the crest, Ferguson sent forward his four battalions in line. The two forces were about equal in numbers, but not in fire power. The British battalions delivered a thunderous volley which wrought havoc among the heads of the French columns. Even more telling, because of its unexpectedness, was the rolling platoon fire from 3,000 British muskets. There were half company volleys delivered precisely from 72 small groups at approximately 15-second intervals. Only the heads of the three French columns were able to return this fire.

The French tried unsuccessfully to deploy into line while under fire, but as a company would separate from its column, it was exposed to withering volleys and was driven back into the mass. After only two minutes, time enough for ten British volleys, all three French columns disintegrated and retired downhill precipitately. Ferguson's four first line battalions followed in a short pursuit only; French guns were taken, together with a number of prisoners.

Ferguson reorganized his force slightly. Bowes's Brigade, the 1/6th, and 1/32nd, was sent back along the eastern ridge towards Vimiero.[1] Nightingall's Brigade, the 1/29th and 1/82nd, reinforced by the 1/71st from Ferguson's own Brigade remained with the captured artillery. Ferguson himself with the 1/36th and 1/40th went off in pursuit of Solignac's routed men. These two battalions scattered with ease the French rearguard and forced Solignac to the north. Ferguson was now cutting off his antagonist from the main French army to the south.

---

[1] Probably because the French grenadier attack had just briefly penetrated into the village. Bowes's Brigade was certainly in the second line when Solignac attacked, and was *not* engaged with Brennier, who attacked a short time after.

Meanwhile, the 1/71st, 1/82nd, and 1/29th (in that order from north to south) were facing east with a line of pickets before them overlooking Ventosa. They seem to have forgotten the presence of the French force commanded by General Brennier which had moved north earlier in the morning. But Brennier had been attracted back to the battle area by the firing during Solignac's attack. Brennier's command advanced on to the flank and rear of the three British battalions, and attacked with four battalion columns abreast. The fighting was confused, for the French had first to climb the northern slope of the eastern ridge before covering 200 or 300 yards across the broad irregular crest, and were in some disorder. The British had time to reverse their formations to some extent, but the flanks of the 1/71st and 1/82nd were assailed while they were endeavouring to change front. Brennier's men were at first successful and retook the guns lost by Solignac.

The 1/29th abandoned its position on the right flank, circled around the fighting area and fell on the French flank from the west. This battalion used an unusual formation; it advanced four ranks deep. The reason for this was the presence in Brennier's force of squadrons of French dragoons. In spite of their formation, the attack of the 29th was sufficiently strong to bring the four French battalion columns to a stand; the 82nd and 71st reformed. A stabilized front at musketry range was established.

For the fifth time that day, British lines were firing regular volleys into French columns. The French enjoyed a numerical superiority of about 3,200 to 2,400, not including their dragoons. But their formation was inferior; furthermore Bowes's Brigade with 1,800 additional muskets could be seen hurrying back from above Vimiero. By the mysterious telepathy of battles, the French realized that they had lost elsewhere and would lose here also. They broke and scattered down the northern face of the ridge after less resistance than their fellows had made earlier. Brennier was wounded and captured; his command, under protection of their cavalry, managed to stream back to the southeast. These Frenchmen actually passed behind Ferguson and his two battalions, who had forced the majority of Solignac's men into a pocket of hills from which there was no easy retreat.

Wellesley was himself present during the latter part of this action and may have brought round the 29th. He witnessed the complete discomfiture of Brennier, who lost not only the three guns he had briefly recaptured, but also the three he brought with him. When the French commander was taken, Sir Arthur questioned him immediately. The four battalions of grenadiers which had already been beaten in front of the hill and village of Vimiero—Brennier did not know this—constituted the entire French reserve. Every single French infantry battalion had been broken. The French could attack no more, and would suffer a complete defeat if pursued industriously. Putting spurs to his thoroughbred, Wellesley galloped a mile along the eastern ridge to where Sir Harry Burrard stood.

'Sir Harry,' Wellesley urged, 'now is your chance. The French are completely beaten; we have a large body of troops that have not yet been in action. Let us move on Torres Vedras. You take the force here straight forward; I will bring round the left with the troops already there. We shall be in Lisbon in three days!'[1]

At this time a message arrived from Ferguson. He had cut off some 2,000 Frenchmen in a cul-de-sac of hills and asked permission to attack with his own brigade together with those of Nightingall and Bowes. It was now only midday; the brigades of Hill, Craufurd, and Bowes had not suffered a single casualty. Acland's men had only skirmished. British morale could not have been higher, nor that of the French lower.

But Sir Harry was a general of the old school. He knew little of battles and less of winning them. He would not pursue for the same reasons that had caused him to forbid Wellesley to advance further the previous evening. Sir Arthur remonstrated forcefully, but to no avail. Burrard was incapable of fully appreciating what had happened, much less the opportunity offered. Sir Harry declared that the army had done enough for one day and ordered everyone back to their bivouac areas. Even the French trapped by Ferguson were allowed to escape.

Sir Harry Burrard commanded the British army for a few hours only. He was superseded next day by Sir Hew Dalrymple, from Gibraltar, who was to be C-in-C in Portugal. Dalrymple was older than Burrard, but had even less experience in the field. Both men were full of years and honours, but lacked military ability, either inherent or acquired.[2]

---

[1] A direct quotation from Wellesley, given by *Fortescue*, VI, 231.

[2] Dalrymple was born in 1750 and entered the army in 1763. He was a lieutenant colonel in 1781, but saw his first active service under the Duke of York in 1793. He was never again in command of troops in combat, but served long and honourably in other capacities: *National Biography*, V, 408. Burrard was born in 1755 and was commissioned in the Coldstreamers in 1772. He served in America without distinction. He was also with the Duke of York in Flanders and in Denmark in 1807, but Wellesley did the fighting. He was never in independent command before Vimiero and never present at any other major British victory. Ibid., III, 440. Wellesley referred to them collectively as 'the Gentlemen'.

Even if Sir Hew and Sir Harry were unable to realize that the French had been disastrously defeated, Junot did. While the three British lieutenant generals were in stormy conference debating what should be done, an alarm was given. The French were said to be attacking again, but it was only General Kellerman accompanied by a squadron of cavalry advancing under a flag of truce to propose an armistice and negotiate for a surrender. The French were willing to give up all Portugal, without damaging anything, if they could be conveyed back to France by sea. A truce of forty-eight hours to consider further the terms of a convention was immediately drawn up; Sir Arthur signed the armistice when ordered to do so by Sir Hew.

Within the time prescribed, the so-called Convention of Cintra was negotiated. The French gave up intact all forts, arsenals, weapons and military stores not only around Lisbon, but elsewhere in Portugal including the powerful border fortress towns of Elvas and Almeida. Within weeks, the French were transported back to France (La Rochelle) in British ships with no restrictions as to further service. They took with them all personal property, a term which included in some cases articles of small bulk plundered from the Portuguese. French civilians were allowed to remain in Portugal without loss of liberty or possessions.

Both Britain and Portugal profited greatly under the terms of the Convention. The entire objective of the campaign, the freeing of Portugal from French domination, was gained most efficiently by two battles fought within five days. It would have taken months to clear the country by fighting; thousands of lives, including those of civilians, were saved. Damage to property would have been great. Elvas and Almeida might have held out indefinitely and could have been relieved by the French from Spain.

The Convention of Cintra was extremely unpopular in Britain. The British public did not approve of transporting the enemy to France in British ships. Feeling ran so high that the Tory Ministry was obliged to bring before a Court of Inquiry not only Dalrymple and Burrard, but to a lesser extent and more obliquely, Wellesley, who had won the victories which caused the French to surrender. Sir Arthur signed the armistice in accordance with Dalrymple's specific order; he had literally nothing to do with the Convention itself, nor did he even see it.[1] The Court of Inquiry voted six to one for the armistice and four to three for the terms granted to the French under the Convention. There can be

[1] A good account of this is in *Man Wellington*, 148–55, amply documented.

little doubt that almost any convention would have been preferable to allowing either Sir Hew or Sir Harry to conduct field operations with the British army!

What was particularly significant about the battle of Vimiero? A veteran French army attacking in the open field in accordance with Napoleon's cherished tactics, was completely defeated. Nothing like this had happened for years. To the French, from Junot to his youngest drummer, it came as a complete surprise; the rest of Europe was hardly less astonished.

Admittedly, the French were outnumbered, but for years they had ignored odds larger than 13 to 17. The French were not handled with genius for they were defeated in detail, yet this criticism of Junot is subject to question. Had his initial attacks on Vimiero hill and on the eastern ridge above Ventosa been successful, they would have become part of a co-ordinated plan.

Junot's conception of sending more than half his infantry around Sir Arthur's exposed left flank was bold and might easily have succeeded if Wellesley himself had not changed completely his original alignment without delay. This countering of French battlefield strategy by a movement of his own was to become characteristic of Wellesley.

Tactically, British lines overthrew French columns every time the two formations came together, even though the columns frequently outnumbered the lines actually engaged. In its way, this was even more startling to the French than their general defeat. Their massed columns, *tirailleurs*, and artillery had been smashing enemy lines of the Frederick the Great type with ease. What had happened?

Every infantry field officer in Europe appreciated the musketry advantage of an infantry line over a column. The French had so weakened these lines with *tirailleur* fire and close range artillery discharges that the shock potential of the infantry columns outweighed the theoretical musketry advantage of the lines. Wellesley had countered the *tirailleurs* with skirmishers of his own. Fane's riflemen, and to a lesser extent those of Acland, not only prevented the French *tirailleurs* from 'softening up' the British lines, but also did considerable damage to the attacking columns. Sir Arthur had sheltered his main lines behind hill crests and achieved a certain surprise with their sudden appearance. The French artillery brought forward with their infantry was never able to deliver a telling fire; several field pieces were captured before they had fired a single round.

It should also be noted that Wellesley had unused reserves available behind both his right and left centres and could have committed fresh troops in either or both sectors, if the French attacks had achieved an initial success. If Vimiero had been taken, Hill's and Acland's Brigades would have descended on the victors immediately. If the French had won above Ventosa, Acland, Craufurd and Trant were in reserve. This inter-relationship of units for mutual support, a form of dynamic defence, was to become characteristic of the British commander.

Finally, although the French were greatly superior in cavalry, this advantage did them no good. Wellesley chose positions which mounted units could not attack effectively. On the other hand, the British cavalry had a remarkable opportunity which they wasted by their undisciplined bravery.

THE CONTENDING FORCES, AND LOSSES AT VIMIERO[1]

THE BRITISH ARMY UNDER WELLESLEY   TOTAL = 16,778

Eight Infantry Brigades, 20¼ Battalions   = 16,312

1st Brigade, Rowland Hill	2,658
1/5th, 1/9th and 1/38th	
2nd Brigade, R. Ferguson	2,449
1/36th, 1/40th and 1/71st	
3rd Brigade, M. Nightingall	1,520
1/29th and 1/82nd	
4th Brigade, B. F. Bowes	1,813
1/6th and 1/32nd	
5th Brigade, Catlin Craufurd	1,832
1/45th and 1/91st	
6th Brigade, H. Fane	2,005
1/50th, 5/60th, 4 Cos. 2/95th	
7th Brigade, Robert Anstruther	2,703
2/9th, 2/43rd, 2/52nd and 2/97th	
8th Brigade, Worth Acland	1,332
2nd, 7½ Cos. 1/20th, 2 Cos. 1/95th	

[1] I have followed *Oman*, I, 246–7 and 250–1. *Fortescue*, VI, 219, reaches a similar conclusion.

Part of the 20th L. D., Charles D. Taylor		=	240
Three Artillery Batteries, William Robe		=	226

(Probably five 9-pounders, ten 6-pounders, and three 5·5-inch howitzers)

Portuguese auxiliaries (none actually engaged)   Approximately 2,000

THE FRENCH ARMY UNDER JUNOT   TOTAL = 13,050

Six Infantry Brigades, 15 Battalions   = 10,400

Delaborde's Division

Brennier's Brigade	3,000
4 Battalions	
Thomiere's Brigade	1,400
2 Battalions	

Loison's Division

Solignac's Brigade	2,800
3 Battalions	
Charlot's Brigade	1,100
2 Battalions	
Reserve of Grenadiers	2,100

Organized into 2 Brigades of 2 small Battalions each

Margaron's Cavalry Division   = 1,950

Four Artillery Batteries, 23 or 24 guns   = 700

LOSSES AT VIMIERO

	French	British
Killed	450	135
Wounded	1,200	534
Prisoners and Missing	350	51
	———	——
Total	2,000	720

The French lost 13 or more artillery pieces.[1]

[1] There should have been 17 captured French artillery pieces in British hands at the end of the battle: seven from the first Vimiero hill assault; four from the grenadier advance, three from Solignac's attack above Ventosa, and three after Brennier's attack. The totals officially given vary from Wellesley's 13 to Robe's 22; see *Fortescue*, VI, 231, note 1.

TOPOGRAPHICAL OBSERVATIONS

The terrain over which this battle was fought is much more complicated than indicated in the simplified sketch. Fortescue, VI, 221–2, note 1, points out that Vimiero hill is not really 'commanding', although Napier, VI, 134, calls it 'a rugged height with a flat top, commanding all the ground to the southward and eastward for a considerable distance'. Fortescue's opinion was based on observations 100 years later when trees and vineyards seem to have been more numerous than in 1960. The two ridges, however, certainly dominate the entire area. The exact locations of the fighting near the hill and village of Vimiero can be found today easily, but those above Ventosa are uncertain. The cul-de-sac into which Ferguson forced Solignac has the appearance of a V-shaped ravine and is so shown on the modern Portuguese military map. It is not easy to climb out of this, even when unencumbered.

IV

SIR JOHN MOORE AND CORUNNA

THE Convention of Cintra cleared Portugal not only of the French army, but also of Sir Hew Dalrymple and Sir Harry Burrard, who were recalled to stand trial. Sir Arthur Wellesley had returned earlier; his relations with Dalrymple had deteriorated to such an extent that political employment at home, or no employment at all, was preferable to continuing on active service.[1] These departures left Sir John Moore in sole command of a fine army of nearly 30,000 British soldiers.

Before Wellesley left for England, he met Moore in an informal conference.[2] Circumstances had developed a rivalry between their supporters, but Moore and Wellesley never entered into this personally. They treated each other with the most scrupulous candour and honesty.

During the summer of 1808, the war in Spain developed remarkably. Murat considered, at the time of his retirement across the border in June, that he had completed the subjugation of the country for the intrusive king, Joseph Bonaparte. The latter appeared to be firmly on the throne and had more than 90,000 French troops in Spain to keep him there.[3] While Junot was losing Portugal, the French commanders in Spain fared little better. Marshal Moncey failed to take Valencia. The militia of Zaragoza heroically and successfully resisted every attack

---

[1] Even though officially commanding only two battalions, Wellesley was consulted by the various staff departments in regard to their duties as if he had been C-in-C; even Moore remarked on this. Sir Arthur reached England on 4th October and resumed his duties as Chief Secretary for Ireland.

[2] A full and unbiased account of this meeting can be found in *Oman's Moore*, 513-4.

[3] The quality of some of these was questionable; *Oman*, I, 103-5, says: 'The victors of Jena and Friedland were left in their cantonments on the Rhine, the Elbe, and the Oder, while a new force, mainly composed of elements of inferior fighting value, was sent across the Pyrenees.'

made by French regular troops in and around their antiquated walls. The French were only able to keep open their communications with Madrid by defeating the Spanish on 17th July at the battle of Medina de Rio Seco. But when an entire French corps under Dupont was forced to capitulate at Baylen later in the month, the French abandoned Madrid and retired towards the Ebro. Their concentrated armies, 70,000 strong, were in defensive positions on that river by 15th August; Marshal Jourdan took command on the 25th.

The enthusiasm and optimism of the Spaniards after Baylen ran high; semi-independent Spanish commanders had grandiose plans for pushing the French back across the Pyrenees. Even the British Ministry had visions of a real military disaster for Napoleon. There were at least 20,000 disposable British troops in Portugal; another 10,000 could be added to this force from Britain. With this army to assist them, the Spaniards might achieve their objective. Time could be saved if Moore commenced his advance from Portugal and united well inside Spain with the force sent from Britain. The geographical logic of this is obvious; the distance from Corunna to Burgos is only 250 miles, while that from Lisbon to Burgos is 380. But the simultaneous advance of two inexperienced armies separated by a hundred miles of impenetrable mountains was hardly wise. Perhaps the first mistake of Moore's campaign was in dispatching this second force under Sir David Baird to Corunna rather than to Lisbon.

Sir John Moore was a soldier's soldier noted for his integrity, professional efficiency, and unique ability in training both officers and men. He had served in the Low Countries, Sicily, Calabria, Egypt, Ireland and the West Indies, always with honour. In his forty-seventh year, he was both handsome and of commanding presence; although frequently wounded, he was strong, vigorous, and energetic. He was not always fortunate in his associations with civilians and ministers, but this did little to hurt his great military reputation.

Moore received orders to advance on 6th October. By the 18th, he had his army marching towards Salamanca. Sir John sent most of his artillery by a separate and circuitous route to the south. This decision was unfortunate, and based upon the false information that no artillery road existed between Lisbon and Almeida.[1] Moore realized that the

---

[1] *Oman*, I, 496–7, carefully evaluated all evidence and concluded that the artillery could have travelled with the rest of the army. *Fortescue*, VI, 307, declares for Moore, as did Napier. *Moore's Diary*, II, 318–19, criticizes Oman severely. Wellington was able to transport his guns over the roads in question without undue delays.

commencement of the rainy season in Portugal was imminent, and made every effort to enter Spain before the roads became impassable. The main force reached Salamanca between 13th and 23rd November, but the artillery, protected by the cavalry and some infantry commanded by Sir John Hope, did not join him until 4th December.

Meanwhile, Moore was beset with difficulties. His orders from London were to march towards Burgos and there meet Sir David Baird. As senior general, Moore would command the combined force. He was then to advance to the Ebro and co-operate with the Spanish armies against the common enemy. Moore was nominally under the Spanish C-in-C, but received private instructions from his Government not to allow his command to be separated, nor to obey orders which might endanger the British army.

No Spanish supreme C-in-C existed; the pride and jealousy of individuals made such an appointment impossible. An infinitely greater danger was Napoleon himself, who at the head of 200,000 additional soldiers had crossed the Pyrenees. The French broke out of the Ebro valley, smashing first one Spanish army and then another. Napoleon entered Burgos on 11th November, two days before the first British soldiers arrived at Salamanca. The original plan by which Moore was to unite his army was now impossible.

Late in November, the three British forces in north central Spain were separated from each other by longer distances than any one of them was from powerful French units. Moore's only advantage was that he had knowledge of the French dispositions, but Napoleon had no accurate information concerning the British army. Moore now considered carefully his alternatives. From a purely military point of view, the best choice would be to retreat. On 28th November, he ordered Baird's force which had reached Astorga to return to Corunna; Hope was also to retrace his steps unless he felt sure that he could join Moore safely at Salamanca. Hope decided on the latter and more daring alternative; he managed to reach Alba de Tormes, a day's march from Salamanca, on 4th December.[1]

Between 28th November and 4th December, Moore informed the Spanish government through John Hookham Frere, the British Minister in Madrid, of his decision to retreat. Their opposition was instant and voluble; even some within Moore's own army were against retreating. To retire without fighting was to abandon Spain as a future ally.

[1] *Napier*, I, 286–7, commends Hope highly for the execution of the last stages of this march through enemy dominated territory.

Moore received intelligence from various sources at about this time indicating that Napoleon was not moving on Salamanca, but across his front towards Andalusia. The Emperor seemed to take it for granted that the British would retreat, and disregarding them, set about the systematic conquest of Spain. Such a situation offered opportunities which Moore was too good a soldier to ignore. Even though outnumbered by nearly ten to one, he could still strike a blow at vital French communications.

Late in the evening of the 4th, Moore made a courageous decision. The British armies would unite and converge on Burgos which lay on the great road from Bayonne to Madrid. Sir John believed he could take pressure off the capital, which had not yet capitulated, and draw the French away from the southern, unconquered areas of Spain.

Considering the odds, and the defeated state of the Spanish armies, this plan was dangerous and warranted only by the political situation. No one realized this more thoroughly than Moore; 'I was aware that I was risking infinitely too much, but something must be risked for the honour of the Service, and to make it apparent that we stuck to the Spaniards long after they themselves had given up their cause as lost.' [1]

On 6th December, Baird's force turned about and headed again for Old Castile. On the 14th, Moore came into possession of a French dispatch giving accurate, up-to-date information on all French forces in central Spain; he shifted his own line of march slightly to the west, veering away from Valladolid, and united with Baird at Mayorga on the 20th. The British cavalry under Lord Henry Paget surprised a large force of French horse at Sahagun at daybreak on the 21st. In the action that followed, 167 French cavalry were taken prisoners, together with horses, mules, and baggage. Two days later, early in the evening, Moore advanced his entire force from Sahagun towards Carrion in the hope of similarly surprising Marshal Soult's army. After the movement had begun, alarming news reached British headquarters. Napoleon had finally noticed the British army and was proceeding northwest at speed. Such an eventuality was no surprise to Moore; he had counted on getting such advance warning. But there was now no time to surprise Soult. Battalions already approaching Carrion were recalled; the entire army retired on Mayorga.

The movements of both the British and French armies during the last days of December were violent. Marshal Ney passed northwest across the Guadarramas on the 21st during a blizzard; Napoleon followed

[1] *Oman's Moore,* 559.

next day leading his horse through shoulder-high snow drifts. Soult was alerted to his danger and ordered to advance southwest cautiously. Had Moore been at Valladolid instead of Sahagun on the 21st, as was reported to Napoleon, it is probably that the British army would have been caught between these two forces and cut off from their only practical line of retreat, to Corunna. But Moore had made his calculations carefully; he was not trapped. On the afternoon of the 27th, when Soult's force joined up with that of the Emperor, Moore had crossed the Esla to the west.

Lord Henry Paget's cavalry was posted advantageously on both sides of the river defending the bridges and fords which the French would have to use, if they intended to follow Moore. Paget was perhaps the most skilful British cavalry officer of the Napoleonic period and during the next few days added considerably to his reputation won at Sahagun.[1] He checked the French cavalry before Benavente on the 29th, under the eyes of the Emperor himself. Those French horsemen who crossed the river were beaten back with 150 casualties, including a general officer made prisoner.[2] The British infantry and artillery retreated at leisure to Astorga.

Moore was joined on the 30th by what remained of the Spanish army of Galicia (under the gallant and patriotic Romana) which had suffered a singularly unnecessary defeat at the hands of Soult's dragoons at Mansilla the previous day.[3] This rout threw Romana's army back on to the same road of retreat as that which the British army would now have to take. Moore had with him about 25,000 of all arms, not counting Romana's force of about 9,500 deficient in everything, including muskets and boots!

Moore had been condemned for not fighting at Astorga. He had a good defensive position; his combined army was not much inferior in numbers to the French actually present. But Napoleon was in personal

[1] Lord Henry Paget, later Earl of Uxbridge and Marquis of Anglesey, was a talented professional soldier who took a real interest in his job. He fell in love with the wife of Henry Wellesley, Sir Arthur's younger brother, with whom he eloped in 1809. Paget and Wellington were estranged for a time, but in the Waterloo campaign Paget was second-in-command and received the greatest confidence that Wellington ever bestowed on a cavalry officer. Anglesey, *One-Leg*.

[2] General Charles Lefebvre-Desnoettes, who commanded the cavalry of the Guard; Oman states only 'General Lefebvre'. There were several high-ranking French officers of both names.

[3] Marquis de la Romana was in command of Spanish troops serving in Denmark and northern Germany when Napoleon treacherously attacked Spain. In a most dramatic operation, described in *Oman's Studies*, 127-39, most of the Spanish force was rescued by Britain and taken to Galicia.

command with some of his best troops and subordinate generals; without question, the Emperor wanted a battle. To have fought under such conditions a hundred long miles from safety would have been foolhardy, but many of his officers and men wished to do exactly this. When a further withdrawal was ordered, they showed their dissatisfaction in a variety of ways. This discontent within the army had been building up since the first decision to retreat at the end of November. Perhaps the success of the Rolica-Vimiero campaign had brought overconfidence. 'The root of all this mischief lay in the fact that certain subordinate Generals, in the plenitude of their ignorance, had made up their own minds, and by loose talk had persuaded their inferiors, that the duty of a Commander-in-chief was to fight and not to retreat.'[1]

The trouble was far more serious than mere complaining; the morale and discipline of many infantry battalions declined rapidly after the countermanding of the advance from Sahagun towards Carrion. Benavente was the scene of looting, wanton destruction of private property, and drunkenness. The weather was terrible. Carts, wagons, and even pack animals began to break down; the army behaved progressively worse at Villafranca and Bembibre.

> 'Our sufferings were so great that many of the men lost their natural activity and spirits, and became savage in their disposition. The idea of running away, without firing a shot, from the enemy we had beaten so easily at Vimiero, was too galling for their feelings. Each spoke to his fellow, even in common conversation, with bitterness: rage flashed out on the most trifling occasion of disagreement. The poor Spaniards had little to expect from such men as these, who blamed them for their inactivity. Every man found at home was looked upon as a traitor to his country. "Why is not every Spaniard under arms and fighting? The cause is not ours: are we to be the only sufferers?" Such was the common language, and from these feelings, pillage and outrage naturally arose.'[2]

Some infantry battalions took leave of their officers and scattered over the countryside in search of wine, women, and plunder. Hundreds became helplessly drunk. Yet the rearguard fought a creditable action at Cacabelos on 3rd January (1809), in which the French General Colbert was killed by Rifleman Thomas Plunket. The rearguard, and

---

[1] *Fortescue*, VI, 360.   [2] *T.S.*, 53.

those units with experienced officers and NCO's, retained their order and discipline admirably.

Napoleon personally followed Moore no further than Astorga, where he turned over the pursuit to Soult, and returned to France. Soult continued to press the British back along the road to Corunna (Plate 6). The French army in direct pursuit had fewer infantry than Moore after 3rd January, but Soult could call on Ney's corps, never more than four days away, for ample reinforcements if required.

Moore made several decisions during his retreat to Corunna which have been severely criticized. The first of these was the detaching, on 31st December, of General Robert Craufurd, with his own brigade and that of Alten of the K.G.L., to Vigo, well to the south of Corunna.[1] Craufurd drove his troops over wintry mountain roads without regard to personal hardships; they embarked for Britain with relatively little loss. Not one Frenchman pursued Craufurd, nor were his five brigades of any further use to Moore. Craufurd personally could have been of great assistance to the army as a whole, if he had remained with it.[2]

It has been suggested that Moore should have fought at Lugo between the 6th and the 9th of January. The prospect of battle filled up the ranks of most battalions; morale and discipline returned when men believed that at last they would have a chance to fight rather than suffer dismally in the cold and wet mile after mile in retreat. The British army had checked its adversaries whenever ordered to do so. The rearguard remained throughout an efficient fighting force, as did the brigade of Guards. The position was good; Soult's army was slow in concentrating. But Moore considered a victory almost useless and a defeat the prelude to complete disaster. At 10 p.m. on the 8th, the army was again in motion northwest in drenching freezing rain.

Even if Moore had not wished to fight, his progress was more rapid than necessary. The army made several long marches, and one continuous effort of thirty-six hours. This haste was probably occasioned by Moore's natural distaste of fighting with an army badly demoralized by retreat, reduced in numbers, and still far from safety. Over 900 prisoners were lost to the French on the 4th, and another 500 on the 9th; death from exhaustion, and at the hands of Spanish peasants, was not uncommon. Yet the French were not much better off. Their supply

[1] Craufurd's Brigade was essentially what later became his famous Light Division, the 1/43rd, the 1/52nd, and the 2/95th.
[2] Craufurd's ability to keep men under control is vividly described in *Rifleman Harris*, *passim*.

system had broken down completely. The pursuers had less food than the pursued, and lost almost as many animals.

Moore's staff, particularly the Commissariat, did not function well. This was to some extent due to the indiscipline of the troops who would not wait for the proper issue of rations. There was enough food and other supplies along the road for all, if distributed efficiently. Schaumann, a commissary in the K.G.L., reported that

> 'The storekeepers and other Spanish officials were driven from their posts at the point of the bayonet; every soldier took what he liked, everything was plundered, carried away, and trampled under foot; the casks of wine were broken open, so that half their contents were spilt over the floor, and the general fury and unruliness of these hordes of men was such that those officers who attempted to maintain order had to make haste to fight their way out of the crowds, if only to save their lives. Aye, towards the end, the men even used to fight among themselves and kill one another, and one frequently saw a regular battle fought over the debris of a stores depot.' [1]

Perhaps a military commander should not be blamed for the failings of what was then a predominantly civilian department. Yet all those who fought in Spain were to learn that rations were often more important than any other consideration. A brilliant strategist and tactician unable to feed his army might be defeated by a less able commander who could.

Moore's advance troops reached Corunna on 11th January; British transports had not yet entered the harbour, but did so a few hours later. Corunna was situated on a promontory, almost as defensible as Cadiz, but Moore did not wish to stand a siege, and made preparations to embark as soon as possible. Although an enormous quantity of stores, carts, baggage, and *matériel* had been lost or destroyed in the retreat, including 125,000 silver dollars, there was much here that could not be transported back to Britain. New muskets, blankets, and boots were issued to men who needed them. The able-bodied infantry was then deployed to protect the loading of the transports. Artillery, cavalry, and the sick and wounded were sent aboard first. All supplies that could not be shipped were destroyed. [2] Time was short; by midday on the 15th,

---

[1] *Schaumann*, 110.

[2] The blowing up of 4,000 barrels of gunpowder on the 13th, certainly one of the largest explosions in the world until that time, is mentioned with awe by several diarists.

Soult closed on the British position. There was some skirmishing towards evening with no definite advantage to either side. A battle appeared certain the next day, for the transports were not yet loaded.

Moore's field force consisted of about 15,000 infantry and nine 6-pounders, but no cavalry; it occupied high ground south of the promontory. The left flank rested on an impassable river, but the right was more or less exposed. Moore made ample provision to cover this weakness by posting half his strength there in considerable depth.

Early on the 16th, Soult, with a force about equal to Moore's, launched an attack against the entire position. Their thrusts were of widely varying strength. Those against the centre and left were little more than feints; their real power was concentrated against the British right where the position was weak, but the defenders numerous. Soult's wide sweep against this flank was defeated by Moore's dispositions and the fighting qualities of Edward Paget's Brigade, often the rearguard during the retreat.

There developed, however, a stubborn struggle at the pivot between the French holding attacks on the east and their attempted penetration to the west. The assault against the British right centre, covered by a concentrated artillery fire, resulted in bloody fighting. The village of Elvina changed hands repeatedly. At the crisis of the battle above Elvina, Sir John was mortally wounded by a solid shot from the French battery overlooking the right of the British line. Sir David Baird had been wounded a few minutes earlier; the command devolved on Sir John Hope, then with his brigade on the extreme British left. By the time he could exercise any general control, the battle had degenerated into desultory artillery firing at long range.

Hope considered the embarkation of the army to be his first responsibility, and undertook no offensive movement. The French army was exhausted by its exertions; even their attack at Elvina had achieved no permanent penetration. The battle of Corunna drew to a quiet end; both armies occupied approximately their original positions. Losses were never determined with any precision, but were probably even, approximately 900 on either side.[1]

[1] *Fortescue*, VI, 387–8, states

'The French lost rather over six hundred killed and wounded, of whom three hundred and ninety-six belonged to Mermet's division, and between one and two hundred prisoners, or say nine hundred in all. The 31st Light alone lost three hundred and thirty killed, wounded, and taken. The losses of the British were never actually ascertained, but were set down by Hope at eight or nine hundred men.'

Napier who was closely connected with Moore and violently partisan writes, I, 332,

Hope was able to embark his entire force during the night and early next day, although harrassed by a battery of artillery which fired at the transports at long range, doing damage to some of them.[1] The fleet reached England after four or five days at sea. Englishmen were no strangers to unsuccessful expeditions, but rarely had one returned so soon after a major battle and in such poor condition. The campaign led to severe political controversy.

The Whigs championed Moore against the Tory Ministry. Sir John was made to appear the victim of deliberate lack of support. In the same partisan spirit, Tories, who knew better, criticized Moore unduly. Charles Stewart, who had served under Lord Henry Paget as a cavalry brigadier in the campaign, and who was also Castlereagh's brother, was particularly severe in his censure. Robert Craufurd was not by any means pleased with the way things had turned out and was equally outspoken.[2] Moore's sterling virtues and personal popularity made objective judgment difficult.

Yet Moore's advance on Napoleon's communications saved the southern half of Spain from French domination for several months. Had Moore not done so, British prestige in Spain would have suffered irreparably. Moore lost between 5,000 and 6,000 men, but left a legend of courage, efficiency, and human virtue that still endures. It is possible that if Napoleon had overrun the entire country during the winter of 1808-9, the Spanish will to resist might have collapsed.[3] Without this, the guerilla armies, which aided Wellington greatly, would not have existed.

'The loss of the British, never officially published, was estimated at eight hundred; of the French at three thousand. The latter is probably an exaggeration, yet it must have been great, for the English muskets were all new, the ammunition fresh; and whether from the peculiar construction of the muskets, the physical strength and coolness of the men, or all combined, the English fire is the most destructive known.'

[1] *Schaumann*, 133-4, gives a vivid account. One transport was lost and several others hit.

[2] Both Stewart and Craufurd were members of Parliament.

[3] This was, I believe, what Wellington was referring to when he said years later, 'You know, Fitzroy, we'd not have won, I think, without him.' See Christopher Hibbert, *Corunna*, London, 1961, 199.

TOPOGRAPHICAL OBSERVATIONS

The actual battlefield of Corunna is much as it was at the time of the conflict; the hamlet of Elvina can have changed hardly at all. The place where Moore fell may be established to within a few yards. Corunna itself has grown considerably; the old walls have been mostly demolished and the entire area built over.

The modern main road from Madrid to Corunna, passing through dreary and inhospitable country, seldom follows the old roadbed along which the retreat from Benavente to Lugo was made. There are stretches, particularly in and out of villages, where the original road can be identified without difficulty.

V

MOORE AVENGED

THE temporary destruction of the British army, and the comparative ease with which Napoleon had routed the Spaniards, did not discourage Castlereagh and the Tory Ministry. Wellesley was asked to write a memorandum on the defence of Portugal; this was produced on 7th March 1809. Sir John Moore had stated that Portugal could not be held. Wellesley was willing to stake both his military and political future on holding the country under certain conditions.[1] On the basis of this report the Government decided that Britain should fight on in the Peninsula.

Sir Arthur was formally appointed to command in Portugal on 6th April and reached Lisbon on the 22nd. He had resigned all his political appointments. He was still a junior lieutenant general, but, after Rolica and Vimiero, had the confidence of the nation, the army, the King, and even the Horse Guards. No European victory since Malplaquet had done so much for British prestige as Vimiero.

The situation in Portugal, however, was not auspicious. Sir John Cradock had been sent out to command what remained of the army there, over 10,000 troops, but half were sick. Cradock laboured under many disadvantages, particularly after Moore's army had been driven from Spain. He wished to evacuate Portugal, and was only prevented from doing so by specific orders from home. Cradock accomplished little of military importance, but managed to clash with the Portuguese.[2] There was even some fighting between his men and local inhabitants.

---

[1] Both *Oman*, II, 286-7, and *Fortescue*, VII, 125-6, discuss this difference of opinion between Moore and Wellesley. Sir Arthur's memorandum can be found in *Dispatches*, IV, 261-3.

[2] Wellesley appears to have been Cradock's only admirer, treating him with both respect and consideration. *National Biography*, III, 937-8, also *Supplementary Dispatches*, VI, 221-2. Wellesley did not want to take over the command if Cradock had been victorious.

Wellesley's previous service in Portugal had left him well acquainted with part of the country; he was also extremely popular there. He had been instrumental in having his friend William Carr Beresford appointed C-in-C of the Portuguese army with the rank of field marshal and ample powers for reorganizing completely the entire Portuguese military establishment.[1] Sir Arthur counted on obtaining considerable support from the Portuguese, and had been promised additional British troops.

Wellesley was informed that Napoleon had ordered Soult's and Victor's armies to overrun Portugal completely during the winter. Due more to logistics and geography than armed opposition, they had not accomplished this. Soult had reorganized his force after Corunna, and advancing into Portugal took Oporto on 29th March. French infantry had pressed as far south as the Vouga river, half way between Oporto and Coimbra, but Soult's control over the country extended only a musket shot from each infantry battalion. The marshal had about 20,000 men with him, but was said to be supported by Ney in Galicia with as many more.

A larger French army under Marshal Victor lay at Merida ready to enter Portugal by either the valley of the Guadiana or the Tagus. General Lapisse with a reinforced infantry division had been operating further north around Ciudad Rodrigo, endeavouring to keep open communications between Soult and Victor. But even as Wellesley considered the situation, Lapisse was reported to be in motion to join Victor. The French under Soult, Victor, and Lapisse outnumbered Wellesley by more than two to one, without including Ney's forces. The French armies, however, were separated from each other by hostile country; any contact between them was undoubtedly tenuous.

Within thirty-six hours of taking command, Wellesley decided to march north, attack Soult, drive him from Portugal, then return south before Victor and Lapisse were able to take advantage of the absence of the bulk of the British army from central Portugal. He would then thrust east against the French at Merida. Seldom had a general conceived so detailed a plan in so short a time.[2]

With the position of the enemy and his own future movements determined, Wellesley concentrated on the reorganizing of the internal

[1] The Portuguese had asked for Wellesley; Castlereagh knew of Sir Arthur's coming appointment to the British command, and presumably sent out Beresford on Wellesley's recommendation.

[2] *Oman*, II, 289, gives details, largely in Wellesley's words.

economy of his army. It would have to move fast and far; if it was not well fed, it would be incapable of fighting and might even alienate the Portuguese by marauding. The commissariat was rudely awakened from the *siesta* it had enjoyed since Sir Arthur sailed home six months before. Ox-carts were again to be used as the primary means of transportation. All private baggage had to be carried on horses or mules. Many of the latter, however, were taken from battalions and squadrons which in Wellesley's opinion did not require them.[1]

On the 27th, five days after his arrival, Sir Arthur was appointed marshal general of the Portuguese; there could be no doubt then as to his right to command Beresford. Wellesley immediately ordered a concentration of both British and Portuguese forces on the Mondego, and reached Coimbra himself on 2nd May. The Allied forces were at once reorganized, in a way remarkable for three important innovations. For the first time, the infantry was divided into divisions for both command and logistical purposes.[2] (The Appendix to this chapter gives details of this new alignment.)

Wellesley's second innovation was to place one Portuguese infantry battalion in each of five British brigades. This was a means not only of extending the limited strength of British infantry, but also greatly increasing the combat effectiveness of the Portuguese. Under Beresford's reorganization of the Portuguese army, infantry battalions already contained several British officers and had been drilled and trained by British NCO's. All units were armed and organized approximately after the British fashion; many of them were paid, clothed, and fed by Britain.[3]

Wellesley's third innovation aimed at making permanent the advantage that the British skirmish line achieved at Vimiero, particularly Fane's riflemen. A company armed with rifles was permanently attached to each infantry brigade that did not already contain such men.[4] This not only improved the accuracy of fire, but also increased the strength of the light troops in each brigade by 33 to 50 per cent.

[1] The 23rd L.D. wanted mules for its gallopers (3-pounder field guns with double trails). Wellesley replied that, 'he could find better employment for mules . . . and would provide horses for the guns if he thought it necessary to retain them at all.' *Fortescue*, VII, 197.

[2] Temporary command of two or more brigades had, of course, been exercised by one senior subordinate in the past, but the autonomous division in the British army was Wellesley's creation.

[3] Initially, some 20,000 men were to be paid and clothed at British expense, but the entire nation was carried throughout the war by the British subsidy.

[4] The K.G.L. light infantry companies had 10 riflemen in each, or 100 per battalion, considerably more than a company per brigade.

The Allied army as now constituted was divided into three parts, each suitable for the mission assigned to it. Beresford was to command a force of 6,000, including only 1,875 British, with the primary objective of preventing Soult, if he was forced to leave northern Portugal, from turning east and joining Victor. Beresford left Coimbra for Vizeu and Lamego on 6th May.

Even though Wellesley expected to be back in central Portugal before long, it was necessary to leave some force there to prevent a French flying column from taking the capital. General Mackenzie with 12,000 men was given detailed instructions should Victor so attack. The British and Portuguese outposts across the border in Spain would give early intelligence of any enemy movements and perhaps delay their approach for several days.[1] If the French should advance south of the Tagus, Mackenzie should hold the line of the Tagus. If they marched north of the river, he was to hold the line of its major northern tributary, the Zezere. At this time of the year, both rivers were running deep and were not fordable. Mackenzie had 4,500 British soldiers with him, including 1,500 excellent cavalry, and could hold his own.

Wellesley retained for his own thrust up the main road from Coimbra to Oporto 16,000 British and 2,400 newly-trained Portuguese. He also had twenty-four pieces of artillery, probably five 3-pounders, ten light 6-pounders, five long 6-pounders, and four 5·5-inch howitzers. At this time, a French officer named Argenton twice entered the British lines claiming to be at the head of a conspiracy to mutiny against Soult. Little of importance developed from this, but it enabled Wellesley to confirm his suspicions that the French marshal was out of contact with both Ney and Victor. Argenton also revealed that Soult's actual strength was 24,000 men, more than Wellesley had estimated.

Wellesley gave Beresford two days start, to enable him to push ahead far inland, before setting out from Coimbra himself on 8th May. The main Allied army was in contact with the French on the Vouga next day.

A trap was planned for Soult; Wellesley sent Hill, using a fleet of small boats, to the enemy's rear through a lagoon area parallel to the coast. Cotton's cavalry was moving north along the main road soon after midnight, and at daybreak was engaged in skirmishing with French mounted units at Albegaria Nova. The French cavalry was

[1] Particularly, a part of the Loyal Lusitanian Legion under Sir Robert Wilson, a brilliant but unpredictable officer. This legion was raised, paid, and equipped by Britain, but not incorporated in the Portuguese army until 1811; *Wellington's Army*, 229.

supported by both infantry and horse artillery. Cotton wisely decided not to attack until Allied infantry came up, and spent the morning manoeuvring. When the infantry arrived, the French withdrew rapidly. By then, Hill, with one brigade, was in position to intercept their retreat, but could do little against a force four times his size, even though it marched across his front.[1]

Wellesley's scheme for encircling a part at least of the French force failed, but during the day the Allied army advanced almost twenty miles through defensible country at a cost of a few British troopers killed and wounded.[2] The following night, the French concentrated in a strong position around the village of Grijon. Early on the 11th, Wellesley again sent Hill's Division in an outflanking movement to the west while the main Allied army attacked frontally. Again the French gave way after a few minutes of severe fighting in which one of the new Portuguese battalions did well.[3] Two squadrons of British light dragoons dashed headlong after the retreating French infantry.[4]

The enemy retired to Vila Nova, the southern suburb of Oporto, and crossed the wide, deep river there by means of a bridge of boats. Once across, they blew up the bridge. This occurred at 2 a.m. on the 12th.

In two days of fighting and manoeuvring, Wellesley had forced back a strong French force, inflicting slightly over 300 casualties with an Allied loss of only 150. Sir Arthur's flanking manoeuvres with Hill's

[1] There were only enough boats to bring forward a brigade at a time; Hill's own came first. The boats were immediately sent back for Cameron's Brigade, but had not yet returned.

[2] The plan appears to have been given away by Argenton, perhaps unwillingly.

[3] 'You are in error,' Wellington wrote to Mackenzie, 'in supposing that the Portuguese troops will not fight. One battalion has behaved remarkably well with me.' *Dispatches*, IV, 350.

[4] Adjutant General Charles Stewart had taken temporary command of these, but they were not particularly effective.

Wellesley	Beresford
	6 May—Left Coimbra for Vizeu and Lamego
Left Coimbra for Oporto— 8 May	
Albergaria Nova fight;—10 May—Arrived Lamego and Poso da Regoa	
Hill crosses lagoon	
Grijon fight—11 May—Reached Amarante	
Oporto taken—12 May—Drove French from bridge at Amarante	
	13 May—Moved on Chaves
March on Braga—14 May	
Contact with French on—15 May	
Braga—Chaves road	
Fight to the Ponte Nova—16 May—Arrived at Chaves exhausted	
HQ at Montelegre—18 May	

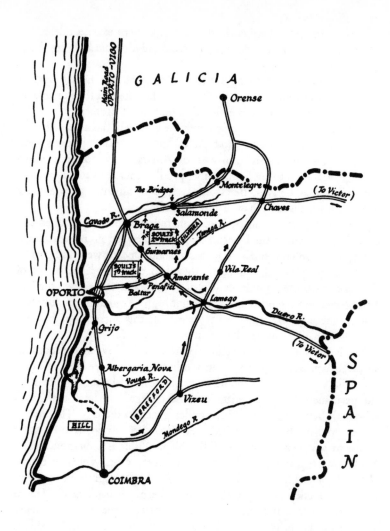

III. CAMPAIGN IN NORTHERN PORTUGAL

force had prevented the French from making use of excellent defensive positions; these, if forced by frontal attacks only, would have cost both time and men.

Beresford was also moving north, but far to the east; he had reached Vizeu on the 8th and Lamego on the 10th. There he met the Portuguese General Silveira, who commanded all militia in the northern part of the country and was in partial contact with the French in this area.[1] Already Beresford had cut Soult's most direct line of communications with Victor. He could either turn east to Amarante or continue north through Vila Real to cut Soult's other possible route towards a junction with Lapisse at Chaves. Beresford decided to advance with Silveira towards Amarante and so informed Wellesley.

Meanwhile, Sir Arthur had been gathering information about enemy dispositions north of the Duero.[2] Soult had received no reinforcement from Ney. The French troops in and around Oporto were well armed and in good physical condition; they had captured large stocks of British arms and ammunition as well as food and wine when the city fell. Morale, on the other hand, was not high; Argenton's mutiny was still simmering. Wellesley never relied on this succeeding, but did nothing to hamper its development.

The heads of three Allied columns entered Vila Nova on the morning of 12th May. Both Oporto and its southern suburb were built on steep, high hills with the river running between. Soult had not only blown up the permanent bridge of boats, but also collected all small craft from the south bank and placed them under guard in the city. The French appear to have been convinced that Wellesley would have to bring round by sea the boats used by Hill in his amphibious flank movements; Soult was keeping a good lookout towards the west. Wellesley, from a point of vantage in a convent garden in Vila Nova high above the river, could see French cavalry pickets along the north bank of the Duero between Oporto and the sea.[3] To the east of the city the enemy appeared to be depending on the width of the river and the Allied lack

[1] The Portuguese military establishment consisted at this time of three classes of troops: The Regulars, the Militia, and the *Ordenanza*. The latter were local forces, poorly armed and indifferently commanded by district leaders. These would have been called militia elsewhere; but in Portugal, the militia was a separate type of organization, neither *Ordenanza* nor a regular force. Silveira succeeded Freire in general command after the latter was killed by the Portuguese themselves for an inefficient campaign and suspected designs to surrender Oporto to the French without a fight.

[2] The river Duero, or Douro, which passes through both Spain and Portugal, is spelt throughout as Duero, to avoid confusion.

[3] The convent still stands, but the gardens are now partially covered by army barracks.

of boats to protect them; there were no pickets nor patrols visible. Wellesley also noticed that the hill formation on both sides of the river would conceal any river crossing immediately east of the city, unless the French were almost on the edge of the northern heights.

While Sir Arthur was personally making observations, using his telescope, valuable information was being brought to him. A ferry at Avintes, four miles upstream from Oporto, had been damaged by the French, but was already being repaired and could be put back into service by noon. A barber who had come over from Oporto in a large skiff, now concealed on the south bank, was willing to help in any way that he could. There were four wine barges on the north side of the river east of the city which the French had neither destroyed nor guarded.

Wellesley ordered Murray with a part of his double brigade to cross by the ferry as soon as possible.[1] Colonel Waters, who had found the barber, was ordered to bring the four barges over to the south bank. The Prior of Amarante, who happened to be at Vila Nova, and the barber, persuaded some boatmen to assist them.

Wellesley saw at short range opposite him a strong stone building surrounded by a wall which stood by itself some 300 yards north of the river bank and east of the city. Both the building and the approaches to it were within range of the 18 artillery pieces which Sir Arthur now ordered up to where he was himself standing. Colonel Waters had returned with the barges and also reported that this building was the Bishop's Seminary and had been unoccupied half an hour before.

'Well, let the men cross!' With these words, Wellesley began one of his most daring offensive strokes. To cross a river of this size with four barges only at 10.30 a.m. on a bright spring morning in the face of an army of almost equal size was to tempt the devil, for each barge held no more than 30 men in addition to its ferrying crew; all four could only transport about 600 men per hour.

A lieutenant and his platoon of the Buffs (3rd Foot) ferried over on the first barge, ran up the hill to the Seminary, closed and secured the iron gate in front, and began fortifying the place. They were soon joined by others including General Edward Paget; reinforcements were passed over slowly, but continuously. The wall surrounding the Seminary was between eight and nine feet high, so that a firing step was

---

[1] *Oman*, II, 335n says, '1st and 2nd Line Battalions of the K.G.L., also a detached company of rifles of the K.G.L.' *Fortescue*, VII, 159, says, 'The First Line Battalion, and the massed riflemen of the German Legion . . .' They agree on two guns and two squadrons for the 14th L.D.

required. The Seminary roof was flat, but had a strong parapet. Its walls were thick, but pierced by ample windows, ideal for infantry armed with muskets. The whole building could hardly have been better situated or designed.

For an hour, the French made no effort to interrupt the ferrying operations.[1] Then a line of *tirailleurs* appeared on the crest of the hill above the Seminary and advanced towards it followed by three battalion columns. Paget had with him in and around the Seminary only about 600 men, but they were enough, since they were protected by fortifications for which the French were unprepared.

At about this same time French artillery were brought up to open fire on the Seminary and on the crossing barges. The first piece to unlimber was put out of action by a shrapnel shell from one of the British howitzers across the river which burst in front of and above the target. The gun was dismounted and every gunner and draft animal assigned to it was either killed or wounded. Wellesley's artillery were now firing at both the French artillery and infantry advancing on the Seminary. The French attack failed; their artillery was withdrawn or abandoned.

Wellesley from his point of vantage could overlook the Seminary, much of the town, and to either side of it. Soult appeared to be abandoning Oporto: a column of all arms was marching out to the east towards Amarante. A second French attack was delivered against the Seminary, better co-ordinated and stronger than the first. But Hill, who had taken the place of Paget, who was wounded, had by now an ample garrison and was even better supported by the artillery across the river. In the face of regular rolling musketry fire from three or four levels and both shot and shell, the French infantry broke and fled.

About this time, the French guards over the boats assembled on the north bank of the river in Oporto were removed, preparatory to abandoning the city. Portuguese civilians by the hundred immediately rowed them over to Vila Nova. The Brigade of Guards and the 1/29th were soon across the Duero and ascending the steep streets into the upper town. So quickly did they advance that they took in flank some of the enemy who were preparing to attack the Seminary for the third time. The French withdrawal now developed into a rout; prisoners were taken with ease. Soult's whole army was streaming towards Amarante, passing across the front of Murray's troops. This unfortunate

[1] General Foy happened to observe one of the barges from a hill-top and ordered forward the first poorly-co-ordinated attack.

officer did not make the best use of his position and force: the French escaped.[1] Charles Stewart took command of a squadron of the 14th L. D. and charged after the retreating French, taking a few prisoners and in turn losing a number of dragoons.[2] The French were completely defeated, but were pursued only three miles.

Wellesley's plan was brilliantly conceived and well executed. The city had fallen in less than six hours to a force attacking from the south with initially only a single skiff. Sir Arthur certainly had confidence in himself and his army. The entire Allied loss was only 123 killed, wounded, and missing. The French loss was considerably greater, more than 300 killed and wounded in addition to prisoners. Soult abandoned some 1,500 men in the Oporto hospital, and much equipment, including some 70 guns. Six field pieces were taken around the Seminary.

Because of fatigue, and difficulties in transportation, the Allied force was not able to follow Soult until the afternoon of the 13th. Wellesley ordered Murray with his double brigade, two squadrons of cavalry, and two guns, to Baltar on the road to Amarante.

Meanwhile, Beresford's advance west from Lamego had been most successful. Wellesley had not given him specific orders, but had stressed that the marshal should not fight an even battle, for he had but one British brigade. Even the Portuguese militia under Silveira fought well, however, and beat a French force under Loison which attacked them not far east of Lamego on the 10th.[3] The French retreated on Amarante with the Allies on their heels. Silveira and Beresford occupied the eastern bank of the Tamega on the morning of the 12th, except for a bridgehead held by the French. Later in the day, Loison gave up Amarante completely and retired north towards Guimaraes.

Beresford exercised his discretionary privileges perfectly. His orders were to prevent Soult from moving east. To have followed Loison would have left open to the French the secondary road through Chaves. He ordered Silveira to march across country towards Salamonde. Beresford himself with his original force countermarched to Lamego and then headed north for Chaves. Many hours later, while on the march, he received instructions from Wellesley to do exactly this.

[1] Sir John Murray had not done well in India; and proved himself more incapable later on, yet became a full general in 1825, *National Biography*, XIII, 1286-7.

[2] Stewart's habit of taking over isolated cavalry units temporarily must have infuriated their officers; he managed to lose 35 of 110 troopers in this dash into difficult country in column.

[3] Loison reported a loss of only 80 men of his 6,500 at Peso da Regoa; *Oman*, II, 344, proves this to be an understatement.

79

Early in the morning of the 14th, Murray's force at Baltar heard a series of explosions and saw large fires raging above the road to Penafiel. This was reported immediately to Wellesley, but was unexplained until 5 p.m. when a prisoner or deserter was questioned. Soult did not know until about 1 a.m. on the 14th that Loison had abandoned Amarante and retreated north towards Guimaraes on the afternoon of the 12th. With Beresford at Amarante, the main French army was caught on a section of road held at both ends by the Allies. To avoid another Baylen, Soult destroyed all his wheeled transport, abandoned plunder, blew up guns and then set off by mule tracks over the mountains towards Guimaraes.

Once Wellesley understood what was taking place, he ordered Murray to follow Soult, and Beresford to move on Chaves. He marched at dawn on the 15th with the rest of the Allied main force for Braga in two columns, one along each of the available roads. Sir Arthur entered Braga on the afternoon of the 15th to receive unwelcome news from Guimaraes. Soult's force had united on the 14th with those of Loison and Lorges.[1] The French army in spite of its various losses still numbered over 20,000 and was concentrated. Yet Soult was once again on a single road both ends of which were already, or would soon be, in the hands of the Allies. Loison's and Lorges's artillery, baggage, and wheeled transport were destroyed. The entire army plunged again into the mountains in the direction of the Braga-Chaves road.

British cavalry operating on this road reported contact with a strong force of French cavalry with infantry support. For two or three hours, Wellesley was of the opinion that Soult might be approaching Braga in order to use the good road running from there north towards Vigo. This French force was identified as a rearguard only; Soult was pressing east towards Chaves. Beresford would probably cut that road before Soult could reach the town, but there was another branch road from near Salamonde leading to Montalegre and Orense.

The condition of Wellesley's army was not good. It had marched about 120 miles and fought a battle in the last seven days; his men had toiled long hours passing guns, ammunition, and other necessaries across the Duero. Rain had been falling steadily since the afternoon of the 13th. The carriage roads soon broke up: the treacherous mire hid in its ooze many axle-breaking and ankle-twisting rocks. The terrain was incredibly rugged; the Braga-Chaves road runs for miles over ridges and through defiles, all with steep gradients.

[1] Lorges had been dispatched by Soult to collect together the isolated French garrisons in northern Portugal and had now completed this task.

In such country, a pursuit of the French from the rear could accomplish no more than the inflicting of a few casualties and the gathering up of stragglers not already murdered by the Portuguese peasants. If the French could be intercepted at any point along their route, even by a small force of well disciplined soldiers, they would suffer severe losses. Wellesley now knew of Beresford's instructions to Silveira to move on Salamonde from Amarante; Silveira had only about half the distance that Soult had to cover to reach this mountain village, but he was too late. The Portuguese delay has never been satisfactorily explained.

Soult was opposed only by the *Ordenanza*, who were, in this area, little more than mobs of poorly organized peasants armed with pikes and fowling pieces. Even these could have caused the French much trouble. At dusk on the 15th, Soult reached a bridge over a turbulent tributary of the Cavado. Two enormous beams still crossed the chasm, but the planking between them had been removed. The local peasants were intrenched on the far side. The French column extending five miles back over the narrow road was brought to a halt and forced to bivouac in the rain without food or fuel. There were no lateral roads across the mountains, not even mule tracks. Their situation was desperate; Wellesley was not far behind.

Napier describes the scene brilliantly:

> 'In this extremity, Soult, addressing Major Dulong, an officer justly reputed one of the most daring in the French ranks, said, "I have chosen you from the whole army to seize the Ponte Nova, which has been cut by the enemy; select a hundred grenadiers and twenty-five horsemen, endeavour to surprise the guards and secure the passage of the bridge. If you succeed, say so, but send no other report, your silence will suffice." Thus exhorted, Dulong, favoured by the storm, reached the bridge, killed the sentinel before any alarm was given, and being followed by twelve grenadiers, crawled along a narrow slip of masonry, the only part undestroyed. The Cavado was flooded and roaring in its deep channel, and a grenadier fell into the gulf, yet the waters were louder than his cry. Dulong and the others surprised the nearest post, and then the main body rushed on, ... mounting the heights, shouting and firing, scared the peasantry, who imagined the whole army was upon them. Thus the passage was won.' [1]

[1] *Napier*, II, 111. This description undoubtedly came direct from Soult, who aided the great British historian. The bridge, however, was of wood.

The bridge was repaired early on the 16th, but the French were far from safe. As soon as it was light, Wellesley led the brigade of Guards forward, and had at the head of his column two 3-pounders. At noon, this force was heavily engaged with the French rearguard near the bridge. Soult had the more advantageous position, since he fought on a limited front with flanks relatively secure. Sir Arthur ordered his three light companies to scale a precipice before delivering a flanking attack; the French rearguard broke and streamed back across the ill-repaired Ponte Nova. Night, hastened by the continuous rain, was falling fast, but there was enough light for the two British 3-pounders to fire grape at point blank range. The mountain torrent entering the Cavado here was almost dammed by the bodies of men and horses which fell from the bridge. Scores of prisoners were taken.

During the night, Wellesley received a dispatch from Beresford. The road to the east was safely blocked at Chaves, but Beresford's army in all probability could do no more. There was still a chance however, that a stone bridge on the Montalegre road might have been blown up, or held in force by the *Ordenanza*.[1] Wellesley issued orders for the pursuit to be continued at dawn and instructed Beresford to send a strong column from Chaves towards Orense.

The pursuit was maintained during the 17th, but only brief contacts were made with the French, who had the advantage of having neither baggage nor artillery.[2] The country was everywhere defensible and the weather appalling. British soldiers were dropping from exhaustion brought on by lack of food. On the 18th, Wellesley slept in a cottage at Montalegre which Soult had occupied the night before; the French had crossed the border into Spain some hours earlier. To follow further would be both impractical and dangerous. Sir Arthur had received a dispatch from Mackenzie intimating that Victor with his entire force had crossed the border and reached Castelo Branco. It was time to turn south.

[1] A British officer of Portuguese birth from Beresford's staff, William Warre, had endeavoured to persuade the *Ordenanza* to destroy the bridge. They refused because it was their only means within miles of crossing the river. They barricaded and entrenched it instead; the French lost only 19 men in capturing the bridge and dispersing 1,000 peasants.
[2] Wellesley's own words in this connexion are interesting:

'I hope your Lordship will believe that no measure which I could take was omitted to intercept the enemy's retreat. It is obvious, however, that if an army throws away all its cannon, equipments, and baggage, and everything which can strengthen it, and can enable it to act together as a body; and abandons all those who are entitled to its protection, but add to its weight and impede its progress; it must be able to march by roads through which it cannot be followed, with any prospect of being overtaken, by an army which had not made the same sacrifice.' *Dispatches*, IV, 344.

Wellesley's campaign in northern Portugal had lasted less than two weeks. Even though no major battle had been fought, the French army lost all its baggage, transport, and artillery. Many dead lay beside the terrible roads and mule tracks which Soult had been forced to use. Many more perished at the hands of peasants whenever they strayed from the main line of march in search of food. Soult lost 4,000 men; many of those who survived lacked knapsacks, shoes, and muskets.[1] Months would pass before they would be in fighting trim again. The total Allied loss had been 300 killed and wounded, with an additional 200 stragglers and sick.

The French most directly connected with Moore's disastrous retreat had in turn been even more soundly beaten. They had not lost quite so many men, but more equipment; they were in even worse shape. Throughout the entire ten days of fighting they had done little of which they could be proud.

Wellesley had achieved precisely what he had set out to do and came close to accomplishing even more than he had thought possible at first. Now he would turn on Victor. Silveira was left to guard the northern frontier. The main army marched south by easy stages; Wellesley himself rode ahead to meet Mackenzie.

THE CONTENDING FORCES IN PORTUGAL
DURING MAY 1809

THE ALLIED ARMY UNDER WELLESLEY—HIS PERSONAL   TOTAL = 17,378
     COMMAND

Infantry British 12,821 Portuguese 2,400		= 15,221
Sherbrooke's Division		= 6,706
Guards Brigade, Henry Fred Campbell	2,552	
1/Coldstreamers, 1/3rd Guards, 1 Co. 5/60th		
4th Brigade, John Sontag	2,079	
97th, 2nd Batt. of Detach., 1 Co. 5/60th, 2/16th Portuguese		
5th Brigade, Alexander Campbell	2,075	
2/7th, 2/53rd, 1 Co. 5/60th, 1/10th Portuguese		

---

[1] At Orense on 19th May, Soult had an accurate count made. *Oman*, II, 360–1, carefully determines and apportions the loss suffered between the 9th and the 18th.

Paget's Division   = 5,145
  6th Brigade, Stewart   2,050
    29th, 1st Batt. of Detach., 1/16th
      Portuguese
  K.G.L. Brigade, John Murray   3,095
    1st, 2nd, 5th and 7th Line Batts.
      K.G.L.
Hill's Division   = 4,370
  1st Brigade, Rowland Hill   2,274
    1/3rd, 2/66th, 2/48th, 1 Co. 5/60th
  7th Brigade, Alan Cameron   2,096
    2/9th, 2/82nd, 1 Co. 5/60th, 2/10th
      Portuguese
Cavalry, Stapleton Cotton   = 1,504
  14th L. D. (2 squadrons), 16th L. D.,
  20th L. D. (part), 3rd L. D., K.G.L.
  (small part)
Artillery (4 Batteries = 24 pieces), Wagon Train.   = 653
  engineers, etc.

ALLIED ARMY—BERESFORD'S COMMAND   TOTAL = 6,000
      British 1,825   Portuguese 4,175
British
  3rd Infantry Brigade, Christopher   1,659
    Tilson
    2/87th, 1/88th, 5 Co's 5/60th, 1st
      Portuguese Grenadiers
  2 Squadrons 14th L. D. Cavalry   164
Portuguese
  5 Batts. Infantry, 2 squadrons cavalry,
  2 batteries (12 guns)

ALLIED ARMY—MACKENZIE'S COMMAND   TOTAL = 12,000
      British 4,575   Portuguese 7,425
British
  2nd Infantry Brigade, Alexander   2,989
    Mackenzie
    3/27th, 1/45th, 2/31st, 2/24th[1]

[1] The 2/24th was newly arrived in Lisbon and not formally attached to Mackenzie's Brigade, but was under his command for this entire period.

Cavalry, Henry Fane	1,466
3rd Dragoon Guards, 4th Dragoons	
1 Battery (six 6-pounders)	120
Portuguese	
10 Batts. Infantry, 5 squadrons cavalry,	
3 batteries (18 guns)	

THE FRENCH ARMY UNDER SOULT	TOTAL = 25,000
The Oporto Command	= 11,000
Merle's and Delaborde's Infantry Divisions	
Parts of Lahoussaye's and Lorges's Dragoons	
Franceschi-Mermet Command (Initially south of the Duero)	= 6,300
Franceschi's Cavalry	1,200
Mermet's Infantry Division[1]	5,000
1 Battery (6 guns)	100
Loison's Command (Initially around Amarante)	= 6,500
Heudelet's and Sarrut's Infantry Divisions and Marisy's Dragoons	
Minor Garrisons in North (collected by Lorges)	= 1,200

TOPOGRAPHICAL OBSERVATIONS

The combat areas around Albegaria Nova and Grijon are hard to identify. Oporto has increased greatly in size; the area around the Seminary was open in 1809, but is now choked with dwellings and industrial buildings. The original Seminary, which was being altered when Fortescue visited Oporto circa 1911, is easily seen from Vila Nova, but retains a portion only of its old wall and grounds. It is shown correctly in Wyld's Atlas but not in some other maps and sketches. The Duero is probably narrower today than in 1809, as are most rivers adjacent to growing cities. The Amarante bridge and nearby buildings are, apart from the necessary widening of the former, little changed. Soult's route from Baltar to Guimaraes can be approximately followed over a minor modern road. The way from Braga to Montalegre still abounds in difficulties; the original location of the two bridges can be determined precisely. An artificial irrigation and waterpower lake, utilizing the waters of the Cavado, covers them throughout most of the year.

[1] According to both Oman and Fortescue, Mermet's whole division was initially south of the Duero. I have, therefore, shown a strength of 5,000 based on Oman, II, 625, rather than page 328.

VI

TALAVERA

WELLESLEY found, as he suspected, that Mackenzie's account of a French advance over the border was an exaggeration. There had been a reconnaissance in force but the French soon retired. Sir Arthur reorganized and re-equipped his army near Abrantes. Shoes were in a sorry state; some gun carriages required repairing. Discipline had suffered in some battalions; infractions were not so easily punished under the new system of courts-martial. There was still a shortage of hard money, and experienced, qualified officers, but by 15th June, he was ready to march against Victor.

Wellesley was finding it difficult to co-operate with the Spanish commanders and their government although he was by nature and training more adept at such negotiations than Sir John Moore. He had sent a dispatch to Cuesta, the Spanish captain general in Estremadura, from Oporto on 22nd May, while riding south from Montalegre to Abrantes, suggesting combined operations against Victor. Both Cuesta and the Supreme Junta of Spain were enthusiastic, and promised not only to feed Wellesley's army, but also to supply transportation as soon as it crossed the border. Sir Arthur sent officers from his staff to discuss such details, although a mutually acceptable plan was not agreed to for some time.

It was finally decided that the British army would unite with Cuesta's in the Guadiana valley east of Badajoz. This was the best of several alternatives proposed by the Spanish. Victor had been at Merida for several weeks, but suddenly retreated to Talavera in the Tagus valley.[1] This allowed the Allied armies to meet further north in a position more convenient for the British. Wellesley marched east from Abrantes on

[1] Joseph and Jourdan issued orders allowing Victor to do this only after the unwelcome news of Soult's expulsion from north Portugal reached Madrid.

27th June along two roads, one south and the other north of the Tagus. The British army—all Portuguese units were to remain in Portugal—reached Castelo Branco on 1st July and crossed the border two days later near Zarza la Mayor. Wellesley again divided his force into two columns which entered Plasencia on the 8th and 9th. The weather was hot and dry; a week's rest for the rank and file was welcome.

The new divisions were taking on definite form, and settling down as independent units. The four major infantry units were still greatly dissimilar in size. Sherbrooke's 1st Division consisted of four brigades and was half as large again as either the 2nd or 3rd Divisions, and twice the size of the 4th.

The cavalry was separated into three brigades. There were five batteries of field artillery armed with 3- and 6-pounder guns and 5.5-inch howitzers.[1] The weakness of Wellesley's force was transport; there were not at this time sufficient bullock carts and pack animals to carry even essential ammunition, medical stores, and tools, let alone food. The Spaniards had promised ample supplies, vehicles, and animals, but had delivered nothing.

On 10th July, Wellesley left the army at Plasencia and rode with his staff to Almaraz on the Tagus for his first meeting with Cuesta. Everything went wrong from the start; Spanish guides appear to have lost their way, causing Cuesta and his army to be kept waiting for five hours. Sir Arthur did not arrive until after dark and inspected his new allies by torchlight. Even such poor illumination could not conceal their faults. The individual soldiers were satisfactory, but their arms, equipment, clothing, and shoes were in poor shape. Neither officers nor men gave any indication of having mastered the art of close order drill, nor of weapon handling for efficient fire in combat. The cavalry was numerous, but poorly mounted, and even less efficient at their drill than the infantry.

Wellesley's greatest disappointment, however, was Cuesta himself, who was over seventy years of age, yet appeared to lack the wisdom of maturity. He spoke neither English nor French. At the disastrous battle of Medellin a few weeks earlier, his own cavalry had ridden over him in their panic. He was so infirm physically that he had to be lifted into his travelling coach which was drawn by nine mules. He was at

---

[1] *Fortescue*, VII, 205, note 1, is, I believe, in error; he says, 'Six batteries without their howitzers.' I have checked his reference to *Duncan*, II, 248–9, and find only a recommendation which was never acted upon. *Hawker*, 100–1, an arms authority seriously wounded at Talavera, wrote, 'We had thirty pieces of artillery—viz. nineteen six-pounders, five five-and-a-half inch howitzers, and six three-pounders.' Oman follows Hawker.

odds with the Supreme Spanish Junta; each distrusted and intrigued against the other.[1]

Cuesta, who was not brilliant, nor even professionally competent, exhibited a kind of animal cunning. He was excessively proud and antagonistic towards Wellesley. His attitude was understandable, in the views of later revelations. Frere, the British minister to Spain, had been behaving most undiplomatically. He had been recommending that Wellesley be appointed Commander-in-Chief of the Spanish armies, and suggested that Cuesta be replaced by Albuquerque. Both these schemes were known to Cuesta, although apparently not to Sir Arthur.[2]

Hours were consumed in argument. What Wellesley proposed, Cuesta refused. Finally when it appeared likely that the British army would retrace their steps to Portugal, Cuesta gave way to a certain extent; a joint plan was agreed upon. The old man, with his many faults, was as anxious as anyone to defeat the French.

Wellesley and Cuesta knew the French dispositions in central Spain to a certain extent. Victor had slightly over 20,000 men at Talavera, 50 miles east of Almaraz and 70 miles southwest of Madrid. Another French army, 22,000 strong, under General Sebastiani, lay at Madridejos, 75 miles southeast of Madrid in the valley of the Guadiana. Joseph Bonaparte, and his Chief of Staff, Marshal Jourdan, who were theoretically in command of all French armies in Spain, had another 12,000 men in Madrid.[3] All three forces could be concentrated within two days at Toledo, a place of considerable strategic importance. The French could form a field army of 50,000 veterans in addition to the Madrid and Toledo garrisons.

The combined force of Cuesta and Wellesley was about 55,000; 35,000 Spanish and 20,000 British. To fight the concentrated French army would be extremely dangerous on account of the known limitations of the Spanish units which were unable to manoeuvre under fire.

[1] *Guedalla*, 184–5, says,

'His present collaborator was Don Gregorio de la Cuesta, Captain-General of Estremadura. This paladin, now rising seventy, was less menacing as an adversary than as an ally; for he looked back upon an uninterrupted record of sanguinary (and frequently avoidable) defeat. Composed in equal parts of pride and failing health, he was the embodiment of Spain at its very worst—old, proud, incompetent, and ailing—and Sir Arthur could hardly hope to have a more instructive object-lesson in the joys of allied operations.'

[2] John Hookham Frere was academically brilliant, and a life-long friend of Canning. His intrigues in Spain, however, did little to help either Moore or Wellesley; *National Biography*, VII, 708–10.

[3] Napoleon allowed French army commanders to correspond directly with him; he issued orders directly to them, and even let them disobey Joseph openly.

There was, however, a practical scheme which could prevent such a concentration. The Allies were fortunate in having another Spanish force of almost 30,000 men under General Venegas located in the mountains south of Sebastiani; Cuesta was senior to Venegas and was authorized to issue orders to him. Venegas, by marching on Madrid from the southwest, would probably prevent Sebastiani from advancing on Toledo. If Sebastiani did insist on moving away from Venegas, the latter could retake Madrid.

The plan eventually adopted was for a junction of Cuesta and Wellesley on 21st July at Oropesa, 30 miles west of Talavera. Both would then advance together against Victor. Venegas was to move north on 16th July along the direct road through Madridejos and Aranjuez towards Madrid. He was to keep sufficient pressure on Sebastiani to enable him to inform Cuesta should the French forces endeavour to disengage. The Spanish capital was not only of great importance politically, but also the main ordnance and supply depot of the French in Spain.

A combined force of a few hundred British, Spanish, and Portuguese under Sir Robert Wilson was to advance eastwards along the valley of the Tietar, north of, but parallel to, that of the Tagus. Wilson was to prevent any surprise attack from Old Castile to the north where the corps of Soult, Ney, and Mortier were known to be, and also alarm Joseph and Jourdan for the safety of the capital on that side. The danger of the French interrupting Wellesley's communications with Portugal was real, although Soult's corps would need time to recover from its recent defeat in northern Portugal. Wilson could not effectively oppose even one French corps, but he could give timely news of its approach.

Wellesley set his army in motion from Plasencia on 17th July, crossed the Tietar next day, and joined Cuesta at Oropesa on the 21st. The following day both armies moved along parallel paths towards Talavera.[1] At noon, the Spanish advance guard skirmished with French dragoons and horse artillery at Gamonal, half way between Oropesa and Talavera, but the more numerous Spanish Horse, even when infantry support caught up with them, could make little impression on the French. Spanish generals endeavoured to manoeuvre, but their convolutions were futile. The sudden appearance of Anson's British and German cavalry on the French right altered the situation; the enemy retreated precipitately three miles past Talavera to the Alberche, which

[1] *Fortescue*, VII, 213, has the British army to the south of the Spanish. *Oman*, II, states the opposite. *Londonderry*, II, 402, and *Schaumann*, 169, are Oman's references and were both present.

enters the Tagus here. Victor had placed both infantry and artillery in position behind this stream.

The French commander at Talavera was in ignorance of the presence of the British army until the 22nd; the Allied plan was working perfectly. Cuesta and Wellesley had 55,000 men in position. Victor, across the Alberche, had at this time only 22,000. The French position was strong if attacked from the west, but was easily flanked to the north; the Alberche flows diagonally from the northeast into the Tagus and was fordable. Wellesley persuaded Cuesta to push across the bridge on the main Talavera-Madrid road, which was still intact, and to either side of it, while the British army would sweep down from the north, taking the French in flank and rear. Cuesta promised to attack at dawn.

Wellesley mustered his army at 3 a.m., and aligned it north of the Alberche under cover of thick groves of cork and olive trees; the left flank was well to the rear of the French position. Daylight came, but there were no sound of the Spanish. Sir Arthur waited patiently for three hours, and then rode into the Spanish camp between Talavera and the Alberche to find Cuesta asleep. The old man, when roused, gave the excuse that his army was too tired to fight that day.

Had the Allies attacked on the 23rd as Wellesley had planned, a decisive victory was almost a certainty, but as so often happens in war, an opportunity once missed is gone beyond recall. Cuesta again agreed to attack at dawn on the 24th, but Victor marched east soon after night-fall on the 23rd.[1] Cuesta was now as full of enthusiasm to pursue as he had been reluctant to attack the previous day.[2]

Wellesley appreciated fully the magnitude of the lost opportunity and could hardly conceal his disgust with Cuesta. Sir Arthur refused to pursue the French for two reasons. Firstly, his own intelligence system reported rumours that a French field army of 50,000 men would be formed soon in spite of Allied precautions. To fight such an army even further inside Spain with Cuesta for a colleague was unappealing. Secondly, the British army had come into Spain depending on Spanish promises to provide both food and transportation. Practically nothing had been received in either category.[3] There was little chance of over-taking Victor; to thrust further east was to lengthen communications

[1] There was talk at the time, and later, of treachery on Cuesta's staff: *Napier*, II, 157; also *Fortescue*, VII, 217.

[2] In the interval, Cuesta had found out that the Supreme Junta had given Venegas permission to proclaim himself C-in-C of all Spanish armies, if he took Madrid.

[3] *Dispatches*, IV, *passim*, abound with complaints about lack of food and transportation, yet there was plenty of both in the area, *Leslie*, 132.

with British bases in Portugal, while every step the French retreated brought them closer to their natural point of concentration, Toledo.

Cuesta was now so self-confident that he decided to pursue Victor alone. The Spanish army swarmed after the French throughout the 24th, covering more than two-thirds of the distance to Toledo. Had Victor realized that Wellesley was still on the Alberche, he would have turned on Cuesta; 22,000 French veterans were more than sufficient to crush 35,000 Spaniards in the open. The French general probably missed as great an opportunity here as the Allies had on the 23rd.

At noon on the 25th, Cuesta received positive intelligence that Sebastiani was reinforcing Victor; an additional French force had left Madrid. Cuesta now retreated more rapidly than he had advanced; the French, who had achieved their concentration at Toledo, were in hot pursuit.

Wellesley crossed the Alberche with two of his four divisions ready to support Cuesta, but the position facing east at this point was weak and dominated by higher ground. Cuesta with his usual stupidity and stubbornness declared that he would retreat no further. On the morning of the 27th, Wellesley was forced in fact to go on his knees in order to humour Cuesta into crossing the Alberche to save himself and his army from annihilation.[1] Sir Arthur indicated to Odonoju, Cuesta's Chief of Staff, where he wished the Spanish army to be placed. For once, Cuesta readily acquiesced, perhaps because his force would have by far the more favourable half of the position that Wellesley had chosen.

Wellesley now withdrew his two divisions from across the stream to the vicinity of the Casa de Salinas, a large, half-fortified building located in a wooded area between the Alberche and Talavera itself.[2] Mackenzie's Division remained here while Sherbrooke's moved further to the west. Donkin's Brigade stayed in the groves east of the Casa.

Silently, a strong line of French *tirailleurs* crossed the Alberche and pushed through the trees, followed by battalion columns. They took by surprise a part of Donkin's battalions which were resting with muskets stacked.[3] The *voltigeurs* did a good deal of damage and took prisoners,

---

[1] Such childish behaviour seems improbable even for Cuesta, but is sufficiently well supported to be included in *Fortescue*, VII, 223.

[2] This building still exists and can be positively identified from the large scale plan of it in *Wyld's Atlas*, Talavera Map, on which it is called 'Palacio de Salinas'. Modern maps refer to the structure, now used largely for storage, as 'Casa de Serranillas'.

[3] *Oman*, II, 504, says 2/87th, 1/88th, and 2/31st (Mackenzie's Brigade) were all broken. *Fortescue*, VII, 227, says the 2/31st 'behaved remarkably well' and that the 2/87th was the battalion most damaged.

but the disordered French columns behind were brought to a halt by five companies of the 5/60th and Mackenzie's Brigade. Some of Donkin's men were not rallied for half an hour.

Just before this unfortunate fight commenced, Wellesley had ridden forward to the Casa. He could see nothing from the ground through the trees and ascended one of its towers which rise to a considerable height (Plate 9). He had hardly reached the top when he noticed French light infantry envelop the eastern end of the building. He had just time to dash down the stairs, mount, and ride from the courtyard to the rear followed by a ragged volley from those *voltigeurs* who happened to be loaded.

Wellesley took temporary command of Mackenzie's Division in the open country behind the Casa. Donkin's two broken battalions were allowed to retreat towards the main army strung out north from Talavera. Mackenzie's own Brigade and the 5/60th covered the retreat and were annoyed only by some long range fire from French horse artillery. This initial skirmish cost the British 440 casualties; French losses were about 100.

The Tagus flows east and west past the old fortified town of Talavera (Plate 7). The walls were no longer defensible against a formal siege, but were valuable protection for poorly trained infantry opposing an enemy in the open. The country to the east was covered by small farms, vineyards, and orchards. To the north of this area of encumbered territory along the river, there was a level open plain more than a mile wide terminated abruptly by a ridge of high ground. A shallow stream, the Portina, flows from north to south across this plain and into the Tagus. The Portina in summer is of no military importance; it can be crossed at any point even by artillery. But it did serve to align the

---

The Fifth Attack was started at 2 p.m. on the 28th, but never pressed home.

The First, Second, and Fifth Attacks were all delivered by the same French Division, Ruffin's (9 Batts.).

The First Attack was delivered by three columns at 10 p.m. on the 27th.

The Second Attack was delivered by the same force in the same area soon after dawn on the 28th.

The Fourth or Main Attack was delivered at 1.30 p.m. on the 28th by 12 Battalions.

The Third Attack was delivered at 1.15 p.m. on the 28th by 9 Battalions.

Because of drastic changes in the British alignment to receive the 1st and 2nd French attacks, no positions can be more than indicated on eastern end of the Medellin.

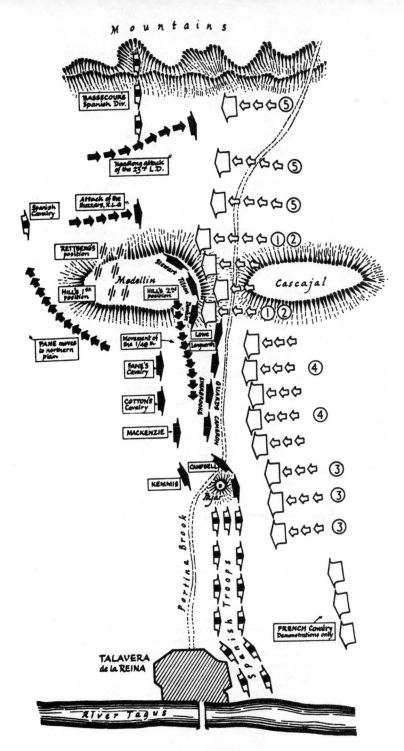

IV. TALAVERA

Allied defence. The stream cuts through the northern ridge splitting it into two segments which lie end to end. These lozenge-shaped hills dominate the low lying area between them and the Tagus. Wellesley had chosen the western hill, the Cero de Medellin, as the anchor for his left flank. The Allied right rested on the Tagus. The eastern hill, the Cero de Cascajal, was somewhat lower, and would remain undefended.

Cuesta's army was positioned between the Tagus directly east of Talavera and a slight eminence overlooking the Portina, known as the Pajar de Vergara, lying about half way between the Tagus and the Cero de Medellin (Plate 8). The British army was to continue the line from the Pajar to the Medellin. The two sectors were roughly equal in length, but not in strength. The Spanish army improvised field fortifications in accordance with Wellesley's instructions.[1] The British force, except for protected artillery position at the Pajar farm, was entirely in the open.

To the north of the Medellin and the Cascajal, there was another plain about three quarters of a mile wide, north of which rise rugged hills, running parallel with the Tagus. This area was initially unoccupied by either side.

Wellesley retired with Mackenzie's Division across the plain to a position near the Pajar. About this time, a force of French cavalry advanced through the olive and cork trees masking the Spanish position by the river. Cuesta was not about; Wellesley and his staff were marshalling the Spanish army behind its extemporized breastworks. The appearance of French dragoons trotting about by squadrons and letting off pistols at real or imaginary Spanish pickets caused an astonishing development. Without orders, the entire Spanish line of infantry between the Tagus and the Pajar fired one thunderous volley.

The resulting noise was great. As the French dragoons were still at least 1,000 yards away, no harm was done to them, but four Spanish battalions threw down their arms and took to their heels in panic.

[1] *Napier*, II, 166, says,

'Sir Arthur taking Talavera, which was built close to the river, as his fixed point, placed the right of the Spaniards there; drawing them up in two lines, their left resting upon a mound where a large field-redoubt was constructed, and behind which a brigade of British light cavalry was posted. The front was covered by a convent, by ditches, mud walls, breastworks and felled trees; the Spanish cavalry was posted behind their infantry; and their rear was supported by a very large house in the wood, well placed, in case of defeat, to cover a retreat to the main roads leading from Talavera to Arzobispo and Oropesa. In this position they could not be attacked seriously, nor their disposition be even seen; thus one-half of the line of battle was rendered impregnable, yet held by the worst troops.'

'Nearly 2,000 ran off on the evening of the 27th ... (not 100 yards from where I was standing) who were neither attacked, nor threatened with an attack, and who were frightened only by the noise of their own fire; they left their arms and accoutrements on the ground, their officers went with them, and they ... plundered the baggage of the British army which had been sent to the rear.' [1]

This performance, in which Cuesta's own coach was seen to have taken part for a short time, caused surprisingly little change at the front. The fugitives ran back for miles, spreading rumours of defeat, but Wellesley, Odonoju, and later Cuesta himself, replaced the missing battalions without difficulty.

Meanwhile the sun was setting. Wellesley had been unable to place his British units in their correct positions in accordance with his original plan. Hill's Division should have occupied the crest of the Medellin above the Portina, but a staff officer blundered. Both brigades were not only placed too far to the west, but were also given to understand that they were in the second line behind Lowe's and Langwerth's Brigades, K.G.L., of Sherbrooke's Division.

As darkness settled over the field, Donkin on his own initiative placed his somewhat shaken command in position on the Medellin east of Hill. Campbell's Brigade held the Pajar and a short line to the north of it, with Kemmis's Brigade in a second line directly to his rear. Sherbrooke's Division of four brigades extended from Campbell's left flank well up the southern slope of the Medellin. Mackenzie's Brigade and some British cavalry formed a second line behind Sherbrooke. This serious misalignment on the summit of the Medellin, which was the key to the entire British position, was to cause trouble.

Many British and German battalions had been on their feet and skirmishing for fifteen hours. Since few of them had anything to cook, they settled down for the night immediately darkness fell. Wellesley was to the rear of the Pajar receiving reports and making adjustments, when firing broke out in the vicinity of the Medellin at about 10 p.m. The sudden roar of musketry and the muzzle flashes from the eastern end of the ridge caused him to mount and ride towards the threatened sector. But even Sir Arthur was at a loss for some time to know what was happening. Finally, the British position was restored by Hill; a fairly clear idea of what had transpired was obtained from several sources, including prisoners.

[1] Wellesley to Castlereagh, *Dispatches*, V, 85.

An entire French division had crossed the Portina unopposed in three separate columns of three battalions each. The centre force was ordered to descend into the defile between the two ridges and ascend the Medellin itself; the two flanking columns were to cross the Portina well to the north and south, and then converge on the summit of the western ridge. The night was dark; the Portina defile was broken and precipitous. The centre column swerved to the south and struck Lowe's Brigade while most of the Germans were still asleep.[1] The 7th Line Battalion, K.G.L., suffered severe casualties including prisoners. The 5th were able to form and deliver half a dozen volleys before it was forced south by superior numbers.

This also caused the French centre column to swerve north again and pass by Donkin's Brigade without either force realizing the presence of the other. The French held the summit of the Medellin for several minutes before Hill investigated personally the 'dark mass of troops' between himself and Donkin. At first, he believed them to be the 3rd Foot, 'the old Buffs as usual making some blunder.' Hill with his brigade major rode up to the French and narrowly escaped capture. Hill broke away from a French *voltigeur* who tried to drag him from his horse, but the major was killed and Hill's mount seriously wounded by a volley from the crest. Hill managed to regain his division, and immediately formed the battalions of Stewart's Brigade into open columns of companies and advanced towards the crest of the Medellin.[2] The 1st Battalion of Detachments were the first to meet the French, and was checked.[3]

The 29th, however, thrust two enemy battalions right off the crest while still advancing in column. It formed into line and closed with the third French battalion which was ascending the ridge from the east in close column. The 29th opened fire with regular volleys at a range of under 40 yards. The French soon broke up into scattered groups and endeavoured to recross the Portina; many succeeded, but others, hopelessly confused as to direction, were captured.

The fighting just described involved the French centre column of three battalions only. The southern column, also of three battalions, had

[1] Lowe believed himself to be in the second line, *Oman* II, 516.

[2] More precisely, a column in which each company was in a two-deep line one behind the other with sufficient intervals between the companies to allow a line to form by moving obliquely. *Dundas, passim; Nineteen Movements*, 62, and plate 8.

[3] The two 'Battalions of Detachments' were made up from those remaining of several battalions left in Portugal by Sir John Moore the year before, and had, according to many authorities, little internal cohesion.

difficulty crossing the Portina and exchanged ineffectual volleys at long range with Langwerth's Germans. The northern French column never made contact; it veered off in the darkness and lost itself completely.

The losses in Lowe's Brigade were severe, but Donkin's and Langwerth's were not seriously engaged. Stewart's successful counter-attack cost less in casualties than might have been expected. The total British loss was 313; French casualties were approximately the same.

Wellesley realigned his troops as best he could in the darkness; Hill's Division was brought forward to a position originally marked out for it. The 29th retained the crest of the Medellin which they had retaken so gallantly, flanked by the 1st Battalion of Detachments and the 1/48th. Tilson's Brigade was aligned on Stewart's right, with Donkin's two and a half battalions further to the south. Wellesley slept on the Medellin wrapped in his cloak; he had his army under arms long before dawn.

At 5 a.m., a single French gun was fired from the summit of the Cascajal. It was the signal for others in this area and further down the French line to open a concentrated fire against the British position on the Medellin.[1] The French fire was both fast and accurate, but Wellesley ordered the British infantry to retire behind crests, or to lie flat. Not many men were hit. Less numerous, but equally well-served British pieces replied from their more commanding positions. Rettberg's long 6-pounders from the Medellin were particularly effective. In a few minutes, the entire upper half of both ridges were enveloped in clouds of smoke and morning fog. A light breeze from the Cascajal carried a continuous protective blanket of smoke back over the Medellin.

Wellesley on the crest could see nothing, but could guess what was going on from the sound of skirmish firing below. The light companies and riflemen had been posted in a strong line along the Portina. Heavy but irregular musketry indicated that these were being driven back on a narrow front by French *tirailleurs*. The fighting here was bloody, as the range was greatly restricted by the smoke and mist, but the British had an advantage both in numbers and arms. They could have defeated the *voltigeurs*, if the heads of three French infantry columns had not supported their attack. The British skirmishers continued to exchange fire with the *tirailleurs* and the heads of their columns; they were only brought back behind the main line with difficulty. They finally passed

[1] This concentration of artillery fire from several angles against a single point just before it was attacked by infantry was in accordance with the French theory. There were between 50 and 60 pieces firing; see *Fortescue*, VII, 238, note 1, for the difficulty in determining the number of guns used by the French at any particular time.

through Hill's brigades when the three enemy columns were no more than 100 yards away.

Each French column was composed of three battalions, but approached in a different formation from that employed at Vimiero. They were now twice as wide, but only half as deep, measuring about 60 men across and 24 ranks deep, altogether a total of 4,300 men in the three columns.[1] From the top of the Medellin they had the appearance of squares; they were separated laterally by about 400 yards. Two of them were heading for the centre and right of Stewart's Brigade; the third column reached out into the northern plain below the Medellin.

Hill's infantry had been kept under cover; it was now brought forward over the brow of the hill. The French columns were advancing along courses which prevented the matching of the head of each column with a British battalion in line. The northernmost column never really entered the action; the left wing of the 29th exchanged fire with it ineffectually at long range.[2]

The centre column smashed into the right centre of Stewart's two-deep line; that to the south hit the extreme right flank of Stewart's Brigade where it abutted Tilson's. Stewart and Tilson opened fire when the French were approximately 90 yards from their lines at the closest point. Stewart's two-deep line alone was 900 men broad and measured about the same in yards. Even though the northern half of the 29th was not firing against the French frontal attack, there were still 1,500 muskets opposed to only 400 which could actually fire from the central and southern French columns.

The centre French column received about two-thirds of Stewart's fire, approximately 1,200 muskets. The first volleys brought the French to a halt. They tried vainly to reply with 200 inefficient musketeers against six times as many good ones. They also endeavoured to deploy into line. The bloody contest lasted less than three minutes, long enough for British infantry to fire about ten volleys by platoons.

Meanwhile, the southern column fared little better. Since it was directed at the junction of Stewart's right and Tilson's left, it had a tactical advantage. Stewart's Brigade could spare only 300 muskets for them; Tilson's fire was in part ineffective because at long range. The Frenchmen here were able to make their way ahead a few yards at a

[1] This formation was known as a 'column of divisions'; two companies were formed abreast.

[2] This right column of the French attack was composed of the same troops who had done all the serious fighting the night before. This movement toward unoccupied territory may have been intentional on their part.

time, but suffered greatly as the extremities of two British brigades wrapped tightly around the head of their column. Meanwhile a force of riflemen and light infantry from Lowe's Brigade took them in flank.

As often happened in close order fighting, the French formation appeared sound, even though absorbing great punishment; suddenly their central column broke and made for the rear in confusion, as did their southern column a few seconds later. The British pursued immediately, inflicting heavy casualties; prisoners were taken before the French were able to recross the Portina. Some of their pursuers followed across the brook, but ran into severe opposition from fresh forces there.

It was not yet 7 a.m. The infantry fighting was over temporarily; a long range artillery duel continued for an hour and then ceased. The day was already intensely hot. An informal truce followed during which the British and French soldiers mingled to quench their thirst at the Portina.[1] At about 11 a.m., the French were recalled to their positions.

From the top of the Medellin, Wellesley could see them preparing for another attack. This would be more general in nature and would probably extend from the Pajar to the Medellin. There was also some activity in the plain to the north between the ridges and the mountains. Since an advance there would turn the Allied left flank, steps were taken to counter this possible threat. Rettberg's long 6-pounders were moved into a position where they could sweep the area. The only troops here, a single British light cavalry brigade, were reinforced by a brigade of British heavy cavalry, an entire division of Spanish infantry under Bassecourt, Albuquerque's Division of Spanish cavalry, and two Spanish 12-pounders. The guns were placed with Rettberg's, the cavalry alongside the British horsemen, and the infantry on the lower slopes of the mountains.

Soon after 1 p.m., the French artillery opened fire; there were at least 80 guns between the Pajar and the Cascajal. Wellesley could see approximately 30,000 French infantry ready to move forward. Their southernmost division opposite the Pajar was the first to advance; it had to move through an area of groves and enclosures defended by British light infantry and riflemen before reaching its objective. The Pajar itself was the southern anchor of the main British line. This large stone farmhouse,

[1] *Oman*, II, 526, says,

'This was the first example of that amicable spirit which reigned between the hostile armies all through the war, and which in its later year developed into that curious code of signals (often described by contemporaries), by which French and English gave each other notice whenever serious work was intended, refraining on all other occasions from unnecessary outpost bickering or sentry-shooting.'

situated on the hillock, was partially fortified; a battery of British 3-pounders was nearby. Campbell's Division defended this sector; he had a single battalion with the guns, two of which were placed north of the Pajar and one just west of the Portina.[1]

The *tirailleurs* of Laval's Division succeeded in driving back the British skirmishers.[2] Solid columns partially covered by an irregular line of light infantry broke into the open less than 300 yards from the Pajar. The British artillery, reinforced by four Spanish 12-pounders only just brought up, opened a destructive fire.[3]

The French division was probably using the same formation already employed earlier in the day by that which attacked the Medellin; three columns of three battalions each advancing on a front of two companies.[4] These battalions were somewhat disorganized by their march through the broken country and did not have time to reform. The French centre column was brought to a halt and badly mauled by the artillery and Campbell's single supporting battalion. The column to the south was received by the Spanish infantry with a hot fire. That to the north ran into two British battalions in line. The musketry advantage was again on the side of the Allies.

The French centre column broke first, but was soon followed by that on their right. The left column, which was in contact with Spanish troops only, retreated more slowly. Campbell sent his men forward in a short controlled pursuit. As at Vimiero, the French brought along their field artillery with their infantry; every single piece was captured before it fired a shot. This 'French' division of some 4,500 men—most of them were Germans—was vanquished by a slightly smaller number of British and Spanish combined.

While Campbell was still engaged with Laval, the main French attack developed to the north. Two 12-battalion divisions, a total of 15,000 veterans commanded by experienced officers, crossed the open plain on a front of about 1,500 yards between the Pajar and the Medellin; a line of *tirailleurs* in advance followed by two lines of battalions in column. Each line was composed of 12 infantry battalions, each 30 men broad

[1] Campbell's Brigade consisted of two battalions only, 2/7th and 2/53rd, but he had brought up the 1/40th from the other brigade of his division, Kemmis's, into his first line.

[2] Some British light troops, three or four companies at most, were surprised and nearly surrounded.

[3] A full battery of Spanish 12-pounders loaned by Cuesta to Wellesley was used; four guns at the Pajar and two on the Medellin.

[4] *Oman*, II, 533, '. . . in a single line of battalion columns, with a thick screen of *tirailleurs* in their front.' *Fortescue*, VII, 246, note 2, '. . . in column of double companies.'

and 15 ranks deep, with lateral intervals of 120 yards. The second line of columns followed the first, but some 500 yards to the rear.

Sherbrooke's Division of 6,000 men was ready in a single two-deep line. When the French crossed the Portina, the two opposing forces closed with each other. The British line appears to have divided into twelve small crescents of about equal strength without strict regard to battalion organization, each across the head of one of the French columns. Every British musket could fire effectively; only about 1,300 Frenchmen could reply. The columns were brought to a stand; too late the French tried to deploy into line. The heads of each column melted away under steady rolling fire. From high on the Medellin, Wellesley could see the enemy battalions break one after another.

Sherbrooke's Division surged forward in pursuit. Cameron's Brigade halted just to the east of the Portina and reformed, but the other three brigades went out of control; the Guards and the two K.G.L. Brigades lost all order. Even senior battalion officers seem to have overlooked the fact that for every battalion in the French front line of columns there was another 500 yards to the rear.

The fugitives from the French first line ran back through the intervals in their second, and immediately the tide of battle shifted. The swarm of British pursuers, many with unloaded muskets, were roughly handled. The same men who had crossed the Portina in triumph only five minutes before were swept back in rout. Even Cameron's Brigade was broken, for it had been unable to fire on the enemy until the very last moment, because the French were protected by a screen of retreating British.

This was the crisis of the battle; if the Allied centre collapsed, they would be badly defeated. Already French dragoons and artillery were moving towards this rent in the British line, and there was no second line behind the Guards and Langwerth. But Wellesley had been able to anticipate by a few minutes what had happened. When he saw Sherbrooke's men lose control, he realized that he must form another line behind them. He did not wish to weaken the Medellin, for the French on the Cascajal were obviously preparing to move forward against it. He could spare only one battalion and sent the strongest in the army, the 1/48th, down to support the Guards. He also ordered Mackenzie to move obliquely forward and north.

Four British battalions, a total of about 3,000 men, now formed in the centre, opened out to let their comrades through, and closed to confront at least 10,000 Frenchmen. If this 'thin red line' had not held, the name

Talavera would rank high in the list of French victories. There were 7,000 skilful, well-handled French cavalry ready to exploit a break-through on the open plains north of the Tagus. But the British infantry seems to have been conscious of its destiny. Calmly and silently, they stood in line awaiting orders.[1]

'Make Ready! Present! Fire!' The first volleys from all four battalions struck the advancing French now only 50 yards away. Inexorably, the platoon volleys commenced, one every 15-seconds from each of 80 half companies.

The Guards had lost more than a quarter of their strength in killed and wounded—not one uninjured man had been captured—east of the Portina. They rallied without delay behind Mackenzie's Brigade, reformed, gave a cheer, and rejoined the fight, as did the Germans and Cameron's Brigade on either flank. The French columns were smothered in fire; the northern division, its commander killed, broke first. Cotton's Brigade of British cavalry charged the flank of the southern division; it broke also and streamed back across the bloody brook. The British pursuit was not carried far this time, for heavy masses of French dragoons could be seen close to the front.

The French on the Cascajal, no less than the British on the Medellin, had witnessed what was taking place on the plain to the south; the French had no desire to assault the heights opposite where their attacks had already failed twice. But Wellesley noticed a French movement to the north; an infantry division here was already under fire at long range from Rettberg's Battery and two Spanish 12-pounders. Nine French battalion columns could not be stopped by eight pieces of artillery.[2] Three battalions ascended the foot-hills to the north to hold in check the Spanish infantry there; the other six edged forward cautiously along the northern side of the plain away from the Allied guns.

Wellesley perceived their hesitation and concluded that these units might be successfully attacked by cavalry. At least, they could be forced to stop and form squares more vulnerable to artillery fire than columns in motion. Anson's Brigade of light cavalry was ordered to advance. Two regiments, the 23rd L.D. and the Hussars of the K.G.L., formed a line and cantered forward. The plain appeared smooth and firm; the

[1] The immobility and silence of the British infantry particularly impressed French observers; *Wellington's Army*, 91, quotes Bugeaud, a battalion commander in Spain, '... the English, silent and impassive, with grounded arms, loomed like a long red wall; their aspect was imposing. ...'

[2] Ruffin's Division of Victor's Corps, the troops who had attacked the Medellin on the night of the 27th, and in the early morning of the 28th.

initial deploying could not have been done more perfectly. In the long advance towards the enemy, however, the 23rd L.D. began to increase its pace. There was no reason for this; the enemy was still several hundred yards away. The British horsemen were not under fire, but their officers made no effort to check this tendency and even added to it by personal example. The entire regiment was almost at full gallop when suddenly they came upon an abrupt cleft in the ground hitherto concealed by long grass. In spring, a tributary of the Portina flows here in a deep, wide cut, but the channel was completely dry. If the 23rd L.D. had been advancing at a controlled pace, this obstacle could have been crossed almost anywhere, but not at a gallop. Only one horse in two was able to clear the cut; others ran full tilt into the far bank and the second line ran into the first. Both men and their mounts rolled over each other in utter confusion; limbs and necks were broken.

The French infantry, already in squares, opened fire at long range on the survivors. But Major Ponsonby rallied the regiment and continued the attack, still at uncontrollable speed. Two squadrons passed between the infantry squares to run into a brigade of French *chasseurs* half a mile further to the east. The British horsemen were in disorder, on spent mounts, and outnumbered five to one. They fought with great bravery and individual efficiency, but were beaten. This unfortunate regiment lost about half its original strength in less than fifteen minutes; it is astonishing that as much as half of it got away under cover of the Allied artillery and the Spanish infantry.

The German light cavalry were able to negotiate the dry watercourse, for they were going at a proper pace, but their unassisted attack on the squares was unsuccessful, for the French were within supporting distance of each other. Any cavalry attack on one would come under a withering enfilade fire from others. The Hussars failed to break the squares, and suffered serious loss in consequence.

Throughout most of this cavalry action, the French squares had been excellent targets for the Allied artillery. When the British and German troopers retired, the French did likewise. The audacity of the charge of the 23rd L.D. may have contributed to the French retreat.

French attacks now ceased, although three hours of daylight remained. Wellesley must have been sorely tempted to advance the Allied right (or Spanish flank) and pin the French against the mountains, for he could see from the Medellin that only a single division of cavalry lay before Cuesta's entire army. The French reserve consisted of no more than 5,000 men located some distance behind their centre. If the road to

Toledo and Madrid was cut, the French would have been in a serious plight. Nevertheless such a movement would be dangerous because of the inability of the Spanish army to manoeuvre. It was best to leave them where they were. Behind their extemporized defences, they were formidable; in the open, even a few squadrons of French cavalry might cause panic.

Wellesley regretfully allowed the initiative to remain in the hands of the French. Before dark, the British army reformed, cared for its wounded as best it could, and prepared for another day of combat. But at dawn next morning the plain to the east was empty. The French had not only crossed the Alberche, but were already ten miles nearer Toledo.

In the fighting at Talavera, Wellesley's British army of about 20,000 had opposed 40,000 Frenchmen. French losses were 7,268 compared with total British casualties of 5,365. Although Allied casualties were lower numerically, Sir Arthur had lost over a quarter of his entire force, while the French army was reduced by less than 18 per cent. The Spanish loss was practically negligible, but their part in the victory had been modest. Wellesley had defeated a Napoleonic army with an inferior force.

The most important tactical aspect of Talavera was of course the breaking of French columns by British lines. This result was achieved not only by the superior fire of the latter, but also because Wellesley protected his men by holding them behind hillcrests, or ordering them to lie down if necessary, before they were required for action. He opposed a more powerful line of skirmishers to the French *tirailleurs*, as he had done at Vimiero. Wellesley perceived how easily columns could beat disordered lines, noticeably when Sherbrooke's Division continued their advance against the French across the Portina.

Wellesley's battlefield efficiency has rarely been better demonstrated. He had persuaded Cuesta to be reasonable, had pulled back the entire Allied force from an extremely weak position into a strong one, and had assigned the Spanish army a sector within their defensive capacity. The British army was brilliantly handled, particularly at the time of Wellesley's decision to send down the 1/48th and order up Mackenzie's Brigade.

On the other hand, not all the units of the British army behaved well.[1]

[1] *Oman*, II, 313, says,

'... there were only present five of the battalions which served at Vimiero and knew the French and their way of fighting. The rest were all inexperienced and new

Wellesley was to spend months eradicating some of the weaknesses that appeared. Internal discipline and attention to basic military duties had been found wanting. Donkin's Brigade had been surprised at the Casa; the night attack on the Medellin had caught several battalions unawares. Even the Guards and K.G.L. had gone out of control by impetuosity in their pursuits. Staff work had been far from perfect. All these things could be remedied by training, and making a few replacements. The fiasco of the 23rd L.D. presented an even more serious challenge, for cavalry was not so directly controllable, even by Wellesley.

There was another irremediable problem. Sir Arthur at this time could not expect to be formally in command of the Spanish armies; and yet the latter could not be effective under its own generals. Wellesley would not depend on Spanish units again until he commanded them.

THE CONTENDING FORCES AT TALAVERA

BRITISH ARMY UNDER WELLESLEY		TOTAL	= 20,641
1st Division, John Cope Sherbrooke			= 5,964
Henry Fred Campbell's Brigade	2,045		
1st Coldstreamers, 1/3rd Guards, 1 Co. 5/60th			
Alan Cameron's Brigade	1,364		
1/61st, 2/83rd, 1 Co. 5/60th			
Ernst E. K. von Langwerth's Brigade	1,388		
1st and 2nd Line Batts. and Light Co's. K.G.L.			
Sigismund von Lowe's Brigade	1,167		
5th and 7th Line Batts. K.G.L.			
2nd Division, Rowland Hill			= 3,905
Christopher Tilson's Brigade	1,891		
1/3rd, 2/48th, 2/66th, 1 Co. 5/60th			
Richard Stewart's Brigade	2,014		
29th, 1/48th, 1st Batt. Detach.			

to the field, and the majority indeed were weak second battalions, which were not originally intended for foreign service, and had been made up to their present numbers by large and recent drafts from the militia.'

The point concerning the militia is not accurate; the finest available recruits were these volunteers from militia units which were not only sounder physically and morally, but also had considerable previous military training.

3rd Infantry Division, Alexander Mackenzie   = 3,747
    Alexander Mackenzie's Brigade   2,276
     2/24th, 2/31st, 1/45th
    Rufane S. Donkin's Brigade   1,471
     2/87th, 1/88th, 5 Co's. 5/60th
4th Infantry Division, Alexander Campbell   = 2,960
    Alexander Campbell's Brigade   1,032
     2/7th, 2/53rd, 1 Co. 5/60th
    James Kemmis's Brigade   1,928
     1/40th, 9th, 2nd Batt. Detach.,
     1 Co. 5/60th
Cavalry, William Payne   = 2,969
    Henry Fane's Heavy Brigade   1,070
     3rd Dragoon Guards, 4th Dragoons
    Stapleton Cotton's Light Brigade   989
     14th L.D., 16th L.D.
    George Anson's Light Brigade   910
     23rd L.D., 1st L.D., K.G.L.
Artillery, Engineers, Staff Corps   = 1,096
    Three British Batteries under Lawson,   681
    Sillery, and Elliot
    Two German Batteries under Rettberg and   330
    Heyse

SPANISH ARMY UNDER CUESTA   TOTAL   = 34,800
    Six Infantry Divisions (41 Battalions?)   = 28,000
    Two Cavalry Divisions   = 6,000
    Artillery (30 guns)   800

FRENCH ARMY UNDER JOSEPH AND JOURDAN   TOTAL   = 46,138
    Victor's 1st Corps   = 19,310
     Infantry: Ruffin's Division   5,286
      (9 Batts.)
      Lapisse's Division   6,862
      (12 Batts.)
      Villate's Division   6,135
      (12 Batts.)
     Cavalry, etc.   1,027

Sebastiani's 4th Corps		= 15,456
Infantry: Sebastiani's Division (12 Batts.)	8,118	
Valence's Division, part (2 Batts.)	1,600	
Laval's Division (9 Batts.)	4,537	
Cavalry, etc.	1,201	
Infantry from Madrid (9 Batts.)		= 5,137
Reserve Cavalry, etc.		= 6,335
Artillery (80 guns)	Personnel included in divisional totals	

TOPOGRAPHICAL OBSERVATIONS

Talavera is a most satisfactory battlefield to visit. The town has not expanded greatly, nor the area changed in regard to the use of the land. Both the Medellin and the Cascajal are admirable points for surveying the entire terrain over which the armies fought. There is also an ancient watchtower on the edge of the mountains to the north. The Casa de Salinas, the Pajar, and the chapel to the east of the city are all readily identifiable and remain unchanged. A dam has been constructed across the Portina, between the Medellin and the Cascajal, to form a lake in the valley to the north which floods the area where the 23rd L.D. charged. The Portina below the dam flows in the same channel, and in the summer apparently in the same volume, as at the time of the battle.

VII

FOURTEEN MONTHS WITHOUT BATTLE

WELLESLEY, although victorious at Talavera, was unable to follow up the French retreat on 29th July. His army had been on half rations for several days; he had now given up all hope of receiving any from Cuesta. His wounded were so numerous that fully two-thirds of the British army was engaged in caring for them. Even had there been plenty of food and adequate civilian medical facilities, the position of the Allied army was insecure. Venegas had failed to carry out his orders to march on Madrid from the southeast. Although 85 per cent of the French soldiers in central Spain had fought at Talavera, Venegas had been held back by a few cavalry and his own lack of resolution. Sir Robert Wilson had accomplished more, with less than 2,000 men. His mixed command threatened the capital and caused the French army to retire northeast rather than east from Talavera. Although too weak to accomplish anything of great value, Wilson was certainly confusing the French and might cause them to make false dispositions.

Wellesley received news of a serious development on 2nd August. A new French army of 20,000 men was reported to have taken Plasencia the previous day. British sick and wounded there were made prisoners, and supplies were captured. Wellesley's communications with Portugal were severed. One or more of the corps of Soult, Ney, and Mortier had thrust south. This possibility had always formed a part of Sir Arthur's calculations; if the British army could not use the roads through Plasencia parallel to the Tagus, a better but longer route was available west of Badajoz in the valley of the Guadiana. But the presence of this new force in the immediate theatre of operations greatly complicated matters.

Wellesley's most serious problem was the Spanish army; it could not manoeuvre or fight in the open. Cuesta was even more stubborn and arbitrary than usual. He wanted to split each of the two Allied armies in half, and combine those halves. Wellesley with one could advance against Plasencia while he with the other would march on Madrid. Cuesta not only lacked all military skills, but cared little about what happened to British troops whose discipline and bravery made them particularly vulnerable, if improperly used.

Sir Arthur rejected Cuesta's plan, but offered to march his army either east or west if Cuesta went off in the opposite direction. Both finally decided that Wellesley should move west. Before dawn on 3rd August, Sir Arthur with 18,000 men set out for Plasencia.[1] British wounded at Talavera were left in the hands of the Spaniards; Cuesta had undertaken to care for, defend, and move them if necessary. Wellesley reached Oropesa before noon and soon assimilated all available local intelligence. The French army which had marched from the north on Plasencia was reported to be no more than a single corps, but Wellesley was overtaken by a Spanish officer with a dispatch from Cuesta. The old gentleman with commendable promptness was passing on to Sir Arthur a captured French dispatch outlining their plans and troop dispositions. Cuesta was following with the Spanish army. The force towards which the British army was advancing consisted of not one but three full French corps. Soult was in general command of his own and those of Mortier and Ney, altogether at least 45,000 veterans.[2] Even though Wellesley was surprised that these three corps were so

---

[1] The Light Brigade under Robert Craufurd, the 1/43rd, the 1/52nd, and the 1/95th had marched a prodigious distance, some of it at Sir John Moore's quick step—three steps walking and three steps running—during the 28th, but came up just too late for the battle. Fantastic claims were made as to time and distance covered, but the truth is still remarkable, about 42 *miles in 26 hours* in central Spain in July, each man carrying 50 to 60 pounds weight on his shoulders. This reinforcement from Lisbon of more than 2,500 first-class troops replaced almost half the Talavera caualties.

[2] In his successful search for the dramatic, *Napier*, II, 185, wrote,
  'Sir Arthur estimating Soult's force at fifteen thousand, was marching with twenty-three thousand Spanish and English, to engage fifty-three thousand: meanwhile Soult, unable to ascertain the exact situation of either friends or enemies, little suspected that the prey was rushing into his jaws. The fate of the Peninsula hung by a thread, which could not bear the weight for twenty-four hours, yet fortune so ordained that no irreparable disaster ensued.'
  This is somewhat of an overstatement; Soult's forces were spread out over a large area and divided. Both this French marshal and Marmont had better chances in 1812 and 1813, but refused to attack.

close, he was prepared for such a move against his communications and had countermeasures ready.[1]

Majestically, the Tagus flows between Alcantara and Toledo through arid, but fertile plains. The river is difficult to approach, for it lies in a gorge and runs wide and deep. It is crossed by bridges at Toledo and Alcantara, and at three points between: Talavera, Arzobispo, and Almaraz (Plates 7, 10, 11 and 33).[2] There were also several ferries and, when the river was low in summer, a few fords. The British army could cross in two hours. Once on the south bank, it was probably safe from French attack. A resolute and alert defence of the river line would keep the more numerous enemy on the northern side.

Wellesley halted at Oropesa; his cavalry patrols made contact with the French further to the west during the afternoon. Cuesta arrived with his vanguard on the morning of the 4th, anxious to fight Soult. But Wellesley realized that the French marshal had a force at least equal in quality and size to that which Joseph and Jourdan had at Talavera. Another victory as costly as Talavera in British casualties would be disastrous, while a defeat north of the Tagus would mean annihilation. If Soult should decline battle, but hold the Allies north of the river for forty-eight hours, they might be trapped between two powerful French forces, for Joseph and Jourdan were moving west again at speed.

In another stormy conference with Cuesta, Wellesley refused either to fight Soult or remain north of the Tagus in the open valley between the mountains and the river. The British army was in motion across the bridge at Arzobispo by darkness on the 4th. At dawn, the army marched west towards Almaraz; Craufurd, with his own brigade and Donkin's, was sent ahead to seize and hold the great Roman bridge and the cavalry ford there. These were secured on the 6th.

The bulk of the army toiled more slowly along the appalling road which frequently required widening to allow the artillery to pass. Teams of horses were unable to pull a single gun up some of the

[1] Much has been made of Napoleon's prescience in suggesting this move to Soult: *Napier*, II, 160–1, ' "Wellesley," said Napoleon, "will probably advance by the Tagus against Madrid; in that case, pass the mountains, fall on his flank and rear, and crush him !" ' But Napoleon realized, as did Wellesley, that the Tagus could be used to counter French numerical superiority.

[2] The magnificent Roman bridges at Almaraz and Alcantara are still in use; they cross not only the river, but the entire chasm. That at Almaraz was destroyed by Cuesta in December 1808 'by blowing up the principal arches'; *De Rocca*, 118–19. The sketch of this bridge in *Hay*, II, opposite 69, shows *only* the 145 foot arch destroyed; this confirms that the present structure is essentially the old one widened (Plate 33A). It still carries the main road from Madrid to Lisbon 110 feet above the river.

inclines; entire companies were assigned to help. Both men and animals were exhausted by several weeks of semi-starvation; yet Wellesley was able to support Craufurd on the 8th, and two days later bivouacked his army at Mirabete in an exceptionally strong position.

Cuesta rashly remained on the north side of the Tagus during the entire day of 5th August, although the French in his immediate front outnumbered him. During the night, however, the Spanish army also crossed the Tagus and followed Wellesley toward Mirabete. A Spanish infantry division and another of cavalry were detailed to hold the strong medieval bridge and ford at Arzobispo. Earthworks mounting 16 guns were thrown up on the southern bank to cover the bridge, but only cavalry defended the ford.

On the night of the 7th, Soult discovered the exact position of the ford, which was not easy to identify from the north. During the Spanish *siesta* the next afternoon, squadrons of French cavalry forded the river while their infantry poured over the bridge. Six thousand Spanish were routed and pursued for miles in several directions. All their artillery was taken including not only the 16 pieces in the bridge fortifications, but also at least 14 pieces captured at Talavera and given by Wellesley to Cuesta. Their infantry lost hundreds of men; even their cavalry was severely punished, while French losses were trifling.

Wellesley was fearful that the French might overtake Cuesta's main army before it reached the almost impregnable position above Mesas de Ibor. On the 9th, he retraced his steps to satisfy himself that they were out of danger. By the following morning, Cuesta's army with its remaining guns and its baggage was safely formed facing east along the summit of an extremely steep ridge. The Spanish in defensive positions, together with Craufurd holding the Almaraz river crossings and Wellesley further west, presented insurmountable difficulties to the French. Soult could cross the Tagus at a number of places both east and west of the Allies, but the country was so rugged and the roads so poor that he could not even threaten to envelope them. He had to cross the Tagus at Almaraz, or give up his offensive. He concentrated there on the 12th, but made no effort to force his way across the river.

There was another alternative for the French commander which Wellesley fully understood. Soult was closer to Lisbon than he by almost a week's march.[1] The French appeared to be heading in that

---

[1] Soult could have marched by Plasencia, Zarza la Mayor, Castelo Branco, and Abrantes. Wellesley, if he took his artillery, would have found it easier to move south by Truxhillo and Merida to Badajoz and then west through Elvas and the Alemtejo.

direction; at least one corps marched west in broad daylight. Wellesley assumed, however, that they were moving no further than Plasencia. If Lisbon had been their objective they would have started off secretly, and at night.

Sir Arthur's assumption proved correct; the fighting was over. Soult's advance south, after concentrating three French corps, accomplished next to nothing; the French, who had relinquished their hold on one quarter of Spain to make this move, marched north again. The British army had an even more potent enemy to contend with; the men were actually starving. Neither the Supreme Junta nor local political authorities could produce food in sufficient quantities in spite of repeated promises. Portuguese supplies were temporarily cut off. Rather than allow his army to disintegrate, Wellesley pushed south towards Merida and Badajoz; Craufurd's rearguard at Almaraz retired on the evening of 20th August. The army remained just inside Spain, but were in contact with the Portuguese border fortress of Elvas, where lay supplies.

Wellesley was always fond of anniversaries; he observed those of his first battles in the Peninsula, Rolica and Vimiero, during the hectic month after Talavera. Portugal was free of the French, but his efforts in central Spain, due to circumstances beyond his control, had not been so productive. He had gained much personal distinction, acquiring the titles of Baron Douro of Wellesley and Viscount Wellington of Talavera. On 16th September, he signed his first dispatch 'Wellington'.[1]

However, he was beset by difficulties. The news from northern Europe was depressing; Napoleon's victory at Wagram confounded all opposition to him on the Continent. The Emperor could turn his full attention to the Peninsula and order veteran soldiers by the division into Spain. It was even possible that he would come himself to drive the British leopards into the sea.[2]

Wellington halted at Badajoz on 3rd September. He was persuaded to remain in Spain by Marquis Wellesley, his eldest brother, then Ambassador at Seville.[3] The presence of the army here might prevent the French from moving across its front into Andalusia.

[1] Several letters of the 16th are signed 'Wellesley'. Then, in a letter to Villiers on the ever-present subject of commissariat supplies, he writes 'Wellington', and adds in a postscript, 'This is the first time I have signed my new name'; *Dispatches*, V, 158.

[2] This oft-quoted phrase was made by Napoleon to the French Senate.

[3] Richard Wellesley succeeded to his father's Irish title, Earl of Mornington, while still a minor. He was created Marquis Wellesley of Harragh on 2nd December 1799 for his service in India; *National Biography*, XX, 1122-5.

Wellington had no intention, however, of undertaking further operations in collaboration with Spanish armies. Even if he could manage to feed his own troops, the Spanish systems of supply were so inefficient that as soon as a Spanish army concentrated, it starved.

Cuesta had suffered a stroke and retired from active command, but the Supreme Junta was seized with a fit of overconfidence after 'their' victory at Talavera. They ignored the real military situation and made impractical offensive plans. Wellington told them bluntly that he would have no part in these, yet the Junta announced to the public and even to their own generals that the British army would co-operate. General Carlos Areizaga, a man of no great military ability, was placed at the head of 56,000 Spanish troops and ordered to march immediately on Madrid. He was soon involved with a vastly more competent French army of only 30,000 and suffered a disastrous defeat on Ocaña on 19th November. The Spanish suffered some 18,000 casualties. On the 28th and 29th of the same month, another large Spanish army commanded by the Duke del Parque was completely shattered at Alba de Tormes.[1] Spain was lost at least temporarily. Portugal must be made secure.

Early in October, Wellington visited Lisbon for the specific purpose of organizing, laying out, and commencing work on a system of fortifications later known as the Lines of Torres Vedras. At the latitude of the town of Torres Vedras the width of the peninsula between the Tagus and the Atlantic on which Lisbon is situated is about thirty miles; this gradually decreases to about eighteen as the river flows southwest to Lisbon before turning west to the sea. Three separate lines of fortification were to be constructed; the first, or northernmost, ran inland from the Atlantic along the south bank of the river Zizandre to the town of Torres Vedras and then southeast across country to Alhandra on the Tagus. The second ran approximately parallel to the first about five miles further south, while the third lay entirely west of Lisbon, and enclosed a small semi-circular area from which a re-embarkation could be made.[2]

---

[1] Wellington's comments on these two battles, *Dispatches*, V, 335, were,

'I declare that if they had preserved their two armies, or even one of them, the cause was safe. . . . But no! Nothing will answer excepting to fight great battles in plains, in which their defeat is as certain as is the commencement of the battle. They will not credit the accounts I have repeatedly given them . . . of the French; they will seek them out . . . I wonder whether the Spanish officers ever read the history of the American war; or of their own war in the Dutch provinces, or of their own war in Portugal.'

[2] Wellington's Memorandum for Lt. Col. Fletcher, Royal Engineers, written at Lisbon 20th October 1809, *Dispatches*, V, 234-9, works out in detail this idea.

The whole system was both complicated and extensive; streams were dammed to produce impassable inundations, and the dams themselves were protected by fortifications. The citadel of Torres Vedras and similar stone castles in other towns were reinforced with earthworks. These defensive works crowned every hill along both the first and second lines. The territory itself was rugged in the extreme and was worthy of the efforts expended on it. Thousands of men worked diligently under careful supervision on this vast project for more than a year before the Allied army made use of it.

On 9th December, Wellington ordered the British army out of Spain and into positions more in keeping with his primary responsibility of protecting Portugal. He was counting heavily on the Portuguese nation to assist him. Beresford and a few British officers had greatly improved their army during the summer. One Portuguese infantry brigade was now incorporated in each British division. Portuguese units, partly under British field and company officers, already considerably disciplined, were to become as reliable in combat as any in the Allied army.[1]

Wellington was preparing other means of opposing the French, utilizing Portuguese military forces. The Portuguese militia were to be kept active and under professional control; the *Ordenanza* were to be used in combination with a 'scorched earth' policy which would cause any army such as the French, which depended so heavily on marauder, to starve. To do this effectively, Wellington had to dominate the Portuguese government. The Prince Regent and the court were still in Brazil; the country was ruled in his absence by a Council. The pro-British faction on this were in the majority, but were themselves not always tractable. Wellington was fortunate in having a personal representative on this Council, for the position was filled after January 1810 by Charles Stuart. This able diplomat not only carried out Wellington's instructions precisely, but also humoured his fellow councillors by a combination of personal tact, charm, and the capacity of giving in gracefully over unimportant matters. Portugal depended on the British

[1] Actually, the 1st Division was already partly German and was not to receive a Portuguese brigade for some years. Hill's 2nd Division had no Portuguese brigade, but was continuously associated with the one and only all-Portuguese division. Craufurd's Light Division was formed by uniting British and Portuguese battalions in each of its two brigades. British officers serving in Portuguese units were volunteers from British battalions who had been given two steps in rank; there were usually five or six of these in each Portuguese battalion. Most, but not all, Portuguese brigades were commanded by British officers.

army to retain her national independence and the British subsidy to pay for her government.

Once Wellington had received proper authority from the Council, he issued the necessary orders to the Portuguese local governments. They were to adapt to modern needs their old forms of resistance to Moorish and Spanish invasion. Food, mills, ovens, and bridges were to be destroyed. Livestock was to be driven off. The people would be forced to move behind the Lines or take to the hills. All able-bodied males between sixteen and sixty not in organized units were to fight as members of the *Ordenanza* with whatever weapons they had. These ill-armed local groups could not oppose the French in battle, but could take a heavy toll of stragglers, messengers, sentries, and small foraging parties.[1]

Wellington planned to use all the regular troops at his disposal in a field army which would slowly fall back on the capital. The initial positions of this field army were governed by the topography of Portugal.

The country is roughly rectangular, 125 miles from east to west by 335 miles from north to south. The ocean forms the western and southern boundaries. The northern border follows the river Minho, no considerable military obstacle. An invasion from this direction would involve a march more than two-thirds of the length of the country before reaching Lisbon. Soult, in the late winter of 1809, had taken Oporto without great trouble, but was unable to move further. An advance on the capital from the north was so difficult that Wellington practically disregarded the possibility.

There remained the entire eastern border, but the northern quarter of this could be ignored for the same reasons as an attack across the Minho. A French advance in the extreme south across the lower Guadiana, south of the Sierra Morena, could be similarly discounted.

---

[1] *Napier*, II, 389, states that Wellington

'insisted that his authority as marshal general should be independent of the local Government, and absolute over all arrangements concerning the forces, whether regulars, militia, or *Ordenanza*. His designs were vast, and such as could only be effected by extraordinary means. Armed with this power, and the influence derived from the money supply by England, he first forced the regency to revive and enforce the ancient military law, by which all men were to serve in arms. Then he required that the people should be commanded to destroy their mills, remove their boats, break down their bridges, lay waste their fields, abandon their dwellings, and carry their property away from the line of invasion. He would use the regular troops in such a way as to avoid decisive battles, he would compel the enemy to keep in mass, and let the armed population cut off all resources not carried in the midst of the troops: it was a design of terrible energy.'

There remained 150 miles of border between the Duero and the middle Guadiana which was crossed by three routes. The northernmost of these ran through Ciudad Rodrigo and Almeida and was the classical path for armies invading Portugal from Spain; Wellington considered this the most likely. Far to the south, another good road passes through Badajoz and Elvas and this also had been used by armies in the past.

These two corridors are separated by 120 miles of rugged country; approximately half way between them, a third road enters Portugal. Both Junot, and Wellington himself before Talavera, had used this route which roughly follows the Tagus, but it was unsuitable for artillery and wagons, and Sir Arthur considered it unlikely that a powerful French army would approach from this direction alone.

An invasion along either the northern, Ciudad Rodrigo, corridor, or the southern, Badajoz, corridor presented a comparatively simple problem. Wellington was confident that if the French thus advanced he could concentrate the Allied forces and give battle at a distance from Lisbon. An advance along two, or all three routes at once, would be more difficult to stop.

Wellington planned to make judicious use of all natural or artificial barriers that would delay the French; the border itself was fortified after a fashion in numerous places. There were many walled villages, old citadels, and a few modern fortifications. In the northern corridor Ciudad Rodrigo and Almeida were both strong and well garrisoned. Badajoz and Elvas were even more powerful in the south.[1] Peniche and Abrantes were strengthened; reliable commanders were appointed, but the garrisons were mainly militia.[2] No British army units, and only a few Portuguese regulars, could be spared to go behind walls.

The route from Elvas towards Lisbon runs through a predominantly flat country; little could be done to obstruct it. The Tagus south of Abrantes was practically impossible to cross in the face of British gun-boats and marines.

In the northern corridor, two roads ran from Almeida to Coimbra. That south of the Mondego was blocked by a system of earthworks at Alva. The road north of this river crosses the Busaco ridge, a position so strong that no earthworks were required.

A French army, once past Almeida, might have avoided the Mondego

---

[1] Ciudad Rodrigo and Badajoz were, of course, on the Spanish side of the border, and had Spanish garrisons. Almeida and Elvas were their Portuguese counterparts.

[2] Abrantes, at the 'elbow of the Tagus', was of great strategic importance. Peniche was of value mainly as a port of re-entry.

roads entirely and followed a route from Celorico to Abrantes known as the Estrada Nova, but Wellington had this totally destroyed, a relatively easy job, since it ran along the precipitous sides of mountains in many places and could be blasted into the valley below. The French would be unable to repair it, or make it practicable for wheeled transport, for some months.

On the other hand, roads which the Allies might require for their own concentration were repaired, particularly that from Santarem through Tomar to Miranda do Corvo. A secondary line of communications was prepared along the south bank of the Tagus from Abrantes through Niza to Villa Velha including semi-permanent bridges of boats at both ends. A movement from Abrantes to Castelo Branco could be made two marches quicker by taking the southern route, even though it involved crossing the Tagus twice. A new road was constructed for lateral communications behind the Busaco ridge.[1]

The Anglo-Portuguese army was initially divided into three commands. Beresford, in addition to the considerable administrative work involved in organizing the Portuguese army, commanded a powerful central force stationed at Abrantes. Hill, with his own strong 2nd Division, a full Portuguese division, and some other smaller units, controlled the Elvas-Badajoz area. Wellington himself, with the bulk of the infantry, held the northern corridor with his headquarters in the vicinity of Almeida.[2]

For military purposes, the entrance to the Ciudad Rodrigo-Almeida corridor had a width of about forty miles south from the Duero to the mountains. This entire sector was the personal responsibility of Robert Craufurd who had not only his newly constituted Light Division, but also a regiment of K.G.L. Cavalry and Ross's Battery of Horse Artillery.[3] This force was deployed for the most part behind the Agueda, a southern tributary of the Duero.

Craufurd was one of the few 'scientific' soldiers of the time. He knew precisely how long it would take to concentrate his forces at any given point. His men were not needlessly burdened with parade and close order drills, but at any time day or night could fall in and be ready to

---

[1] *Fortescue*, VII, 508, states that Wellington 'had caused a road to be constructed from end to end on the ridge along the western or reverse side.'

[2] For exact details of this organization see Appendix to Chapter VIII.

[3] The Light Brigade (see note 1, page 110) together with the 1st and 3rd Portuguese *Caçadores* formed the Light Division with a total strength of under 4,000 men. It was smaller than the other divisions, but of high quality. Craufurd had both the 14th and 16th L.D. assigned temporarily to him toward the end of this period.

fight in seven minutes. Within a quarter of an hour, all baggage could be packed and headed towards the rear, and the entire fighting force formed in columns, carrying three days' rations, ready to march as directed. Semaphores by day and beacons by night were in use throughout the entire area to pass orders rapidly between his various units.

There were but three bridges over the Agueda, although the stream was fordable at several points depending upon the water level. Like many Peninsular rivers, the water could rise or fall several feet within a few hours, sometimes without any apparent reason. Readings were taken of the depth of the water at various points and such information was conveyed to all field officers every six hours.

Wellington's system of intelligence had been good during the first year of war; it was now much improved. Throughout the winter and spring Wellington had exact knowledge of enemy movements. He was receiving first hand information gained from reconnaissance by large and small Allied forces and from questioning prisoners and deserters. He was also carefully collecting observations and rumours from his 'correspondents' within the enemy lines.[1] The Spanish guerrillas were gaining in strength and experience. They also supplied information and passed on captured French dispatches. To insure prompt delivery of the latter, British headquarters always paid for them in hard money. A continual flood of newspapers in five languages reached headquarters, also dispatches from home and elsewhere in Europe, and a steady stream of visitors. Wellington's imaginative, yet realistic and logical mind gained from all this material a remarkably clear picture of what was happening 'on the other side of the hill'.

Early in the winter of 1809–10, it was expected that Napoleon would take personal command in the Peninsula during the spring. More than 100,000 additional French soldiers including units of the Guard crossed the Pyrenees; their numbers in Spain rose to 324,996 on 15th January 1810.[2] As the winter wore on, there was less talk of the Emperor coming in person. He was preoccupied with divorcing Josephine and marrying Marie-Louise of Austria.[3] On 18th May, Wellington finally received positive information as to his personal adversary; Marshal

---

[1] These individuals were of every class and society; most were paid, but some probably were not. Their motives were usually patriotic, and collectively they sent along a mass of information. Actual details of the organization were never committed to paper for obvious reasons.

[2] *Oman*, III, 539, for details.

[3] The civil and religious ceremonies took place on 1st and 2nd April.

Massena, in direct command of 138,000 French troops had been ordered to retake Portugal.

Massena reached Salamanca on 28th May, several days after his campaign had actually begun. Ney had used the heavy French siege train to batter Astorga into subjection. Its medieval walls strengthened with earthworks sheltered a strong and courageous Spanish garrison, but it capitulated after thirty-two days, on 22nd April.

Massena chose to use the northern corridor into Portugal for his advance, either exclusively or in combination with the central road through Castelo Branco. His first objective was Ciudad Rodrigo; the French in the area had been making fascines and gabions for this purpose for some time. This fortress was Spain's main bastion against the Portuguese in the northern corridor, but was equally defensible in the other direction. The ancient walled town was situated just east of the Agueda in a rolling plain; it had recently been surrounded by Vauban-type outer works. Its normal population was about 8,000. The present garrison of 5,500 Spanish regulars and militia was commanded by General Andres Herresi, a veteran nearly seventy years old, but still vigorous and ingenious.[1]

The French surrounded Ciudad Rodrigo on 26th April, but did not commence the siege until 30th May. Wellington was considering a surprise attack on the French forces in the area even before Massena arrived. The Allied army might destroy the material collected and fabricated for the siege, inflict severe casualties, and thoroughly disorganize the French units present. But a complete victory was unlikely, for the enemy could concentrate within a few hours well over 40,000 veterans, including 5,000 cavalry. Wellington could muster no more than 32,000 of which only 2,000 were cavalry. The risks involved in leaving the protection of the Portuguese mountains were too great; the project was given up.

Once Massena took command, he endeavoured to persuade Wellington to come out and fight in the open. With a natural craft matured by thirty years of soldiering, the French marshal disposed his forces in such a way as to invite attack. A single corps of 26,000 men conducted the siege; Wellington could have beaten this force, but would have been a long day's march from safety. Massena would have brought up additional forces to defeat the Allies, or drive them back in rout across the border. Even a British victory with losses as heavy as at Talavera would

[1] This garrison was composed in part of militia from the town and the surrounding area; there was but one battalion of regulars.

have reduced greatly Wellington's chances of successfully defending Portugal. There was no possibility of permanently relieving Ciudad Rodrigo unless 36,000 Allies could defeat three times as many French veterans in the open plain.

Wellington endured during this period the taunts of the French, the threats of the Spanish, and the ill-concealed murmurs of his own army. Many high ranking British officers were openly critical not only in their conversation, but also in letters home which found their way into the newspapers. Some even considered his failure to relieve Ciudad Rodrigo to be disgraceful.[1]

On 10th July, Herresi capitulated to save the civilian inhabitants from the plunder, rape, and murder which usually accompanied the taking of a town by storm. The forty-two days gained in holding the town were extremely valuable. Wellington was further encouraged by the slowness with which the French replenished their siege train before transferring it to Almeida. This Portuguese fortress just across the border from Ciudad Rodrigo was finally isolated after a bloody fight between Craufurd's Light Division and Ney's whole corps on 24th July. During the past two months, Craufurd and his command had been involved in almost daily skirmishes and had fought a major action at Barba del Puerco. They had been uniformly successful, but in the fight on the 24th things went wrong. Craufurd not only failed to handle his command properly, but also disobeyed orders.[2] There is no question, however, that the individual companies and battalions behaved admirably. The French forced the Light Division back over the Coa, but were not able either to break its morale or inflict crippling casualties (Plate 31).

Ney then tried to follow up his success by pressing his attack across a narrow bridge. This was the first time that the marshal had fought British infantry under the general command of Wellington. He brought forward his artillery and sent infantry columns in close order across the bridge. Three determined attacks failed. Not more than a score of

---

[1] Even so loyal a supporter of constituted authority as D'Urban, 116–26, was critical of Wellington at this time. Napier, II, 408, 'Nevertheless Wellington absolutely refused to venture even a brigade, and thus proved himself a truly great commander of a steadfast mind. It was not a single campaign but a terrible war he had undertaken. If he lost 5,000 men, his government would abandon the contest; if he lost 15,000, he must abandon it himself.'

[2] Oman is pro-Craufurd and Fortescue severely critical; their accounts differ as do their conclusions. Wellington wrote on 31st July to Wellesley Pole, '. . . if I am to be hanged for it, I cannot accuse a man who I believe has meant well, and whose error was one of judgement, not of intention.' Fortescue, VII, 484.

Frenchmen ever reached the west bank. Ney lost at least 400 killed and wounded to no purpose.

Although Almeida was isolated, the place was strong, well garrisoned, and commanded by an able British officer.[1] It was plentifully supplied with artillery, ammunition, and food. The French did not commence their siege for more than a month; their batteries opened fire for the first time on 26th August. The Portuguese defenders were giving back more than they received in this initial artillery duel when a most unusual accident occurred. Although Almeida contained bombproof casemates, it lacked a central powder magazine. The enormously strong cathedral had been converted to this use and contained many tons of powder; it was strong enough to withstand a direct hit, even by the largest mortar shells. At the commencement of the bombardment, powder was carried from the cathedral to the various ready magazines near the guns on the walls. Kegs and filled cartridges were conveyed through the streets by donkeys. One of these kegs was damaged and left a long trail of powder behind it. A shell falling some distance from the cathedral ignited this train. It burned back, not into the magazine itself, but to the entrance where other cartridges awaiting transportation were set off. This comparatively small explosion, after a short interval, caused the main magazine to blow up.

The cathedral ceased to exist. Only one man survived to tell the story; he dived into an oven after the first explosion. The tops of houses throughout the town were sheared off as if by a knife, but at progressively higher levels depending on their distance from the focal point of the explosion. The outer walls of the place suffered relatively little damage, as most of the explosive force passed above them. However, 500 Portuguese soldiers were killed in an instant.

Although the loss of ammunition alone now made a protracted defence impossible, Cox endeavoured to gain time by exacting the best possible terms from the French; he was betrayed by his Portuguese officers.[2] They insisted on immediate surrender; the French were masters of Almeida by noon on the 28th.

[1] Lt. Col. William Cox, a brigadier in the Portuguese service.
[2] *Marbot*, 412, says of Cox,
    'That brave officer, not suffering himself to be intimidated by the horrible disaster which had just destroyed almost all his means of resistance, proposed to the garrison to continue their defence behind the ruins of the city. But the Portuguese troops, terrified, and led away by their officers, especially by Bernardo Costa, the lieutenant-governor, and Jose Bareiros, commanding the artillery, refused, and Colonel Cox, being unsupported, was compelled to capitulate.'

Had Almeida held out as long as Ciudad Rodrigo, Massena's advance into Portugal would have been delayed until the autumn rains began. With its surrender, Massena assumed that he had nothing between him and Lisbon but the Anglo-Portuguese army. He could move west along the northern corridor only, or he might use both that and the Castelo Branco route. Reynier's French 2nd Corps marched north from Zarza la Mayor on 10th September. By the 17th, Wellington was certain that Massena would advance by the northern route alone. He had stored his siege train in Ciudad Rodrigo, and garrisoned the place, together with Almeida. The French were bringing into Portugal a field army of 65,000 men. Wellington was now forced to concentrate his own armies also; he ordered Hill and Beresford to join him on the Mondego.

The road from Almeida to Abrantes had been destroyed, but there were two from Almeida to Coimbra, one north and the other south of the Mondego. Massena could march by both or either. Skilful British reconnaissance reported the French plan almost as soon as it was known to their own army.[1] Massena chose the northern road. It was considered one of the worst in Portugal, and ran for miles through defiles where the *Ordenanza* would be effective and the French cavalry almost helpless.[2]

Massena forced his army along this atrocious road through country infested by bloodthirsty peasants who well remembered the last time the French were in Portugal. Wellington's regulars were only briefly in contact with the French, but the *Ordenanza* were present twenty-four hours a day. These hardy mountaineers kept mainly to the hillsides during daylight, but descended into the valleys at night. They fired fowling pieces from behind rocks at close range and rolled huge boulders down upon the French. They separated division from division and created confusion all along the line of march. The French had hardly a moment's rest. Sentries had their throats cut; small groups of Portuguese would creep close to French camps and discharge volleys which were both infuriating and deadly.[3] Stragglers were cut off, tortured, and murdered. The road itself took a toll. Gun carriages were

---

[1] Capt. John Somers-Cocks of Wellington's staff was operating with a few well-mounted British and German troopers behind the enemy and sending in intelligence of all their movements which was of great value.

[2] This choice appears to have been based not on ignorance, for Massena had many Portuguese renegades with him, but on his desire to avoid the entrenched position on the southern road at Alva.

[3] The firearms of the *Ordenanza* were often loaded with bird shot. The wounds inflicted were usually considered superficial at first, but these sometimes festered and caused death.

smashed; horses broke their legs and had to be destroyed; baggage and supplies had to be abandoned.

On the other hand, Massena and his army were skilful professional soldiers with years of experience in all types of fighting. They were inconvenienced, but not seriously weakened even in morale. When a better organized Portuguese militia force under Colonel Trant threatened to inflict really serious damage, it was defeated. Massena ordered all peasants taken with arms, but without uniforms, to be shot.[1]

On 24th September the Allied army at the village of Mortagua was again in contact with the French, who were then advancing southwest. Craufurd's Light Division was stationed to the north of the road and Pack's Independent Portuguese Brigade to the south. Wellington was in personal command of both and endeavoured to oppose Massena in such a way as to entice him along this road towards Coimbra. He wanted to make sure that Massena followed him, rather than veer northwest towards Oporto. This alternate route was even worse than the road the French has been following, but it avoided the Busaco ridge.[2] The French marched straight ahead as desired.

On the morning of the 25th, their advance gained impetus. There was bloody skirmishing at the hamlet of Moura, only three miles from the ridge. Wellington ordered the Light Division and Pack's Brigade to pull back past the village of Sula, half way to the crest, and to take up carefully chosen positions (Plate 12). When Craufurd reached the summit, he found the Allied army waiting. During the past week, both Beresford and Hill had arrived in the area. After fourteen months, Wellington was again willing to give battle.

---

[1] This order seems to have been a form only; the French had been following the procedure for several days. The *Ordenanza* kept few live prisoners, although Wellington had instituted a system of payment in hard money for all French soldiers captured and not maltreated.

[2] The track from Mortagua through Avelleira to the Oporto-Coimbra road passed through deep gorges which Wellington had ordered to be held by organized Portuguese units.

VIII

BUSACO

WELLINGTON had concentrated his field army along the summit of the Busaco ridge by 10 a.m. 26th September in accordance with a plan conceived long before. This position completely blocked the northern road from Almeida to Coimbra. If the French wished to advance further in the direction they were moving, they would have to push 49,000 Allied infantry, half British and half Portuguese, from their stations.[1] A total of 60 artillery pieces supported them strategically placed among the Allied battalions.

The Busaco ridge extends north from the Mondego for ten miles (Plate 13). The road from Mortagua through Moura to Coimbra is the only good one across this line of hills and is nearer the northern end than the river. Throughout its entire length the ridge dominates the valley lying to the east, but varies both in height and breadth. The southern section is 1,800 feet above the Mondego and relatively narrow; the central section is 400 feet lower, and broader. The ridge rises again just south of the main road where there was a convent enclosed in a large walled garden. The northern quarter of the ridge, beyond the road, is not so high but no less steep. Many lateral spurs project from the ridge which is penetrated by ravines; the valley to the east is rough and irregular, but there is no place where the ridge can be climbed easily, nor any route by which the French could approach it unseen. There were some secondary roads in the area which were hardly practicable for wagons. The only one which played a part in the battle crossed the central section of the ridge between the village of San Antonio de Cantara on the east and Palheiros to the west.

---

[1] The total Allied force at Busaco was 51,345 as given in the Appendix to this chapter. The cavalry, except for two squadrons, was not present. Wellington had sent it far out to either flank and to the rear at Mealhada and Ponte de Murcella.

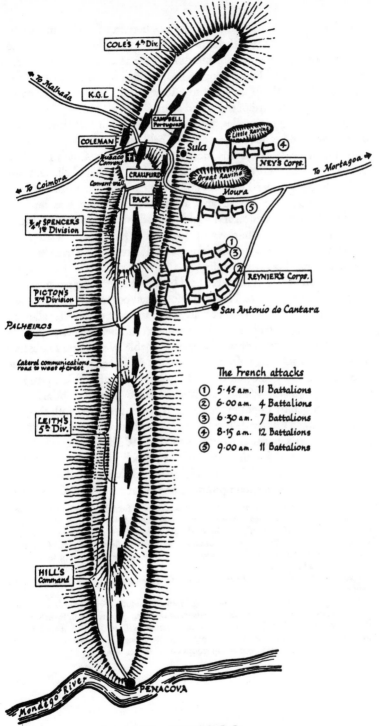

COLE'S 4th Div.

To Malhada

K.G.L.

COLEMAN

Busaco Convent

To Coimbra

Convent wall

CAMPBELL Portuguese

Sula

Little Ravine

NEY'S Corps.

To Mortagoa

CRAUFURD

Great Ravine

Moura

⑤

PACK

¾ of SPENCER'S 1st Division

①
③
② REYNIER'S Corps.

PICTON'S 3rd Division

San Antonio de Cantara

PALHEIROS

Lateral communications road to west of crest

The French attacks

① 5·45 a.m. 11 Battalions
② 6·00 a.m. 4 Battalions
③ 6·30 a.m. 7 Battalions
④ 8·15 a.m. 12 Battalions
⑤ 9·00 a.m. 11 Battalions

LEITH'S 5th Div.

HILL'S Command

Mondego River

PENACOVA

V. BUSACO

Wellington had analysed his entire position and found it more susceptible to attack in its northern than its southern half. The tracks to the south of Moura were bad, and difficult for an army advancing from Mortagua to use without exposing its flank and rear. He entrusted the southern three-fifths of his front to Hill and Leith, who together commanded only one-third of the Allied army.

The remaining four miles, from the San Antonio–Palheiros road to the northern end of the ridge, could be held more strongly; there were 34,000 men available for this more important sector. Cole's Division, and Independent Portuguese brigade under A. Campbell, and the K.G.L. brigade under Lowe occupied the extreme left flank north of the main road. The crucial area about the road itself was held by Craufurd's Light Division and Pack's Brigade supported by Coleman's Brigade. Further south towards Leith and Hill, there were three brigades of Spencer's 1st Division, and Picton's 3rd Division reinforced by some Portuguese units.[1]

The northern four miles were held by about 8,500 men per mile; the six miles further south had less than 3,000 men per mile. The important lateral communications road behind and to the west of the crest allowed easy movement of troops from one point to another. The eastern slope of the ridge was then sufficiently open to enable Wellington to observe any French attack long before it reached the Allied main line.[2] The basic idea was flexibility in defence; not a spadeful of earth had been turned.

During the 26th, Wellington saw the three French corps arrive at Moura and deploy opposite the ridge. Reynier's moved south towards San Antonio de Cantara (Plate 14). Ney's lay between Moura and Sula. Junot's was in a position to support either. Wellington knew almost exactly the size and constitution of the French army; he could now see its precise position.[3] He strongly suspected, however, that Massena knew little of the size, composition, and position of the Allied force,

[1] There remains a problem as to who commanded, and for what length of time, some Portuguese units in the area where Picton's line joined Leith's. Picton certainly had temporary control of the two battalions of the 8th Line of Eben's Brigade of Leith's new 5th Division and the Tomar militia battalion nominally of Spry's Brigade of the same division. The British units of Leith's new division were of fine quality, but some doubt existed as to his Portuguese.

[2] Much of this area has now been re-afforested, although it was still open fifty years ago; *Oman*, III, 360.

[3] Wellington's vantage point overlooking Moura is carefully preserved today, although it is now shrouded in trees. Craufurd's methodical checking of personnel in French formations on the Agueda had been of great value; *Fortescue*, VII, 463, says 'A special department was organized for receiving and comparing the reports of deserters, who came in frequently from the German and Italian troops on the French side.'

and ordered forward a skirmish or security line into the valley to prevent French reconnaissance. As usual, the bulk of his army lay behind the crest of the ridge and could not be seen from below.[1]

On the night of the 26th, the Allied army had to be content with cold food; no fires were to be lit after dark, for Wellington wished to prevent illumination giving away his dispositions. The French could be seen clearly from the ridge; there were three broad areas of bivouac fires, one for each corps.

Wellington's army was under arms by 4 a.m., but the whole valley was shrouded in thick grey fog at dawn. Nothing could be seen below, but there were unmistakable sounds of enemy movements. Wellington was with Lightburne's Brigade, the northernmost of Picton's three, shortly after daybreak. From his observations the previous evening, he expected the first French attack to be made here.[2] This was the lowest part of the ridge; the San Antonio–Palheiros road would assist a French advance. Reynier's whole corps had been concentrated against this position.

By 5.30 a.m. Wellington was convinced that French infantry columns were ascending the slopes towards Lightburne's Brigade. Soon irregular firing could be heard below between the Allied skirmish line and *tirailleurs*. The firing was getting closer; the fog was lifting. First the *tirailleurs* and then French columns began to appear. Wellington counted eleven battalions in three regimental formations, each with a front of a single company. Each column was therefore between 35 and 40 men wide and 45 or 60 ranks deep. The eleven *voltigeur* companies, not being so widely dispersed as Picton's security line, outnumbered their opponents and drove them back towards Lightburne's Brigade.[3]

Wellington ordered forward to a previously selected position two British 6-pounders. These raked the French columns so effectively that they swerved away to the south when only 200 yards from Lightburne's

---

[1] Ney endeavoured to push in the Allied skirmishers so that he could ascend one of the numerous eastern spurs of the Busaco ridge, but accomplished nothing. Both Massena and Reynier believed that Picton was on the Allied right flank, rather than near its centre.

[2] *Fortescue*, VII, 514, tentatively advances an extremely doubtful theory that Wellington intentionally left a gap in his line here to invite French attack. This appears to me to be unlikely.

[3] Col. Williams of the 5/60th, three companies of which were permanently assigned to Picton's Division, was in command of these and the other light companies of both British and Portuguese battalions of the 3rd Division, a total force of perhaps 800 men. These were distributed over a mile of front. The 1,100 *voltigeurs* of the northernmost French attack were advancing on a front of no more than 800 yards.

infantry. There was some exchange of musketry, but at a range too great to be effective.

In spite of the unfavourable terrain, the French artillerymen were trying hard to advance with their infantry. They could not ascend the slopes, but did find a few positions in the western valley from which they could just reach the crest. Wellington ordered Lightburne's Brigade a few yards to the rear out of sight of these gunners. These two battalions, the 2/5th and 2/83rd, took no further active part in the battle, but remained in position with arms ready.

As the first French attack turned away from Lightburne and the two Allied guns, it was again partially enveloped in the fog. These columns marched across the front of Colonel Wallace's 1/88th, the northern battalion of Mackinnon's Brigade; they climbed a spur at right-angles to the ridge, rather than the ridge itself. They then corrected their direction and turned on Major Gwynn's half of the 1/45th, which was defending a position some 600 yards south of the flank of the 1/88th.[1]

Wallace and the 88th immediately moved to Gwynn's aid. Some *voltigeurs* gained the crest of the ridge between Gwynn and Wallace and opened fire on the latter as the 88th moved south in column. Wallace detached three companies to engage the French light troops who were protected by rocks. He then threw his other six companies into line and swept down on the northern flank of the French attack. Meanwhile, Wellington had ordered forward two more British 6-pounders to ply the enemy at close range with grape and canister. Picton sent north the other half of the 1/45th and two Portuguese battalions which closed with the French.

Eleven French battalions had been struggling blindly in fog on a broken, steep hillside, frequently under fire from both infantry and artillery; they had lost their original formation, confidence, and physical freshness. There were only four Allied battalions opposing them at the moment, but these were in line with every musket functioning. The northernmost of the three French regimental columns was in the lead. Steady volleys from fresh, well-ordered Allied infantry created havoc in the disordered mass; the two 6-pounders did their full share. Suddenly, the French broke and streamed back into the valley. The other two regiments did likewise, although their casualties were not so

---

[1] The 1/88th was ordered into its position by Wellington on the evening of the 26th; Picton sent Gwynn's wing of the 1/45th north just after dawn.

severe.[1] The Allies pursued almost to the valley floor before they were checked by the French artillery and retired to their original positions.

The French attack just described began a quarter of an hour before another made nearly a mile further south; however, the second attack followed a more direct route, the San Antonio-Palheiros road, and was actually the first to be engaged. It consisted of a single column of four battalions on a single company front protected by *tirailleurs*. Even though they were moving in fog they had the road to guide their left flank and did not lose their way, and this column struck the Allied line just north of the road where Picton commanded in person. He had not yet sent off the second half of the 1/45th and had in addition the 1/74th, Champlemonde's Portuguese Brigade, and three more Portuguese battalions, together with one, and later two, full batteries of Portuguese artillery, which opened fire as the fog lifted.[2] Colonel Williams had drawn back his skirmishers earlier when the northern French attack had broken through, but now attacked downhill with three companies of Rifles. The French were suffering severely. The road curves south as it approaches the crest, but the attackers continued straight ahead. The head of their column was directed at the middle of the two-deep line of the 1/74th. This strong battalion was flanked and supported by at least six Portuguese battalions; the Portuguese artillery was still firing at the French over the heads of the Allied infantry.

Not only Williams's riflemen, but also Allied line infantry opened fire at unusually long range. This musketry was heavy, but not as effective as usual. Even though outnumbered two to one, the French were not broken. After receiving several volleys and point blank artillery discharges, their column lurched to the north where it was protected from Allied artillery. This action degenerated into a long range 'fire fight'.

Picton was now confident that this attack beside the road would come to nothing. He sent north the second half of the 1/45th and the two Portuguese battalions which were so important in defeating the French

[1] Parts of these disordered French units delivered a secondary attack to the south of the main assault, but were thrown back and mingled with the other fugitives.

[2] *Fortescue*, VII, 514, states that on 26th September Wellington 'ordered Leith to detach Spry's brigade and the 8th Regiment of Portuguese to reinforce Picton.' Yet when Leith came north the following day he still appears to have had Spry's Brigade with him; *Oman*, III, 375, says Leith had 'Spry's Portuguese Brigade at the head of his column.' The Tomar militia was definitely under Picton's command. Arentschildt's Portuguese Battery was always with Picton; Leith brought one of Dickson's two Portuguese batteries with him. Fortescue indicated either an earlier arrival for the latter or an unnamed third battery in action here. See also note 1 page 126.

northern attack, and followed them himself a few minutes later.[1] Mackinnon was left in command at the road.

Wellington, at the time of Lightburne's partial action, had issued a positive order to Leith to march north behind the ridge if he himself was not attacked. At the same time, Wellington had sent off discretionary orders to Hill to move north with most of his force if there were no French troops directly east of him. The C-in-C considered an attack on both Picton and Leith to be unlikely, if not impossible, knowing the position of the French bivouac areas the previous evening.

The battlefield was almost completely free of fog by about 6.45 a.m. Already, the French had failed twice. One rocky outcrop at the summit of the ridge still remained in their hands, but it was held by a few *voltigeurs* only. The survivors of the French second attack were still clinging to an area of the lower ridge. Wellington could see, however, that the French had not yet given up. Two new columns in close support of each other were more than a third of the way up the ridge by 7 a.m.; they were heading towards that small part of the crest still in French control. This force of seven fresh battalions, the northern four slightly in advance of the other three, came on vigorously. They were obviously well handled and did not falter under a crossfire from both artillery and riflemen.

With surprising speed and power, the northern column drove into and broke the five companies of the 1/45th and three Portuguese battalions. The French took the crest of the ridge and were within 200 yards of the lateral communications road. Their able commander, General Foy, was striving to reform his disordered battalions, which believed for a short time that they were completely victorious.[2]

At this moment, Leith's 5th Division struck. In accordance with Wellington's orders, he had moved north along the communications road with his divisional battery, his British brigade, and some Portuguese infantry.[3] When he reached the San Antonio-Palheiros road where Mackinnon commanded, he detached his battery and Portuguese

---

[1] Picton did not arrive at the scene of the defeat of the French first attack until after it was over. He stopped to rally the light companies of the 1/45th and 1/88th and sent them on to take from *voltigeurs* an outcropping of rock on the crest of the ridge south of that against which Wallace sent his three companies.

[2] Foy had discovered the Allies crossing the Duero at Oporto 12th May 1809.

[3] The permanent assignment of a battery to each division became standard at about this time. For details of Portuguese troops see note 1, page 126, and note 1, page 129.

infantry, but continued north along the crest with his British brigade.[1] Leith reached the field of action within seconds of the French passing over the crest.

Leith formed his leading battalion, the 1/9th, into line and advanced diagonally from the southwest supported by the 2/38th. These two battalions took the French by surprise and tore to pieces with their regular platoon volleys the disordered mass of Foy's battalions. Foy was wounded and his brigade hurled back into the valley again. The third French attack carried back with it the *voltigeurs* from the crest and any remaining survivors of their second attack; all suffered considerably in the strenuous Allied pursuit.

By 8.30 a.m., the only Frenchmen west of the original Allied security line were killed, wounded, or prisoners; 23 of the 27 infantry battalions in Reynier's corps had been completely broken, and severe casualties had been inflicted on some of them. Wellington had accomplished this with five British and six Portuguese battalions actually engaged; their losses had been relatively light. Not only Leith, but Hill also, was now in a position to reinforce the front, if the French persisted in their attacks.

Reynier showed no inclination to send more troops up the steep slopes already covered with French casualties. No sooner was the southern fight concluded, than the roar of artillery was heard further north.[2] Wellington galloped towards it, leaving the southern sector in the capable hands of Hill who took over command of what had now become the right wing.[3]

For almost a mile, Wellington passed above a quiet front along which only skirmishing was taking place. But in the area of the main road and to the north of it, Ney's Corps was in motion. This road was paved and in good repair, but narrow. It climbs to the crest of the ridge by means of two sweeping bends along the sides of a steep hill. To the east, there are two deep U-shaped ravines. The Great Ravine, directly north of the road, is just over 400 yards across; the smaller about 600

---

[1] There was, according to Picton, a meeting between himself and Leith; Leith implies that there was no such meeting. Picton's and Leith's accounts of what happened do not agree. *Oman*, III, 376, says, 'Each general speaks as if he had been in command, and I fear that each is using undue reticence as to the other's doings.'

[2] Ney has been criticized for not attacking earlier, but Oman points out that according to Massena's orders he was not to move until Reynier was seen to have gained the ridge. *Oman*, III, 367 and 549.

[3] *Sherer*, 110, quoting Wellington, 'If they attempt this point again, Hill, you will give them a volley, and charge bayonets; but don't let your people follow them too far down the hill.'

yards further north is both narrower and terminates further to the east. The village of Sula is at the western end of an area of relatively level ground between the ravines, but already part of the way up the ridge. The main road passes in its first great bend above and behind Sula and then turns to the west again.

Wellington had placed Craufurd's line battalions on a semi-circular shelf in the hillside just behind the bend in this road west of Sula; the 1/52nd was posted to the north and the 1/43rd to the south. These were ordered to lie down in line, and were invisible from below. Ross's Horse Artillery Battery was a few yards in front of these two strong battalions (1,750 men present) while the 1st *Cacadores* were just to the rear in support.

South of the Great Ravine, in a similar position to the Light Division, were the four line battalions of Pack's Independent Portuguese Brigade. Wellington had three batteries in the area, Cleves's at the head of the ravine, Passos's with Pack, and Lawson's 150 yards further south. All three batteries were in position to rake the main road toward Moura. Between Pack and Craufurd, but initially somewhat to the rear, waited Coleman's Independent Portuguese Brigade.

The skirmishing line in front of Craufurd and Pack was exceedingly strong. The former had sent forward the entire 1/95th and the 3rd *Cacadores*, a total of 1,400 picked men armed with Baker rifles.[1] These had the further advantage of a thin screen of trees running north and south some 600 yards east of Sula. To the south of the Great Ravine, Pack had deployed the 4th *Cacadores* in a thick pine wood.[2] This security line joined Spencer's to the south and Cole's to the north.

Wellington arrived at a point of vantage above Craufurd and Pack just as the powerful French attack commenced.[3] He could see two of Ney's brigades, each of six battalions, advancing between the Great and the Lesser Ravines, with the usual line of *tirailleurs* in front, and artillery struggling forward with them. The twelve *voltigeur* companies were unable to make headway against Craufurd's skirmishers.[4] Each French

---

[1] Whether all *Cacadores* were rifle-armed is subject to question. *Oman*, III, 379, thought so. The museum at Busaco shows several Baker rifles, some with marks indicating issue to these Portuguese units. But were there enough for all the *Cacadores*?

[2] This wood is now greater in extent and the trees larger.

[3] Probably near the site of the larger battle monument today. The area was then far more open.

[4] The French were outnumbered 1,300 to about 1,200, and armed with inferior weapons for this sort of fighting.

line brigade temporarily divided into three individual columns to support their *tirailleurs*.[1]

A line of 1,400 riflemen could not hold back 12 battalions, particularly as they were too far forward for effective support even by Ross's battery. They gave ground stubbornly and in accordance with orders, but rallied at Sula and held the village for a few minutes, before being forced back by weight of numbers. The French columns were now within effective range of the Allied artillery which was firing fast and accurately.[2]

Sula was too small to provide protection for 7,000 men; the French had to advance or retreat. They reformed into a line of *tirailleurs* and two columns and moved forward again. Their artillery could not accompany them and had to be content with opening a harmless fire from the valley towards the crest of the ridge. The distance from Sula uphill to Craufurd's concealed main line was 500 yards, but the French found it tough going. The skirmish line of the Light Division was even thicker than before, for Craufurd had added the 1st *Cacadores*. The riflemen were firing not only on the *voltigeurs*, but the two columns also.

Craufurd, a little black-muzzled man, sitting in an enormous saddle on a fine heavy horse, waited in the artillery position. His two battalions, 20 yards to the rear and on either side of their commander, were ready but invisible to the enemy. Ross's Battery fired one last round of case from each piece and pulled back. When the French saw the guns retire, they let out a shout and surged forward to clear the ridge. Craufurd seemed to be facing them alone. He waited until the two French columns were 25 yards from the edge of the shelf.

'Now!' He roared in his mighty bass voice. His veterans rose as one man, moved forward a few yards, and fired a staggering volley.

'Fifty-second, avenge Moore!' Craufurd bellowed again. The two southernmost companies of the 52nd and the two northernmost of the 43rd fought with their bayonets. The others, eight on each flank, lapped around the columns, firing regular volleys from their two-deep lines.[3]

[1] This probably explains the discrepancies between the various British eyewitness accounts of the French formation.

[2] Some of these six pieces were firing from between rocks as if in field fortifications. These exact positions can be found today.

[3] The Napiers were both in this fight, but confuse small details past understanding: *Napier*, III, 27, and *Napier Autobiography*, 143. The Light Division may or may not have been the best fighting division in Wellington's army, but it has certainly produced more writers of memoirs and history. Many British accounts of Peninsular fighting overemphasize the bayonet; the bullet was the really effective means of inflicting casualties in all but a few actions.

Within a minute, the French columns buckled, broke and disintegrated into a panic-stricken rabble. The men of the Light Division, particularly the riflemen, followed them right down into the valley, killing, wounding, and capturing. Only one French battalion, the rearmost of their southern column, escaped destruction in this holocaust. In climbing the ridge, they had entered the Great Ravine and were south of the 1/43rd.

Major McBean's Battalion of the 19th Portuguese Line of Coleman's Brigade, which had just brought into position south of the Light Division, smashed this French battalion completely just as it reached the military crest near Cleve's guns. McBean's Portuguese two-deep line was just as effective against the French column as a British one would have been. The incline down which the French were pushed was so steep that individual soldiers who lost their footing rolled all the way down, although not always with fatal results.

Ney was also mounting an attack south of the Great Ravine. This appears to have been planned to take place concurrently with that just described, but was later in starting and proceeded more cautiously. Eleven battalions with *tirailleurs* in front emerged one behind the other from the hamlet of Moura. Soon they were under long range artillery fire from two, three, or even four Allied batteries.[1] Their *voltigeurs* ran into stiff resistance from Pack's *Cacadores* in the pine wood; the steep hillside offered continuous shelter and first rate firing positions for the riflemen. In order to clear the wood, the entire leading French brigade had to be deployed and sent into this irregular combat. With an advantage in numbers of 3,200 to 550, the French finally cleared the pine wood, but at a high cost.

Once through the trees, the French reformed and began to climb towards Pack's four Portuguese battalions in line on the crest above. They advanced with confidence, for they saw only a few brown uniforms, indicating Portuguese troops whom they had come to despise three years before. But these well-drilled and disciplined battalions had little in common with the Portuguese of 1807. When the French columns were within range, the Portuguese volleys were hardly less regular, or slower, than those of British units. Pack did not wait as long as had Craufurd to open fire. The French battalion columns

[1] Apparently, Ross fired mainly at the northern French advance, Cleve engaged both. Lawson and Passos concentrated on the southern attack. It is impossible to locate the actual positions of the last three batteries, because of the extensive growth of trees; it would appear, however, that they were scattered over a considerable area, one gun here, two there, etc.

were brought to a halt when still about 100 yards from the Portuguese position. They could not make any further ascent under such fire; although not broken, they retreated on their second brigade which never came to grips with the Allies.

Craufurd to the north had by now dispersed his assailants; Ross's guns were free to concentrate their fire on the French south of the Great Ravine, even though at long range. The French attacks in the northern sector came to an end as abruptly as Reynier's had to the south. Ney's Corps was withdrawn to its starting point before 11 a.m.

Some skirmishing continued along the front of Spencer's 1st Division; during the afternoon, Sula was retaken by *tirailleurs*, but a single company of the 43rd drove them out again. Massena was obviously calling off the assault on Busaco ridge, even though Junot's Corps, one third of Ney's, and four battalions of Reynier's had not been in action at all. Wellington could see through his telescope French infantry beginning to entrench their original bivouac areas. The battle was probably over, unless the Allies were willing to abandon their advantageous position and fight in the valley below. Wellington knew that French casualties had been severe, but not nearly severe enough to tempt him to attack Massena's veteran army.

A tabulation of French losses shows over 4,600 killed, wounded, or prisoners, including more than 300 officers, the highest casualty percentage of officers to men that the French suffered in the entire war. Four French generals were wounded and one killed. The Allied army suffered a loss of only 1,252, half of whom were Portuguese. The battalions which delivered the most stunning counterblows during the morning, the 1/9th and 2/38th of Leith's Division who had cleared Foy from the ridge, and the 1/43rd and 1/52nd of Craufurd's Division who broke Ney's northern attack, lost less than 75 men between them. Casualties in Mackinnon's British Brigade, the 8th Portuguese, and the 21st Portuguese had been more severe. The British and Portuguese riflemen in the north also lost comparatively heavily.

French soldiers never fought more courageously than at Busaco, but their commanders had assigned them impossible tasks. So convinced was Massena of French invincibility that he had rushed headlong into a battle without proper reconnaissance. He would not make that mistake again. The French had forgotten Talavera 14 months before, and were surprised by the change in the Portuguese army which could be said to have come of age on that 27th September. The amalgamation of British and Portuguese units produced divisions whose quality was essentially equal to an all-British force of the same size.

Tactically, Busaco was far more than another example of the superiority of Wellington's line over the French column. The Allied infantry was protected and even concealed by terrain; French artillery and cavalry accomplished nothing. The *tirailleurs* who were supposed to disorder the Allied main line could not even defend their own columns.

Ney's attacks were greatly handicapped by the inability of his *tirailleurs* to push back Craufurd's and Pack's riflemen. Only in Reynier's first thrust early in the morning were the *voltigeurs* able to break through the Allied skirmishers.

Wellington had carried his earlier decision to assign a company of British riflemen to each brigade a step further; each independent Portuguese brigade had a full battalion of *Cacadores*, one fifth of its total strength, armed with rifles. The assignment of a *Cacadores* battalion to every Portuguese brigade was soon to follow. The Light Division already had a high proportion of rifle-armed skirmishers.

Wellington showed as clearly at Busaco as in any future battle his ideas on the proper use of artillery. In direct contradiction to the Napoleonic theory, and in opposition to his own artillery officers, he avoided any massive concentration of fire.[1] He preferred to employ his guns in relatively small numbers, a battery or two at most, at effective range right in line with his infantry. The success of this system over the corps concentrations used by the French was in part responsible for the 'under-gunned' condition of the Allied army in the future.[2]

Strategically, Busaco was a triumph of forethought and planning. Wellington had carefully evaluated every possibility in connexion with Massena's advance into Portugal. The Allied regular units had held every practical route into the country. When the French committed themselves to one only, Wellington achieved a concentration of all his useful field army in a position chosen tentatively months before.

Even though the ridge was naturally strong, it could have been of far less value if Wellington had not built the lateral communications road, the importance of which cannot be overestimated. The fundamentals of

[1] The artillery was not then an integral part of the army, but was under the control of the master general of ordnance. Artillery officers were critical of Wellington and were not so directly under his command as those of the infantry and cavalry.

[2] The ratio of artillery to infantry in the Allied army seldom greatly exceeded one gun to 1,000 men, but was as high as eight to 1,000 in French armies in Central Europe and sometimes reached four to 1,000 in Spain. *Oman*, I, 121–2.

Wellington's system of defence were flexibility and mobility. Allied infantry did not fight behind static field fortifications. His lines of fresh unhampered musketeers were opposed to tired cramped columns regardless of where the French attacked. Wellington could retain his initial superiority by bringing in reinforcements easily and quickly. He was in a position to launch repeated counterattacks against any French penetration.

If Picton and Leith had required additional help, Wellington could have brought into action the Guards and Cameron's and Pakenham's Brigades from the north, and Hill from the south. If Craufurd and Pack had shown signs of weakness, there were immediately available the K.G.L. Brigade and those of Coleman, Pakenham, and Campbell. If these had not been enough, Cole could have been brought down from the north and parts of four divisions up from the south. Perhaps the greatest single virtue of Wellington's defensive positions was that they always allowed a rapid and, if necessary, continuous flow of reinforcements from all parts of his line not engaged to a threatened sector.

THE CONTENDING FORCES AND LOSSES AT BUSACO

THE ALLIED ARMY UNDER WELLINGTON		TOTAL = 51,345
INFANTRY 24,796 British 24,649 Portuguese		= 48,845
1st Division, Brent Spencer		= 7,053
Edward Stopford's Brigade	1,684	
1/Coldstreamers, 1/Scots, 1 Co. 5/60th		
Robert Blantyre's Brigade	1,516	
2/24th, 42nd, 1/61st, 1 Co. 5/60th		
Sigismund von Lowe's Brigade	2,061	
1st, 2nd, 5th and 7th Line Batts., K.G.L., Det. Light Batt. K.G.L.		
Edward Pakenham's Brigade	1,792	
1/7th, 1/79th		

2nd Division, Rowland Hill		= 10,777
William Stewart's Brigade	2,247	
1/3rd, 2/31st, 2/48th, 2/66th, 1 Co. 5/60th		
William Inglis's Brigade	1,818	
29th, 1/48th, 1/57th, 1 Co. 5/60th		
Catlin Craufurd's Brigade	1,672	
2/28th, 2/34th, 2/39th, 1 Co. 5/60th		
Portuguese Division, John Hamilton (Attached to 2nd Division)		
Archibald Campbell's Brigade	2,350	
4th Line (2 Batts.), 10th Line (2 Batts.)		
Fonseca's Brigade	2,690	
2nd Line (2 Batts.), 14th Line (2 Batts.)		
3rd Division, Thomas Picton		= 4,143
Henry Mackinnon's Brigade	1,808	
1/45th, 1/74th, 1/88th		
Stafford Lightburne's Brigade	1,160	
2/5th, 2/83rd, 3 Cos. 5/60th		
Champlemond's Portuguese Brigade	1,175	
9th Line (2 Batts.), 21st Line (1 Batt.)		
4th Division, Lowry Cole		= 7,400
Alexander Campbell's Brigade	2,109	
2/7th, 1/11th, 2/53rd, 1 Co. 5/60th		
James Kemmis's Brigade	2,448	
3/27th, 1/40th, 97th, 1 Co. 5/60th		
Collins's Portuguese Brigade	2,843	
11th Line (2 Batts.), 23rd Line (2 Batts.)		
5th Division, James Leith		= 7,322
Barnes's Brigade	1,896	
3/1st, 1/9th, 2/38th		
Spry's Portuguese Brigade	2,619	
3rd Line (2 Batts.), 15th Line (2 Batts.), Tomar Militia Batt.		
Baron Eben's Brigade	2,807	
Lusitanian Legion (3 Batts.), 8th Line (2 Batts.)		

Light Division, Robert Craufurd   = 3,787
    Sidney Beckwith's Brigade   1,896
        1/43rd, 4 Cos. 1/95th, 3rd Cacadores
    Robert Barclay's Brigade   1,891
        1/52nd, 4 Cos. 1/95th, 1st Cacadores
Three Independent Portuguese Brigades   = 8,363
    Denis Pack's Brigade   2,769
        1st Line (2 Batts.), 16th Line (2
        Batts.), 4th Cacadores
    Archibald Campbell's Brigade   3,249
        6th Line (2 Batts.), 18th Line (2
        Batts.), 6th Cacadores
    Coleman's Brigade   2,345
        7th Line (2 Batts.), 19th Line (2
        Batts.), 2nd Cacadores
Cavalry (2 squadrons 4th Dragoons), Artillery (60   2,500
    guns), Staff, etc.

THE FRENCH ARMY UNDER MASSENA   TOTAL = 65,974

CORPS	INFANTRY				CAVALRY	ARTILLERY[1]	TOTAL
	Divisions	Brigades	Battalions	Personnel			
2nd (Reynier)	2	4	27	14,676	1,397	1,645	17,718
6th (Ney)	3	6	34	21,113	1,680	1,513	24,306
8th (Junot)	2	5	23	14,020	1,863	1,056	16,939
General Reserves	—	—	—	924[2]	3,479	2,608	7,011

[1] This total included also Staff, Engineers, and other military personnel; there were about 114 field pieces with the French army.

[2] A 'battalion' of naval ratings for use as marines or for small boats on the Tagus.

	KILLED	WOUNDED	PRISONERS AND MISSING	TOTAL
Reynier's Corps	226	1,427	364	2,017
Ney's Corps	309	2,147	None reported[1]	2,456
			FRENCH	4,473[2]
British	104	409	31	544
Portuguese	96	510	20	626
			ALLIES	1,170[3]

TOPOGRAPHICAL OBSERVATIONS

Busaco is perhaps the easiest of all Peninsular battlefields to visit, although reforestation has changed the terrain militarily. The Convent is still encircled by the old wall, loop-holed on its eastern side. It has been converted into a luxury hotel and is surrounded by extensive gardens. The villages of San Antonio and Sula show scars from Allied artillery fire. The roads in the valley are only passable by ox-carts, but part of Wellington's lateral communications road has been modernized. A small museum is maintained here by the Portuguese army.

---

[1] General Simon was definitely captured; as Oman points out, he could hardly have been the only prisoner taken by Craufurd, Pack and McBean.

[2] These figures are from *Oman*, III, 552–3, who points out several discrepancies. The French clearly understated their loss which was at least 4,600.

[3] Also from *Oman*; Fortescue says 1,251; 631 British and 620 Portuguese.

IX

THE LINES OF TORRES VEDRAS

WELLINGTON was both delighted and disappointed by the result of the battle on 27th September. The Allied army had functioned superbly; the French thrusts could hardly have been more completely defeated, nor at less cost. If Massena had continued to press his attack, as Napoleon was to do at Waterloo, the invasion of Portugal would have terminated at Busaco. But Massena gave up the frontal assault and ordered his cavalry to discover a route towards the coastal road from Oporto to Coimbra to avoid crossing the ridge. There was such a track, which ran from Mortagua to Avelleira, passing through defiles which Wellington had ordered the ubiquitous Trant and his militia to occupy (Plate 15). A misunderstanding between Trant and his immediate superior, the Portuguese General Bacellar, caused Trant to reach them too late.[1] Wellington learned by mid-afternoon of the 28th that Massena had found this way around the Busaco ridge.[2]

Wellington had to retreat. The next really strong position for the Allied army lay behind the Lines of Torres Vedras. In accordance with a prearranged plan, its divisions were ordered to withdraw south and west over several roads.

The Allied army lit numerous campfires on the Busaco ridge on the evening of the 28th, but left them burning and retired. Hill's divisions crossed the Mondego at Penacova; the others were all south of the river by 1st October. Allied cavalry used a ford well to the west after suffering some casualties in a skirmish with advancing French horsemen. Coimbra, the third city of Portugal, was given up without a fight.

[1] Too much has been made of this, even by Wellington himself. There is no defile along the old Mortagua-Avelleira road so naturally strong that militia could have held back the French army for long.

[2] For an account of the French discovery of this road, see *Marbot*, 421 and 427.

Contact was now lost between the contending armies for four days. The Allies retreated south undisturbed; the French sacked Coimbra, where they captured large quantities of food which had not been removed or destroyed in spite of Wellington's specific orders. Massena proceeded south on the 4th, deployed in battle array.[1] But the Allied army was already approaching its gigantic system of fortifications north of Lisbon. The French commander did not know of the Lines, until two days later, when a handful of Allied prisoners were taken in a petty cavalry action.

Massena, believing as he did that the decisive battle of the campaign would be fought soon, left his travelling wounded under insufficient guard in Coimbra.[2] Trant, with about 4,000 militia, swooped down on the city from the north on the 7th. He took and held the bridge by which the French had left the town and then forced the surrender of two fortified hospitals. He captured 4,500 Frenchmen, including the sick and wounded, and had them all on the road to Oporto before nightfall. By the time Massena was informed of the capture, Trant was beyond pursuit. This was a brilliant stroke, perfectly timed.

The French continued to advance south; some cavalry skirmishing took place. On the 8th, at Alcoentre, a British horse artillery battery was unnecessarily exposed and almost taken.[3] Somers-Cocks and his squadron of the 16th L.D. charged successfully three times their number of French cavalry and saved the guns.

That evening, the autumn rains began. This is an awesome event in Portugal each year; the downpour continues for days, isolating all wheeled transport in mountainous areas, not having access to paved roads. Had Almeida held out a fortnight longer, Massena's entire army would have been immobilized for weeks around the headwaters of the Mondego. In the open, sandy plains south of Coimbra, however, the drenching rain was a discomfort, but did not stop military movement altogether. The Allied army had been entering the Lines since the 8th; the Light Division and some cavalry patrols only remained in the open on the 10th. The French were gradually closing in.

This enormous expanse of fortifications was even further advanced

---

[1] *Fortescue*, VII, 538, considered that Massena 'expected to end the campaign within a week'. He took considerably longer to gain the true measure of his opponent than vice versa.

[2] About 400 desperately wounded men had been left near Moura and were moved back to the Convent by the Allied rearguard on the 29th; *Tomkinson*, 44.

[3] Ibid., 50–1, states that the howitzer of the battery and two ammunition wagons had been abandoned, but were recovered.

VI. CAMPAIGN AREA NORTH OF TORRES VEDRAS

Map labels:

ATLANTIC OCEAN

BUSACO
French flank attack
French retreat from Portugal
Allied retreat from BUSACO
Mondego River
COIMBRA
Miranda
Zezere River
River TAGUS
ABRANTES
Portuguese Militia and Ordenanza
French offer to cross Mondego 10-12 March
Mealhada
Advance of French retreat
Punhete
HILL's defence of the Tagus
Allied 6th Div., Flank march
Pombal
WILSON
French & Portuguese Militia
French subsistance area, used Nov. to March
Tomar
Leiria
PENICHE
Allied Cavalry & Light Infantry Watch.
Santarem
RIO MAIOR
MASSENA's frontward attack on the Lines 11-14 October '40
LISBON
The Lines of the Torres Vedras

143

than Wellington had hoped. After a careful inspection, he decided to hold the northernmost line from the mouth of the Zizandre on the Atlantic to Alhandra on the Tagus, rather than the main line from north of Mafra to Quintella.[1] This outer line was roughly twenty-six miles long; there were artificial inundations at each end which reduced considerably the actual mileage to be defended. The town of Torres Vedras, eight miles inland, had been turned into an extremely powerful bastion; the country to the southeast of it was so naturally strong that only a few mountaintop forts were required. The eastern sector, from near Pero Negro to the Tagus, had been artificially strengthened, at enormous cost; hundreds of guns were already in protected positions. Trenches, palisades, abatis, scarped hills, and masonry citadels were to be found in profusion (Plates 16 and 17)[2]. The navy protected both flanks of the Lines.[3]

Wellington's system of defence was unusual in that not a man of his field army—his British and Portuguese regulars—was intended to fight behind the protection of these fortifications. They had been built to be manned by secondary troops, to enable them to delay the French and allow Wellington to concentrate against any thrust; the lateral communications roads had all been improved. For the field army there were at least a dozen defensive positions here similar to Busaco.

The actual fortifications were held by 25,000 Portuguese militia, Romana's 8,000 Spaniards, and 2,500 British marines and artillerymen.[4] There was a system of semaphores which could transmit messages from

---

[1] The outer or northern line of works had originally been intended for outposts only.

[2] The best plan of the Lines in their entirety is to be found in *Wyld's Atlas*, Plate entitled 'The Lines in Front of Lisbon'.

[3] There were many shallow draft vessels in the Tagus mounting one or two heavy guns, and able to operate as far upstream as Abrantes. A round shot from one of these cut in two the French General Saint-Croix on 12th October.

[4] *Oman*, III, 434,

'The whole of this vast system of redoubts was to be held by the troops of the second line, and by them only. There were altogether some 20,000 men of the second line in the fortifications, composed of (1) the 8,000 (afterwards raised to 11,000) militia infantry. (2) Of about 800 Portuguese regular artillery aided by over 2,000 gunners picked from the militia and *Ordenanca*, trained by the regulars and incorporated with them. (3) Of some 250 British artillery-men from the batteries which had been lying in reserve at Lisbon. (4) Of picked companies of the Lisbon *Ordenanca* (*atiradores*) drilled into a state of discipline not much worse than that of the militia. (5) Of the landing force of 2,000 British marines, partly from the fleet, partly brought specially from England to garrison the proposed lines of embarkation at St. Julian's. (6) Of the depots, convalescents and recruits of the eight Line regiments of infantry raised from Lisbon and Southern Estremadura—about 4,000 strong.'

the Atlantic to the Tagus in seven minutes; a written order could be sent from Wellington's headquarters at Pero Negro to any unit in his field army in very much less than an hour.

Wellington had considered the relative probability of a French attack at various points; he concluded that the sector from Torres Vedras to the Atlantic was the least likely and could be left mainly in the hands of his static force. He disposed his regulars on both sides of Pero Negro.

On the eastern flank, near the Tagus, Hill had his Anglo-Portuguese 'corps'. Next came Craufurd and the Light Division who were responsible for an extensive open area. The bulk of the army lay on either side of headquarters, while Picton and the 3rd Division were in position towards Torres Vedras.

The Lines enclosed an area of over 500 square miles. Even though a large portion of the Portuguese population south of the Mondego had come into this area, there was still living space for all and plenty of food. Supplies could be obtained locally, brought across the Tagus, or imported. This healthy civilian life was, of course, a great military advantage.

Between the 12th and 14th October Wellington observed from various points of vantage the appearance of the French army, and noticed its concentration around Sobral as if ready for an attack on the Lines. He ordered Picton east, since no appreciable French force was reported in the Torres Vedras area. The Allied position south of Sobral was even stronger than Busaco; the entire army was wildly confident.[1]

---

[1] *D'Urban*, 157-8, says,

'At 4 o'clock this morning (15 October) Sir Brent Spencer's advance was withdrawn in silence, and the most perfect good order from the foot of the hill of Sobral, and the Villages of Sta. Quintina and its adjuncts, and the Divisions of the Centre and Right occupied a Position determined upon by the Commander-in-Chief yesterday. The Right is formed by Sir Brent Spencer's Division upon the Hill of Zibreira stretching towards the Great Redoubt No. 14. This Division occupies about 1,000 yds. The 3rd Division on the left of the 1st 800 yds. The 4th on the left of the 3rd 1,500 yds., and the 6th on the left of the 4th, closes the left of the Position in the Mountains of Ribaldeira. The two Portuguese Brigades of Campbell and Colman form a Reserve in the Rear of the left, and the 5th Division in like manner in Rear of the Right. Each individual Division has besides more than sufficient troops to occupy the space allotted to it, and the overplus will form a Reserve to each respectively. If this Force thus posted beats the attacking Enemy, of which there is little doubt, a Telegraphic communication will bring down Hill and Craufurd from Alhandra and Arruda and the affair will be complete. There is much appearance that the Enemy will attack this Position with his whole force. Alhandra is too strong for him to attempt, and Torres Vedras under his present circumstances and the state of the roads, too long a detour for him to make. He cannot well retire, and his distress for provision will it is to be hoped, compel him to bring the thing to a speedy decision.'

Wellington had 10,000 more infantry than he had at Busaco, while Massena had about that number fewer.[1] There was a fierce skirmish on the evening of the 14th, which convinced the French marshal that a Busaco-type assault must be avoided.

Instead of attacking, the French army dug itself in. Even Wellington was surprised. What was Massena's intention? He was known to have only small supplies of food, and was already cut off from Almeida and Ciudad Rodrigo. A waiting game would be dangerous for the French, but for the Allies to attack them behind field fortifications was equally so. Even a drawn battle might enable Massena to escape from his predicament. A Pyrrhic victory might be disastrous for the Allies.[2]

For a month the French army remained in the vicinity of Sobral. Then Massena drew back over thirty miles to a carefully chosen position between Santarem and Rio Maior. This line was fifteen miles long and protected by water, marsh, and earthworks. He was now able to subsist on food from an undevastated district. The French were holding other boundary areas, besides the Santarem-Rio Maior front. On the east they held the line of the Tagus and the Zezere to north of Tomar. French cavalry patrolled a flexible western boundary north of Rio Maior.

Once Massena had pulled back to the Santarem-Rio Maior-Tomar position, Wellington ordered Hill and his 'corps' across the Tagus, together with cavalry and artillery, to hold its eastern bank south of Abrantes. Artillery positions and earthworks were built where a French crossing in force appeared likely; it was known that Massena had ordered the construction of boats and rafts for such an enterprise. If the French crossed the Tagus here, they could use their powerful and numerous cavalry to contact other French forces to the southeast, and

[1] Nine newly arrived British infantry battalions comprising 6,500 men and Portuguese regulars not at Busaco. The 5th Division was brought up to full strength and a new 6th Division formed; (see the Appendices to Chapters X and XI for their exact constitutions).
[2] Wellington wrote to Lord Liverpool on 3rd November, Dispatches, VI, 583, that his army was the only anti-French

'military body in the Peninsula which is capable of taking, much less of keeping, the field . . . if I should succeed in forcing Massena's positions, it would become a question whether I should be able to maintain my own, in case the enemy should march another army into this country. But, when I observe how small the superiority of numbers is in my favour, and know that the position will be in favour of the enemy, I cannot but be of opinion that I act in conformity with the instructions and intentions of His Majesty's government, in waiting for the result of what is going on, and in incurring no extraordinary risk.'

also draw on the fertile plains of the Alemtejo for supplies.[1] The Portuguese-occupied fortress city of Abrantes at the bend of the Tagus was more important than ever, and practically unassailable, for Massena had brought no siege artillery with him.

Wellington closed in on the French north of Rio Maior, but with mobile units of cavalry and irregular infantry operating mainly from Peniche. Trant and Wilson with their militia passed south of the Mondego; the line of the Zezere was loosely but effectively held by the *Ordenanza*. The French were completely cut off; to send a messenger to the Emperor, Massena found it necessary to employ a strong force of cavalry and infantry to break through into Spain. Even then the French had to mask its departure and temporarily seal off Abrantes![2]

Massena continued to sustain himself after a fashion in his constricted territory. He maintained an army of 50,000 in an area where a single British division, according to Wellington, would have starved.[3] There were two basic reasons for this.

Wellington's 'scorched earth' policy had not been carried out fully; he had given orders that all food and livestock, bridges, ovens and mills, which could possibly be of use to the French, should be destroyed or removed behind the Lines. But the frugal peasants would not follow these instructions entirely. Instead of destroying the mills totally, they hid parts of the machinery. Grain and other foods were stored in caves, buried, or walled up inside buildings. Wine was hidden in underground vaults; livestock was driven into the hills.

---

[1] Wellington had knowledge of the general French plan, conceived by Napoleon, in which Soult with a powerful army was to take Badajoz and advance on Lisbon from the east, but no move had yet been made. Both Spanish-held Badajoz and Portuguese-held Elvas barred such an approach.

[2] General Foy left Massena on 1st November and met Napoleon in Paris on the 22nd; *Oman*, III, 455–8, describes this incident fully.

[3] Wellington to Lord Liverpool, 21st December 1810, *Dispatches*, VII, 59–60,

'It is certainly astonishing that the enemy have been able to remain in this country so long; and it is an extraordinary instance of what a French army can do. It is positively a fact that they brought no provisions with them, and they have not received even a letter since they entered Portugal. With all our money, and having in our favour the good inclinations of the country, I assure you that I could not maintain one division in the district in which they have maintained not less than 60,000 men and 20,000 animals for more than two months. This time last year I was obliged to move the British cavalry only from the district which they now occupy with their whole army, because it could not be subsisted. But they take everything, and leave the unfortunate inhabitants to starve.'

The Allied army tried to remedy this situation as much as possible during the winter. A commissary writes:

'My duty was to clear the ground between us and the enemy of all victuals as quickly and as thoroughly as possible. Accordingly, I was given a detachment of hussars from time to time, with which I carried out raids. My people followed us with mules and empty sacks. When we reached a village we sent patrols to the left and right of it; then we would go forward; post sentries, and proceed to plunder the houses and barns which had long lain deserted by the inhabitants. As a rule, the owners had concealed their property badly; everywhere one could see from large damp patches on the walls that something had recently been walled up just there; or from hollow sounding places in the gardens that things had been buried. In all these matters my shoemaker, Joaquim, displayed the utmost virtuosity. We often found large supplies of corn, wheat, oil, flour, ham, pork, sausages and vegetables; . . .' [1]

The French army was adept at living off the country. Massena's command had seventeen years of experience in marauding as a standard military procedure. Officers and men alike seem to have acquired a sixth sense when it came to the discovering of food, wine, and vital parts of machinery. Mills were back in operation; ovens were repaired and baking bread within a week. What ingenuity and resourcefulness could not accomplish, torture and murder of the peasantry did. The French would lie in ambush to catch some poor fellow who, contrary to orders, had stayed near his village. Once taken, he was given the choice of revealing hidden stocks of food or being shot. Various forms of torture were substituted for a quick death, as the French became collectively more hungry.

This continued existence of the French in the area was remarkable, but was purchased at a terrible cost. They had no proper protection from the weather and were weakened by semi-starvation. Thousands were sick; hundreds died each week. The Portuguese peasants were surprisingly capable in their revenge. French soldiers were murdered within a mile of their divisional headquarters. Small parties of marauders were overwhelmed and died horribly.

[1] *Schaumann*, 269.

Twice during the winter, French reinforcements entered Portugal.[1] Toward the middle of November, a column of over 3,000 was marching southeast along the Zezere. On the 25th, it was less than twenty miles from Massena's position when its commander, General Gardanne, was imposed on flagrantly by the garrison at Abrantes. Three volunteer militiamen were sent out; they joined Gardanne separately, all pretending to be deserters. When questioned, each gave the same false information, that Massena was retreating by way of the coast road. Gardanne's presence was known to Wellington, who had ordered Hill with 10,000 men to fall on him immediately. The French turned about, abandoned their baggage and supplies, and hastened back to Ciudad Rodrigo.

The second effort to reinforce Massena was more successful. Napoleon had placed D'Erlon's 9th Corps under Massena's command months before, but its advance from the French border had been delayed through lack of transport, and the fact that D'Erlon wanted to shake down his 26 separate battalions into something like fighting trim before he led them into action.[2] After crossing the Portuguese border, D'Erlon endeavoured to keep communications open between him and Ciudad Rodrigo; he dividing his corps into two parts. One division remained at Celorico, while the other made contact with Massena's cavalry on the Zezere on 26th December. Massena immediately ordered the forward division to Leiria where it reinforced his western flank, but all contact with Celorico and Spain was lost. D'Erlon brought ammunition and 11,000 men, including Gardanne's force, but no food. Even with these reinforcements, Massena's army was weaker on 1st January 1811 than it had been when it reached the Lines two and a half months earlier.

Conditions within the French rectangle grew progressively worse as the winter wore on. Weekly losses of over 500 men from sickness, starvation, and Portuguese retaliation were normal; morale and discipline were deteriorating. Wellington was aware of this, but was unwilling to attack until reinforcements from Britain, expected early in March, reached him. He then planned to launch his entire field army into a great pincer movement, attacking around Rio Maior and across the Zezere west of Abrantes.[3]

---

[1] This is exclusive of the 2,000 men brought back by Foy who arrived in Massena's camp on 5th February 1811 after a hard fight; *Marbot*, 447.

[2] This French general is better known by his title, Count D'Erlon, than by his name, Jean Baptiste Drouet. His corps was composed of fourth battalions, normally a depot cadre, of regiments serving with other corps.

[3] *D'Urban*, 185, gives details of this projected offensive. *Oman*, IV, 83, described this in a somewhat different form before D'Urban was published.

Massena probably knew about the imminent arrival of British reinforcements, and decided not to remain where he was any longer.[1] Wellington received intelligence that the French were in motion on 4th March; during the late afternoon he personally reconnoitered Santarem, but could see little change. The following day, the entire French army retreated thirty miles and concentrated between Leiria and Tomar. Wellington followed at once with all the force he could muster.

Was this just another transference of troops from an exhausted area to a fresh one, similar to the retrograde movement from Sobral to Santarem? Nothing that the French marshal had done so far indicated that he would calmly accept defeat and retire into Spain. He had destroyed his boats, so he obviously was not going to attempt the crossing of the Tagus, but the other side of the Mondego offered an area undamaged by the French for five months. If Massena could gain this, he might survive indefinitely.

Wellington decided that his major objective for the next few days was to prevent the French from crossing this river. Bridges were to be destroyed; Portuguese militia units were ordered to hold fords and ferry sites. But the main deterrent to such a crossing was the close proximity of the Allied field army to the French rear. If Wellington was near enough to attack in force, Massena would not risk a crossing. If the French were kept south of the river and did not win a major battle, they would have no alternative but to leave Portugal. The country south of the Mondego towards the Spanish border was too poor to support them for even thirty days.

Wellington could not concentrate exclusively on Massena. While the French Army of Portugal had been starving and freezing in open bivouacs, Soult's Army of the South had conquered Andalusia and was now approaching the successful termination of its siege of Badajoz. The fortress of Olivenza had already fallen; a Spanish army had been defeated at Gebora. Marshal Bessiers, in Old Castile with 70,000 men, was under orders from Napoleon to co-operate with Massena.

Wellington would have to detach a force to confront Soult on the

---

[1] *Napier*, III, 111, says that Massena 'knew from the *hidalgos* that the long expected reinforcements from England had landed at Lisbon on the 2nd of March, he commenced his retreat, and on the 6th all his positions were void.'

Guadiana.[1] In the manoeuvring and fighting of March 1811, Wellington was handicapped by having his most able divisional commanders absent. Hill, Craufurd, Leith, and Cotton were on leave in Britain; Beresford had taken Hill's place across the Tagus. This force, Hill's old 'corps', was sent south to the vicinity of Elvas.[2]

The Light Division, Pack's Portuguese, and some cavalry were in contact with Massena after 9th March, but the rest of the army had to march fast to keep up. On the morning of the 11th, Picton's 3rd Division joined; later that day, the 4th, 5th, and 6th Divisions came up, with the 1st Division close behind. After a hectic period of marching and skirmishing, Wellington was in force close behind Massena's retreating army. There was serious fighting at Pombal and at Redinha on the following day. Each time Wellington outflanked the French rearguard under Ney and drove it from strong positions.

Meanwhile, Trant with several guns was engaging French horse artillery across the Mondego at Coimbra. French engineers supported by a strong force of infantry were constructing a trestle bridge west of the town. Wellington had already sent the 6th Division directly north to interrupt this bridging operation.[3] Massena's army was concentrated south of the Mondego. The Allied force north of the river could not hold out for long against an attack in strength, but Wellington was not far away. Massena had now to choose between risking the crossing and leaving Portugal. If he passed over safely all would be well, for presumably Soult would soon enter the Alemtejo. If Wellington attacked while Massena was astride the Mondego, the French could be annihilated.

Massena decided not to take the risk and turned east toward Miranda do Corvo on the south bank of the Mondego. The main French army managed with great skill to disengage itself by traversing a desolate, mountainous region. Wellington used mainly the Light and 3rd Divisions to fight several bloody skirmishes with their rearguard; many prisoners were taken. To quicken his retreat, Massena ordered all

---

[1] At no time during Massena's retreat was Wellington's force numerically equal to the French until the newly formed 7th Division caught up with the Allied army on the border.

[2] William Stewart, normally in command of the 2nd Division, was considered 'too venturesome' for a larger independent command, so Beresford was chosen to relieve Hill when the health of the latter broke down.

[3] Several contemporaneous French accounts state that this force was landed from the sea 'behind the French lines'. This was not so; the Allies at all times controlled the coastal roads both north and south of Peniche and used them.

wheeled vehicles except gun carriages and caissons to be destroyed. All animals no longer serviceable were hamstrung.[1]

The Allied army halted on the 16th because their commissariat had broken down. The country, poor to start with, was stripped by the French, and Allied soldiers still had to be fed. Wellington was now convinced that Massena was leaving Portugal, and ordered Cole's 4th Division to join Beresford. Massena now had over 44,000 men with him, while Wellington had 38,000 or less.

Food reached the Allied army during the 16th; the pursuit was continued at dawn next day. Little fighting occurred on the 17th and 18th, but 600 prisoners were taken the following day. The main French army was now far ahead, although the Light Division and some cavalry were pursuing the rearguard and continued to pick up stragglers.

During the evening of the 22nd or the following morning, Wellington received intelligence that Massena at Celorico had ordered his army to proceed southeast to Guarda rather than east to Almeida. A few hours later, this was confirmed. The French were moving in the general direction of Castelo Branco and the Tagus, a region of few roads and no supplies. Unless a fresh force well provided with food and transport had entered the area, Massena was courting disaster. Wellington checked with his many sources of information and learnt that no French army was nearer than Badajoz or Salamanca.

A partial reason for this change in direction was forthcoming on the 24th. A rumour from French headquarters suggested that Ney had disapproved so violently of Massena's decision to move south rather than east that he had been placed under arrest and sent to the rear.[2] The situation remained confused until the Allies reached Guarda on the 29th. Massena had abandoned his scheme of crossing the mountains to the middle Tagus and was again retreating due east. The French occupied a position behind the Coa; Reynier's corps of three divisions had reached Sabugal, where the river, after running from east to west, turns abruptly north across the Almeida plain towards the Duero.

---

[1] *Grattan*, 58,

'The most disgusting sight was the asses floundering in the mud, some with throats half cut, the rest barbarously houghed. What the object of this was I never could guess. The poor brutes could have been of no use to us, for they could not have travelled another league. Their meagre appearance, with backbones and hips protruding through their skin, and their mangled limbs, produced a feeling of disgust and commiseration.'

[2] This was correct; Massena, to save face, wished to remain in Portugal if possible, or at least not retreat the way he had advanced.

At dawn on 3rd April Wellington ordered an attack to be made. The Light Division with two attached cavalry brigades would sweep to the south and east, ford the upper Coa, and take Reynier's Corps in the flank and rear. The 3rd and 5th Divisions, supported by the 1st and the new 7th, were to launch an attack from the west across the river. The frontal attack was not to be commenced until the French were on the point of retiring. It was a promising scheme; if successful, Reynier's corps would be badly mauled, if not annihilated.

A thick fog blanketed the entire valley of the Coa; rain was falling intermittently. From a point of vantage to the west of Sabugal, Wellington could overlook the area fairly well, for he was above the fog, but his division, brigade, and battalion commanders were lost in it. Sir William Erskine, who commanded both the Light Division and the cavalry, could do nothing right.[1] He led part of his force much too far east, while leaving the rest stationary. Almost all units lost their way. Both brigades of the Light Division eventually crossed the Coa, but too late and in the wrong places. The cavalry was delayed for hours and allowed the French to slip away. The Light Division did some of the finest fighting of its long and honourable history in this confused action.[2]

Beckwith's Brigade was particularly heavily engaged, contending successively against all three French divisions. Four companies of the 1/95th followed by the 1/43rd and some *Cacadores* took a steep hill occupied by twice their strength and then beat off three counterattacks. The skirmish line of British and Portuguese Rifles was particularly effective. Captain Tomkins of the 1/43rd distinguished himself, when, on his own initiative, he led his reinforced company 400 yards toward a French force advancing against the Allied flank. He broke up not only their line of *tirailleurs* but a battalion in column as well.

In this fierce combat, the French lost 760 men and a howitzer. The Allied losses were 179; the 1/43rd suffered 80 of these while closely engaged with more than ten French battalions. Seldom was the superiority of British infantry weapons more clearly demonstrated.

Under torrents of rain, the French brigade and division commanders extricated Reynier's corps and retreated in a compact mass in an easterly direction. The rest of Massena's army to the north along the line of the

---

[1] Never a good soldier, Erskine committed suicide while of unsound mind on 14th May 1813.

[2] In Wellington's words, 'one of the most glorious actions British troops were ever engaged in'; *Oman*, III, 196.

Coa was now exposed and had to be drawn back. Almeida was the only town in Portugal still held by the French. Wellington isolated this fortress on 7th April by ordering Trant to advance his Portuguese militia. A French division moved to attack Trant, believing him to be unsupported. Suddenly, six squadrons of British cavalry and a battery of horse artillery appeared on their flank. The French turned tail and precipitately crossed the Agueda.[1]

Massena reached his base at Salamanca on 11th April 1811, almost eleven months after he had assumed command of the Army of Portugal. He had accomplished nothing of military importance and had lost between 25,000 and 45,000 men and vast quantities of guns, baggage, and transport.[2] The remnants of his once proud army resembled that which Soult brought back from Oporto two years before. Massena retained some of his artillery, but lost many more men, and also a higher percentage of his force than had Soult. Those who survived were in worse physical condition.

Massena must be given credit for bringing his army back at all. He dominated his command and kept it efficient; he manoeuvred well. Tactically and strategically, it is hard to fault the French in this campaign after Busaco. It was extricated from half a dozen critical situations. Massena's only obvious error was in venturing southeast from Celorico to Castelo Branco instead of retiring directly on Almeida during the retreat.

After Busaco, Wellington's generalship was sound rather than brilliant. He was in the more advantageous position even though numerically inferior during most of the campaign. He realized fully the responsibility which he carried; any error of judgement at any time would would have changed the whole complexion of the contest. He handled the Allied army both in retreat and in pursuit without a mishap in the face of veteran troops commanded by Napoleon's most able marshal. His manoeuvring, which prevented Massena from crossing the Mondego into fresh territory, was masterly.

Wellington's tactical dispositions were particularly good during the final phases of the French retreat. The Allied army was continually flanking the enemy from strong positions without committing itself to a major contest. The efficiency of the British and Anglo-Portuguese armies in battle under Wellington was unquestioned. During March

[1] This action at Val de Mula cost the French more than 300 casualties.

[2] The upper figure is Wellington's contemporaneous estimate. Napier and Oman thought 30,000, Fortescue says 25,000.

and April 1811, he demonstrated that he could manoeuvre for lesser objectives as well.

Throughout the campaign, Wellington displayed an appreciation of the overall situation rarely equalled by any one in field command. His army alone stood between Napoleon and the complete domination of Continental Europe. It was the only field force in the Peninsula with any offensive capacity, and as such had to be conserved. Solicitous without being overcautious, Wellington would not risk his army unless he was certain of victory. Once he committed his army to battle, as at Busaco, he fought it with resolution.

TOPOGRAPHICAL OBSERVATIONS

The deeply-rutted, narrow road by which Massena turned the Allied left flank can be followed on foot from the hamlet of Pala over the mountains to where it joins the road system north of Mealhada. One would presume from the depth to which this road has sunk in some places that it had been in use for centuries, but it has not been improved or repaired recently. There is no place on it where a few hundred of Trant's militia could have held back for any length of time the well-disciplined French light troops who could have turned the flanks of any Portuguese position.

The towns and villages in the 'northern corridor' through which both armies passed can be found without much difficulty, although the new main road does not often run through them. The road from Lousa to Foz d' Aronce is impassable to motor vehicles. Redinha has changed little; the bridge there remains as it was in 1811. The position of the earthworks on the Alva cannot be verified with any certainty.

The remains of the Lines of Torres Vedras are particularly interesting. There were over 140 masonry and earth closed works in the first line alone, most of which still exist as easily recognizable ruins. They were placed on hill-tops and have a characteristic appearance from below. It is a rewarding climb to many of these; one can often trace the original walls, ditches, gun emplacements, and means of entrance.

Massena personally surveyed the Lines from the village of Arruda. The Allied army was drawn up on the commanding ground to the south and west confidently awaiting him. One can share with Massena his lack of confidence in the result of a French attack. Another Busaco could hardly have been avoided.

X

FUENTES DE ONORO

WELLINGTON drove Massena and his field army from Portugal on 8th April 1811. Only Almeida, which had been repaired and garrisoned, but not adequately provisioned, remained in French hands.[1] The easiest way for the Allies to retake it was to prevent its resupply with food, for Almeida was situated so far west that only a major effort by the entire French army would enable a convoy to enter it.

Ciudad Rodrigo was also short of food and temporarily isolated, but it lay well inside the plain of Leon where the numerous French cavalry was most efficient. The Allied army was at a disadvantage here, but Wellington attempted to blockade this fortress also. Julian Sanchez, a Spanish guerrilla commander of ability, undertook to prevent all small detachments from reaching the town and to warn the Light Division of the approach of any large convoy. This he did on the 13th, but Erskine failed to take advantage of his opportunity. A convoy escorted by a single French division entered the town which was now safe, for the Allies had as yet no siege train.[2] Wellington relaxed his efforts to blockade Ciudad Rodrigo, but kept Almeida isolated.

Over a month previously, Soult, in the southern corridor, attempted to advance into Portugal. Badajoz was at first commanded by a Spanish General, Menacho, who was skilled, brave, and enterprising. He was killed early in Soult's siege, during a successful sortie on 3rd March. His successor had no military virtues and surrendered the powerfully garrisoned and well supplied fortress on the 11th to a French force not

---

[1] The food supplies in both Almeida and Ciudad Rodrigo had been reduced by Massena's starving army as it passed by in retreat.

[2] A British siege train had been for months aboard transports in Portuguese harbours. but had not yet been landed.

greatly stronger in infantry than his own.[1] Badajoz fell before Wellington had prevented Massena from crossing the Mondego, but Soult was unable to invade Portugal because of a development even further south.

A British force under Sir Thomas Graham won a brilliant victory at Barrosa, in the vicinity of Cadiz, on 5th March over a more numerous French Army. A combined Anglo-Spanish army from the long-beleaguered Spanish port made a landing behind French lines, but was itself surprised. Graham received no better co-operation from his Spanish allies than Wellington had from Cuesta, but won unassisted.

Soult's siege of Badajoz caused Wellington to dispatch Beresford to the Alemtejo on 8th March. On the 16th, Wellington sent Cole and his 4th Division south also.[2] On 25th March, Beresford and his Chief of Cavalry, General Long, mismanaged an opportunity to crush a weaker enemy force at Campo Maior. A fine British cavalry charge again went completely out of control. (Cf. Taylor and the 16th L.D. at Vimiero, and Ponsonby and the 23rd L.D. at Talavera.) The French were thrown back on Badajoz and practically blockaded there.

Wellington found his army divided by over one hundred miles of rugged country. He would continue to control both sections himself as far as was possible at that time. Leaving specific instructions with Spencer to cover all likely eventualities, he rode south, accompanied by staff officers only, at dawn on 16th April.[3] He conferred with Beresford and rode completely around Badajoz, which he ordered to be reinvested. He then drew up instructions for the protection of this siege which gave Beresford considerable latitude, including permission to fight a battle.

Wellington started back north early on the 25th and was met half-way by a dispatch from Spencer. French columns from Salamanca, Zamora, and Valladolid were converging on Ciudad Rodrigo. One of Wellington's 'correspondents' within the fortress reported that a house was being prepared for Massena.

Wellington reached Almeida during the evening of the 28th; the French had not yet entered the area. During the next three days, however, intelligence reports indicated that Massena was advancing with every man on whom he could lay hands. His objective was the

[1] *Oman*, IV, 55–61, gives a vivid and convincing account of the misdeeds of Menacho's successor, José Imaz.

[2] Wellington knew of the fall of Badajoz on the 14th, partly by means of semaphores. A signal station at Elvas was constantly in touch with Badajoz during daylight and fair weather.

[3] Wellington sometimes rode 70 *miles* between dawn and dusk.

revictualling of Almeida, only relic of his Portuguese invasion. Massena's Army of Portugal had received only token reinforcements from Bessieres, and numbered about 48,500 in all. Wellington could muster only 37,500 men, but had five veteran Allied infantry divisions as well as the new 7th Division.[1] He was determined to fight if given a favourable opportunity. There was an excellent position for his purposes east of Almeida and the Coa.

The terrain in this area depends on the Duero, and four approximately parallel tributaries which flow into it from the south. The Coa is west of Almeida, but further east there are, in succession, the Turones, the Dos Casas, and the Agueda. Wellington was planning to place his army on some high ground between the Turones and the Dos Casas. These streams are about two miles apart; the main road from Ciudad Rodrigo crosses the Dos Casas at the village of Fuentes de Onoro. North of the village, the Dos Casas enters a gorge which gets deeper and wider until at Fort Concepcion, directly east of Almeida, it is a considerable military obstacle (Plates 18 and 19).[2] Tributaries of the Dos Casas, flow through the Portuguese villages of Poco Velho and Nave de Haver, approximately three and five miles respectively south of Fuentes; they then converge and pass through meadowland immediately before running through the village.

On 2nd May, Massena's army crossed the Agueda at Ciudad Rodrigo. Wellington had the bulk of his force immediately behind Fuentes with the 6th and 5th Divisions extending to the north toward Fort Concepcion. He calmly awaited the French attack.

Early next day Massena in personal command of five divisions advanced directly west towards Fuentes; another three divisions further north proceeded in the direction of Almeida. Wellington saw all this from a hill above Fuentes, and was satisfied that the French main attack

[1] The morale and unity of the Allied army was much improved since the spring of 1810. In infantry, Wellington was only 10 per cent weaker than Massena. Due to losses of draft animals during the recent retreat, the French brought forward only 38 guns to oppose 48 Allied field pieces.

[2] Fort Concepcion was 'blown up' in July 1810, but was still defensible against any attack short of a regular siege.

Light Division: This force moved north to support 6th and 5th Divisions on 3rd May and south to cover the retreat of the 7th Division on 5th May; it remained on the afternoon of the 5th in reserve behind the critical angle in the Allied line.

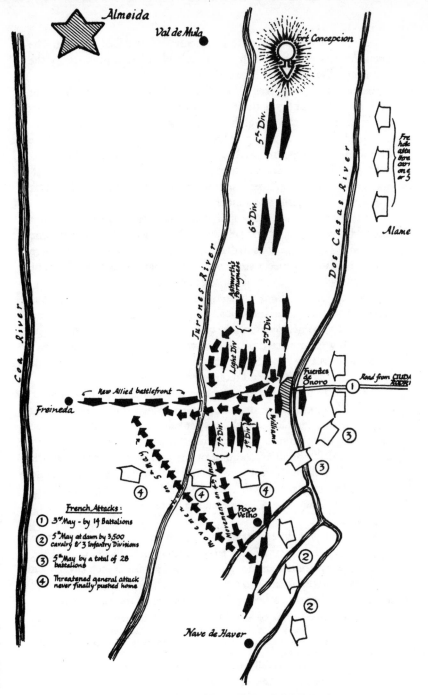

Almeida

Val de Mula

Fort Concepcion

5ᵗʰ Div.

6ᵗʰ Div.

Fre hole astu lltra catri on e ar 5

Alame

Dos Casas River

Turones River

Coa River

Ashworth's Portuguese

3ʳᵈ Div.

Light Div

Fuentes de Onoro

Road from CIUDAD RODRI

New Allied battlefront

Freineda

Williams

7ᵗʰ Div.

1ˢᵗ Div.

Movement on 4ᵗʰ May

No 2 May (?)

Poco Velho

French Attacks:
1 3ʳᵈ May - by 14 Battalions
2 5ᵗʰ May at dawn by 3,500 cavalry & 3 Infantry Divisions
3 5ᵗʰ May by a total of 28 battalions
4 Threatened general attack never finally pushed home

Nave de Haver

VII. FUENTES DE ONORO

was directed towards the greatest concentration of Allied strength. The secondary attack to the north could probably be held in check by the two Allied divisions in that area.

Fuentes had already seen a lot of the war. Some units of the Light Division were so at home there that they knew almost every inhabitant by name. The narrow straggling village lay mainly between the Dos Casas and the crest of a long hill to the west (Plates 20 and 22). There were a few buildings only on the right bank and some enclosed gardens. Inside the village the narrow crooked streets were constricted by high stone walls, and intersected each other infrequently but at irregular angles; the whole place was a maze.

Wellington considered this sprawling village the key to his position and held it with 28 light and rifle companies together with a weak line battalion.[1] This force consisted of 2,260 men, many of whom were picked marksmen armed with accurate weapons. Colonel Williams of the 5/60th, who distinguished himself at Busaco, was in command.

About 2 p.m., Massena directed a whole division of ten battalions towards Fuentes with an impetuosity reminiscent of Busaco. The Allied skirmishers were deployed in a heavy line on the western bank of the stream and were protected by garden walls and buildings. French losses were heavy, but they gained a foothold on the left bank until Williams threw in his line battalion and recaptured the entire village.

The French rallied and delivered a second assault over now familiar ground. This time, more than 4,000 men forded the knee-deep Dos Casas in what resembled a thick line, probably caused by the complete disordering of columns by Allied artillery fire from higher ground to the west and the broken condition of the area over which the attack was made.[2] Williams's men were driven back from the stream, while he himself was severely wounded. Partly because there was no rallying place in the village, the Allied defenders were driven clear of it on to the ridge behind.

Wellington was close at hand and sent in the 1/71st and the 1/79th supported by the 2/24th. These troops retook the village, crossed the stream, took prisoners, and fought successfully with French cavalry on the far side. But Massena also sent in fresh battalions. These were only able to occupy a few gardens and a small chapel on the eastern bank. As

[1] All the skirmishers of the 1st and 3rd Divisions, with the exception of Stopford's Guards Brigade; 13 British light companies, 4 Portuguese light companies, 6 German light companies probably armed with rifles, and 5 companies of the 60th and 95th. The line battalion was the 2/84th.

[2] This area still abounds in small gardens enclosed by thick stone walls.

darkness fell, the Allies retained the entire village west of the Dos Casas.

All the fighting on the 3rd May took place in or near Fuentes. The French made only a demonstration against the Allied 6th and 5th Divisions to the north. Wellington sent the Light Division in that direction, but the French manoeuvres were so obviously not intended to be more than demonstrations, that the division was halted half-way.[1] When night approached, Wellington ordered it back to the rear of Fuentes. Massena's assault on the village had cost him 652 casualties; the Allies lost only 259.

Although Wellington had his command under arms well before dawn on the 4th, no serious fighting occurred. When a thick blanket of fog lifted an hour after daybreak, Wellington could see that the French positions were unchanged. A bickering fire began across the Dos Casas near Fuentes, but lasted only until 10 a.m. An informal truce was established to allow the removal of the dead and wounded. Later on in the day, the French cavalry manoeuvred as if to turn the Allied right, but did not actually do this.

Wellington had plenty of time to consider countermeasures; should the French follow such a plan, he would have two alternatives. He could shift his army south, but this would uncover Almeida. He could remain where he was and continue to protect the siege of Almeida, but then he would have to abandon his communications through Malhada Sorda and Guarda. There was no reason to take either step immediately. Wellington extended his front moderately to the south by moving the 7th Division to Poco Velho and the British cavalry to Nave de Haver. Julian Sanchez and his guerrillas had been holding the latter village for some time already.

At dawn on 5th May, the French struck hard at the weakest sector of the Allied line, the newly formed right wing. The morning was again foggy; Sanchez was surprised and routed at Nave de Haver. The British cavalry there was thrust back towards Poco Velho (Plate 21). French infantry in force attacked the Allied 7th Division and quickly drove out the two battalions posted in Poco Velho.[2] These disordered units retired on the other seven battalions of the division further west. French infantry and cavalry pursued. Before long the entire 7th Division and two squadrons of British cavalry which came to their rescue

---

[1] The Light Division had been on outpost duty until the morning of the 3rd under its senior brigade commander. Craufurd was expected back from leave in England; Erskine had been transferred to the 5th Division.
[2] The 85th and the 2nd *Cacadores*.

were in a hazardous situation. French infantry, cavalry, and artillery were moving forward in earnest against the Allied right flank.

Just when matters became desperate, Craufurd and the Light Division approached Poco Velho; Wellington had ordered them south to support the 7th Division soon after dawn.[1] With unerring instinct he had sensed the power of Massena's southern thrusts. Craufurd was not to extend the Allied flank to the south, but rather to bring the 7th Division back safely to the north. Wellington had no intention of uncovering Almeida, even though his communications were cut.[2]

Meanwhile, Wellington re-aligned his army. The 6th and 5th Allied Divisions with Barbecena's Portuguese cavalry remained where they were, blocking all wheeled access to Almeida. Fuentes was still held by the two Scots battalions with the 2/24th in support. But the Allied line behind the village was changed. Instead of running north and south, it now bent back abruptly to the west just to the rear of the village. Three and a half divisions were redeployed to face south. Picton's 3rd Division was immediately behind Fuentes; Ashworth's Independent Portuguese Brigade came next. Spencer's 1st Division and Houston's 7th Division extended the new line across the Turones toward Freineda and the Coa.

This gave up the line of communications through Guarda. If the Allied army was forced to retreat over the Coa, both baggage and artillery would probably be lost; the only passable bridge at Castello Bon was narrow and difficult to reach along a steep sharply turning road. But Wellington had no intention of retreating; he had confidence in his army and in himself. He was going to prevent the relief of Almeida whatever happened.

At Poco Velho, Craufurd had relieved the 7th Division by the simple expedient of substituting his own Division; the 7th retired towards the new position which Wellington had assigned to it. The Light Division together with Cotton's British cavalry was practically isolated in the open plain surrounded by numerous French cavalry, three divisions of Massena's infantry, and several batteries of artillery. The Allies refused to allow the enemy cavalry to pin them down to a position on which infantry and artillery could converge. This was Craufurd's finest hour; he handled his command with unerring skill. He kept his line battalions in mobile squares, but used his riflemen in small groups of one or two

[1] Craufurd had finally arrived the previous evening.

[2] Wellington realized that the French were faster, due partly to their superiority in cavalry. If he conformed to their pressure in the south, Massena could force him further and further in that direction until the cavalry escorted convoy could pass into Almeida.

companies as skirmishers.[1] This area, although predominantly flat, abounds in low outcroppings of rock; wherever one of these gave some protection, riflemen would take cover and open fire. Their accurate fire was galling to the enemy cavalry and artillery even at 250 yards. If they were charged, they would sprint for protection under the muskets of a square. All slowly retired to the north.

The French artillery approached to short range so as to fire on the British squares effectively, but Cotton's cavalry would counter this by making partial charges which forced back the guns. Craufurd was moving his line battalions to the rear alternately. Bull's Horse Artillery gunners and drivers in three sections of two guns each had taken up positions between Craufurd's squares and fired on the French cavalry, artillery, and infantry. The Light Division retired at a carefully controlled speed and in perfect order. Its discipline, courage, confidence, and physical fitness was remarkable; total losses in a difficult retreat of over two miles were trifling.[2]

During this movement an incident occurred which was to start a tradition. Sometimes a section of Bull's Horse Artillery would stay behind firing after its protective square had pulled back. Captain Norman Ramsay's two guns were completely enveloped by the French cavalry. He ordered his pieces and caissons to be limbered up, surrounded them with mounted gunners with drawn sabres, and cut his way through the encircling mass at a gallop.[3] They were aided considerably by a squadron of the 14th L.D. and a squadron of the Royals (1st Dragoons).

The French followed Craufurd and Cotton to their new positions

---

[1] The British infantry at this period could form three different types of squares; one of these could be taken up by troops either stationary or in motion: *Nineteen Movements, Dundas*. There were now three line battalions in the Light Division; the 1/43rd, the 1/52nd, and the 2/52nd.

[2] The entire Light Division lost only 67 (*Fortescue*) or 44 (*Oman*) casualties during the whole day.

[3] *Napier*, III, 150-1, describes this brilliantly.
'Their leading squadrons (French), approaching in a disorderly manner, were partially checked by fire, but a great commotion was observed in their main body; men and horses were seen to close with confusion and tumult towards one point, where a thick dust and loud cries, and the sparkling of blades, and flashing of pistols, indicated some extraordinary occurrence. Suddenly, the multitude became violently agitated, an English shout pealed high and clear, the mass was rent assunder, and Norman Ramsay burst forth sword in hand at the head of his battery, his horses, breathing fire, stretched like greyhounds along the plain, the guns bounded behind them like things of no weight, and the mounted gunners followed close, with heads bent low and pointed weapons, in desperate career.'

and managed to cut off and capture some skirmishers of the Guards.[1] Their entire southern force, a total of about 22,000 Frenchmen, closed to within artillery range of Wellington's new line, but did not attack. Massena was obviously waiting to take Fuentes first. It was now the anchor of the Allied left as it had been of their right two days before.

The Allied position facing south had been chosen with care by Wellington. Behind the crest of the east-west ridge, there was a reverse slope except where it was cloven by the narrow valley of the Turones. Artillery was in position along the crest with open fields of fire; a heavy and continuous security line was pushed well forward. But this position, like that at Sobral the previous autumn, was destined not to be attacked.

Before the Light Division had completed its withdrawal, the French were again attacking Fuentes from across the Dos Casas. Ten battalions pushed the 1/71st and 1/79th back through the village to the ridge and church behind. The Scots rallied and with the assistance of the 2/24th, thrust the French back almost to the stream again. During this struggle, two companies of the 79th were trapped in culs-de-sac and practically annihilated; a few only surrendered unwounded.

The French attacked again, and again forced the three British battalions back to the high ground around the church. But Fuentes was no more than about 400 yards from Wellington's personal point of vantage. He fed in more reinforcements in the form of light companies from the 1st and 3rd Divisions and the 6th *Cacadores*, who already had fought in the village.[2] Once more the French were thrown back.

Massena now ordered forward 18 fresh battalions, probably two full divisions. By sheer weight of numbers, the Allies were pushed right through the village and on to the plain behind it. Again Wellington had an adequate force moving in the right direction towards this critical pivot of his line. He had ordered forward the 1/88th and the 74th of Mackinnon's Brigade of Picton's Division. These were advancing in two columns abreast when they met the French pouring in disorder across the plain from the western end of Fuentes. For once the British battalions attacked in column; the wild Irishmen of the

[1] The total loss of Stopford's Brigade on 5th May was 135, only 26 of whom were missing, but this small reverse was magnified in some contemporary French accounts to three battalions of Guards laying down their arms: Oman, IV, 328, based on narratives of French Generals Fournier and Fririon.
[2] The 6th *Cacadores* were from Ashworth's Independent Brigade who had suffered 'nearly all' the Portuguese casualties on 3rd May: Oman, IV, 622.

Connaught Rangers (the 88th) used their bayonets with considerable effect. Behind these two intrepid units, the Scots rallied and counter-attacked.

The blood-soaked streets were gorged with fighting men. Columns from both armies were trying to force their way forward through its maze of high walls and narrow passages. A party of over 100 French grenadiers was cut off in a cul-de-sac and killed almost to a man by the 1/88th. Volleys were exchanged at point blank range, and casualties mounted quickly on both sides. Once more the entire village was in Allied hands. The gallant but hard to control men of Connaught poured across the Dos Casas to kill and be killed among the walled gardens to the east.

This last defeat did not terminate French efforts to take the village. The last reserves of the three French divisions now came forward on a front of 1,000 yards; they were joined by some troops which had already entered Fuentes six times. But this last attack was not pressed home; the French knew when they were beaten and hardly cleared the right bank of the stream. Many units did not even advance to musketry range. Fuentes remained in possession of the Allies.

Other French divisions west of Fuentes had been awaiting orders to attack as soon as the village fell. The Allied troops facing them under Ashworth, Spencer, and Houston remained equally inactive. The artillery of both armies had been in action sporadically, but the Allies had an advantage both in number of pieces and in their position.[1] Finally the French guns were silenced.

During the artillery duel, Captain Knipe of the 14th L.D. put to a practical test a theory he had that cavalry could take a battery of artillery by charging them in front. He led a squadron of his own regiment and one of the Royals in a disastrous attempt which cost him his life.[2] An equally unsuccessful and more costly attack was made by French *voltigeurs* among the rocks on either sides of the Turones. They were stopped dead by five companies of British Rifles which had been stationed in this defile earlier in the day by Craufurd.

Finding he could not take Fuentes, Massena's further schemes were impracticable. To attack west of the village while it remained in Allied hands, would have divided his army in two. The serious fighting was

[1] See note 1, page 158, regarding the artillery ratio.
[2] *Oman*, IV, 326–7, places this episode earlier; I have followed *Fortescue*, VIII, 167, who was aware, of course, of Oman's timing but deviated from it on the eyewitness evidence of a member of Knipe's squadron in *Maxwell's Peninsular Sketches*, I, 194.

over by 2 p.m. Both armies remained within artillery range of each other, but no offensive move was made.

During the night of the 5th, Wellington entrenched his position.[1] The entire line from Fuentes to Freineda, a distance of four miles, was dug in and protected by abatis; the artillery to the immediate rear was placed in epaulements. Feuntes with its stone walls rising up in tiers became an almost impregnable bastion.

Massena made no attack on the 6th; his cavalry manoeuvred both north and west, but could find no way through the Allied defences. How could he force a position protected by earthworks, which had defied him when still open? The chasm of the Coa arrested the French to the west; to the north lay Allied troops calm and confident in strong positions between the Dos Casas and the Turones. Still further north were Fort Concepcion and chasms cut by these two streams. Wellington could not be manoeuvred out of position; to relieve Almeida, Massena had first to beat the Allies in battle, which meant attacking Fuentes again.

Massena ordered the supplies that he had brought forward to throw into Almeida to be distributed to his field army which otherwise would have gone hungry. He endeavoured to get a message secretly into Almeida instructing the governor to blow up the place and try to escape.[2] Massena maintained his position until the morning of 10th May, then withdrew his whole army east of the Agueda.

In two days of bloody fighting, the Allies lost 1,545 and the French 2,192. Casualties on 5th May were not so one-sided as on the 3rd, because of Houston's early losses in Poco Velho.

The most important tactical aspect of Fuentes was the ineffectiveness of the numerically superior French cavalry against properly handled, steadfast infantry. Massena gained nothing after the initial surprise in the south, even though he had a three or four to one advantage in numbers.[3]

[1] This was the first and only time during the Peninsular War that an army in the field commanded by Wellington used earthworks, although occasionally they were thrown up around detached positions, such as at Maya in the Pyrenees.

[2] One of the three French volunteers disguised in peasant costume succeeded; the other two were caught and shot as spies. Receipt of the message was acknowledged by Brennier, the Governor of Almeida, by firing three salvos at a designated time.

[3] Both Tomkinson and Napier state that Allied cavalry actually present for duty numbered no more than 1,000.

No lines met columns at Fuentes, but the British system of open order fighting proved more effective than the French mass, even inside the village. The Allied light companies and riflemen were more at home in street fighting than Frenchmen used to attacking in column.[1] The French in their various assaults on the village do not appear to have used their *voltigeurs*.

For the first time in the Peninsula, Wellington had a numerical superiority in artillery which led to a silencing of the French guns along the southern flank. Yet a careful reappraisal of this long range duel would indicate that field pieces so used made a great deal of noise which might improve morale, but rarely caused decisive casualties.[2]

The British cavalry at Fuentes, with the exception of Knipe's abortive effort, had an almost flawless record. In small units, the horsemen did not get out of hand in charges. Their courage, fine mounts, and superior physical strength made them more than a match for an equal number of the enemy.

Wellington again displayed an unique ability to anticipate what units would be required, and have them ready when they were needed. The 1/88th and 74th could not have appeared at a more opportune moment. Dispatching Craufurd and the Light Division changed the entire complexion of the fighting at Poco Velho.

Both Wellington and Massena have been criticized for their control of this battle; historians have brought forward endless conjectures. Should Wellington have placed the 7th Division in an exposed position and then 'risked' the Light Division in its rescue? His critics forget that the raw 7th Division although attacked in force, had only two of its nine battalions mauled at Poco Velho, and suffered only slightly when

[1] The skirmishers were apparently much more efficient inside the village than line troops; both Costello and Napier criticize the 1/71st and 1/79th for standing 'shoulder to shoulder': *Fortescue*, VIII, 172.

[2] *Maxwell's Peninsular Sketches*, I, 193-4.

'a brigade of Portuguese artillery, commanded by a German, thinking it was an attack by the French infantry, as indeed it appeared to be, opened upon them with spherical case. The shells appeared to burst over the heads of the skirmishers, when a mounted officer came from the canonaded party at a gallop, waving a handkerchief. It proved to be a body of the Brunswick Oels, who were dressed in a peculiar manner, and something like the French. The poor German was in sad distress—"Have I shed the blood of my gallant countrymen!" he exclaimed; while he paced to and fro in great agitation, another officer now arrived from the Brunswickers (though they were usually called the *Owls*). He came to console the captain; not a man was touched. This only changed the cause of distress; the professional skill of the gunner was called in question, and the gallant German was in still deeper despair.'

retreating to a new and stronger position. The Light Division was never in real danger.

Massena had been criticized particularly for not manoeuvring more with his cavalry so as to mask an even greater concentration of infantry, which should have been used to attack even more powerfully at a single point. Massena and his professional army now had almost a year's experience in fighting Wellington, but had accomplished nothing.[1] He had the good sense at both Busaco and Fuentes not to continue unsuccessful attacks indefinitely and expose his army to total defeat. Both Marmont at Salamanca and Napoleon at Waterloo were to make this error.

THE CONTENDING FORCES AT FUENTES DE ONORO

ALLIED ARMY UNDER WELLINGTON   TOTAL = 37,614[2]

INFANTRY	23,026 British	11,471 Portuguese	= 34,497
1st Division, Brent Spencer			= 7,565
Edward Stopford's Brigade		1,943	
1/Coldstreamers, 1/Scots, 1 Co. 5/60th			
Sigismund von Lowe's Brigade		1,914	
1st, 2nd, 5th and 7th Line Batts. K.G.L., 2 Cos., Light Infantry K.G.L.			
Nightingall's Brigade		1,774	
2/24th, 2/42nd, 1/79th, 1 Co. 5/60th			
Howard's Brigade		1,934	
1/50th, 1/71st, 1/92nd, 1 Co. 3/95th			
3rd Division, Thomas Picton			= 5,480
Henry Mackinnon's Brigade		1,863	
1/45th, 74th, 1/88th, 3 Cos. 5/60th			
Colville's Brigade		1,967	
2/5th, 2/83rd, 2/88th, 94th			
Power's Portuguese Brigade		1,650	
9th Line (2 Batts.), 21st Line (2 Batts.)			

[1] Massena was only fifty-four, nine years younger than Graham was at the time of Barrosa, but aged by wounds, privation, and excesses.
[2] Includes 266 Engineers, Train, Staff, etc.

5th Division, William Erskine   = 5,158
  Hay's Brigade   1,770
    3/1st, 1/9th, 2/38th, 1 Co. Brunswick Oels
  James Dunlop's Brigade   1,624
    1/4th, 2/30th, 3/44th, 1 Co. Brunswick Oels
  Spry's Portuguese Brigade   1,764
    3rd Line (2 Batts.), 15th Line (2 Batts.), 8th Cacadores

6th Division, Alexander Campbell   = 5,250
  Richard Hulse's Brigade   2,041
    1/11th, 2/53rd, 1/61st, 1 Co. 5/60th
  Burne's Brigade   1,072
    2nd, 1/36th
  Madden's Portuguese Brigade   2,137
    8th Line (2 Batts.), 12th Line (2 Batts.)

7th Division, William Houston   = 4,590
  John Sontag's Brigade   2,409
    2/51st, 85th, Chasseurs Britanniques, 8 Cos. Brunswick Oels
  Doyle's Portuguese Brigade   2,181
    7th Line (2 Batts.), 19th Line (2 Batts.), 2nd Cacadores

Light Division, Robert Craufurd   = 3,915
  Sidney Beckwith's Brigade   1,631
    1/43rd, 4 Cos. 1/95th, 1 Co. 2/95th, 3rd Cacadores
  Drummond's Brigade   2,284
    1/52nd, 2/52nd, 4 Cos. 1/95th, 1st Cacadores

Ashworth's Independent Portuguese Brigade   = 2,539
    6th Line (2 Batts.), 18th Line (2 Batts.), 6th Cacadores

CAVALRY   = 1,864
Slade's Brigade   776
  1st Dragoons, 14th Light Dragoons

Frederick Arentschildt's Brigade   776
    16th Light Dragoons, 1st Hussars, K.G.L.

Barbacena's Portuguese Brigade   312
    4th Line, 10th Line

ARTILLERY   8 Batteries = 48 guns,   =   987
    4 British (Ross's, Bull's, Lawson's   437
         and Thompson's batteries)
    4 Portuguese   550

THE FRENCH UNDER MASSENA   TOTAL = 48,268

CORPS	INFANTRY				CAV-ALRY	ARTILLERY		TOTAL
	Divisions	Brigades	Battalions	Personnel		Personnel	Guns	
2nd (Reynier)	2	3	21	10,382	682	—	—	11,064
6th (Loison)	3	5	34	16,806	334	—	—	17,140
8th (Junot)	1	1	10	4,714	—	—	—	4,714
9th (D'Erlon)	2	2	18	10,304	794	—	—	11,098
Reserves	—	—	—	—	1,187	1,327	32	2,514
Bessiere's Army					1,665	73	6	1,738
				42,206	4,662	1,400	38	48,268

TOPOGRAPHICAL OBSERVATIONS

The lower village of Fuentes remains today almost as it was at the time of the battle. The original bridge over the Dos Casas still stands; the walled gardens on the right bank are little changed. To the north, the ruins of Fort Concepcion are in much the same condition as when Craufurd blew up the place in July 1810. As Harry Smith wrote, this is a 'most perfect work', and can be inspected in detail by anyone who ascends the broad low hill between the Turones (the Spanish-Portuguese border at that point) and the Dos Casas. Both Poco Velho and Nave de Haver are in Portugal. The swamps are greatly diminished, but the great flat plain, where Craufurd accomplished so much, is unmistakable. The Allied line between Fuentes and Freineda is difficult to follow, being partially obscured by the modern town, railway station, and the new border crossing point. The main road now passes to the north of Fuentes and south of Almeida.

XI

ALBUERA

O N 5th May 1811, Sir William Beresford finally commenced the siege of Badajoz in accordance with Wellington's orders. The French had not yet fully restored the fortifications; supplies were low. Almost immediately, however, Beresford heard that Soult was preparing to relieve the place.[1]

Two Spanish armies in this area would co-operate with Beresford's Anglo-Portuguese force. Both Blake and Castaños, the Spanish commanders, magnanimously waived any rights to overall command and acknowledged Beresford as chief of their joint army. Beresford had plenty of time for a concentration of all forces. The siege was to be abandoned temporarily, but Soult was to be stopped far enough south of Badajoz to ensure that the town could not be materially aided, and that the garrison could not take any part in an ensuing battle.

Spanish scouts reported that two French columns, one from Seville under Soult himself and another from further east in Andalusia under Latour-Maubourg, had joined on the evening of the 12th with a total strength of about 25,000 men including powerful cavalry and probably 50 guns. The Allied cavalry was in contact with the French on the 13th, but following Wellington's instructions of 25th April made no effort to stop the French advance. General Long was in command and had some 1,400 sabres. The French cavalry was more skilful and nearly three times as strong, but Beresford considered Long inefficient in not creating more of a delay and replaced him on the eve of the battle.[2]

[1] Soult made a speech in Seville to this effect on the 8th of which Beresford heard on the 12th.

[2] Long certainly abandoned country more quickly than was necessary. His successor, Lumley, was his senior in rank and a former Light Dragoon, but had been in command of an infantry brigade of the 2nd Division. Long's own memoirs were published, under the title of *Peninsular Cavalry General*, in 1951.

Beresford had marched from Badajoz to Valverde on the 13th, commanding Hill's 'corps', endeavouring to anticipate Soult's route.[1] The French marshal was reported at Santa Marta at noon on the 14th; he was definitely committed to the road passing through Albuera, a small town rather than a village, situated adjacent to the most defensible position in the area.[2]

Beresford reached Albuera at 2 p.m. on the 15th. He added at this time to his Anglo-Portuguese force both Alten's Independent German Brigade and Collins's Independent Portuguese Brigade.[3] Blake brought in his army that night; Cole's 4th Division and Castaños's infantry came up early next morning.[4]

The town of Albuera is situated west of a river of the same name which flows roughly north from south. The river is formed some 500 yards south of the town where two brooks, which have run parallel to each other for a couple of miles, finally come together. The narrow tongue of land between these brooks is comparatively high and was then covered by trees.

The main road to Badajoz from the southeast, on which Soult was advancing, crossed the Albuera river by a bridge just north of the junction of the brooks and then passed through the town (Plate 23). This road lies at an angle of about 30 degrees to the stream. At the time of the battle both sides of the streams were clear and open; but the woods between them shielded that portion of the road over which the French advanced from Allied observation behind Albuera. Neither of

[1] There were three possible road systems which Soult could use from Los Santos to Badajoz; Valverde was astride the middle one.

[2] *Oman*, IV, 373. Wellington criticized the actual manner in which the position was occupied, *Wellington at War*, 219.

[3] I have followed *Oman*, IV, 631; *Fortescue*, VIII, 207, assigns Alten's Brigade to Cole's 4th Division. For simplicity, K.G.L. units and some other foreigners in the British service are usually included in British totals.

[4] Due to a mistake, the too early removal of a pontoon bridge, and deepening water over a Guadiana ford, only three companies of Kemmis's Brigade, 165 of about 2,250, accompanied Cole; the remainder had to march 30 additional miles to cross by another ford, arriving too late for the battle.

French Attacks:

(1) 8 a.m.	4,000 infantry, 550 cavalry, 12 guns; serious fighting, but attack not pressed home.
(2) 8 a.m.	6,000 + with 12 guns. A threat only; no actual fighting.
(3) 9.30 a.m.	8,400 infantry and 18 guns with cavalry and artillery flank guard.
(4) 10.30 a.m.	Polish Lancers.
(5) 12.15 p.m.	French Cavalry attack; 4 regiments of dragoons.
(6) 12.20 p.m.	French Infantry attack with 9 battalions; 5,600 men with close artillery support.

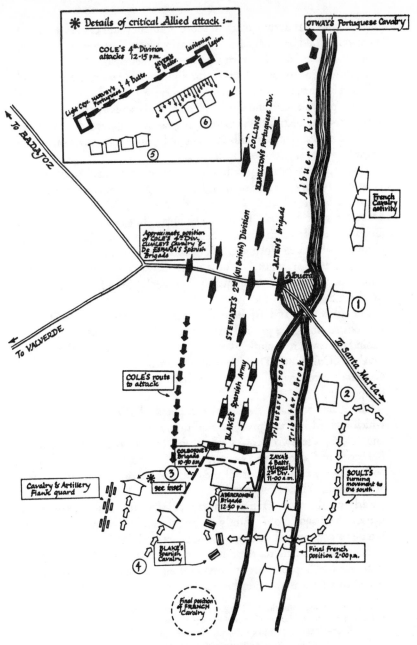

* Details of critical Allied attack :—

COLE'S 4th Division attacks 12·15 p.m.

Lusitanian Legion

Myer's 3 Batt.

Light Coy. Harvey's } 4 Batts.
Portuguese }

6

5

OTWAY'S Portuguese Cavalry

Albuera River

French Cavalry activity

COLLINS

HAMILTON'S Portuguese Div.

ALTEN'S Brigade

To BADAJOZ

To VALVERDE

Approximate position of COLE'S 4th Div., LUMLEY'S Cavalry & De ESPANA'S Spanish Brigade

STEWART'S 2nd (2nd British) Division

Albuera

1

To Santa Marta

COLE'S route to attack

BLAKE'S Spanish Army

Tributary Brook

Tributary Brook

2

COLBORNE'S Brigade 10·30 a.m.

ZAYA'S 4 Batts. relieved by 2nd Div. 11·00 a.m.

SOULT'S turning movement to the south.

Cavalry & Artillery Flank guard

* see inset

3

ABERCROMBIE Brigade 12·30 p.m.

BLAKE'S Spanish Cavalry

4

Final French position 2·00 p.m.

Final position of FRENCH Cavalry

VIII. ALBUERA

173

these brooks was deep enough to prevent infantry and cavalry fording; even guns could be dragged across in many places. There was, however, a perpendicular bank between the river and the town.

A number of topographical features in the Albuera area are termed hills and heights, in many accounts. All these are much lower than those at Vimiero, Talavera, and Busaco. The town is actually surrounded by plains; the undulations which rise progressively toward the south on the west of the river are hills in name only, and in comparison to the completely flat land east of the streams.

Beresford occupied a position in the expectation that Soult would cross the river by the bridge, or at least near the town. Alten's Germans were placed in Albuera. To the north in line with this brigade was Hamilton's Portuguese division; Collins's Independent Portuguese Brigade was placed in support in a second line. The Allied left flank consisted of eleven Portuguese battalions, approximately 6,200 men, and extended for a distance of a mile. Otway's Portuguese cavalry, about 800 sabres of doubtful quality, was deployed in front and on the northern flank.

The all-British 2nd Division commanded by Sir William Stewart was posted on rising ground some 700 yards west of the streams and behind the town in a single two-deep line. To their rear was the British cavalry.[1] Cole's 4th Division and de España's Spanish infantry of Castaños's army, which came up at dawn on the 16th, remained here temporarily.

The Allied southern flank was composed of Blake's Spanish army which arrived late the previous night. It was being deployed in two lines facing the two brooks when the French attack commenced. Beresford had a force of 35,000 men with 48 guns posted in a strong position against an attack from the east, but his right flank, composed of Spaniards, was not yet settled.

Early on the 16th, French infantry, cavalry, and artillery advanced against the town from slightly south of east.[2] Six French infantry battalions approached Albuera and menaced Alten; two Spanish battalions were sent in to reinforce him. Another French force of all arms was seen approaching the bridge along the road.[3] Beresford concluded that he was about to be attacked in his centre and on his right

[1] Lumley had with him the 3rd Dragoon Guards and the 4th Dragoons; the 13th L.D. was detached to cover the west banks of the streams south of the town.

[2] Goudinot's Brigade of 3,924 infantry, Birche's light cavalry, and twelve guns.

[3] Werle's Brigade of 5,621 infantry, two brigades of dragoons, and another twelve guns.

flank from the east; French infantry was already fighting with Alten near the town.

Suddenly, French cavalry appeared much further south, already west of the brooks, followed by a column of infantry.[1] This cavalry routed the Spanish horse here while 19 battalions of French infantry emerged from the trees and formed deliberately before advancing to roll up the Allied flank (Plate 24).

Beresford immediately ordered Blake to form a new front facing south. There was plenty of time for the Spaniards to do this, for they were not actually engaged with the French.[2] Beresford rode off under the impression that Blake was already in the process of changing the position of at least two of his three divisions; the British 2nd Division was sent south to support the Spaniards.

But Blake did not obey Beresford's orders; he still believed that the major French attack would be from the east. He formed his southern line with four battalions of Zaya's Division only, about one quarter of his infantry. This force deployed properly and advanced to the crest of a low hill, awaiting the French attack.[3] Before they actually began fighting, they could see the 2nd Division coming up to support them.

The French now delivered the most massive single attack of the Peninsular War. Two full infantry divisions comprising more than 8,400 men advanced in what appeared to be a solid column with only a light skirmish line in front. The first division advanced in the 'mixed order' favoured by Napoleon personally. This formation had a central core of five battalions in column of double companies in line one behind the other. On each flank, there was first a battalion in line and then a battalion in column of single companies. The central mass had a front of approximately 50 men and was 45 ranks deep. To either side, the battalions in line were three men deep by about 150 broad. The flanking battalions were about 25 men wide by 18 ranks deep.[4]

[1] From Beresford's position behind Albuera, the point where the French appeared was clearly visible. The whole field of battle was unusually open except for the area shielded by trees and high ground between the two brooks behind which Soult manoeuvred to turn the Allied right flank.

[2] Where the brooks join is marshy; the French infantry never actually crossed the streams here. The 13th L.D. required no help to hold this front.

[3] The Spanish position appears to have been across slight ridges in the predominantly north-south 'heights'; the whole area was a wheat field in 1957, 1960 and 1962. There are only minor undulations.

[4] *Oman*, IV, 380, says, 'At last I found the required information in the Paris archives (those at the War Ministry, not the Archives Nationales), in the shape of an anonymous criticism on Soult's operations, drawn up (apparently for Napoleon's eye) by some officer who had been set to write a report on the causes of the loss of the battle.'

The second French division followed closely, and was composed of ten battalions drawn up initially in four columns of double companies; the two outer columns consisting of three battalions each, while those on the inside contained only two. There was an interval between the rear of the first division and the head of the following division, but this soon disappeared and the divisions merged. The breadth of the attack was about 400 yards with a total depth of 600 yards before the telescoping process began. Artillery went forward as usual with the French infantry. Their left flank was protected by 3,500 cavalry and more guns.[1]

This powerful force first struck the four Spanish battalions who were apparently in three-deep lines. The Spaniards behaved unusually well and brought the leading division to a stand. Blake's only battery went into action on their left. The firing was at close range and destructive on both sides; the French were held, at least temporarily.

The Spanish infantry was weaker numerically, but presented more usable muskets because of their three-deep array. In spite of their unaccustomed bravery, they would have broken had not the 2nd Division come up on their right flank. The leading brigade, Colborne's, was deployed in line to the southwest by William Stewart and sent against the west flank of the massive enemy column.[2] This flank attack was made on Stewart's initiative and against Beresford's specific orders; he had been instructed to form his three brigades into a second line to the rear of the Spaniards.

All went well at first; Colborne's line had opened fire, when the weather, which had been threatening all morning, suddenly broke. A thunderstorm swept across the field. Under cover of sheets of rain, two regiments of 'French' cavalry charged the flank of Colborne's Brigade with disastrous results. These Polish lancers, veteran professional soldiers armed with a weapon seldom seen in Western Europe, approached undetected and broke against the extremity of the British line. The sudden downpour had put most of the British muskets out of action. The first three of Colborne's battalions were practically annihilated in three minutes; only the northernmost, the 2/31st, which had time to form square, withstood the cavalry effectively.[3]

---

[1] The cavalry to the east of Blake's initial position hurried round and joined the southern attack once it began.

[2] This was a superb opportunity which Stewart seized avidly; 2,000 British muskets on the exposed flank of the French column could have been decisive. Stewart refused to allow Colborne to form the leading battalion, the Buffs, in a protective column.

[3] The Poles had a distinct weapons advantage; lances wielded by trained horsemen in formation had no equal offensively. Accounts of this tragedy stress the ruthlessness of the

This cavalry broke into the Spanish rear, doing a good deal of damage. Beresford and his staff were taken by surprise; the marshal had not drawn his sword, when he saw a Polish lancer heading directly for him. But the Anglo-Irishman was powerful and alert; he thrust aside the lance, seized the Pole by the neck, and dashed him senseless to the ground.

Cleve's Battery of K.G.L had moved up with Colborne's Brigade and had hardly gone into action when the lancers swept over the guns, killing and wounding many artillerymen. The pieces were soon recovered except for the howitzer which the French carried off. The situation in the rear of the Spanish infantry was confused; clouds of smoke further reduced visibility. The French cavalry cut in between Hoghton's Brigade which was just coming up, and the Spaniards. Both, in firing at the common enemy, did damage to the other; the Spaniards suffered severely. Lumley sent two squadrons of the 4th Dragoons against the French and drove them back, but these were in turn defeated by fresh French cavalry.

About this time part of Zaya's infantry broke, but was rallied and led back to the front. Beresford ordered these gallant Spaniards, who had lost 30 per cent of their original strength in killed and wounded, to be replaced by the brigades of Abercrombie and Hoghton and the 2/31st from Colborne's Brigade. The rain had ceased, and muskets on both sides were again functioning.[1]

The seven British battalions, about 3,700 men in a two-deep line now engaged the survivors of two French divisions, at least 7,800 men, in a fire fight at close range perhaps never equalled in military history. The French had lost most of their original formation and now appeared to be one enormous column about 200 men wide by 40 ranks deep. The British line was thin indeed, but was firing continuous volleys. If musketry only had been used, the French in column would have lost quickly, for the British line extended around both their flanks. But French artillery more than offset their musketry disadvantage. Several

cavalrymen, even against wounded who tried to surrender. The percentage losses of the 1/3rd, 2/48th, and 2/66th amount to 85·3, 75·9, and 61·6, not including a sizeable number of men who were taken prisoners, but escaped during the night following the battle and rejoined their units.

[1] Artillery could function almost normally even during a heavy shower, but muskets required dry priming once they had been fired. Cartridge pouches kept the individual rounds—paper packages containing a ball and powder both for the propellant charge and the priming—dry, but they could not be brought out and loaded successfully into a musket in rain.

batteries were not more than 300 yards back from the head of the French column; these were partially enfilading the flanks of the British line and crossfiring through the centre with grape and canister.

The quantity of fire on both sides was enormous, but was inaccurate. Smoke, heavy clouds, and damp atmosphere tended to obscure the targets. Nevertheless, the carnage was frightful, particularly in Hoghton's Brigade.

> 'Survivors who took part in this fight on the British side seem to have passed through it as if in a dream, conscious of nothing but dense smoke, constant closing towards the centre, a slight tendency to advance, and an invincible resolution not to retire. The men stood like rocks, loading and firing into the mass before them, though frightfully punished not so much by the French bullets as by grape shot from the French cannon at very close range. The line dwindled and dwindled continually; and the intervals between battalions grew wide as the men who were still on their legs edged in closer and closer to their colours; but not one dreamed for a moment of anything but standing and fighting to the last.... Nearly four-fifths of Hoghton's brigade were down, and its front had shrunk to the level of that of the French; but still it remained unbeaten, advanced to within twenty yards of the enemy and fired unceasingly.' [1]

This terrible contest went on for almost an hour. Hoghton fell, together with most of his field officers. All this occurred in an area not larger than a cricket field. Beresford realized that he must reinforce Hoghton and Abercrombie.[2] Carlos de España's Spanish Brigade was ordered forward from behind the Allied centre, but refused to advance into effective range. Beresford seized one of their colonels, his powerful right hand gripping his epauletted shoulder. He dragged the officer ahead, hoping that his regiment would follow him, but it would not. When Beresford released his grip, the Spaniard ran away.

Reliable reinforcements had to be found. Cole's 4th Division was the logical answer, but Beresford preferred to draw on Hamilton's and Collins's Portuguese further north.[3] He ordered Alten and his weak

---

[1] *Fortescue*, VIII, 200-1.

[2] Abercrombie's Brigade was to the east of Hoghton's and opposed mostly by *voltigeurs*. Abercrombie suffered severe losses mainly from the French artillery.

[3] Beresford later maintained that he had to keep Cole where he was to protect the Allied army from French cavalry to the southwest; Wellington was probably correct thinking that Beresford wished to keep open his line of retreat. *Fortescue*, VIII, 210-11, a full discussion of this with references.

battalion out of Albuera to reinforce the right, but his instructions to Hamilton went astray. One A.D.C. was hit; another could not find Hamilton, who had moved east towards the river.

At this critical point, Lowry Cole and one of Beresford's staff, 26-year-old Henry Hardinge, collaborated in a decision to attack the French on Stewart's western flank.[1] Cole apparently was already considering such a move when Hardinge recommended it most strongly. After a brief conference with General Lumley, the advance commenced. Cole's line was supported on the west by Lumley's cavalry, but supplied its own tactical defence against local cavalry attacks. The 4th Division was arrayed in one long line facing southeast, but formed in an unusual manner. The centre was composed of three British battalions on the left next to Stewart and four Portuguese line battalions on the right. Cole had taken the seven light companies from these battalions, added the three light companies from Kemmis's Brigade, and formed them in a mobile square on the extreme right of his line as a protection against cavalry. His inner or left flank was similarly protected by a Portuguese light battalion, the 1st Lusitanian Legion.[2] This divisional line was composed of 4,000 men and was deployed on a front of more than three-quarters of a mile.

Cole's line bore down obliquely on the enemy mass to be met by two French counter-manoeuvres. On the west, French cavalry surged forward; to the east, fresh French infantry, which had just arrived, advanced more slowly. Cole's right flank was first tested. The French cavalry, four regiments of dragoons composed of about 1,600 sabres, charged in two continuous lines. The massed British light companies in square were thrust well forward. The cavalry would have to deal with them before it reached the two-deep Allied line. Further, the French horsemen appear to have moved directly north against an Allied line facing southeast; the cavalry charge would make contact successively rather than simultaneously. The Allied units opened rolling fire as the French came within range. The enfilading volleys from the light company square into the line of cavalry careering past was particularly destructive. The French attack failed all along the line; apparently no horsemen ever approached to sabre range.

This cavalry attack extended no further east than the junction of the British and Portuguese battalions in Cole's line; Myers's British Brigade

---

[1] Hardinge was later a field marshal and C-in-C of the British army; *National Biography*, VIII, 1226-9, which discusses in detail the origin of Cole's movement at Albuera.

[2] This unit may have been armed with Baker rifles; it was later designated *Cacadores*.

and the Lusitanian Legion were not charged, although the western battalion did halt and fire obliquely at the French horsemen on their right. The second French counterattack was directed exclusively towards Cole's left. What appeared to be a French infantry division came forward directly against Myers's Brigade in three columns of three battalions each.[1] Each column advanced against one of the three British fusilier battalions, the 1/7th, the 2/7th, and the 1/23rd. Although each column outnumbered the line opposed to it by about three to one, the active weapons were in the reverse ratio. The musketry disadvantage of the French was, however, counterbalanced by their numerous and effective artillery. The struggle continued stubbornly. Even though charges of grape were tearing rents in the thin red lines, the blue columns were suffering heavier casualties.

The Lusitanian Legion on Cole's left abandoned its square and formed a line joining the 4th Division with the 2nd. The two armies were locked together, but the Allies were on a wider front. Abercrombie's three British battalions on the extreme Allied left and Cole's light companies and Portuguese line battalions on the right began to swing inward. The French were now in a most destructive crossfire; those opposite Myers began to waver. The three fusilier battalions charged. The French opposite them were thrust back and disintegrated. Panic spread quickly to the two divisions opposite Stewart. Soon, all that remained of 14,000 superb French infantry was a crowd of exhausted individual soldiers making for the rear. Their retreat was covered, however, by Soult's last reserve, a strong battalion of massed grenadiers.[2] The French artillery retired also, but continued to be effective.

Beresford now finally brought south his Portuguese and drove the French back across the westernmost of the brooks. Soult formed a new line on the high ground between them and supported it with his still powerful artillery; to the south and east their numerous cavalry hovered menacingly. The Allied army did not press their counterattack in the south, although Alten's Germans recovered Albuera and the area around it.

After four hours the fighting came to an end. Rain now came down

---

[1] This unit of French infantry was actually Werle's Brigade, even though it was composed of 5,600 men, 20 per cent more than the divisions of Gazan and Girard. The French were in columns of double companies, about 70 men broad (Werle's battalions were unusually strong) and 18 ranks deep. There appear to have been few *tirailleurs* detached in front.

[2] Eleven grenadier companies from French 1st and 4th Corps battalions; *Oman*, IV, 634, note 4 for details. The line companies of these battalions were not present.

in torrents again. The armies remained where they were throughout the afternoon and most of the following day, during which Kemmis's brigade reached the field. The French finally retired southeast along the road by which they had come, covered by their cavalry and horse artillery.

The immediate result of the battle was that Badajoz remained unrelieved; the place was free of the Allied blockade for only three days. Casualties were heavy on both sides, but about 6,000 to 8,000 in favour of the Allies. The Allied losses had fallen disproportionately on the British infantry. Casualties totalling 4,039 were suffered by units which had a combined initial strength of 8,738. Three of the four British brigades had insufficient survivors to take care of their wounded.[1]

The battle of Albuera was the basis of controversy and recrimination for forty years. Beresford clashed with Napier. Groups supported and condemned Long. Even Hardinge and Cole failed to see eye to eye in later life. Napier in particular, and later historians in general, have been unfavourable to Beresford.[2] Sir William was more unfortunate than culpable. He cannot be blamed for the disaster of Colborne's Brigade while William Stewart was acting on his own initiative and against Beresford's specific instructions. Had Blake carried out his order to change front with his three divisions rather than four battalions only, the Spanish contribution to the Allied effort would have been greater.

Wellington's own opinion of Beresford's handling of his force during the battle showed more understanding. He wrote to Sir William three days after Albuera saying, 'You could not be successful in such an action without a large loss. We must make up our minds to affairs of this kind sometimes, or give up the game.'[3] Wellington, who arrived in the southern corridor soon after the battle, had to take over temporarily the direct command of Beresford's army. Even though he comforted his lieutenant, he must have found it hard not to complain of the loss of so many men, for whom there were no immediate replacements.

The Allied army did not take advantage of the tactics used in the recent past with so much success by Wellington personally. There were

[1] Their losses were 51·9, 63·1, and 68·4 per cent of their initial strengths.

[2] Napier, for all his brilliant writing, was violently partisan. He idolized Sir John Moore, Napoleon, and all Whig statesmen, but was unfair to many personal enemies in the British army and made Beresford his special devil. He appears never to have seen the Albuera battlefield.

[3] *Dispatches*, VII, 573.

virtually no skirmishers; infantry remained in the open, instead of out of sight and harm behind crests. For the first and last time in the war French artillery was allowed to fire alongside its infantry in an attack. Wellington would never have risked a whole brigade of fine infantry being caught in line and destroyed by cavalry from the flank.

Shortcomings in strategic dispositions are not so obvious. Had Wellington been in personal command he would not have defended his weaker flank with his worst troops. If he had ordered the Spaniards to change front, he would have personally supervised the execution of the manoeuvre. Wellington would have occupied the only really good position in the area, the high ground between the brooks. He certainly would not have allowed Soult to use it to surprise the Allied army.

Even if Wellington had assumed the Allied position at Albuera, he would have changed his defensive alignment immediately Soult shifted his axis of attack from the east to the south. No man was so quick to divine the intentions of an enemy and make immediate adjustments. The French in the south would have been confronted successively by well-ordered Allied units reinforcing each other at regular intervals. Wellington usually managed to have equal or superior numbers at critical points, even when considerably outnumbered overall. Beresford had more men on the field, but was outnumbered where Soult attacked.

Wellington would not have let Stewart or Cole fight with French infantry while their artillery was also in action at point blank range on either flank. In order to prevent such tactical stupidity, Wellington almost invariably placed his divisions on defence himself and launched them personally in their attacks. He never lost a battalion to French cavalry, much less a brigade. Artillery, which accompanied almost all French infantry attacks, was usually captured before it was able to open fire.

A comparison between Albuera and Fuentes de Onoro comes naturally. In each case, a French army advanced to relieve the siege of a border fortress, lost a major battle, and was forced to retreat. The main difference between the two is that Wellington won with an inferior force and suffered only 1,804 casualties; Beresford, in spite of a numerical advantage over the French, lost 5,916 men, of whom 4,159 were British.

A story is told of Wellington's visit to the wounded of the 29th Regiment.[1] He is reported to have said, 'Men of the 29th, I am sorry to see so many of you here.'

[1] *Maxwell's Peninsular Sketches*, II, 331, and elsewhere, with variations.

'If you had commanded us, My Lord,' a veteran sergeant replied, 'there wouldn't be so many of us here.'

Yet if Beresford had fought Albuera at any other period in the history of the British army, the victory that he certainly gained would have appeared to better advantage. He was not a battlefield genius; he did not have Wellington's eye for terrain nor his long experience in handling troops of all descriptions under all conceivable circumstances. Few commanders have. Further, the Albuera army, British, German, and Portuguese, missed Wellington's presence. They may not have loved him, but they wanted 'Our Artie', or 'Nosey', or 'Douro' with them when their lives were at stake. They did not have the same confidence in Beresford.

Beresford was personally as brave as a lion and as strong as a bull. He was loyal and talented, but not eloquent; yet his official tribute to his British infantry is magnificent. 'It is impossible by any description to do justice to the distinguished gallantry of the troops; but every individual nobly did his duty; and it is observed that our dead, particularly the 57th Regiment, were lying as they fought, in ranks, and every wound was in the front.'

THE CONTENDING FORCES AND LOSSES AT ALBUERA

ALLIED ARMY UNDER BERESFORD		TOTAL =	20,310
INFANTRY 8,738 British	9,131 Portuguese	=	17,869
2nd Division, William Stewart		=	5,460
John Colborne's Brigade	2,066		
1/3rd, 2/31st, 2/48th, 2/66th			
Hoghton's Brigade	1,651		
29th, 1/48th, 1/57th			
Abercrombie's Brigade	1,597		
2/28th, 2/34th, 2/39th			
Divisional Light Troops	146		
3 Cos. 5/60th			
4th Division, Lowry Cole		=	5,107
William Myers's Brigade	2,015		
1/7th, 2/7th, 1/23rd			
James Kemmis's Brigade	165		
1 Co. each of 2/27th, 1/40th, 97th			
Harvey's Brigade	2,927		

11th Line (2 Batts.), 23rd Line (2 Batts.), 1st Batt. L.L.L.

Hamilton's Portuguese Division		= 4,819
Fonseca's Brigade	2,429	
2nd Line (2 Batts.), 14th Line (2 Batts.)		
Campbell's Brigade	2,390	
4th Line (2 Batts.), 10th Line (2 Batts.)		
Alten's Independent German Brigade		= 1,098
1st Light and 2nd Light Batt., K.G.L.		
Collins's Independent Portuguese Brigade		= 1,385
5th Line (2 Batts.), 5th Cacadores		

CAVALRY   1,146 British   849 Portuguese   = 1,995
British: 3rd D.G., 4th Dragoons, 13th L.D.
Portuguese: 1st, 5th, 8th, 7th Line

ARTILLERY   225 British   221 Portuguese   = 446
4 British and K.G.L. Batteries—24 Guns
2 Portuguese Batteries—12 Guns

SPANISH ARMIES UNDER BLAKE AND CASTAÑOS   TOTAL = 14,644

INFANTRY		= 12,593
Three Divisions (Blake)	10,815	
One Brigade (Castaños)	1,778	
CAVALRY		= 1,886
Loy (Blake)	1,165	
Penne Villemur (Castaños)	721	
ARTILLERY		= 165
One Battery (Blake)	103	
One Battery (Castaños)	62	

FRENCH ARMY UNDER SOULT   TOTAL = 24,260

INFANTRY   = 19,015

UNIT	BATTALIONS	PERSONNEL
Girard's Division	9	4,254
Gazan's Division	10	4,183
Werle's Brigade	9	5,621
Goudinot's Brigade	6	3,924
Grenadier Brigade	—	1,033

```
CAVALRY                                        =  4,012
   Three Brigades and three unattached Regiments
ARTILLERY, TRAIN, STAFF, ETC.                   =  1,233
```

		ALLIED LOSSES		
NATION	KILLED	WOUNDED	MISSING	TOTAL
British	882	2,773	544	4,199
Portuguese	102	261	26	389
Spanish	258	1,110	—	1,368
				5,956

FRENCH LOSSES

The official return of French casualties to units shows a total of 5,936.
Oman, IV, 395 and 635, states that this cannot be complete, for it
conflicts with Martinien's exact list by name, rank, and battalion. Soult
gives the number as 241 officers, but with no further details; Martinien
lists 362 officers and 'others' in detail. Oman estimates French casualties
at a total of 7,900; *Fortescue*, VIII, 208, says, 'fully eight thousand'.
In his first dispatch to the Emperor, Soult stated his casualties to have
been '2,800 killed and wounded'; on 6th July 1811, he filed a detailed
return showing 5,936. Even the partisan French historians, Belmas and
Lapene, place Soult's actual losses at 7,000.

TOPOGRAPHICAL OBSERVATIONS

*The predominantly flat terrain surrounding the town of Albuera is little
changed. The two streams which converge to form the Albuera river, the high
ground between them, and the probable point of the main French crossing of
this tongue of land, can all be determined with ease. The 'hill' on which most
of the fighting took place is little more than a tract of rolling arable land.
Beresford's dispositions are certainly open to question by anyone walking over
this battlefield.*

XII

CIUDAD RODRIGO AND BADAJOZ

THE tide of war commenced to turn when Massena began his retreat from Sobral in October 1810. The victories at Albuera and Fuentes established Allied ascendancy in both corridors between Spain and Portugal. This was not apparent at the time; the French still seemed to be winning. There were at least 250,000 French soldiers present with their units in Spain; Napoleon was capable of pouring further tens of thousands into the Peninsula. The Anglo-Portuguese army was not more than a fifth the size of the French. Every Spanish army that had taken the field had been defeated. In all Spain, only Cadiz and Valencia held out; all other areas were either already dominated by French armies, or incapable of defending themselves against enemy thrusts.

The French had failed in their onslaught upon Portugal, but they still held Ciudad Rodrigo and Badajoz; from either of these fortresses they could advance again. If Wellington was to undertake an offensive himself, these towns must be recaptured.

The situation in Spain was not so bad from Wellington's point of view as it might seem. The guerrillas controlled more territory than the French. These irregulars were not only a nuisance to the enemy, but in their way were militarily effective and useful to Wellington.[1] If the French could be forced to concentrate, the guerrillas could overpower small garrisons, take over civil control of large areas, and spread insurrection against the French even into regions long ruled by Joseph's puppet government, which, if allowed to work undisturbed at the civil

---

[1] Julian Sanchez operated mainly between Salamanca and the Portuguese border, and was most useful to Wellington. But there were many others, particularly in the mountainous north and south; all passed along information, isolated and killed enemy soldiers. See *Oman*, V, 611–18 for a fascinating description of dispatches captured largely by guerrillas and preserved by George Scovell, Wellington's cipher expert.

and political conquest of Spain, would probably accomplish it. Wellington and the Anglo-Portuguese army could by forcing the French to concentrate, keep alive the spirit of Spanish resistance.

The later part of the year 1811, after Fuentes and Albuera, was remarkable for manoeuvre; large French armies concentrated, but were not able to catch Wellington at a disadvantage; nor were they willing to fight him in positions he had chosen. The Allied southern army recommenced the siege of Badajoz on 19th April. Wellington brought south, by way of his lateral communications inside Portugal, sufficient reinforcements to make up for the heavy casualties at Albuera.[1] Spencer was again left in command of the northern army, but with detailed and specific instructions which would enable him to avoid battle.

Badajoz was still short of supplies. The French would have to go to its aid promptly or it would fall into the hands of the Allies. As Wellington foresaw, Soult's Army of the South and Marshal Marmont, who had succeeded Massena in command of the Army of Portugal, co-operated to relieve Badajoz. Soult had 80,000 men in Andalusia. He held Seville in strength and had smaller garrisons at Cordoba, Granada, and Jaen. This left not more than 25,000 men as a field army. Marmont in the centre, behind Ciudad Rodrigo, had 35,000 men and fewer responsibilities. Bessieres with 60,000 men had to hold in subjection not only the most enterprising and able of the guerrillas, but also some of the most rugged territory, which extended from Salamanca to the Bay of Biscay.

Early in June, Wellington heard that Soult was marching north again toward Badajoz. Spencer also wrote to advise him that Marmont was moving west. Wellington considered this highly unlikely, and warned Spencer that it was probably a feint. Actually, Marmont imposed upon Spencer to the extent of causing him to blow up Almeida again, destroy supplies, and retreat before half his strength.[2] Marmont's reason for such a manoeuvre was to enable him to transfer most of his army to the valley of the Guadiana. Wellington had anticipated this, and planned to defend the northern corridor mainly with Portuguese militia. He had his entire field army, including Spencer, concentrated within one march of Badajoz by 13th June.

[1] There were several roads, but the Tagus was usually crossed at Villa Velha. Portalegre to the south of that river and Penamacor to the north were road junctions.

[2] Wellington wrote to Spencer on 8th and 9th June 1811 concerning the true nature of Marmont's movements. *Dispatches*, VII, 651-2. He speaks in frank displeasure on the 10th, ibid., 652, and the 11th, ibid., VIII, 1-2, of the destruction of Almeida. Spencer, according to *Harry Smith*, I, 47, was an 'old woman' and by no means up to Beresford and Hill, who had just returned to take command of his old 'corps'.

The second siege of Badajoz was going badly. Ground had been broken on 29th May both north and south of the Guadiana. Since time was short, Wellington had to attack those parts of the defences which, if taken, would be immediately decisive. The San Christobal fort north of the river and the Castle to the south were chosen, but they were the two strongest sections of the fortifications (Plate 30).

The Allied army laboured under several disadvantages. The northern approaches to San Christobal had to be made in an area almost completely bare of soil. The British engineer officers not only lacked practical knowledge of siege operations, but had neither trained sappers and miners nor proper equipment.[1]

Wellington solved the problem of erecting siege works on bare rock by using bales of unwashed fleece freshly sheared. These were found to stop cannonballs as well as clay-filled gabions, and were more resistant to weather. Fire was opened on 4th June, but ranges were overlong for breaching.[2] The ancient Portuguese siege pieces, the only guns available at first, were all inaccurate; some blew up, blew out vents, or drooped at the muzzle.[3]

An effort was made to storm San Christobal on the night of the 6th. This failed, for the French had removed from the ditch all debris knocked from the wall (Plate 29). The storming party had to first climb down into the ditch, cross it, and then set their ladders on the other side under a constant heavy fire from the admirably handled, efficient garrison. Besides, the ladders were too short. An inaccurate, long range bombardment was continued both on San Christobal and the castle; another unsuccessful attack on the former was delivered on the night of the 9th. In each of these attacks the total number of Allies engaged was less than 500. Casualties were a little over 200; a high proportion of those involved.

On the 10th, fire from the batteries was more effective; some iron guns brought up from Lisbon were in action for the first time. The breach in the castle wall was soon practical.[4] But Wellington had just received definite intelligence of the probable junction of Soult, D'Erlon and Marmont in the neighbourhood of Badajoz within a week in such

[1] The British army, unlike all other major European forces at that time, lacked specially trained siege units; the necessary tools were limited in number and poor in quality.

[2] In excess of 650 yards.

[3] Both *Oman*, IV, 419, and *Fortescue*, VIII, 222-3, describe in detail these deplorable siege pieces which were 100 years old, brass, and cast in poor moulds.

[4] The term 'practical' in siege terminology indicates that a soldier could enter by the breach without using his hands.

1. *A typical ox-cart of the type used by Wellington. The wooden axle was solidly connected to both wheels, and revolved in two wooden journals.*

2. *Rolica valley from the southern fortifications of Obidos.*

3. *Delaborde's second position at Roliça lay on the central section of these hills; the two larger breaks in the ridge protected the French flanks.*

4. The French second position at Roliça seen from the village of Columbeira. The central cleft was the defile entered by Lake.

5. The Maceiras river and the hills northwest of Vimiero, which lies on the far side of these ridges; here British reinforcements came ashore.

6. *A section of the old road along which
Sir John Moore's army retreated to Corunna.*

7. *The long bridge across the Tagus at Talavera. This structure, important in 1809, now abandoned.*

8. *The Paja de Vegara in the centre of the Allied position at Talavera from west of the Portina.*

9. *The Casa de Salinas (or Serranillas) east of Talavera.*

10. The Roman bridge across the Tagus at Alcantara. After being blown up early in the war, it was kept in operation by a simple form of suspension-bridge.

11. The town of Arzobispo and the bridge spanning the Tagus. The fortifications which rose on either side of the main arches have been demolished.

12. The terrain over which Ney's corps attacked at Busaco. The village to the right is Sula. Craufurd and the Light Division were on the summit of the hill to the left.

13.
The southern end of the Busaco ridge from an adjacent ridge occupied initially by the Allies. The area shown here was not fought over during the battle.

14. *The chapel just south of the village of San Antonio de Cantara, scarred during the battle of Busaco. Portuguese artillery from the main ridge to the west controlled this area.*

15. *The road by which Massena turned Wellington's left flank after Busaco. This road is now used only by ox-carts and pedestrians.*

16.

A ruin, typical of the earth and masonry fortifications erected on hillcrests across the Lisbon peninsula in 1809 and 1810 to form the Lines of Torres Vedras.

17. A view from the citadel of Torres Vedras looking west along the valley of the Zizandre, showing ruins of first line fortifications on the skyline.

18. *Fort Concepcion showing the main entrance
and one of the original breaches.*

19. *Another view of Fort Concepcion. This structure was blown up in 1810
but was used by the Light Division intermittently for the next three years.*

20. The 'main street' in Fuentes de Onoro. The whole village is, and was, a maze.

21. The church, Poço Velho, south of Fuentes de Onoro. Allied troops were thrust from this village by Messena's left flank attack on 3rd May.

strength that the Allies would have to retire into Portugal.[1] To take the city and have insufficient time to repair its fortifications would only waste those lives lost in the assault. Wellington ordered the siege to be given up and all useful *matériel* to be moved into Elvas.[2]

Wellington placed his army in a carefully chosen position stretching from Elvas northeast for 15 miles through Campo Maior, a strong minor fortress, to Ouguela (Plates 25, 26 and 32). The river Caia ran at a right angle through this position at its mid-point.[3] There were convenient crests and reverse slopes with good, concealed lateral communications behind. The flanks were protected by fortified places and were hard to turn. A line of old Moorish watchtowers near the border had been occupied as semaphore stations; orders could be sent to any unit in the Allied army from headquarters in a few minutes.

Wellington had no more than 44,000 men, but his position was as strong as Busaco. Marmont and Soult, who were known to have joined forces at Merida on 18th June, had at least 60,000. They entered Badajoz on the 20th, the day on which the garrison's provisions were finally exhausted. On the 22nd and 23rd, the two French marshals made a reconnaissance in force against the Allied positions on the Caia. The local fighting did not please Wellington; Long, with his usual inefficiency mishandled some raw British squadrons and retreated precipitately. But the French did not press their advantage; the British cavalry lost a few troopers and some excellent horses.

From the French point of view, this reconnaissance was a failure. They saw scattered British and Portuguese soldiers and guns on hill crests, but had little idea of what lay behind. The two marshals were convinced, however, that Wellington was not going to retire further. They could attack the Allies here, or retreat, but the French system of supply would not allow them to remain concentrated for more than a few days. Besides, a prolonged absence by Soult from the south could be fatal to his personal aspirations to rule a kingdom.[4]

On the 27th Wellington heard that the French had blown up the

[1] D'Erlon was subordinate to Soult, but had been operating independently.

[2] The Portuguese fortress is only eleven miles from Badajoz; everything was taken back except the heavy timber gun platforms.

[3] This position was strong, but unpleasant. *Schaumann*, 312, says, 'All day long we were infested by snakes, blowflies, and other vermin, while our water came from a dirty stream known as the River Caya, in which the whole army bathed, the cattle went to drink, and dirty clothes were washed. At night we were plagued by scorpions, mosquitoes, and a piercingly cold wind.'

[4] Both in Portugal in 1809 and in Andalusia later, Soult aspired to a crown after the style of Murat and Bernadotte.

captured border fort of Olivenza and sent an infantry division southeast of Valverde. The marshals would not have done either if they were planning an attack on the Caia. Two days later, Soult with at least one more infantry division was reported in motion towards Seville.

For a time Marmont held a position on both banks of the Guadiana at Badajoz with 47,000 men. An Allied attack in the open plain against a considerable cavalry superiority would be dangerous. Wellington knew that his adversary was short of food and could not remain concentrated any length of time unless he subsisted on supplies brought into Badajoz. The French army retired north and east on 15th July.

Wellington did not renew the siege of Badajoz now that it was well supplied. Instead, he placed his troops in cantonments along his lateral communications between the northern and southern corridors. The army had possessed a modern siege train for years, but it had remained afloat on transports in Portuguese harbours. On 18th July, the C-in-C ordered it to be unloaded at Oporto, taken up the Duero as far as possible by boat, and then carried overland toward Almeida.[1] Ciudad Rodrigo was to be his next objective.

Wellington personally moved north early in August and established his headquarters at Fuenteguinaldo on the 12th. Hill was left in command of the southern corridor. Sir Thomas Graham, the victor of Barrosa, came north from Cadiz to replace Spencer who went home on sick leave.[2] Ciudad Rodrigo was blockaded, but no siege operations were undertaken for the time being.

Marmont was soon reported to be concentrating in the vicinity of Salamanca; Dorsenne, who had replaced Bessieres in command of the Army of the North, was marching south with part of the latter force; both marshals obviously intent on relieving and revictualling Ciudad Rodrigo. They would have at least 50,000 troops between them to oppose no more than 46,000 Allies.[3] This French junction took place on the 23rd in the valley of the Tormes.

[1] The overland stage started at Lamego and ended temporarily at Villa de Ponte, twelve miles short of Trancoso. The whole operation was under Major Dickson's supervision, who required 160 river boats and over 1,000 carts.

[2] This was about as close as Wellington was ever able to come to replacing an unsatisfactory lieutenant with a more able man. But Graham already had sufficient seniority to take independent command of several divisions when necessary. The C-in-C wished to use him as Hill's counterpart in the north.

[3] On 3rd September, Wellington received an intercepted dispatch from Foy, now one of Marmont's divisional commanders, giving many details of French plans.

Then Wellington received intelligence indicating a total enemy force of about 60,000 men. It would be as imprudent to fight Marmont and Dorsenne in the plain around Ciudad Rodrigo now as to have fought Massena here the year before, or to have fought Soult and Marmont near Badajoz. The blockade was given up; the Allied army moved southwest toward the mountains. An Allied force of 1,000 infantry, 500 cavalry, and two batteries of artillery fought 2,500 French cavalry and one battery on 25th September at El Bodon. The results were creditable to the discipline and training of the Allied infantry and the tactical ability of Wellington and the field officers involved. The action was similar to Craufurd's retreat at Fuentes de Onoro, but on a smaller scale.[1] The casualties were 149 to 200 in favour of the Allies.

The following day, Wellington took up a strong position at Fuenteguinaldo. He had chosen this some time before as the best available in the area; there were some old trenches along the hill-tops here. The position was strong, but the Allied force in it weak. Graham, in command of the northern wing of the army, was at least a day's march away. Craufurd had the Light Division, contrary to orders, in a dangerous situation which might become desperate if Wellington retreated. The C-in-C chose to oppose a further French advance with an inferior force rather than risk losing the Light Division.

Marmont and Dorsenne were not aware of their opportunities; their reconnaissance was similar to that made by Marmont and Soult on the Caia in June. They had seen nothing other than the usual fringe of troops and guns along the hill-tops. Wellington seemed ready to fight for every foot of his position. Again the French decision was not to attack. Craufurd came up in the early afternoon.[2]

Wellington could have had his entire army in position at Fuenteguinaldo by daylight of the 27th; he chose, however, to retreat that night to an even stronger position inside Portugal across the great bend of the Coa. The French army also retired shortly after dark, but the commander of the rearguard noticed that the Allied campfires appeared to be going out, and investigated. As soon as Marmont realized that

[1] The Allied units involved were 1st Hussars, K.G.L., two squadrons 11th L.D., 2/5th, 77th, and 2/83rd. One of the Portuguese batteries was lost temporarily, but retaken.

[2] *Oman*, IV, 573, note 2, 'Wellington was vexed that the Light Division had not done the night march, and, according to Larpent's Journal (p. 85, 3rd edition) observed to Craufurd, with some asperity, "I am glad to see you safe." The answer was, "Oh! I was in no danger, I assure you." "But I was, from your conduct," answered Wellington. Upon which Craufurd observed, "He's d——d crusty today." ' *Fortescue*, VIII, 265, and Rev. A. H. Craufurd, *General Craufurd and His Light Division*, 184, repeat the story and give the same reference.

Wellington was retreating, he countermanded his own orders and advanced in pursuit. He was brought up short on the morning of the 28th by the Allied army in its new position.

Wellington was no longer bluffing; he was now anxious to be attacked in spite of the odds, but Marmont retired cautiously and allowed Ciudad Rodrigo to be isolated again; there was no other strongly held French post nearer than Salamanca.

On 22nd October, Hill advanced into Spain south of the Tagus; by a series of hard marches and skilful manoeuvres in atrocious weather he destroyed a force of some 2,500 Frenchmen at Arroyo Molinos. On 4th November, he returned with more than 1,300 prisoners, after inflicting between 700 and 800 other casualties, at a cost of just over 100 men of his own Anglo-Portuguese force. Hill had been able to accomplish this mission in part because his advance into Spain was not detected by the French until too late for their countermeasures to be effective.

Towards the close of the year, Wellington learned of impending transfers from Marmont's army to Suchet's for use in Valencia. By this time, the British siege train was close behind the Allied front. On 8th January 1812, the Allied army suddenly pushed forward to begin the siege of Ciudad Rodrigo.[1]

This town was oval in shape, about 700 by 550 yards, and occupied the entire top of a flat hill more than 100 feet above and to the north of the river Agueda. It was surrounded originally by massive masonry walls. There was no central citadel, but an ancient castle rose immediately adjacent to the river, overlooking the bridge.

By the beginning of the nineteenth century such masonry walls, no matter how thick and substantial, could not withstand siege artillery. They could be covered, however, by a complicated system of earth and masonry outworks which made them much more formidable.[2] Ciudad Rodrigo had been so modernized, but because of the height of the hill on which the original walls were built, the new outworks gave them only partial protection (Plate 27). There was no question, however, that

[1] *Harry Smith*, I, 55, says that Wellington widely 'advertised' a field 'sports day' to be held on the 8th at Fuenteguinaldo so as to lull the French into false security.

[2] There were several systems of providing these outworks; the most famous is described by Sebastian Vauban, *The New Method of Fortifications*, many editions.

Details of Assault - 19ᵗʰ January 1812

1. Light Cᵒ 2/83ʳᵈ & 2ⁿᵈ Cacadores
2. 2/5ᵗʰ, 77ᵗʰ } CAMPBELL'S Brigade
   94ᵗʰ
3. MACKINNON'S Brigade
4. Light Division
5. PACK'S Independant Portuguese Brigade

The Light Division

Convent of San Francisco

Lesser breach

Greater Teson

French outwork taken by COLBORNE night of June 9ᵗʰ

Teson

MACKINNON'S Brigade

Great breach

Lesser

3ʳᵈ Divn

2/83ʳᵈ

94ᵗʰ

CAMPBELLS Brigade

Convent of Santa Cruz

3

77ᵗʰ

2/5ᵗʰ

CIUDAD RODRIGO

S Castle

Outwork

Bridge

Protective outworks added in 18ᵗʰ Century

Original walls

PACK

O'TOOLE

Agueda River

IX. CIUDAD RODRIGO

the town was strong; in the summer of 1810 it withstood the veteran French siege engineers with ample troops and *matériel* for twenty-five days of actual attack.

The principal weakness of Ciudad Rodrigo was that two connected hills known as the Lesser and Greater Tesons rose to the north at distances of 200 and 700 yards respectively. The Greater Teson was actually 14 feet higher than the ramparts. The French in 1810 had placed their first batteries here and ran communications trenches down to the lower hill directly in front, where they established additional batteries. They breached the walls and blew in the counterscarp by means of a mine.

Once in their hands, the walls were repaired and the trenches on the Tesons filled up. The French improved the works to some extent and placed a redoubt of considerable strength on the Greater Teson. They realized that the town was not impregnable, but counted on it holding out long enough for Marmont and Dorsenne to relieve it, as they had done in September. Wellington had to take it quickly, or not at all.

On the night of the 8th, Colborne with ten companies from the Light Division attacked the Greater Teson redoubt. These troops were not discovered until they were within 50 yards; four companies encircled the work, lay down at the top of the glacis, and fired at anyone who showed his head above the wall. Four more companies climbed down into the ditch, reset their ladders on the far side, and ascended; two companies burst through the palisade which always closed the rear of these outworks.[1] About the only resistance the garrison made was to throw grenades and shells over their walls blindly. The storm succeeded in 20 minutes. The garrison of some 60 men were almost all killed or captured; Colborne lost 26 only.

Immediately the redoubt fell, the Allies began working on trenches following in general the earlier French pattern.[2] The weather was cold, and the surface of the earth frozen to a depth of an inch or so. But the soil dug easily and piled well. The fire from the walls was continuous and heavy, for the garrison still had Massena's original siege train which provided ample guns and ammunition. However, the Allied troops did their work with enough enthusiasm to make up for their lack of skill.[3]

[1] For obvious reasons, these outworks were built so as to be of as little use as possible to besiegers once they were captured. The garrison could quickly knock down the rear palisade with artillery fire from the main walls.

[2] Digging was easier; besides, the new masonry in the outer wall here was thought to be weaker than the older portions.

[3] Since there were no sappers and miners available, Wellington used line battalions.

Each division did duty for twenty-four hours within the trenches. They had not only to defend themselves against possible sorties, but also to extend the trenches under the direction of engineer officers, make gabions and fascines, and repair any damage done by the heavy fire of the French. The Allied batteries opened on 13th January at about 4.30 p.m.; the enemy were driven from the fortified suburbs in vicious night fighting. Fire was interrupted by a heavy fog for twenty-four hours on the 16th, but great progress was made with the system of trenches. Rifle pits were placed in front of the incomplete 'second parallel' on the Lesser Teson from which marksmen could check the fire of the artillery on the town walls.

By the 19th, there was a breach in the same place as the French had made theirs, and another of smaller size some 250 yards west of it.[1] These appeared practical, although not as satisfactory as they might have been.[2] Wellington now ordered the artillery to seek out and destroy any guns which might be used against storming columns while he himself sat down in a trench to work out a plan for making an assault that night.

Picton's 3rd Division and Craufurd's Light Division were to attack the main breach and the lesser breach respectively.[3] The assault on the main breach would be preceded by two ingenious subordinate attacks. Campbell's Brigade was to advance from behind the Convent of Santa Cruz on the outworks in front of the main walls. The 2/5th, working its way between the river and the fortifications, would cut through the gate into the main ditch, mount the outer wall by means of scaling ladders, and sweep the French from the outer works as far as the main breach. Colonel O'Toole with the 2nd *Cacadores* and the Light Company of the 2/83rd was to advance south of the Agueda, cross the bridge, escalade in silence the outwork in front of the castle, and capture the two guns pointing west along the main wall[4] (Plate 28).

The 94th would attack the outworks 300 yards north of where the 2/5th struck, sweep along the outer ditch, and overpower any ravelins which might bear on the main breach. The remaining nine companies

---

[1] A tower had been knocked down near where the main road now enters the town.
[2] The breaches were far steeper than was desirable and the counterscarp only partially broken down; there were no close protected approaches.
[3] Both divisions were fresh for the assault, for at noon the 4th Division had relieved the 1st for general duty in the trenches.
[4] *Fortescue*, VIII, 358, emphasizes that these two pieces covered at their most effective range the first point to be attacked by the 2/5th. This is obvious to anyone going over these fortifications today.

of the 2/83rd were to man the western section of the second parallel and fire on the main walls, while the 77th would remain in reserve.

Mackinnon's Brigade was to storm the main breach from the eastern half of the second parallel. As soon as these troops moved out, their places were to be taken by the line battalions of Powers's Portuguese Brigade. Mackinnon would be supported on his left by three companies of Rifles who, after clearing any French-occupied ravelins in their area, would be firing on the main wall in the same manner as the 2/83rd, but at closer range.

The Light Division had similar detailed orders. They were to assemble behind the suburb of San Francisco; Vandeleur's Brigade (1/52nd, 2/52nd, 4 Cos. 1/95th, and 3rd *Cacadores*) would undertake the actual storming with Barnard's in close support. Pack's Independent Portuguese Brigade would meanwhile attack the eastern and opposite side of the town to the breaches; this diversion might or might not be pressed home according to the amount of resistance encountered.

The initial attacks began at about 7 p.m.[1] O'Toole took his outwork and the two enfilading cannon. The 2/5th, accompanied by the 77th by mistake, broke into the inner ditch, scaled the counterscarp against some opposition, and cleared the outworks. They reached the main breach before Mackinnon's men and were joined almost immediately by the 94th. Campbell launched his brigade up the mass of debris into the main breach followed by Mackinnon's Brigade.

These two brigades were stopped short at the top of the breach. The French had cut two ditches across the solid masonry of the terreplein ten feet wide by ten feet deep, isolating the breach itself. Behind each ditch, there were lateral breastworks at right-angles with undamaged parapets, each mounting 24-pounder howitzers. It was impossible to push straight on into the town without negotiating a 16-foot drop onto sharp obstacles and a new semi-circular wall from which a heavy fire was being maintained.

The head of the British column suffered grievously, not only from musketry and the howitzers, but also from shells set off by powder trains and thrown grenades. The survivors crossed both 'ditches' and took the French artillery pieces before they could fire a third time. The retrenchment to the right was crossed by planks found nearby; on the left, some wild men of Connaught discarded their muskets, helped each other across the masonry cleft, and fought with bayonets only.

Suddenly, a powerful explosion shattered the area. The French had

[1] O'Toole's was ten minutes earlier.

contrived to place a large mine directly under the breach which had been detonated when the situation seemed desperate. Many of the 3rd Division were blown up, Mackinnon among them. But the mine had been too powerful, and the French were likewise mutilated and the fortifications themselves were damaged. The two intermingled British brigades continued to enter the breach, and could now walk either into the town or along the walls.

Further east, the Light Division had assaulted the lesser breach. One artillery piece took them in the flank in a manner similar to that of the howitzers at the main breach, but fired only once. The lesser breach had neither 'ditches', secondary walls, nor was it mined. The garrisons delivered a heavy fire for a brief interval, and wounded both Vandeleur and Craufurd. But the French defence deteriorated rapidly. The Light Division cleared the walls and pushed the defenders back into the town so quickly that some of the 'Light Bobs' were close enough to the main breach to be burned by the explosion there.[1]

Meanwhile, both Pack and O'Toole had broken into the town. The entire French garrison, under General Barrie, surrendered with little further fighting. Considering the quality of the French veterans, the strength of the place, and the necessarily incomplete preparations, the assault could hardly have been more successful. It cost the Allies 568 casualties, a total of about 1,100 for the whole siege. The French lost approximately 530 killed and wounded; the rest of the garrison of 1,937 were taken prisoner.[2]

The Allied forces which stormed the city did not behave well. Three buildings were set on fire; soldiers drank themselves into insubordinate intoxication, some actually drowning in brandy casks. The incorrigibles set out to plunder private homes as well as French warehouses. But the riot was quelled long before morning. Picton himself, wielding a broken musket barrel, was damning all and sundry, and was ably assisted by officers who risked their lives to restore order. Apparently, no one in authority had considered that the unwritten privilege of storming parties might be claimed at Ciudad Rodrigo, a Spanish, not a French town. However, no Spanish civilians were killed and only a few physically molested.[3]

[1] Harry Smith, I, 57, was burned; he claimed that the 3rd Division required the help of the Light Division to take the main breach!
[2] Oman, V, 587.
[3] There is no doubt that this 'right' existed even in the British 'rules' of war. James Wolfe refers to it clearly in a letter to his mother in connexion with the siege of Louisbourg; Robert Wright, The Life of Major-General James Wolfe, London, 1864, 446.

Craufurd died from the wound received while directing his division from the top of the glacis close to the lesser breach. He was the most able of Wellington's lieutenants for some types of service. His record on outpost duty was brilliant; his handling of the Light Division at Busaco and at Fuentes was beyond praise.

The Light Division were to pay him an unique and unpremeditated tribute. In life, he had always been an exacting disciplinarian; he never allowed a formation to be broken or diverted, unless unavoidably, merely to avoid physical discomfort. Streams were forded in column. Officers were not to be carried over by their men, nor to seek out bridges. After burying Craufurd beneath the lesser breach, the Division, moving west to their encampment, came to a marshy pool about 50 yards wide around which the road looped. Instead of following the road, the leading files marched straight ahead, thigh deep in icy water. Every officer and man followed in silence. As a soldier's soldier, Craufurd rates high; Wellington and the Light Division were to miss him in the fighting which lay ahead.

Wellington set about filling in trenches, repairing breaches, installing an adequate Spanish garrison, and victualling the place. He wished to be ready, if Marmont and Dorsenne concentrated and attacked. Since Ciudad Rodrigo had fallen in twelve days, however, there was little likelihood of the French appearing before the middle of February. By that time, the fortifications would be as strong as ever.

Wellington now turned again to Badajoz. On 28th January 1812, he semaphored for his iron guns to be sent forward to Elvas from the coast, while his divisions passed along familiar roads to the south. By 26th February, only the 5th Division and the K.G.L. Hussars remained in the northern corridor. Wellington did not move south himself until 6th March so as to confuse the French as much as possible.

Reinforcements from Britain and additional regular Portuguese units increased the Allied field army in the southern corridor to almost 60,000 men. The French force in the area under D'Erlon was much weaker and retired south leaving the Badajoz garrison to its own devices. Graham with 19,000 men was sent to the south in pursuit of D'Erlon and would at the same time observe Soult in Andalusia. Hill with 14,000 men was dispatched northeast toward Merida to watch out for Marmont.

Close investment of Badajoz south of the Guadiana was completed

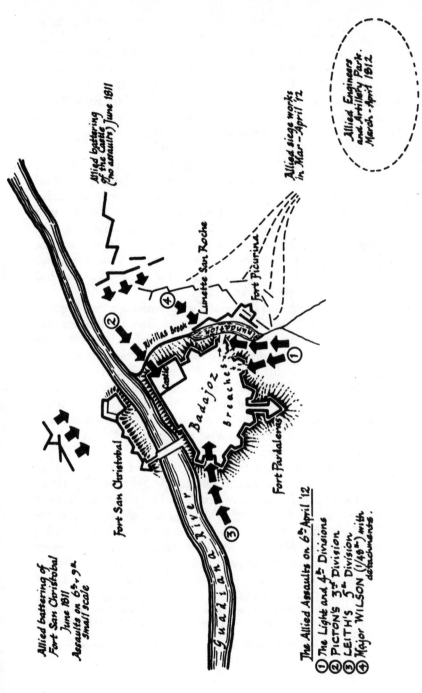

Allied battering of
Fort San Christobal
June 1811
Assaults on 6ᵗʰ-9ᵗʰ
Small scale

Fort San Christobal

Guadiana River

Allied battering of
the Castle
(no assaults) June 1811

Urrillas brook

Fort San Roche

Fort Picuriña

Allied siege works
in Mar.-April '12

Badajoz
Breaches

Rivillas

Fort Pardaleras

Allied Engineers
and Artillery Park.
March-April 1812

The Allied Assaults on 6ᵗʰ April '12
① The Light and 4ᵗʰ Divisions
② PICTON's 3ᵗʰ Division
③ LEITH's 5ᵗʰ Division
④ Major WILSON (1/48ᵗʰ) with
   detachments.

X. BADAJOZ

on 17th March. Wellington made a personal reconnaissance of its defences on both banks of the river and noticed that the French had made several changes since the previous June. The Pardaleras outwork had been strengthened and was now attached to the main defences; substantial earthworks had been raised in front of the southwestern fortifications. The southeastern face of the town had been strengthened by an outwork on the far side of the Rivillas brook known as Fort Picurina. This stream had been damned so as to inundate the approaches to the main walls for a distance of about 600 yards.

Wellington decided to break into Badajoz from the southeast; neither the castle nor Fort San Christobal was to be battered.[1] Colonel Dickson, who had commanded the artillery successfully at Ciudad Rodrigo, was again in charge of the guns. Colonel Fletcher, who supervised the construction of the Lines of Torres Vedras, was chief engineer. Even though the army still lacked miners and sappers, artillery engineer's *matériel* was in plentiful supply. Time was not so short as it had been at Ciudad Rodrigo; the Badajoz garrison had provisions for only seven weeks.

At dusk on the 17th, in wild rain and wind, working parties began to open the first parallel no more than 200 yards from the Picurina outwork; their communication trenches stretched back over the San Miguel hill. The weather drowned the sound of picks and shovels. By morning, the first parallel was defensible and covered the continuing digging behind. But Phillipon, the French governor, was a man of unusual ability and industry and battered down the newly-raised parapet with a storm of fire. That night it was replaced; two batteries were laid out in front. But the French extended their earthworks also, so as to impede seriously Allied working parties next day.

At 1 p.m. on the 19th, a French sally from Fort Picurina and the Lunette San Roche nearer the Guadiana surprised the working parties unarmed and up to their hips in water. Considerable damage was done and entrenching tools carried off.[2] There was no panic; covering forces advanced and pushed the French back behind their earthworks with a loss of 180 men including 13 officers. The Allied casualties were about 150, including Colonel Fletcher, who was seriously wounded. A musket ball hit his money purse, forcing a Spanish silver dollar an

[1] Wellington was never better informed as to enemy dispositions. A French sapper sergeant had deserted to the British with plans showing the position of many newly constructed mines. However, Wellington's choice of positions to be attacked has been criticized often.

[2] Knowing of the scarcity of these in the Allied army, Phillipon paid bounties for them.

inch into his groin. It was said that the most painful of injuries for a Scot was to be hit in the purse!

The first parallel, which initially ran roughly east and west in front of Fort Picurina, was now extended north toward the Guadiana, bringing the entire southeastern side of Badajoz under fire from a distance of less than 700 yards. Phillipon, seeing that no operations were being conducted against Fort San Christobal on the other side of the Guadiana, ordered his garrison to extend an earthwork to the east so as to enfilade with field guns the Allied operations south of the river. Wellington countered on the 22nd by ordering Leith's 5th Division to invest San Christobal; the temporary earthwork was immediately abandoned by the French. The same afternoon, rain fell with such violence that the Allies were flooded from their trenches. The Guadiana rose several feet and swept away their pontoon bridge, cutting Wellington's army in two.

The weather cleared on the afternoon of the 24th. That night six batteries of artillery in front of the 1st parallel were armed with 28 heavy cannon. At 11 a.m. next day they opened fire, mainly on the Picurina works. Phillipon replied with every cannon that would bear, but Wellington now had guns far more efficient and powerful than the ancient Portuguese bronze pieces used in the two earlier sieges. Fort Picurina was silenced and its ramparts suffered great damage. The French could be seen occasionally making frantic efforts to clear away debris and restore the parapets, but the Allies stormed the place soon after nightfall.

Instead of climbing down into the ditch, taking the ladders across it, resetting them, and then ascending the other side, a detachment of the 3rd Division found that they could balance them on the lip of the ditch and then let them fall forward to form a bridge to the parapet. In a moment, three ladders stretched across, swaying and bending, but holding as the infantry ran over. The fort was carried, although a simultaneous attack in the rear failed. The French garrison of about 250 were mostly casualties, but the Allies lost as many. Phillipon tried to retake the place, but was beaten back.

Additional batteries were established, one in the gorge of Fort Picurina; the main walls of Badajoz were now exposed to fire in the sector of Wellington's choice. By 30th March, a total of 38 guns were firing on the bastions of Santa Maria and Trinidad and the wall between, but Allied losses were heavy from courageous and efficient French counter manoeuvres. The inundated Rivillas brook prevented the Allies from using saps and mines, even if they had known how to dig them. But there was plenty of ammunition for a continual pounding of the walls. Wellington was informed on 6th April that the three breaches would be practical by nightfall.

Badajoz was taking more time than Wellington had expected. Soult was stirring to the south, but Graham was capable of holding him back. A more serious situation was developing in the north where Marmont was threatening Ciudad Rodrigo. Although Marmont had no siege train, he might be able to scrape together enough siege pieces to impose on Carlos de España.[1] General Imaz's stupid and unnecessary surrender of Badajoz the year before did not inspire Wellington with confidence.

Badajoz would have to be stormed without further delay, although if the French fought courageously, as must be expected, the cost would be high.[2] With a heavy heart, Wellington gave orders for a general assault that evening. It was at first scheduled for 7.30 p.m., but was postponed to 10 p.m. Of five separate assaults, only two would be made on the breaches; the Light and 4th Divisions were to storm these. Picton's 3rd Division was to escalade the castle, and Leith's 5th Division would climb over the walls at the northwest corner of the town. The important Lunette San Roche, which protected the dam across the Rivillas, was also to be attacked by about 1,000 men under Major Wilson of the 1/48th.

The Light and 4th Divisions marched across a narrow, open corridor towards the two breaches only to find that all debris had been cleared away from the ditches; there was enough water in some places to drown the men.[3]

> 'The first shot from us brought down such a hail of fire as I shall never forget, nor ever saw before or since. It was most murderous. We flew down the ladders and rushed at the breach,

[1] Wellington had turned over the captured Spanish fortress to General Carlos de España after making temporary repairs. He was given money to pay for new masonry walls and ample supplies for a strong garrison was delivered into the magazines for emergency use. De España issued the food for regular use and had hardly started on repairing the stonework.

[2] Some critics assume that Wellington was not aware of his faulty preparations, and was ignorant of proper siege procedure. This is patently ridiculous. Few generals knew more of the theory of war in all its forms, but a commander's knowledge cannot make up for the lack of experienced engineer officers and NCO's, nor for skilful spademen proud of their special abilities. British Line infantry hated the work and considered it beneath them.

[3] The centre and easiest breach was ignored.

but we were broken, and carried no weight with us, although every soldier was a hero. The breach was covered by a breastwork from behind, and ably defended on the top by chevaux-de-frises of sword-blades, sharp as razors, chained to the ground; while the ascent to the top of the breach was covered with planks with sharp nails in them. However, devil a one did I feel at this moment. One of the officers of the forlorn hope, Lieut. Taggart of the 43rd, was hanging on my arm—a mode we adopted to help each other up, for the ascent was most difficult and steep. A Rifleman stood among the sword-blades on the top of one of the chevaux-de-frises. We made a glorious rush to follow, but, alas! in vain. He was knocked over. My old captain, O'Hare, who commanded the storming party, was killed. All were awfully wounded except, I do believe, myself and little Freer of the 43rd. I had been some seconds at the revetement of the bastion near the breach, and my red-coat pockets were literally filled with chips of stones splintered by musket-balls. Those not knocked down were driven back by this hail of mortality to the ladders.' [1]

Although more than forty separate attacks appear to have been made, no single Allied soldier passed the sword barriers; the ditches and the breach slopes were clogged with dead and wounded.

Meanwhile, Picton and the 3rd Division were escalading the castle. At first, their ladders were either thrown back, or the men who ascended killed at the top. Other positions were found and a lodgement was made in a single embrasure; a handful of British infantry fought desperately against frantic efforts of the garrison to push them off the battlements. Every few seconds another man climbed up the single ladder. As the hold on the walls widened, other ladders were set up; the 3rd Division carried the castle completely, although Picton and many of his men were casualties.

Leith and the 5th Division were more than an hour late in commencing their attack. Initially, their efforts, like those of Picton, met stubborn opposition and failed. But officers and men continued to reset and mount their ladders regardless of casualties. Suddenly, they too were successful. Leith's men pressed impetuously round the walls and through the city to take the breaches from behind. Picton's men joined Leith's in firing on the defenders from the rear. French resistance collapsed; Phillipon collected all the men he could and retreated across

[1] *Harry Smith*, I, 64-5.

the river to Fort San Christobal, but he had no rations there and surrendered next morning. Of the original garrison of 5,003, about 4,500 effectives, only a handful of cavalry escaped to take news of the disaster to Soult.

Had Picton or Leith broken into the town earlier, the storming of the breaches would have been unnecessary. Even Wilson's attack on the Lunette and Rivillas dam, which was completely successful, would have forced a French surrender. But each of the five assaults gained much from the others; it is hardly conceivable that any one could have succeeded alone.

Of the 4,760 Allied casualties suffered during the siege, the Light and 4th Divisions lost 2,500 at the breaches. Picton and Leith sustained only about half as many. Wellington lost more British soldiers in taking Badajoz than in any major battle except Talavera and Albuera.[1] More men fell at the breaches in two hours than were lost at Busaco or Fuentes.

The British and Portuguese troops who finally flowed into the town went out of control.

> 'The place was eventually completely sacked by our troops; every atom of furniture broke; beds ripped open in search of treasure; and one street literally strewed with articles, knee deep. A convent was in flames, and the poor nuns in dishabille, striving in vain to burrow themselves into some place of security; however, that was impossible; the town was alive and every house filled with mad soldiers from the cellar to the once solitary garret.'[2]

This was no temporary lapse in discipline, but a beastly mutiny which lasted altogether for forty-eight hours. It made no difference that Badajoz was a friendly town. Females of all ages were raped; children were foully murdered. Officers who tried to restrain their men were shot. Yet to condemn is to fail to understand one of the horrid truths of war. Soldiers who face death in mounting breaches such as those at Badajoz are maddened; for milleniums such men have behaved abnormally immediately afterwards. Furthermore, civilians in this part of

[1] Comparative British casualties: Talavera—5,365, Albuera—4,159, Siege of Badajoz—3,660, Vitoria—3,475, Salamanca—3,127, Storming of Badajoz—2,983 (2 hours).
[2] *Maxwell's Peninsular Sketches*, I, 285–6.

Spain had been hostile to British troops since Talavera. The larger Spanish towns were often pro-French; civilians in Badajoz had fired on Allied soldiers.

Severe losses and the misbehaviour of British troops should not obscure the astonishing success of Wellington's operations. Ciudad Rodrigo fell in twelve days and Badajoz after twenty. Central Spain was now open to Allied attack. As if to emphasize this shift to an overall offensive, Wellington had taken the French siege train in Ciudad Rodrigo and captured in Badajoz their main pontoon train. The means of making offensive war were lost to the French; the tide had truly turned. Wellington had manoeuvred and applied his 60,000 men so as to confound three times as many French veterans under four of Napoleon's most illustrious marshals. He gave not only hope but many opportunities to the Spanish people to help themselves. The guerrillas took full advantage of them.

TOPOGRAPHICAL OBSERVATIONS

This campaign area can now be covered by using modern paved roads which follow the old ones fairly closely. At Ciudad Rodrigo, the castle is now a state-owned hotel. From a bedroom there, one can toss an orange onto the exact position of the two guns taken by O'Toole. The repairs made by Wellington at the main breach can be recognized easily from the Greater Teson. The narrow streets within the old town can be negotiated with early nineteenth century military maps.

Badajoz has grown, but the old fortifications remain, including the castle, Fort San Christobal, and certain walls. The breaches were repaired, but the walls themselves have been in part taken down. The town is a sad, depressing place; memories of the tragedies of a century and a half ago seem to linger in the old streets.

XIII

SALAMANCA

Aᴼ sᴛᴇʀ the fall of Badajoz, Wellington turned his attention to Marmont's threat to Ciudad Rodrigo, Almeida, and Castelo Branco. The French were quickly thrust back into central Spain.[1] A substantial section of that country was now in Allied hands.

Wellington set about consolidating the area occupied, particularly with regard to transportation. During the next two months, he cleared the Tagus and the Duero of impediments and blasted channels where necessary, enabling boats from Lisbon and Oporto to travel right across Portugal and into Spain. The Roman bridge at Alcantara was made serviceable.[2]

On 12th May 1812, Wellington sent Hill with three brigades of British and Portuguese infantry, a regiment of cavalry, and a battery of heavy artillery from Merida against fortified positions on both banks of the Tagus at Almaraz. The main French crossing place over the river west of Toledo was situated here.[3] Hill took the fort on the south side of the Tagus by surprise and forced the precipitate abandonment of that on the north (Plate 34). Direct communications between Soult and Marmont were severed.

---

[1] Marmont actually took Castelo Branco on 12th April, but retreated when he learnt of the fall of Badajoz. In recrossing the Agueda, he had a narrow escape, for Allied divisions were only a few hours behind him.

[2] This was a remarkable achievement involving the replacement of 30 yards of the central arch rising 140 feet above the river. Wellington discussed with Col. Sturgeon of the Royal Service Corps the possibility of using a form of suspension frequently employed in India. Sturgeon took 17 cartloads of materials from Elvas to Alcantara; a few days later, the bridge was carrying heavy artillery. Hand-operated capstans could adjust the cables for changes in length due to moisture; the whole thing could be taken up or set in place within a few hours when necessary.

[3] The original bridge was broken and not repaired, but the French were using a temporary pontoon structure. The other places where the French could have crossed the river, such as Talavera and Arzobispo, led to almost impassable roads south of the Tagus.

The news from northern Europe was mixed; Napoleon had enormous armies in being, but was finally resolved on invading Russia. There was plenty of local news too. Wellington's system of intelligence, and Scovell's ability in decoding cipher communications was particularly important at this time. The Emperor was reorganizing his units in Spain; all Polish battalions and squadrons were being replaced; the Imperial Guard was withdrawn. Joseph Bonaparte, with Marshal Jourdan as his Chief of Staff, was to command in Spain while Napoleon was in Russia.[1] The Intrusive king was not a military genius, nor did he have the drive of his younger brother, but he was neither cruel nor a fool. Even the most patriotic Spaniards called him 'Uncle Joe'; Wellington was impressed by his realism and common sense.[2]

The French armies in Spain were reduced to five. Suchet, who had finally taken the city of Valencia on 9th January 1812, had about 60,000 troops, all on or near the east coast. In central Spain, there were the Army of the North under Dorsenne, soon to be replaced by Caffarelli, and Marmont's Army of Portugal. These numbered 48,000 and 52,000 respectively. In Andalusia, the Army of the South, commanded by Soult, consisted of approximately 54,000, while Joseph with Jourdan had 18,500 men in and around Madrid. In all, there were more than 230,000 French soldiers fit for service and present with their units in spite of heavy casualties and some withdrawals. But there was much territory to hold against numerous, active, and now experienced guerrilla bands.

Wellington had slightly over 60,000 regulars. Even though outnumbered by four to one, he had several advantages, the most important of which were an efficient system of supply, command of the sea, the general goodwill of the Spanish people and the guerrillas, a vastly superior intelligence system, and a complete control of his command. The government at home now supported him to the limit of its ability. The organizations he had created in the Peninsula knew their jobs and were both reliable and loyal. Even his detractors were to some extent subdued.

Wellington could move against Soult in the south, or Marmont in the centre. The retaking of Andalusia offered political advantages. The

---

[1] The history of the French command in the Peninsula is a study in itself. Even though Joseph and Jourdan had nominal command for some long time, Napoleon had in fact been exercising overall control of half a dozen armies from Paris. This was ridiculous during active campaigning, for dispatches could take a month or more each way.

[2] 'Tio Pepe' in Spanish. Wellington studied a captured copy of Joseph's estimate of the military situation and found little to criticize: *Oman*, V, 303–8.

Supreme Junta of Spain was in Cadiz, which had been besieged for months. It would be relatively easy to free the city.[1] But Soult would probably just withdraw north and join Marmont, or northeast and combine with Suchet. Either concentration would mean a French army too strong to oppose in the plains, particularly in view of French cavalry superiority.

An advance on Marmont at Salamanca would threaten the main lines of French communications. Marmont could not give up central Spain. Even a check in this area would cause the French to make drastic adjustments elsewhere. Wellington realized, however, that the French were sure to try to reinforce their Army of Portugal, if the Allies moved against it from Ciudad Rodrigo. He planned to prevent this concentration against him by keeping other French forces occupied elsewhere.

In Soult's area, the Spanish regular army under Ballasteros was stirred into action directly, and by the Supreme Junta. Wellington, who was by this time corresponding with all Spanish army commanders, took pains to explain the advantages that he, Ballasteros, would gain from a joint offensive, even though separated by hundreds of miles.[2] This Spanish army in Andalusia was supplied with British munitions through Cadiz and Gibraltar. A similar effort was made to provoke the Spanish regular forces in the Asturias into taking the initiative, which would have the full co-operation of the Portuguese militia forces east of Oporto. At the least, French-held Astorga and Toro were to be besieged.

Guerrilla leaders throughout Spain were encouraged and supplied with arms where possible. This was particularly so on the Biscay coast where a British naval commander, Sir Home Popham, was to co-operate with the local guerrillas in besieging ports held by Caffarelli's garrisons. Popham, Porlier, and Longa were to conduct their operations in such a way that their forces appeared larger than they were. Two battalions of British marines and a battery of artillery were magnified to simulate an expeditionary army in size.

Wellington was also able to organize a diversion further east. Sir William Bentinck, commanding in Sicily, threatened a descent on Suchet's territory with an army composed of 17,000 British, Neapolitan, and Spanish troops. Bentinck accomplished little of a positive

---

[1] In fact, Wellington had been at some pains *not* to raise the siege. Nowhere in Spain except at Gibraltar could a French force be employed so uselessly. The city was situated at the end of a long isthmus, heavily fortified, and easily supplied by sea.

[2] With the passage of time, Wellington had begun to exert an influence on Spanish generals which approached actual command.

nature, but he and the guerrillas on the east coast kept Suchet from sending a single soldier into central Spain. Hill with 18,000 regulars was to hold the southern corridor.[1]

Early in June, Wellington assembled on the Agueda seven infantry divisions, Pack's and Bradford's Independent Portuguese Brigades, four cavalry brigades, and nine batteries—in all 48,000 men and 54 guns.[2] He advanced in three columns towards Salamanca before dawn on 13th June.

The Allies met no serious opposition, and entered the town early on the 17th. Marmont had constructed some fortifications in the western suburbs among university and religious buildings, and left them garrisoned when he retired. Wellington immediately laid siege to these, even though he had but three suitable guns with 100 solid shot for each. A single division, the 6th, under Clinton, was to conduct the siege; Wellington with the rest of the field army took up a position north of the city on a range of hills near the village of San Christobal, hoping that Marmont, whose army in the area almost equalled that of the Allies, would attack to save the Salamanca garrison.

On the evening of the 20th, Marmont advanced against San Christobal. The two armies were within artillery range on the 21st and the 22nd, but fought only a partial action over a single village which remained in Allied hands. The total combined casualties were less than 200. On the night of the 22nd, Marmont marched east; the armies had remained for more than forty-eight hours in close proximity without serious fighting.[3]

---

[1] Hill's 'corps', Powers's Independent Portuguese Brigade (until recently the garrison of Elvas), cavalry, and artillery.

[2] British, 28,000; Portuguese, 17,000; and 3,000 Spaniards (de España's Division which had been at Albuera).

[3] This situation was perhaps the most tantalizing of the Peninsular War for both commanders. Marmont almost attacked on the 22nd, but was dissuaded by Foy and Clausel, his two best divisional commanders. Many on Wellington's staff considered that the Allies should have attacked on the morning of the 21st when they had a numerical superiority of 8,000; this was neutralized by the arrival of Thomieres's and Foy's divisions during the afternoon. *Tomkinson*, 166, says,

'We could have attacked them with our whole force in half an hour, and their only chance of getting away was by defending the villages; by sending a large force against one we might have expected success, and so on to the other. Had they both been carried by us, they would then have had to cross the plain before a superior force. The opportunity for an attack was so favourable, we all agreed Lord Wellington had some unknown reasons for not availing himself of their situation.'

Meanwhile, the Salamanca fortifications had withstood one attack. Trenches and mines had been dug; Wellington brought up further supplies of ammunition for the three long iron 18-pounders, and some iron siege howitzers.[1] At dawn on the 27th, the French commander signalled to Marmont that he could hold out for no longer than three days. He was over-optimistic; the 18-pounders smashed the walls of one fort; the howitzers firing red hot shot set the other two on fire. All three were taken that afternoon. The Allied casualties (all British) were 430; French losses were 800, including 600 unwounded prisoners.

Wellington was now free to give Marmont his undivided attention; the French army was still close, within a half day's march, at Huerta, on the great bend of the Tormes. Cavalry, and Wellington's 'correspondents', reported that Marmont was moving southeast against Allied supply lines with at least two French divisions. After appropriate counter movements by Wellington the French drew off to the north, but he pressed after them the next day. The armies were separated by the Duero between Toro and Tordesillas, until 16th July.

During this interval, Wellington made good use of his intelligence facilities. He knew the strength of Marmont's force to within 100 men, the position of every other French unit in central Spain, the route and time of arrival of Marmont's 8th Division under Bonnet then moving south. When the latter came up, the contending armies would be numerically equal. But there were no further French reinforcements on the way; Wellington's diversions in the north and south were working to perfection. Both Caffarelli and Soult advised Joseph and Jourdan that not a man could be spared; Suchet was writing similarly from Valencia.

Joseph and Jourdan realized the serious consequences of even a drawn battle in central Spain. If Marmont were forced to retreat either north or east, they would be badly compromised. They decided to strip Castile of all garrisons except for those in Madrid and Toledo, and add 13,000 men to the Army of Portugal. Joseph marched northwest with this force on 21st July.[2]

Since Marmont was in ignorance of these reinforcements and had with Bonnet's arrival his entire army concentrated, he began on the

[1] These were powerful weapons capable of firing solid shot, different from the lighter brass field howitzers, although nominally of the same size, 24-pounders or 5·5-inch.

[2] This entire movement was unknown to Marmont; however, *Fortescue*, VIII, 480, and *Oman*, V, 383–5 do not agree as to how much Wellington knew of it. The intercepted cipher dispatch from Joseph to Soult of 26th May certainly indicates that such a movement would take place, but is not specific.

16th some complicated manoeuvres designed ultimately to throw the Allies back on Ciudad Rodrigo. The French army occupied the north bank of the Duero for about twenty miles. It marched west, crossed the river with a strong vanguard, and threatened the Allied left. Marmont then counter-marched his entire force east behind the Duero, crossed it again, and appeared in great strength on Wellington's right. This was all well done but accomplished nothing, for each threat was countered. It was characteristic of Wellington that he preferred to ride from one part of his army to another, explaining exactly what he wanted done, or even take personal command of a division for a few hours, rather than send orders to nervous detached subordinates.[1]

By the afternoon of the 18th, both armies were facing each other closed up in battle array, their lines running north and south but separated by the trickling Guarena river. Marmont began to move south; Wellington did the same. They were marching along parallel courses within artillery range of each other from dawn until 6 p.m. on the 20th, more than twenty miles under a pitiless sun, across the dry, dusty plain. Artillery was in action on both sides from time to time, but no serious fighting took place.

This gruelling operation indicated a slight French superiority in marching.[2] Marmont gained a few hundred yards on the Allies, but Wellington changed direction slightly to the west. By the evening, the Allied army was back in the San Christobal position, while Marmont occupied his earlier bivouac area at Huerta. If the French crossed the Tormes, Wellington would have to follow, or risk being cut off from Ciudad Rodrigo; Salamanca might have to be abandoned. The alternative was to attack the French, but this Wellington did not want to do unless he could secure some advantage. All was going well; why risk an even battle? Wellington cared nothing for his personal reputation. He was prepared to take all the criticism that would accompany a 'cowardly' retreat to Portugal rather than fight a battle on ground not

---

[1] One of these rides might have had serious consequences. The C-in-C and his staff found themselves in the midst of French cavalry. Even Beresford and Wellington had their swords drawn and were defending themselves until British cavalry galloped to the rescue. Had Wellington been killed, wounded, or taken, it is probable he would not have been succeeded by his brilliant military lieutenant, Sir Rowland Hill, nor by politically wise and logistically sound Sir William Beresford, but by the more senior Sir Stapleton Cotton of the cavalry. In spite of many soldierly and gentlemanly virtues, the latter had no conception of Wellington's way of making war, nor of battlefield command, let alone non-military problems.

[2] This ability of the French was more organizational than physical; every man in their army travelled lighter than his British counterpart and had less unit baggage.

of his own choosing. Meanwhile, he kept his army well in hand and was ready to seize any opportunity.

Early on the morning of the 21st Marmont was reported to be in motion south across the great bend of the Tormes. There are several fords at Salamanca as well as the Roman bridge, but for a distance of about twelve miles upstream to the next bridge at Alba de Tormes the river can be crossed without boats only at two fords near Huerta and adjacent to the right-angle bend. Marmont used these; Wellington crossed at Salamanca. A Spanish force under Wellington's orders occupied strong fortifications at Alba, covering the bridge there. By nightfall, the bulk of both armies was across the Tormes. The opposing cavalry pickets were in touch with each other on a line approximately 5,000 yards long.

An hour after dark, 100,000 men within a radius of three miles were exposed to a remarkable thunderstorm.

'It was late when the Light Division crossed the river, and the night came suddenly down with more than common darkness, for a storm, that common precursor of a battle in the Peninsula, was at hand. Torrents of rain deepened the ford, the water foamed and dashed with increasing violence, the thunder was frequent and deafening, the lightning passed in sheets of fire close over the column or played upon the points of the bayonets, and a flash falling amongst the fifth dragoon guards near Santa Maria killed many men and horses; hundreds of frightened animals then breaking loose from their piquet ropes and galloping wildly about were supposed to be the enemy's cavalry charging in the darkness, and indeed some of their patrols were at hand. But to a military eye there was nothing more imposing than the close and beautiful order in which the soldiers of that noble light division were seen by the fiery gleams to step from the river to the bank and pursue their march amidst this astounding turmoil, defying alike the storm and the enemy.' [1]

The territory inside the great bend of the Tormes north of Alba and east of Salamanca is roughly square, about nine miles on each side. The area is not particularly rugged, except for two hills, but is remarkably blind because of its rolling wooded nature. There are glacis-like slopes

[1] *Napier*, IV, 262. Every British diarist mentions this storm not only because of its violence, but also as an omen of victory.

where slightly tilted plains are open for up to two miles; there are also areas in which a division could be hidden from sight completely. Towards Alba there were cork, olive, and oak woods.

Two unusual hills known as the Arapiles dominate this area.[1] They extend east and west and are about 600 yards apart; they are steep, but not rugged, and are flat-topped. The Greater Arapile to the south is larger, slightly higher, and more isolated. The Lesser Arapile to the north has other high ground nearby. West of both Arapiles, at a distance of about 800 yards, there is a lower, flatter hill with the village of Los Arapiles below it (Plates 36 and 37). Further south, across a 1,200 yard wide valley, there is a slight ridge two miles long which merges into broken country to the west.

Two roads led from Salamanca to Ciudad Rodrigo. The one nearer the Arapiles passed through Aldea Tejada; the other was further north and close to the Tormes. Wellington was already sending baggage, ammunition, and supplies back toward Portugal along both roads. Although the two armies were nearly equal in numbers, the slightly greater speed of the French gave Marmont the capacity to turn the southern flank of the Allied army. Wellington had to cover his lines of communication; in all probability, he could hold Salamanca only one more day. With iron resolve, and without a word about lost opportunities, Wellington was ready to retreat.[2]

At dawn on the 22nd, both armies were northeast of the Arapiles, but marching southwest along parallel paths. Neither force had yet reached the Arapiles. The French vanguard had occupied the village of Calvarrasa de Arriba as their foremost point of advance on the 21st. Early next morning an Allied force endeavoured to take a chapel on top of a hill directly west of this village. This brought on desultory fighting which continued nine hours, but was never very serious.[3]

A more spirited action began before 8 a.m. when the French made a rush for the Greater Arapile. Wellington had already begun to occupy the Lesser; the 7th *Cacadores* of Cole's 4th Division were in this area. The Portuguese riflemen tried to seize the Greater Arapile also, but

[1] Both the French and Spanish refer to the 'Battle of the Arapiles'; Salamanca is five miles away.
[2] The situation at San Christobal on 21st June may have been the most promising of these opportunities.
[3] This fighting was done for the Allies by light companies of the 7th Division to whose support Wellington sent the 68th and the 2nd *Cacadores*. They were relieved about noon by some companies of the 95th from the Light Division. The hill and ruined chapel would have provided the French with a fine observation post.

four French battalions pushed them back in a bloody fight. Throughout the morning, both armies continued moving in a southwesterly direction. Wellington kept most of his divisions concentrated, but hidden behind a range of hills extending northeast from the Lesser Arapile and to the south behind the low hill to the rear of Los Arapiles. Only Pakenham's 3rd Division, which crossed the Tormes early in the morning, was detached from this group and was progressing towards Aldea Tejada to act either as an independent force on the exposed right flank, or as a reserve.[1]

Some little time later, Wellington observed the French dispositions and movements from the flat summit of the Lesser Arapile and the hill behind Los Arapiles. He saw enough to be certain of the position of Marmont's eight divisions; the French commander appeared to be taking advantage of the slowing up of the Allied army and the open country southwest of the Greater Arapile where he could turn their right flank. Wellington redeployed his right, bringing Leith's and Cole's Divisions into line running approximately east and west through the village. Clinton's 6th Division supported Cole; Hope's 7th Division was withdrawn from the line north of the Lesser Arapile and brought back to the rear of the 5th. The 3rd Division, accompanied by D'Urban's Portuguese cavalry, was nearing Aldea Tejada.

At about 11.15 a.m. Wellington believed that his new line through Los Arapiles would be attacked. French *tirailleurs* pressed forward resolutely and obtained a lodgement in some outlying houses; their artillery was active on a wide front. Such an attack would be most

[1] Pakenham had temporarily replaced Picton, whose wound received at Badajoz had re-opened early in the campaign.

See figures in black circles opposite.

(1)	3.30 p.m.	3rd Division (5,800), D'Urban's Portuguese Cavalry (450), Arentschildt's British and German Cavalry (700).
(2)	4.15 p.m.	5th Division (6,500), Bradford's Portuguese (1,800).
(3)	4.45 p.m.	Le Marchant's Heavy Cavalry (1,000) supported by G. Anson's Light Cavalry (1,000).
(4)	4.30 p.m.	Two brigades of 4th Division (3,900).
(5)	4.30 p.m.	Pack's Brigade (2,500).
(6)	5.30 p.m.	6th Division (5,500) aided by Spry's brigade under Beresford and part of W. Anson's brigade (4th Div. from lesser Arapile).

Positions of the French Infantry Divisions—see figures in white circles.

(1)	Foy—4,600	(5)	Maucune—5,000
(2)	Clausel—6,300	(6)	Brennier—4,300
(3)	Ferrey—5,400	(7)	Thomieres—4,500
(4)	Sarrut—4,700	(8)	Bonnet—6,400

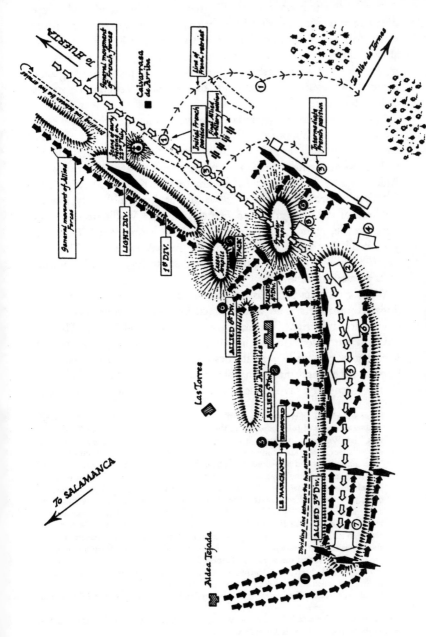

XI. SALAMANCA

welcome, but it hung fire. Wellington took some food, and while doing so was informed that Marmont was thrusting part of his force westwards along the low ridge to the south. The French army was already spread out over a full four miles of front; Marmont was extending his left even further without pulling in his right. A glance through his telescope was enough to convince Wellington that his chance had come.[1]

Marmont's divisions were marching west along the broad low crest away from their supporting forces, for French infantry and artillery were still holding a line northeast from the Greater Arapile to Calvarrasa de Arriba. Wellington outdistanced his staff in a gallop to Aldea Tejada, and ordered Pakenham to lead the 3rd Division and D'Urban's Portuguese cavalry in an all-out attack obliquely against the head of the most advanced French column.[2] Wellington's orders were precise, ending '.... drive everything before you!' 'Give me your hand, My Lord, and I will do it!' Pakenham replied. The two shook hands solemnly and parted, Pakenham to lead the 3rd Division to its greatest triumph.[3]

Wellington rode back east to give similar orders to his other divisional commanders. The whole Allied line would move forward in echelon from the right. Wellington reached Leith and Cotton. The 5th Division was to form in two lines each two-deep and attack as soon as Wellington personally sent it forward.[4] Cotton's cavalry, with the brigade of Le Marchant leading, was to advance on Leith's right and to charge whenever a favourable opportunity was presented. This whole

[1] There are several different accounts of this: *Guedalla*, 220-1, summarizes them well: 'The morning of July 22 passed in this agreeable manner, Marmont's "manoeuvring" (as Wellington wrote) "in the usual French style, nobody knew with what object". But about lunchtime the French lapse became manifest. Wellington was "stumping about and munching" in a little farmyard among the brown cottages of Los Arapiles, lunching apparently off alternate bites of chicken and glances at the French through a telescope. (The occasion lingered in Alava's memory because, for once, there was not cold meat.) The Peer's lunch was interrupted by a final look towards the French. "By God," he suddenly exclaimed, "that will do"—and scandalized Alava by flinging far over his shoulder the leg of chicken which he had been eating in his fingers. Then he cantered up the hill for a more comprehensive view, and the whole field was spread before him—the red masses of his own command, the still country, and the marching French. The game was in his hands. "Mon cher Alava," he said cheerfully, "Marmont est perdu," and rode off to launch the attack.'

[2] Wellington added Arentschildt's cavalry to Pakenham's force.

[3] Pakenham was no military genius, but he carried out courageously and efficiently his brother-in-law's orders.

[4] Bradford's Independent Portuguese Brigade was formed on Leith's right and was apparently temporarily under his orders.

co-ordinated movement was to begin immediately after the 3rd Division struck the French.

Wellington rode further east to give Cole and Pack instructions to be carried out when Leith's attack was well under way. Pack was to storm the Greater Arapile; Cole with two only of his three brigades—W. Anson's was holding the Lesser Arapile—was to advance between the village and Pack. Wellington now returned to Leith under a heavy artillery barrage. All the guns of both armies seem to have been in action, although at long range. The enlisted men of the Allied army were lying down in accordance with orders, but their officers were standing.[1] The light troops of both armies were bickering in front of Los Arapiles.

Suddenly, the roar of musketry and the deep bark of field pieces could be heard further west. Pakenham and the 3rd Division had struck. He had formed his infantry into three columns in such a manner that the whole could be deployed into three lines, one brigade in each, without coming to a halt. The 12th *Cacadores* and three companies of the 5/60th, all riflemen, were acting as skirmishers in front.[2] The exposed southern flank was covered by D'Urban's Portuguese cavalry. The divisional battery was on the left, ready for action.

The initial impact was caused by the cavalry, which broke up and routed the leading companies of the enemy infantry.[3] Pakenham's infantry was in action a moment later; so were his field pieces. Thomieres division was strung out in a line of battalion columns more

[1] The field, general, and staff officers remained mounted. This custom of British officers of exposing themselves, even though their men were to some extent protected, continued at least into the Boer War.

[2] There is some evidence to support the assertion that the Allied skirmishers did not cover the front until after the French were sighted, but this is illogical.

[3] D'Urban says little of this in his Journal, but wrote a complete account later, part of which is quoted by *Oman*, V, 441,

'The enemy was marching by his left along the wooded heights, which form the southern boundary of the valley of the Arapiles, and the western extremity of which closes in a lower fall, which descends upon the little stream of the Azan, near the village of Miranda. As the head of our column approached this lower fall, or hill, skirting it near its base, and having it on our left, we became aware that we were close to the enemy, though we could not see them owing to the trees, the dust, and the peculiar configuration of the ground. Anxious, therefore, to ascertain their exact whereabouts I had ridden out a little in front, having with me, I think, only my brigade-major Flangini and Da Camara, when upon clearing the verge of a small clump of trees, a short way up the slope, I came suddenly upon the head of a French column of infantry, having about a company in front, and marching very fast by its left. It was at once obvious that, as the columns of the 3rd Division were marching on our left, the French must be already beyond their right, and consequently I ought to attack at once.'

than a mile long and only imperfectly protected by cavalry.[1] The French were taken by surprise by the sudden emergence from the woodland to the west of the 3rd Division at a range of less than 500 yards. They endeavoured to present a defensive front with artillery and cavalry, but were caught by Pakenham's leading brigade in line. Every musket—almost 1,800 of them—in Wallace's three veteran battalions, from left to right the 74th, the 1/88th, and the 1/45th, was blazing away regularly.

All was confusion within the first French division. The ill-formed open mass was being plied with rolling volleys and grape. Allied cavalry was moving up on both flanks of the advancing British and Portuguese infantry, although partially concealed by dense smoke and dust. Thomieres was killed; his leading battalions suffered appalling casualties within a few minutes.[2] The French dissolved, panic-struck; all their divisional artillery was captured.

Eventually some French cavalry cantered up and delivered a half-hearted charge against the right flank of the 3rd Division, but was driven off by Arentschildt's five squadrons. Pakenham's whole force now began to 'drive the enemy before them' to the east. They had so far encountered only one French division.

Once the sound of battle to the west were unmistakable, Wellington sent forward Bradford and Leith.[3] The formation here was a line of skirmishers composed of the *Cacadores* and Leith's ten light companies followed by two main lines each two ranks deep. These probably extended for more than a mile.[4] Leith had in his first line, right to left, the 1/4th, and 2/4th, both of Pringle's Brigade, and then the 3/1st, the 1/9th, the 1/38th, and the 2/38th of Greville's Brigade. Similarly, the second line was composed of the 2/44th and the 2/30th from Pringle's Brigade and then Spry's four Portuguese line battalions.

[1] Curto's Brigade of French light cavalry, 1,700 sabres at least, should have been covering this movement, but did not enter the action until after their leading infantry division had been broken.

[2] His leading regiment lost 1,031 of 1,449 men. The second suffered 868 casualties of 1,123 originally present, but the third only lost 231 of 1,743: Oman, V, 445.

[3] Wellington rode with them for some distance between the first and second lines, which were about 100 yards apart: Hay, II, 56.

[4] The distance depends upon whether Bradford's men were formed to extend Cole's lines to the east. This is probable; but there is less accurate information concerning Portuguese units. Cole's front would have consisted of 1,500 men in a single line, perhaps 1,500 yards; Bradford's would have covered an additional 350 yards at least. Hay, II, 58, gives Bradford full credit with the 5th Division for the victory and indicates that the two operated together. However, Oman, V, 449, states that Bradford's Brigade was beyond the extreme French left.

This force, 8,300 strong including Bradford, was sent against the second French division pushed west by Marmont, which consisted of nine battalions, about 5,000 men. There were at least four French field batteries in front of this force. A third division was hurrying west to support the second, but arrived too late to take part in the impending action.

The Allied light companies and riflemen threw back not only the French *tirailleurs*, but their artillery too.[1] The French infantry had imitated one of Wellington's characteristic alignments and was formed 50 yards beyond the crest of the low ridge. But the French divisional commander had placed his nine battalions in square, perhaps because Allied cavalry could be seen to the west and northwest. A dense square may be ideal for receiving cavalry, but was less effective by 50 per cent than the usual French column of double companies, when resisting infantry in a two-deep line.[2] Leith's first main line suffered considerably in their long advance over the open plain from French artillery, but when Greville's and Pringle's men came to grips with these squares, they slaughtered them in three volleys. Brave French soldiers were stupidly betrayed by their formation. The survivors broke and fled.

Wellington had ordered Le Marchant to charge with his heavy cavalry at the first opportunity. These 1,000 sabres cantered past Bradford on his right, wheeled slightly to the east, and approached the French infantry just as Leith's men had caused them to disintegrate. Le Marchant's eye was keen and his control of his dragoons unique in the British service.[3] The opportunity was no sooner presented than taken. Down swept the heavy dragoons in awesome array and with a terrible roar always remembered by the few who survived the onslaught.

The first two French battalions tried to form together before the holocaust. Many still had loaded muskets, but shot wildly. Le Marchant

[1] *Hay*, II, 54–5, says,
   'The general desired me to ride forward, make the light infantry press up the heights to clear his line of march, and if practicable make a rush at the enemy's cannon. In the execution of this service, I had to traverse the whole extent of surface directly in front of the 5th division: the light troops soon drove back those opposed; the cannon were removed to the rear; every obstruction to the regular advance of the line had vanished.'

[2] The musketry efficiency of a square depends upon its depth along a side; a battalion never formed a solid square, but had, under the French system, probably six or nine ranks facing outwards. A six-deep formation would mean—even with three ranks firing—that only one man in eight could defend himself.

[3] Paget, who appears to have been the only other British cavalry commander who could handle more than a squadron or two in action, was unacceptable to Wellington at this time. See note 1, p. 63.

and his men rode over them with ease, sabring some, but leaving for Leith's infantry those who threw down their arms.[1] The dragoons, still in fair order, next reached three more broken battalions which had slightly more time to prepare. A few saddles were emptied as the heavy horsemen thundered into the confused infantry, sabres slashing rhythmically.[2] The French broke and scattered.

Le Marchant had now smashed utterly five battalions; he could have halted and reformed, but in front there lay an even finer opportunity. The third French infantry division was coming up out of breath and in disorder 500 yards to the east. Le Marchant resumed his charge after some hurried dressing and filling in had been done. Although the three British cavalry regiments were intermingled, they still presented an even front and were under control.

This French division had not been in action yet and had time to form squares across Le Marchant's front. Absolutely steady infantry in square could stop the best cavalry. But the French were just formed, and blown from a mile at double time; the heavy dragoons were battle crazy. The French held their fire a little too long; mortally injured horses smashed into the squares together with those that were unwounded; Heavy cavalry sabres did the rest.

The dragoons were now out of the control of even Le Marchant. The terrified French fled in every direction, closely pursued. The brigade commander kept about one squadron together, and engaged in a sharp action at the very edge of the wood to the southeast. Here Le Marchant was killed instantly, shot through the spine. This loss was probably the most serious single casualty Wellington suffered in the Peninsula, apart from that of Robert Craufurd.[3]

Three French divisions had been destroyed in about 30 minutes. Some scattered survivors managed eventually to get back to the Greater Arapile. Wellington's first three attacks had all succeeded

---

[1] These two battalions were of the 66th Line of Maucune's Division.

[2] These were of the 15th Line, also Maucune's Division. The remaining four battalions of this division were not charged by the British cavalry.

[3] *Oman*, V, 452,

'Thus fell an officer of whom great things had been expected by all who knew him, in the moment when he had just obtained and used to the full his first chance of leading his brigade in a general action. One of the few scientific soldiers in the cavalry arm whom the British army owned, Le Marchant had been mainly known as the founder and administrator of the Royal Military College at High Wycombe, which was already beginning to send to the front many young officers trained as their predecessors had never been. He was the author of many military pamphlets, and of a new system of sword exercise which had lately been adopted for the cavalry.'

22. The bridge over the Dos Casas at Fuentes de Onoro showing the western bank defended by the Allies.

23. The bridge at Albuera in the background, from the southeast.

24. The main fighting area at Albuera showing in the left centre background the church, and in the right middle-ground the bridge.

25. *Fortified Portuguese village of Ouguela, the 'anchor' of the Allied left flank on the Caia.*

26. *The extreme right flank of Wellington's position on the Caia, a separate fortification 600 yards southwest of Elvas.*

27. *Ciudad Rodrigo from the greater Teson. The breaches repaired by Wellington after the siege are still discernible.*

28. The Castle of Ciudad Rodrigo and the bridge across the Agueda seen from the main wall. O'Toole crossed this bridge and took the outwork below the castle before the main attack developed.

29. The 'ditch' of the San Christobal fortification across the Guadiana from Badajoz.

30. The northwest wall of Badajoz, looking east towards the Castle. A road has been built between the town and the Guadiana.

31. *The chasm of the Coa southwest of Almeida. The stream itself could be forded at several places, but the steep sides of the gorge were almost impassable to vehicles.*

32. *Campo Maior, approximately the centre of Wellington's position on the Caia.*

33. *The Roman bridge at Almaraz from the west taken from just above the river level. It was destroyed during the Talavera campaign, but ingeniously repaired by British engineers. The contemporary drawing (33A) is taken from Leith Hay's Narrative, Vol. II, opp. p. 69.*

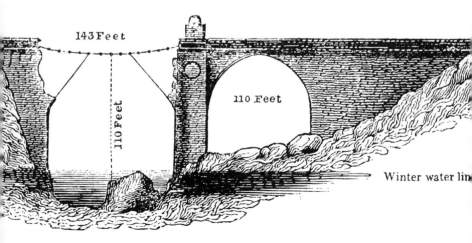

34. *The bridge at Almaraz seen from the ruins of Fort Napoleon south of the Tagus. Hill took this fort on 18th May 1812.*

35. *The castle ruins at Burgos seen from the upper part of the town.*

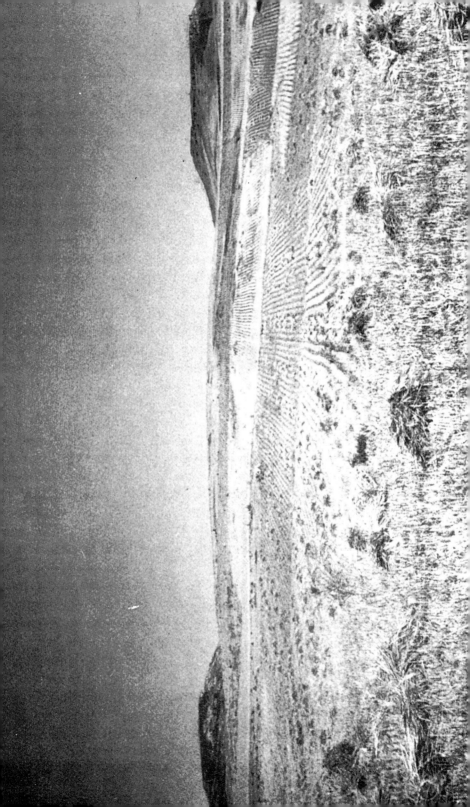

36.
The Arapiles
as seen from
the hill
north of
Los Arapiles.
On the
right is
the Greater
Arapile,
which was
occupied by the
French until
late in
the battle.

37.
View from the
Lesser Arapile
showing Los
Arapiles, the hill
to the north of
the village, and
the plain where
'40,000 French-
men were
defeated in 40
minutes'.

38. The mountainous region through which the Allied army thrust before the battle of Vitoria. The French considered this area impassable for artillery.

39. The western section of the valley of the Zadorra and the entrance to the gorge of Puebla as seen from the southern heights.

40.
The bridge of Nanclares over the Zadorra in the western end of the Vitoria valley. The Allies did not attack here until Hill put pressure on the French left flank.

41.
The western valley of the Zadorra from an underfeature of the Arinez knoll looking southwest towards the gorge of Puebla.

43. *One of the principal buildings in Lesaca, Wellington's headquarters during the Battle of the Pyrenees. This structure was probably occupied by the Staff.*

← **42.** *The village of Arinez from the knoll. The mountains in the centre and right from the southern boundary of the Vitoria valley; the left background 'pass' leads to Logrono.*

44. *Looking south over the country between Roncesvalles and Pamplona.*

45. *The* Chemin des Anglais *follows the ridge crest. The road in the centre is modern.*

46. *The* Chemin des Anglais. *Half a battalion of the 92nd in a two-deep line across this crest held up a French division.*

47. *The valley of the Ulzana from Cole's ridge looking northwest. The western end of Clausel's ridge partially shields the village of Sorauren.*

48. *The village of Sorauren with Cole's ridge in the right background. On the bridge Wellington wrote his dispatch to Murray.*

49. *The San Marcial hill with the chapel on the skyline to the right, as seen from the French bank of the Bidassoa immediately downstream from the bridge at Behobie.*

50. *La Rhune from southwest of the village of Sare. This mountain dominates the entire terrain. It varies considerably in appearance depending on the point from which it is viewed.*

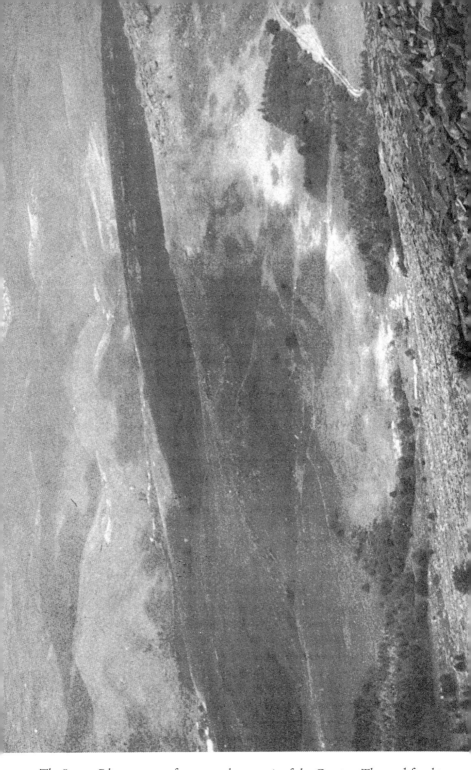

51. *The Lesser Rhune as seen from near the summit of the Greater. The 43rd fought along the ridge in the right centre clearing it from left to right.*

52. *The bridge at Vera, defended by Cadoux and his riflemen.*

53. *The church of Arcangues from the position occupied by the French artillery in its duel with the 43rd.*

54. *The bridge of Amots. This was the only French lateral communication immediately behind their main line at the battle of the Nivelle.*

55. *The bridge at Orthez. The central fortification was virtually impregnable if the passageway beneath was blocked.*

56. *The village and church of St Boes as seen from the northern wall of the Roman Camp from which Wellington directed the Allied army during the battle of Orthez.*

57. *The village church at St Boes. The village beyond was badly damaged in the battle of Orthez and was rebuilt further east.*

58. *The approximate site of the northern end of the bridge of boats across the Adour between Bayonne and the sea.*

astonishingly well and at small cost. Allied advances to the east of Los Arapiles were to meet with more stubborn resistance.

Wellington had ordered Cole's 4th Division forward in an attack on the hinge of the enemy line before Leith's thrust had reached the French position.[1] From the start Cole had to contend with a crossfire from batteries of artillery ahead of him and on his left flank, particularly from the summit of the Greater Arapile. Further, Cole was attacking two full divisions. In order to alleviate this situation, Wellington ordered Pack and his Portuguese to storm the Greater Arapile.[2]

Cole sent forward as skirmishers the 7th *Cacadores* on his left and four British light companies on his right. Since he covered almost a mile of front and had only 3,000 line infantry in his seven battalions, he formed them into a single two-deep line. Ellis's Brigade, from left to right, 1/48th, 1/23rd, and 1/7th, stood next to Leith; Stubbs's Portuguese Brigade of four line battalions was next to Pack. All went well at first; the Allied skirmishers pushed back the *tirailleurs*. French artillery fire was heavy, but not effective. The French infantry division directly south was clearly the objective of the Allied 4th Division.[3]

Soon after beginning his long advance, Cole noticed several other French battalions, particularly three on his left flank a mile west of the Greater Arapile. These were thrust back in a short, hard fight by the four Portuguese line battalions, but retreated east rather than south. The 7th *Cacadores* were taken from the skirmish line and detached to follow them, but the whole situation was dangerous in that Cole was outnumbered by about three to one.

Meanwhile, Pack was approaching the Greater Arapile. He had his 2,600 infantry in an unusual formation; the 4th *Cacadores* formed his skirmish line, supported by the four grenadier companies of his line battalions in separate small squares, probably short columns. These were followed by two columns each composed of two line battalions. Presumably Pack did not yet have sufficient confidence in his Portuguese infantrymen to use them in a two-deep line when attacking.

Pack's Brigade crossed the valley, ascended the long hill, and approached the precipitous crest, under a continuous and heavy artillery

---

[1] Cole had with him only Ellis's British and Stubb's Portuguese Brigades; W. Anson's was holding the Lesser Arapile.

[2] I have followed *Fortescue*, VIII, 494. *Oman*, V, 447, following the narrative of Charles Vere, Assistant Q.M.G. of the 4th Division, states that Pack received discretionary orders to attack or to 'contain' the French force in this area. Wellington almost never gave discretionary orders except to Hill and Beresford, and later to Graham.

[3] This was Clausel's Division which contained 6,300 men.

fire which became more effective as the range decreased. Near the summit, there was a bank four or five feet high.[1] As the *Cacadores* clambered up this, the French fired a volley from 40 yards and charged with the bayonet. Outnumbered more than five to one and in an impossible situation, the *Cacadores* broke; the grenadiers fought valiantly for a few moments, but were thrown back also. The two line columns, attacked in front and flank, were beaten. The entire brigade was pursued down the long slope of the Greater Arapile and into the valley below. Pack and his men were rescued half-way across by the 1/40th of W. Anson's Brigade coming from the Lesser Arapile.

During this action, Cole was advancing against the ten strong battalions of Clausel's division, five of which were arrayed in column of double companies in a first line. The French formation was a line of five rectangles 70 men wide by 9 ranks deep separated from each other by intervals of 200 yards. There was an identical second line 200 yards to the rear. They had suffered little so far and were too distant to have observed the French disasters further west. For the first time in the war, *tirailleurs* were able to operate against Wellington as called for in the French regulations. They were inflicting casualties on Cole's main line, for four small British light companies—the 7th *Cacadores* had not returned from the east—could not contend successfully against ten large ones.

Cole continued to advance, however, reforming and filling in. Finally, the long thin Allied line was within musket range of the first five French columns. As usual, the line broke up into segments each concentrating a concave fire on the column ahead of it. Along each section of the front, the French could fire but 210 weapons against over 600. The Allies pressed closer with their terrible rolling fire. Cole's men advanced to less than 60 yards before the French broke. But this was no real panic; they retired and reformed on the flank of each column of their second line. Essentially, the French formation was now ten rectangles instead of five, with less than half the original interval between each.

The two contending divisions now came together in a ferocious musketry duel; the French had numerous and well served artillery enfilading the Allied line from both flanks. Cole's men suffered terribly and were beaten; their retreat was near panic. Cole himself was badly wounded.

[1] The side of the Greater Arapile up which Pack climbed is extremely steep, yet is still tilled almost up to the top. This bank is at the upper edge of the ploughed land.

In order to understand what happened next, it is necessary to appreciate facts not then known to Wellington. In the earlier long range artillery duel, Marmont was hit by a piece of shrapnel. The French second in command, General Bonnet, was also a casualty.[1] General Clausel was now in control of the army, two-fifths of which was already defeated. But when his own division defeated Cole, and Pack had been thrown back, Clausel believed there was an opportunity for a Napoleonic counterstroke. He sent French cavalry in pursuit of Cole and Pack; Sarrut's fresh division was deployed to hold back Pakenham, who commanded the Allied 3rd and 5th Divisions and Bradford's Brigade after Leith was wounded. The strong infantry divisions of Bonnet and Clausel himself were sent into the gap between the Lesser Arapile and Los Arapiles. More than 12,000 men were launched in this attack, all either fresh or previously victorious. The conception of this movement was brilliant; it was executed flawlessly. Against any other contemporary commander, excepting only Napoleon and Wellington, Clausel would probably have succeeded in making it a drawn battle.

But Wellington had anticipated the possible defeat of Cole and Pack, and such a counterattack. With unerring instinct, he had ordered Clinton's 6th Division forward and had himself deployed it into line diagonally southwest from the Lesser Arapile. Beresford was sent to bring up Spry's Portuguese Brigade from the 5th Division, practically undamaged because of its position in the second line, into line with Clinton's division. The genius of this lay in the fact that Wellington had started both these forward movements before Clausel's advance. Any breach in the Allied line was stopped before it formed.[2]

Wellington had arrayed the 6th Division with its two British brigades in a two-deep first line; the Portuguese brigade was similarly aligned

---

[1] Marmont's wound was caused by a shrapnel shell from the howitzer of Dyneley's British field battery which was firing from the Lesser Arapile. *Oman*, V, 438, says in a note, 'Many years after, when Marmont, now a subject of Louis XVIII, was inspecting some British artillery, an officer had the maladroit idea of introducing to him the sergeant who had pointed the gun—the effect of the shot in the middle of the French staff had been noticed on the British Arapile.'

[2] The French cavalry accomplished little other than the cutting down of a few infantry caught in the open. Most of the 4th Division closed together in impromptu squares of British and Portuguese. A few squadrons rode against the 2/53rd, which also formed square. These experienced and talented French horsemen had an independent efficieny developed by years of war; but they realized now the folly of charging formed British infantry. They could ride through a 'thin red line', but not a square. Cavalry would take 60 seconds to cover 400 yards; Wellington's infantry required but half that time to form square and commence firing volleys.

200 yards to the rear.[1] W. Anson's Brigade lay on Clinton's left and Spry's Portuguese Brigade on his right. This formation was supported by a crossfire of Allied artillery from the hill behind Los Arapiles and from the summit of the Lesser Arapile. The Allies met the French towards the middle of the valley.

The struggle followed a familiar pattern. Wellington's line met French columns; Clausel's men had neither artillery nor *tirailleur* superiority, although they were slightly more numerous. The French fought valiantly for a short time, perhaps five minutes, and suffered almost as severely as their comrades to the west. They were finally driven back completely broken.

Five of the original eight French divisions were now dispersed; the Greater Arapile was abandoned as Clinton's men pressed forward. Even the division left to oppose Pakenham was badly mauled. Clausel managed to thrust Ferrey's Division, which had previously only bickered with the Allied 1st and Light Divisions, into position across the Alba de Tormes road as a rearguard to stem the Allied pursuit. For the first time in the war, almost a complete French division formed in line; seven battalions were arrayed in a continuous three-deep line, with a single battalion at either end in square. Darkness was fast approaching when Wellington ordered Clinton's victorious formation to break through this rearguard. Numbers were about even, but the French were fresh; the usual musketry advantage of British line was absent.[2] The gallant Frenchmen held their ground. Clinton was forced to retire momentarily and shift from his British to his Portuguese line.

Meanwhile, Wellington himself brought up the divisional batteries of the 1st and Light Divisions, which went into action obliquely against the French line. Taken in front and flank, Ferrey's Division finally broke, but not until its talented commander had been cut in half by a round shot. There was one further action among the trees to the south-east; but the French army, except for one division, had disintegrated.

---

[1] The importance of the Portuguese in the Allied army is nowhere more vividly brought out than in the fact that some Portuguese brigades were, as in this case, almost the numerical equal of two British brigades.

[2] Apparently, neither Spry nor W. Anson moved forward in this final action alongside Clinton. Physical freshness was not the only factor; the muskets of the 6th Division were fouled from firing at least 30 rounds each. The Brown Bess was more effective for the first few rounds than later. Even though some men claimed to have fired over 100 rounds from one weapon in one combat, the musket usually gave trouble after about 25 or 30 shots. Flints would need resetting or replacement in order to spark freely; bores would foul to such an extent that balls could be pushed home only with difficulty.

Foy's men alone remained between the French and annihilation, but this division made no stand anywhere near the field of battle.

A vigorous pursuit was now required; Wellington spurred himself, but was handicapped by the fact that his army was physically exhausted after days of marching and a battle fought under a tormenting July sun. The greatness of the British army lay in its regularity, a disciplined force directed by a dominating will. The infantry, and its subordinate officers lacked spontaneity and the 'killer' instinct in pursuing a defeated opponent; even the cavalry were limited in operations of this type.

Wellington would probably have been able to drive his army after the retreating French and accomplish far more, had not an almost unbelievable blunder been committed by Carlos de España, senior Spanish general in the area. The Tormes east of the battlefield could not be crossed between the Alba bridge and a ford six and a half miles further north; there was another ford at the great bend at Huerta two miles beyond. Since the bridge at Alba was closed to the French by the Spanish garrison, Wellington naturally assumed that the French must retreat towards the fords.

It was not until nearly midnight that Wellington realized that, apart from a few stragglers, the French were not heading for the fords at all, but were crossing the Tormes by the bridge. Against Wellington's positive orders, de España had withdrawn the Alba garrison days before. The Spanish general could not bring himself to admit this to Wellington. Hours after he had let the garrison leave Alba undefended, he suggested to Wellington that such an order should be issued.

'No! Certainly not,' Wellington replied. 'We need them right there!' De España had neither the courage to admit his error nor the sense to order the garrison back.

By the time Wellington was informed of the true state of affairs, even he was exhausted.[1] The French accomplished their retreat with relatively small loss, more by good luck than by good management. Marmont's army had suffered 30 per cent casualties on the battlefield and lost 20 guns. At least another 30 per cent was making off in all directions; only Foy's Division retained any semblance of fighting efficiency.

---

[1] At this time, Wellington was forty-three years old and 'in the prime of life, a well made man, 5 foot 10 inches in height, lean and muscular, with broad shoulders and well-developed chest. Of the cruiser, rather than the battleship build, the greyhound, rather than the mastiff breed, he seemed made all for speed and action, yet strong as steel, and capable of great endurance.' *Man Wellington*, 211–12.

After 22nd July 1812, even the French who had forgotten Rolica admitted that Wellington could fight an offensive battle and fight it superbly well. Foy wrote six days later:

'The battle of Salamanca is the most masterly in its management, the most considerable in the number of troops engaged, and the most important in results of all the victories that the English have gained in these latter days. It raises Lord Wellington's reputation almost to the level of Marlborough. Hitherto we had been aware of his prudence, his eye for choosing a position, and his skill in utilizing it. At Salamanca he has shown himself a great and able master of manoeuvres. He kept his dispositions concealed for almost the whole day: he waited till we were committed to our movements before he developed his own: he played a safe game: he fought in the oblique order—it was a battle in the style of Frederick the Great.'[1]

There are several tactical lessons to be learnt from Salamanca in addition to the obvious fact that the line when properly employed was as much a master of the column offensively as defensively. Wellington achieved a complete tactical surprise with Pakenham's attack on Thomieres, and then used the 'oblique order' referred to by Foy to crush Maucune and Brennier. Marmont's blunder of too widely separating his army was his downfall. Wellington managed to have considerable superiority in numbers at each critical point, until Cole and Pack advanced.

Wellington's ability to be at the right place almost continuously is astonishing; he personally directed almost every manoeuvre and controlled the advance of division after division in turn. If Clinton's Division had not been moved immediately into the threatened area at the real crisis of the battle, an Allied victory would not have been assured.

A more numerous and more powerful artillery proved advantageous to the French, particularly against Cole and Pack. They did not have their usual cavalry superiority.[2] Clausel's own division in its contest

---

[1] Oman, V, 472–3, translating Foy's *Vie Militaire*, 178.
[2] Wellington complained of the heavier metal of the French artillery, yet all seven French 12-pounders, the only pieces larger than those available to the Allies, were among the 20 pieces taken. Earlier in this chapter I have followed Oman and Fortescue in stating that Thomiere's complete divisional battery was taken, but the French must have carried away their howitzer. There were 13, one for each of 13 batteries, on 15th July, and again on 1st August: *Fortescue*, VIII, 636 and elsewhere.

with Cole confirmed the efficiency of their columns when supported by powerful flanking artillery and properly protected by numerous *tirailleurs*. At the very end, the French imitated the 'thin red line' with considerable success until Wellington personally set artillery in an enfilading position against it.

In the larger sense, Salamanca shattered more than Marmont's army. It was the beginning of the end of French domination of Spain, although much remained still to be done. Joseph's seat on the Spanish throne was thoroughly shaken. Rolica, Vimiero, Talavera, and the rest, had established Wellington's reputation in Britain, but Salamanca carried it throughout Europe. From now on, Napoleon's favourite form of referring to Wellington as 'the Sepoy General' fooled few besides himself, and him fatally.

THE CONTENDING FORCES AND LOSSES AT SALAMANCA

ALLIED ARMY UNDER WELLINGTON		TOTAL = 48,569[1]
INFANTRY 25,577 British 17,421 Portuguese		= 42,998
1st Division, H. Campbell		= 6,423
Fermor's Brigade	1,972	
1/Coldstreamers, 1/Scots, 1 Co. 5/60th		
Sigismund von Lowe's Brigade	1,823	
1st, 2nd and 5th Line Batts., K.G.L.		
Wheatley's Brigade	2,628	
2/24th, 1/42nd, 2/58th, 1/79th, 1 Co. 5/60th		
3rd Division, Edward Pakenham		= 5,877
Alexander Wallace's Brigade	1,802	
1/45th, 74th, 1/88th, 3 Cos. 5/60th		
J. Campbell's Brigade	1,878	
1/5th, 2/5th, 2/83rd, 94th		
Powers's Portuguese Brigade	2,197	
9th Line (2 Batts.), 21st Line (2 Batts.), 12th Cacadores		
4th Division, Lowry Cole		= 5,236
W. Anson's Brigade	1,261	
3/27th, 1/40th, 1 Co. 5/60th		

[1] This figure includes 246 Engineers, etc., but not any of de España's Spaniards who numbered about 3,300, but suffered six casualties, four of whom were missing.

Ellis's Brigade   1,421
 1/7th, 1/23rd, 1/48th, 1 Co. Brunswick Oels
Stubb's Portuguese Brigade 2,554
 11th Line (2 Batts.), 23rd Line (2
 Batts.), 7th Cacadores

5th Division, James Leith   = 6,691
 Greville's Brigade   2,606
  3/1st, 1/9th, 1/38th, 2/38th, 1 Co.
  Brunswick Oels
 Pringle's Brigade   1,780
  1/4th, 2/4th, 2/30th, 2/44th, 1 Co.
  Brunswick Oels
 Spry's Portuguese Brigade 2,305
  3rd Line (2 Batts.), 15th Line (2
  Batts.), 8th Cacadores

6th Division, Henry Clinton   = 5,541
 Richard Hulse's Brigade 1,464
  1/11th, 2/53rd, 1/61st, 1 Co. 5/60th
 Hinde's Brigade   1,446
  2nd, 1/32nd, 1/36th
 Rezende's Portuguese Brigade 2,631
  8th Line (2 Batts.), 12th Line (2
  Batts.), 9th Cacadores

7th Division, John Hope   = 5,183
 Halkett's Brigade   1,659
  1st Light, 2nd Light, K.G.L., and
  remainder Brunswick Oels
 De Bernewitz's Brigade 1,356
  51st, 68th, Chasseurs Britanniques
 Collins's Portuguese Brigade 2,168
  7th Line (2 Batts.), 19th Line (2
  Batts.), 2nd Cacadores

Light Division, Charles Alten = 3,548
 Barnard's Brigade   1,702
  1/43rd, Cos. of 2/95th, 3/95th, 1st
  Cacadores
 Vandeleur's Brigade   1,846
  1/52nd, 1/95th, 3rd Cacadores

Independent Portuguese Brigades   = 4,499
    Pack's Brigade   2,605
        1st Line (2 Batts.), 16th Line (2
        Batts.), 4th Cacadores
    Bradford's Brigade   1,894
        13th Line (2 Batts.), 14th Line (2
        Batts.), 5th Cacadores

CAVALRY   3,543 British   482 Portuguese   = 4,025
Stapleton Cotton
    Le Marchant's Brigade   1,022
        3rd Dragoons, 4th Dragoons, 5th
        Dragoon Guards
    G. Anson's Brigade   1,004
        11th L.D., 12th L.D., 16th L.D.
    V. Alten's Brigade   746
        14th L.D., 1st Hussars, K.G.L.
    Bock's Brigade   771
        1st Dragoons and 2nd Dragoons,
        K.G.L.
    D'Urban's Brigade   482
        1st and 11th Portuguese Dragoons

ARTILLERY   1,186 British (54 guns)   114 Portuguese (6 guns)=1,300

FRENCH ARMY UNDER MARMONT   TOTAL = 49,999
INFANTRY   = 41,575

DIVISIONS	BRIGADES	BATTALIONS	PERSONNEL
1st, Foy	2	8	4,635
2nd, Clausel	2	10	6,385
3rd, Ferrey	2	9	5,462
4th, Sarrut	2	9	4,773
5th, Maucune	2	9	5,028
6th, Brennier	2	10	4,329
7th, Thomieres	2	?	4,541
8th, Bonnet	2	12	6,422

CAVALRY   = 3,390
    Boyer's Heavy   1,508
    Curto's Light   1,882

13 Batteries of 78 pieces

NOTE: In both armies, the actual number present was probably 1,000 less than shown, for these are exact figures for 15th July, a week of hard marching and some fighting before the battle of Salamanca proper.

SALAMANCA LOSSES

	KILLED	WOUNDED	PRISONERS AND MISSING	TOTAL
British	338	2,714	74	3,176
Portuguese	304	1,552	182	2,038[1]
Allies	692	4,266	256	5,214
French	Impossible to determine, but at least 14,000.[2]			

TOPOGRAPHICAL OBSERVATIONS

The two Arapiles define the area of fighting from afar. The long hill behind Los Arapiles is immediately identifiable, as is the long low ridge along which Thomieres advanced. The final French position can be traced, even though the forest is now cut back to the southeast by several hundred yards. Alba de Tormes, like the city of Salamanca, has grown and changed, but much remains from the Napoleonic era. The fortification which de España left undefended survives in ruins; the bridge here has been widened.

On the other hand, the route from Aldea Tejada along which Pakenham took the 3rd Division is not clear; the roads today do not seem to be in the same place; the exact point of the first collision with Thomieres cannot be determined within half a mile.

[1] I have followed Fortescue rather than Oman; they are almost in agreement as to British casualties, but not for the Portuguese. Oman shows a British total of 3,129 which is close, but only 1,627 Portuguese which is too low. We have here and elsewhere a strange condition; the ratio of wounded to killed in the British army was usually greater than in the Portuguese. From chance observations in diaries, one wonders if British regiments did not report every scratch as a battle casualty, even though the soldier concerned was not out of action at all. If this were true, Wellington's actual losses over the years may have been considerably below those given officially.

[2] *Fortescue*, VIII, 504–6, and *Oman*, V, 604–6, agree on this approximate total by careful estimates based on all known facts. There were probably 20 field pieces captured, seven 12-pounders, three 8-pounders, nine 4-pounders, and 'one 3-pounder'. The last is inexplicable. Marmont was responsible for artillery standardization in Napoleon's armies; it is unlikely that a field gun of this old size was used by the French at so late a date. Even though the metric system of weights was in common use in France by this time, the artillery was still using the old French pound; 8 French pounds equalled roughly 9 British pounds.

XIV

BURGOS, AND RETREAT

A T dawn on 23rd July 1812, Wellington led the cavalry brigades of Bock and Anson after the retreating French army, but did not come up with their rearguard until the middle of the afternoon near the village of Garcia Hernandez. An action ensued between four squadrons of K.G.L. heavy dragoons and three battalions of French infantry. Less than 450 Germans were actually engaged; they lost about 30 per cent of their strength, but inflicted 1,400 casualties on the enemy. They broke one formed square and scattered a column, two-battalions strong. They forced Foy's Division into static defensive positions; if the infantry had been in close support, Wellington could have accomplished far more. But the French army moved much faster than the Allies; the C-in-C gave up the pursuit on the 25th at Arevalo.

Wellington now received definite intelligence of the army which Joseph and Jourdan had brought north from Madrid to the aid of Marmont.[1] This force of 17,000 might endeavour to join Clausel rather than retire on the capital, particularly if Clausel wished to defend the line of the Duero. Clausel's beaten divisions were retreating in disorder northeast along the main road toward Burgos and Vitoria. Wellington in person, with some cavalry, entered Valladolid on the 30th.

Wellington's strategic problem was how best to take advantage of his victory at Salamanca. The French Army of Portugal was completely defeated and might be pushed right back into France, but there were still four other French armies in Spain. Three of these were fully occupied with the diversions Wellington had set in motion during the late spring.

[1] As referred to in note 2, page 210, Wellington knew of this movement before Salamanca; a cavalry picket from the approaching French army had been captured south of Arevalo on the 25th.

The Army of the North under Caffarelli was still engaged in defending itself from incursions by Sir Home Popham and co-operating guerrilla forces. Not a single soldier from the Army of the North had fought at Salamanca. A force of cavalry and artillery only, less than 2,000 strong, had been sent south, but too late. Caffarelli still maintained that he could not spare infantry.

In the far south, Ballasteros was operating unpredictably. He had been defeated at Bornos on 1st June, but not routed. As usual, when in difficulties, this army retired under the guns of Gibraltar. Soult was unwilling to send troops away from his area, particularly as Hill had advanced against D'Erlon south of the Guadiana.[1]

The news from the east coast was less satisfactory. General José O'Donnell with a Spanish army of 12,000 had managed to get himself beaten at Castalla on 21st June by about 3,000 Frenchmen. Spanish casualties exceeded the entire French force and included 2,135 un-wounded prisoners. O'Donnell's army was not, however, totally destroyed and was still fit for some service. It retired to Alicante where William Bentinck was supposed to have landed with his entire disposable Anglo-Sicilian force. A part only had arrived and was commanded by General Maitland. Suchet expected this descent on the east coast; he was no more willing to send men to Castile than Caffarelli or Soult.

Wellington concluded that for a time at least he could do almost as he pleased in an area some 200 miles square in the centre of Spain. Joseph's army of 17,000 men was no problem. The Allied system of supply and the opening up of the Duero and the Tagus enabled Wellington to move throughout this area and remain concentrated without fear of a breakdown of discipline caused by shortages.[2]

Wellington had not yet brought his infantry north of the Duero, but moved his headquarters and most of his army to Cuellar on 31st July. If Joseph and Clausel were still trying to join forces, the presence of the Allies at Cuellar would make this extremely difficult. Joseph's army was reported as late as 1st August to be in Segovia after passing near Arevalo on 25th July. Intelligence reaching Wellington led him to believe that it was possible that the French would have to evacuate the south of Spain altogether. In all probability, Soult would move with his entire force by Toledo on Madrid.[3]

[1] This manoeuvring took place north of Llerena.

[2] Wellington was acutely conscious of the fact that if his army was hungry it would plunder, and that if it did so, Spanish civilians would detest the British equally with the French.

[3] Joseph and Jourdan dispatched such an order on the 29th.

If Soult was marching north immediately, a further pursuit of Clausel toward Burgos would place the Allied army in grave danger of being cut off from Portugal. On the other hand, if Wellington approached Madrid, a junction with Hill could take place. If the entire Allied field army were concentrated, Wellington could face Soult and Joseph combined. Further, Madrid was certain to fall; Joseph's army unaided was far too small to hold the capital which Soult could not reach in time to prevent its capture. It was even possible that Joseph might allow himself to be shut up inside the city. Madrid was more than just the seat of Joseph's tottering government; it was the largest military depot in French-controlled Spain.

On 6th August, Wellington marched on Madrid via Segovia, leaving at Cuellar only Clinton's reinforced 6th Division and Anson's cavalry. Contact with the French was made on the 11th at the village of Majadahonda. D'Urban's Portuguese cavalry, which did well at Salamanca, panicked here when opposed to inferior numbers. Three horse artillery guns were temporarily lost, but were retaken.[1] The casualties were almost equal, about 200 on each side.

On the 12th, the Allied army entered Madrid. The capital was free of the French for the first time since December 1808, and gave Wellington a spontaneous and sincere welcome. Joseph, with his main army, and an enormous train, were already across the Tagus at Aranjuez and heading for Valencia. He had left a garrison of 2,500 men in the citadel of Madrid, the 'forts of the Retiro'; this place was proof against guerrillas and the civilian population, but surrendered when confronted by artillery. It was found to contain 180 guns, 20,000 muskets, much other military *matériel*, and two eagles.[2]

Wellington did not pursue Joseph for the same reasons which had prevented him following Clausel; an overextension of the Allied army

---

[1] A similar loss and recapture had occurred at El Bodon; Wellington never lost a field place under his immediate personal command.

[2] The loss of these through carelessness—they could have been destroyed—must have amounted to a crime in the sight of the French. Napoleon's eagles were more significant than battalion colours. There was but a single eagle for each French regiment, which usually contained three or four active battalions; the little gilded statuette could be taken from its staff in a moment of peril and either concealed or destroyed. More were captured by troops commanded by Wellington than by the other enemies of France combined, throughout the entire period of their use. The 87th, for their exploit at Barrosa, was at first called the 'Eagle Takers', but this was soon corrupted to 'Bird Catchers': *Maxwell's Peninsular Sketches*, I, 152.

to the southeast would be as dangerous as to the northeast. Besides, he would be leaving the areas in which his transportation and supply system functioned best. Wellington now learnt that Joseph had in fact ordered Soult to abandon all Andalusia and retire northeast. The Allied C-in-C therefore instructed Hill to move to the north and east if and when Soult carried out Joseph's orders.[1]

During the next two weeks Wellington remained in Madrid. He spent long hours with Spanish generals and politicians trying to stimulate the Castiles and Leon into using to advantage the enormous supplies of war *matériel* found in Madrid. His intelligence system had never been more demanding of his own time, and rarely more productive. The French in Andalusia were moving north slowly. Clausel meanwhile had turned about, chased Santocildes and his Spaniards from Valladolid, and had sent Foy to relieve French garrisons in Toro, Zamora, and Astorga. This flying column was successful in the first two instances; Astorga fell to the Spanish besiegers thirty-six hours before Foy could reach it. It was gratifying to Wellington that none of these detached irregular forces suffered any considerable casualties; they carried out to the letter his instructions to retire and avoid risking pitched battles.

The situation on the Duero required Wellington's personal attention; he would be able to return quickly to Madrid if needed there. He left on 31st August and reached Arevalo on 3rd September. He had sent north ahead of him the 1st, 5th, and 7th Divisions, Pack's and Bradford's Independent Portuguese Brigades, and Bock's and Ponsonby's cavalry brigades, about 23,000 in all to add to Clinton's 7,000.

On 6th September, Wellington crossed the Duero unopposed; Clausel was still suffering from the demoralization of Salamanca. Although the French forces were superior in number to the Allies, Clausel again retreated toward Burgos. Wellington hoped to fight a battle immediately, but was disappointed. He followed Clausel nearly 100 miles, through and past Burgos which he entered on the 18th.

During this advance Wellington finally received positive intelligence that Soult was actually abandoning Andalusia. The siege of Cadiz was given up on 24th August. An Allied army in which Skerrett commanded some 5,500 British troops, took Seville on the 27th and found there over 500 cannon and a great deal of other war *matériel*. Both

[1] Wellington to Bathurst, *Dispatches*, IX, 370, 'Any other but a modern French army would now leave the province, as they have absolutely no communication of any kind with France, or with any other French army; and they are pressed on all sides by troops not to be despised, and they can evidently do nothing. But I suspect that Soult will not. stir....'

Soult and D'Erlon were moving towards Valencia. The Tagus valley was free of French troops. A concentration of French armies for offensive action against the Anglo-Portuguese army in central Spain appeared unlikely. Hill could certainly be ordered to march on Madrid; Skerrett could join him on the way.

Wellington decided that he could make no better use of his army than to drive Clausel further along the road to France. There was one local problem; the old castle at Burgos had been recently refortified and was now held by a well-supplied French garrison.[1] This fortification would have to be taken before following Clausel further. A careful reconnaissance showed the place to be stronger than indicated by 'correspondents'. It would be harder to take than Wellington had supposed, but if it did fall it could be quickly repaired and regarrisoned. This would serve the same purpose as a victory over Clausel in the field. The Army of Portugal would not advance south or southwest, if it meant leaving a hostile Burgos in its rear.[2] The military advantages to be gained in taking the place were certainly worth the gamble. Besides, Clausel might be lured into fighting a battle to relieve it.

This fortification was situated on a steep hill north of the city and was about 450 yards long by 300 yards wide (Plate 35). The tall medieval walls had been reinforced with new masonry and were protected by earthworks. New and powerful batteries had been installed and amply supplied with ammunition. The French garrison totalled approximately 2,200 men under General Dubreton, who was not inconvenienced by any civilian population. The main military weakness of the place was that another hill equally lofty rose some 500 yards to the northeast. The French had constructed an outwork on this second hill.[3]

The great objection to besieging these fortifications was that Wellington's siege train, the three 18-pounders which had been used to knock to pieces the forts of Salamanca, was too small for battering

---

[1] Burgos was the capital of Old Castile; the castle was the residence of royalty until gutted by fire in 1736. When in 1808 Napoleon was passing the empty shell, he ordered it to be restored and modernized as a fortress.

[2] With an Allied garrison in the castle and Mina, Longa, and other guerrillas of this area in the surrounding hills, no French commander would have dared move past Burgos.

[3] French authorities state that it was unfinished, yet Dubreton risked over one-fifth of his entire garrison there.

Burgos. The only other pieces that could be brought up within three weeks were the iron 24-pounder siege howitzers still at Salamanca.[1]

During the afternoon of 19th September, riflemen and light troops cleared French sharpshooters from three fleches around the outwork on the detached hill; that night the outwork itself was taken by assault. The tactics used were the same as those which succeeded on the Great Teson at Ciudad Rodrigo; a firing line was to overwhelm the garrison from the crest of the counterscarp while another force climbed down into the ditch and ascended the far side. The main attack became confused and failed, but Major Somers-Cocks, in command of the light companies of the 1/24th, the 1/42nd, and the 1/79th, converted what was planned for a false attack on the gorge into a real assault, and took the place.[2] The Allies suffered 421 casualties compared with 198 French, but captured the outwork intact including some field guns. If the other attacks on the castle had been as successful, all would have been well.

The next month was probably the most frustrating of Wellington's military career. He divided his time between the covering army which Clausel refused to attack, and the siege which was carried on by Pack's Portuguese and units of the 1st Division. After the initial success, nothing went right. There was insufficient ammunition even for the few guns. Rain came down in torrents. Only the Guards did their duty; the lack of miners and sappers and efficient engineers was particularly obvious because of the artillery shortage.[3] Several separate

---

[1] Critics have made comments in connexion with the transporting of siege guns from Madrid, from Ciudad Rodrigo, and from British ships-of-war at Santander. Some of these have not appreciated that a long iron 18-pounder weighing 5,600 lb. and its carriage of 3,000 lb. is quite different from a field gun with a gross weight of 800 lb. It was certainly possible to send guns from Santander, but the two pieces dispatched from there on 9th October were only at Reinosa on the 19th, an average of four miles per day over rela-- tively easy territory. Oman, VI, 40, glibly states that there were only fifty miles left to go, but this is a point to point measurement on a map. These pieces could not have reached Burgos until the middle of November at the earliest. In any event, would two guns have altered the situation appreciably? A dozen siege guns, even if ordered up on 19th September, could not be expected to reach the town until the end of October. For an historian to fault Wellington in regard to military transportation in an area which he knew and controlled is as dangerous as to criticize his tactical dispositions.

[2] Somers Cocks of the 16th L.D., originally on Wellington's staff, was an extremely talented intelligence officer. He transferred to the 79th, and was later killed at Burgos. See Fortescue, VIII, 580, for a testimonial from Wellington as to his value. See also Tomkinson, 212-21.

[3] Oman, VI, 26, in a note states that there were eight miners, seven of whom were hit during the siege, and five engineers. The Guards because of their internal discipline and esprit de corps could be relied on to carry out the work regardless of circumstances, but others considered the work beneath them.

attacks were launched after limited bombardments and mine explosions, but Dubreton defended his fortifications well, and made both sorties and counterattacks. The outer walls were finally taken, but the French continued to hold both the inner ring wall and the old keep.

A final attack was delivered on 18th October at 4.30 p.m. by two parties of 300 men each from the K.G.L. and the Guards. During the first ten minutes these two forces were successful, but Dubreton was able to drive them back eventually, for he still commanded 1,400 veteran soldiers. French casualties throughout the siege were 623; the Allies lost 2,059.

Meanwhile, Wellington was also conducting distant Allied operations and advising the Spaniards. On 2nd October he received from the Cortes a formal offer of the command of all Spanish military forces. The various Spanish commanders had been endeavouring to carry out Wellington's suggestions for some months. Wellington might be held responsible for future Spanish failures, but would not gain any greater co-operation from the Spanish army than he had already.[1] There was no chance of organizing and training Spanish soldiers as Beresford had the Portuguese.[2]

On 9th October, Wellington received intelligence of the junction of the armies of Soult, Joseph, and Suchet, which had taken place on the 30th of September approximately fifty miles west of Valencia. On the 19th, Wellington heard from Hill, now commanding an Allied army of 36,000 men at Madrid, that this combined French army was approaching the capital. Neither Hill nor Wellington then knew the strength of this force, but in all probability it would be too strong for Hill to oppose unaided. Wellington decided to abandon the siege of the Castle of Burgos and move south. But his covering army had first to be brought back through the town.

Since the commencement of the siege, Souham had replaced Clausel in command of the Army of Portugal, which now numbered 42,000 men. Further, Caffarelli had finally beaten back Popham and the guerrillas and brought south an additional 11,000 men. By 18th October, Wellington with 24,000 British and Portuguese, including those

[1] This controversy dragged on for months; Wellington did not wish to accept merely a title, and the Spaniards were unwilling to give him any real control of the internal organization of their army which alone could produce good soldiers in well-disciplined units.

[2] Whittingham's Spanish Division, organized and trained in the Balearic Islands, was completely provided for by Britain, but it would have been impossible to do this on a large scale.

conducting the siege, together with 10,000 Spaniards, was confronting 53,000 Frenchmen.[1] On the 20th, Souham sent forward two divisions to determine the strength of the Allied army covering Burgos. Wellington checked them in a sharp action; the French retreated precipitately. Losses were small on both sides, but the psychological advantage lay with the Allies.

Wellington began his own retreat immediately after dark on the 21st. As the field army passed Burgos, Pack's Portuguese left the trenches silently and joined the columns. All military *matériel* that could not be withdrawn had been destroyed.[2] By daybreak on the 22nd, Wellington was ten miles west of Burgos. He allowed his forces some hours rest and then proceeded towards Valladolid.

Shortly after dawn next day, a force of 6,000 French cavalry pressed in on the Allied rearguard which was composed of 1,300 British and German horsemen plus some Spanish irregulars incapable of formal action. Anson's Light Brigade manoeuvred well; Bock's heavy cavalry gave them all necessary support. When the Allies were pressed, Wellington reinforced them with two battalions of K.G.L. infantry under Halkett, and a battery of horse artillery.

All was going well until Cotton and Anson collaborated in a blunder not unusual for British cavalry. They had reached a position about two miles northeast of the village of Villodrigo where a deep tributary flows into the Arlanzon from the north; This stream was crossed by a sound stone bridge which would take time to be destroyed. Bock's and Halkett's Germans and the horse artillery had taken up a position directly behind the bridge; the light cavalry hurriedly retired over it, but reformed on the wrong flank. Instead of passing behind the guns, they rode in front, masking them completely. The French took advantage of this to cross the bridge and charge. When finally able to fire, the British gunners were unnerved, misjudged the range, and inflicted not a single casualty. They had to limber up and retire headlong to avoid capture.

[1] Wellington estimated Souham's army to be less than 40,000 when it was in fact over 50,000. Wellington consistently underestimated the forces opposed to him. This quality is unusual and refreshing in military history, but difficult to understand. His information was extremely accurate; did he intentionally overcompensate for the natural human tendency to exaggerate the size of an opponent? It may be significant that this never got him into serious trouble.

[2] The three 18-pounders were destroyed on the retreat, an indication of the difficulty of moving heavy guns, even over good Spanish roads during the autumn.

Bock and Anson were thrown back, but Halkett's rear battalion, already in square, opened fire. The French cavalry reined in, but a fresh regiment of dragoons came up and charged under the eyes of Souham and Caffarelli. There was always the possibility in such a situation that some accident caused by the presence of wounded horses, or the behaviour of a few frightened infantrymen, would cause a gap to develop in the defence. But the Germans were ready; their continuous volleys began at a range of 180 yards. The squadron in the centre of the French line could not face the fire and bright steel, and dividing, it passed round the square without closing in. The dragoons now reached Halkett's other battalion in open column, but these Germans also formed square and took a severe toll of the enemy. For a period of some twenty minutes, Halkett's two weak battalions, not more than 1,000 bayonets in all, were surrounded by a far more numerous cavalry force, but kept both their formation and their discipline. They drew off gradually, each battalion aiding the other, giving the Allied cavalry ample time to reform and resume their rearguard duties. The Allies lost during the day 230 men; French casualties exceeded 300.

Meanwhile, the main Allied army did no fighting, but marched during daylight an average of twenty-six miles, leaving only a few stragglers. Wellington took up a strong position behind the Carrion. The Army should have been relatively safe, for they held all three bridges across this swollen river, but the French were able to push the Spaniards back on the northern flank and crossed one of the bridges. Wellington managed to fight and manoeuvre so that no advantage could be taken of this, although his army showed signs of disintegrating.

'It is impossible for any army to have given themselves up to more dissipation and everything that is bad, as did our army. The conduct of some men would have disgraced savages, drunkenness had prevailed to such a frightful extent that I have often wondered how it was that a great part of our army were not cut off. It was no unfrequent thing to see a long string of mules carrying drunken soldiers to prevent them falling into the hands of the enemy. It would not be fair in me to mention any particular Corps, all partook in some degree a share of the disgrace. At Validolid (sic), the—was punishing several hours, the sides of the roads were strewed with soldiers as if dead, not so much by fatigue as by wine. But there is some excuse, from Burgos to Salamanca is chiefly a wine country and as there had been a good harvest, and the new wine was in tanks particularly about Validolid the soldiers ran mad. I remember seeing a soldier fully accoutred with his knapsack on in a large tank, he had either fell in or had been pushed in by his comrades, there he lay dead. I saw a Dragoon fire his pistols into a large vat containing several thousands of gallons, in a few minutes we were up to our knees in wine fighting like tigers for it.' [1]

Instead of moving southwest to the Duero, Wellington crossed the Pisuerga at Cabezon on the 26th and again interposed a river between himself and the French. The Pisuerga was here unfordable and crossed by only a single narrow bridge. On the 28th, the French endeavoured to force their way over the river at Valladolid, but were easily repulsed by the Allied 7th Division. Further downstream, Halkett's two K.G.L. battalions did an excellent job defending the bridges at Simancas. The third battalion of Halkett's Brigade, the Brunswick Oels Regiment, were at Tordesillas. They had destroyed the centre of the bridge across the Duero here, and occupied a fortification at its southern end. [2] A party of 56 Frenchmen swam the river with their muskets and ammunition on a kind of a raft and stormed this tower. Both the subaltern in charge of the half company garrison and the battalion commander, who at that moment was several hundred yards away in a wood, panicked. The French secured a foothold on the south bank of the river and were reinforced; they were strongly supported by artillery on the north bank and soon strengthened their position.

Many commanders would have attacked this bridgehead and lost heavily, or abandoned the line of the Duero. Wellington did neither; he merely contained the small area occupied by the French by advancing an entire division and constructing a semicircle of earthworks around it. If Souham and Caffarelli tried to break out while the river was high, they would have to place a large force in a cramped space not easily reinforced nor protected.

Wellington in his retreat from Burgos had fought the French to a standstill on numerous occasions in spite of his numerical inferiority. But the situation in the south was not good. Hill was holding a position on the Tagus south of Madrid with 28,000 British and Portuguese plus 8,000 Spaniards against a French army under Joseph, Jourdan, and Soult

[1] *Wheeler*, 105-6.

[2] Spanish bridges were often so fortified. This Brunswick regiment was popularly called the 'Owls'.

of at least 60,000 men. The Tagus gave relatively little protection; a retreat was necessary.[1]

Before dawn on 28th October, Hill retired to a position running roughly north and south behind a tributary of the Tagus north of Aranjuez; his army was now in actual contact with the French. Next morning, he received a dispatch dictated by Wellington early in the evening of the 27th; the two forces were now but thirty-six hours, or about 130 miles, apart. Wellington would hold his position on the Pisuerga and Duero as long as possible before retiring on Arevalo. Hill was to retreat at once and join him there. Wellington pointed out that he was opposed by a force greatly exceeding his own, and conceivably might be forced back on Ciudad Rodrigo. Hill must be ready, therefore, to retreat if necessary by the valley of the Tagus.[2] The implication was that Hill should retreat in a manner which would allow him to follow either route. Wellington assured Hill that a message would immediately be sent to him if he was unable to reach Arevalo.[3]

Hill ordered part of his command to retire on Madrid and Escorial as darkness set in on the 29th. The rest, with the exception of Skerrett's force now attached to Cole's Division, moved back at dawn. Skerrett, under Cole's experienced direction, acted as a rearguard; he occupied a strong position north of Aranjuez and held back the French all day. At nightfall this force also fell back. Close contact with the French was now lost, although the Allied army straggled badly.[4] Hill's army had passed the Guadarramas and was in the vicinity of Villacastin by 2nd November. Wellington was continuing to hold the line of the Duero; a concentration at Arevalo was still possible.

But Wellington now decided that a junction at Salamanca would be preferable. He instructed Hill to march to Alba de Tormes; the Allied northern Army retired on San Christobal. The entire Allied force was

[1] By October this river should have been in flood, but the autumn rains, so abundant in the north, had not begun further south.

[2] During the retreat he had seen with his own eyes most of the enemy and had a clearer idea of their strength.

[3] For once, Wellington's meaning is not clear. I cannot see how Hill was to follow a route by which he could at the last moment cross the Guadarramas or march west in the Tagus valley. I believe that Hill solved his problem by simply concluding that if Wellington intended to stay on the Duero, he would do so, while he (Hill) would be safe in moving on Aravelo.

[4] Hill's force found new wine at Valdemoro. Enemy cavalry captured hundreds dead drunk the next morning, but also picked up information that stopped the French in their tracks! Wellington had arrived personally in Madrid; the whole Allied army might be just over the next crest in battle formation. The rumour was false, but it gave Hill an unmolested retreat.

concentrated by the 8th on a front of twenty miles running from San Christobal southeast to Alba and numbered 52,000 British and Portuguese, plus 18,000 Spaniards.

Meanwhile, Wellington knew that the French had occupied Madrid on the 1st, but had evacuated it on the 8th. By the 10th, there was not a French soldier in New Castile; Soult was moving north and west toward a junction with Souham.[1] When their forces concentrated, Wellington estimated that they would number about 80,000 men.[2]

From the 8th to the 14th, the Allied army remained in the San Christobal-Alba position. Fighting only occurred when Soult attacked a brigade of Hill's 'corps' holding Alba. Allied casualties were less than 100; the French lost over 200. Wellington appreciated the strength of his position, but realized that the French had sacrificed the southern half of Spain to achieve their concentration. To bring such a force together at such great cost and then not fight a numerically inferior enemy was unthinkable. Wellington calmly and confidently awaited the attack which never came. The French cavalry reconnoitred all along the line, but there was no forward movement of infantry.

Early on the morning of the 15th, the French crossed the upper Tormes some distance south of Alba, but too far away to be caught in motion as Marmont had been on 22nd July. Soult showed no signs of attacking but did have his enormous army closed up and in battle formation as if to receive an Allied attack. Slowly and cautiously, the French began to extend their left flank to the west, threatening Allied communications with Ciudad Rodrigo.

Wellington first assumed a new position south of the Tormes facing south and southeast and waited, hoping for an attack. His army was concentrated, strongly posted, and favoured by good concealed lateral communications. But when the French moved west, Wellington had either to attack them or retire. He could not risk being cut off from his sources of supply.

At 2 p.m., Wellington ordered a retreat to the west; at about the same time, it started to rain. The entire area was soon swamped. Diarists have likened this rain to a tropical deluge; the army were forced to wade for miles. Nothing more was seen of the French that day; darkness descended before 4 p.m. After covering about ten miles, the Allied army bivouacked in miserable circumstances. Fires were

[1] Joseph and Jourdan allowed Soult to command the combined French armies of the South and the Centre as regards field manoeuvres.

[2] Wellington was underestimating his enemies as usual; the total French strength was at least 95,000 men.

impossible to kindle; rations were short. The men were used to receiving regular issues of bread, meat, and other provisions, but all that most battalions got that evening was tough beef.[1] The natural grumbling at having to retreat without fighting was aggravated by the weather and meagre rations.

The 16th was a day of trial and tribulation for everyone. It rained almost constantly. No French infantry was seen, but their cavalry harassed the Allies continuously. They never charged, but picked up 600 prisoners, mostly stragglers. The roads were quagmires which sucked off shoes and even stockings.

'The effects of hunger and fatigue were even more visible than on the preceding day. A savage sort of desperation had taken possession of our minds, and those who lived on the most friendly terms in happier times now quarrelled with each other, using the most frightful imprecations, on the slightest offence. A misanthropic spirit was in possession of every bosom. The streams which fell from the hills were swelled into rivers, which we had to wade, and many fell out, including even officers. It was piteous to see some of the men, who had dragged their limbs after them with determined spirit, fall down at last among the mud, unable to proceed further, and sure of being taken prisoners if they escaped death. Towards night the rain had somewhat abated, but the cold was excessive, and numbers who had resisted the effect of hunger and fatigue with a tardy spirit were now obliged to give way, and sank to the ground praying for death to deliver them from their misery. Some prayed not in vain, for next morning before daylight, in passing from our halting-ground to the road, I stumbled over several who had died in the night.'[2]

The 17th was even worse. The centre column of the Allied army was left without the cavalry assigned to it and had to fight French cavalry and artillery.[3] Unnecessary losses were suffered, including the capture of Sir Edward Paget, commander of the 1st Division and senior to every-

---

[1] Many tons of biscuits and other food was available in the area; Commissary General Kennedy was not at fault. James Willoughby Gordon, the interim Q.M.G., from 2nd August to 11th December 1812, ordered these supplies back to Portugal by a route inaccessible to those responsible for feeding the troops.

[2] *Oman*, VI, 145-6, quoting Sergeant Donaldson of the 94th.

[3] *Tomkinson*, 224, attributes this to Q.M.G. Gordon, but the cavalry cannot have been blameless.

one in the British army except Wellington himself.[1] The Light Division fought an action near the village of San Munoz on the Huebra river; casualties were slight, but the French cavalry carried off over 1,000 Allied stragglers during the day.[2]

The southern column of the Allied army was not disturbed by the enemy, but their breaches of discipline were even greater. Peasants were plundered and molested; herds of pigs were slaughtered far beyond the need for food. British soldiers discovered more wine and brandy than they could drink. The Portuguese were better disciplined, but suffered more from the severity of the weather.

To complete the dismal story, three divisional commanders received specific marching orders from Wellington for the 18th, but decided that they knew their business better than their C-in-C. They moved off by another route to find their way blocked by a Spanish army. For two hours Wellington waited for them where they should have been; guessed what had happened, and rode across country to find their divisions in hopeless confusion. But he brought order out of chaos; the whole army was safe, well-fed, and dry by the following evening.[3]

The retreat from Salamanca to Ciudad Rodrigo cost 3,000 men, more by nearly half than were lost at Burgos. Fully four-fifths of these were unnecessary. The Allied army had not distinguished itself.[4]

Wellington wrote on 28th November a scathing communication intended to be delivered to general officers, colonels commanding brigades, and the heads of staff departments only. He minced no words in his condemnation of the recent behaviour of officers and men alike. This confidential memorandum soon became public and was even printed in British papers.[5] Individually and collectively the Allied army

---

[1] Paget had just come out again to the Peninsula and joined the Army during the siege of Burgos. When taken by three French dragoons, he was accompanied by his Spanish orderly only. He had lost an arm in the Seminary at Oporto and was practically defenceless while on horseback.

[2] Here French infantry appeared at the front for the first time during the retreat, but their artillery did most of the fighting. Both round shot and shells were smothered in the sodden soil; hardly anyone was hit.

[3] The generals involved were Clinton, Stewart, and Dalhousie. There were no serious consequences because Soult did not cross the Huebra.

[4] This disintegration was similar to that which occurred in Sir John Moore's army four years before. Even after losing battles, the French did not go to pieces in this way. Massena's army in Portugal withstood greater privations for over five months than the Allied army knew for four days.

[5] The whole memorandum should be read, *Dispatches*, IX, 582-5, but a single paragraph contains the principal accusation,

'It must be obvious to every officer, that from the moment the troops commenced

considered themselves unjustly accused. But the facts remain that drunkenness, insubordination, and brutality toward Spanish civilians were common. The armies of Hill and Wellington were not defeated in battle, nor even in actions. The French hardly ever pursued closely, nor were Allied armies ever called on to make unduly long marches, except on one day, 23rd October. Wellington's armies rested for considerable intervals during the course of their retreats, and would have been tolerably fed were it not for the errors of some officers to whom this communication was sent.

The retreats from Burgos, Madrid, and Salamanca tended to conceal from the army itself, and even the British public, the preponderant success of 1812. There had never been any question that if the French concentrated even half their 250,000 veteran soldiers in Spain against Wellington, the Allied army would be in danger. The enemy had done precisely this, yet Wellington suffered no serious loss. Even though he was forced back in November to a position he had held in May, he had freed the entire southern half of Spain. After years of French occupation, New Castile, including Madrid, became a 'no-man's-land.' The capital was lost by the French in August, retaken for a period of eight days only in November, and then reoccupied temporarily in the early winter.

The change in morale in the two contending armies is also significant. After a few comfortable days, the Allies made light of their reverses and began to appreciate their overall success. Few understood Wellington's strategic and logistic achievements, but all could appreciate the tangible benefits they brought about. The outlook for the future was bright.

The French, on the other hand, had almost nothing of which to be proud, nor did they anticipate much success in future. In spite of having relinquished territory to enable three of their armies to concentrate in

their retreat from the neighbourhood of Burgos on the one hand, and from Madrid on the other, the officers lost all command over their men. Irregularities and outrages of all descriptions were committed with impunity, and losses have been sustained which ought never to have occurred. Yet the necessity for retreat existing, none was ever made on which the troops had such short marches; none on which they made such long and repeated halts; and none on which the retreating armies were so little pressed on their rear by the enemy.'

Wellington undoubtedly would have preferred to have spoken to his officers face to face rather than write this, but those addressed were scattered over 1,500 square miles of territory. Most of those who felt unjustly condemned base their case on the fact that their battalion behaved a little better than another they had heard about.

central Spain, little had been accomplished.[1] The French knew nothing of the sufferings of the Allies between the 15th and 19th of November; they were equally exposed to the abominable weather, in no more comfortable surroundings, and had even less food.

The year 1812, after Salamanca, was more notable for strategy than tactics, yet Wellington's retreat from Burgos to the position south of the Duero was brilliantly carried out considering the odds against him and the misbehaviour of his troops. The actions were on a small scale, but were fought well. His extemporaneous manoeuvres and re-alignments were cleverly conceived and carried out with professional efficiency, particularly the shift to the south side of the Pisuerga at Cabezon, halting the French on the Duero, and sealing off the bridge-head at Tordesillas. Soult's refusal to attack 52,000 Anglo-Portuguese with almost 100,000 Frenchmen is indicative of the respect now felt for Wellington by his opponents.

TOPOGRAPHICAL OBSERVATIONS

The road and river systems in the valleys of the Duero and the Tagus and in the extensive areas between them remain much as they were 150 years ago. The smaller towns such as Arevalo, Villacastin, and Tordesillas have not changed greatly. The larger cities, in particular Madrid, have grown enormously; a few ruins only remain of the Forts of the Retiro.

Wellington's positions around Salamanca, particularly those between San Christobal and Alba de Tormes, can be traced easily, as can Hill's between Valdemoro and Aranjuez.

The ruins of the castle at Burgos and the French fortifications on the hill to the east are fascinating. The trenches and mine craters were filled in by its defenders after Wellington abandoned the siege, but the entire place was badly damaged by the intentional explosion of the magazines when the French abandoned it. With a good map of the siege operations one can follow exactly each episode in this gallant but futile effort.

---

[1] *Fortescue*, VIII, 624, quotes Foy's *Vie Militaire*, 192-3,

'Lord Wellington has retired unconquered, with the glory of the laurels of Arapiles, having restored to the Spaniards the country south of the Tagus, and made us destroy our magazines, our fortifications—in a word all that we have gained by our conquest, and all that could assure the maintenance of it.'

XV

VITORIA

THE Allied army, once in winter quarters around Ciudad Rodrigo, was soon restored; practically overnight health, discipline, and morale returned. The army was now in the northern corridor only; no British troops were required in the Elvas-Badajoz area, for there were no French units south of the Tagus.

As the winter wore on, Wellington heard rumours, and then had confirmation of French disasters in Russia. The French army in Spain could not be greatly reinforced for the next campaign, while the Allies would have more regulars with them, both British and Portuguese, than ever before. Protracted negotiations concerning the command of the Spanish army continued; Wellington would have at least their co-operation, together with that of the guerrillas, now more numerous and efficient than at any time in the past.

In order to take full advantage of the situation, Wellington had to remedy first the shortcomings apparent in 1812. The most serious of these was the weakness of internal discipline in many battalions. His officers strove to prove him wrong in his recent criticism. Slackness in all forms was eliminated; schools for NCO's and enlisted men were set up in every unit. Tons of powder and lead, and thousands of flints were expended in weapons practice. Every battalion was drilled to the extent that they could move from open column into line, or from line into square, in 30 seconds, even in rough country.

Wellington planned to improve the health of his men and had the full co-operation of Surgeon General McGrigor. Central hospitals were instituted; delivery of sick men to them was expedited. Damp bivouacs had probably caused as many casualties amongst the troops as had the

French; tents were to be provided for all infantry.[1] The heavy cast iron camp kettles which had been carried on mules were discarded and replaced with light, sheet-metal cooking pots which the men could carry themselves. This would help to avoid delay in the preparation of food. A reduction in total load to be carried by each infantry soldier was achieved in the spring by the elimination of greatcoats. With tents available, a single blanket and ground sheet per man would be sufficient, except in really cold weather.

Wellington had seen the benefits derived from the position and prestige of senior NCO's in the Guards; these men by example, admonition, and informal physical punishment, were largely responsible for the discipline of these great battalions. The C-in-C encouraged this intervening socio-military strata between officers and enlisted men. He demanded and obtained increments in pay for some sergeants.[2] A military police corps was formed; Judge Advocate General Larpent was continuously prosecuting delinquents. Wellington stubbornly insisted, in opposition to the Duke of York, that he should be allowed to retain veteran battalions, and combine them with others when reduced in numbers, rather than send them back to Britain to recruit.

Wellington was more guarded now in what he committed to paper than he had been in 1809. He had learnt through bitter experience that there were leakages of information even in high places.[3] It was clear, however, that he planned to take the offensive without undue delay and to strike toward France directly. The army had to be in good state, physically, mentally, and materially, for a long sustained attack. Exactly how this was to be ordered depended on the French.

Wellington carefully considered all intelligence received. Napoleon's defeat in Russia and subsequent return to Paris to organize a new Grand Army could lead to large withdrawals from the Peninsula. This did not take place; veteran soldiers and cadres of officers and NCO's were taken from Spain, but were replaced. The total French force south of the Pyrenees still exceeded 200,000 men.[4] Suchet's army, between Valencia

---

[1] These tents were issued on about 1st March 1813 and appear to have been large and round, capable of accommodating up to 25 men each. They were carried on 'public' mules: *Ward*, 200-1.

[2] Wellington's proposal for increasing the pay of all sergeants could not be accepted because of lack of money, but one per company was chosen to receive more pay and a new badge: *Fortescue*, IX, 100.

[3] James Willoughby Gordon, Wellington's interim Q.M.G., actually gave military secrets to the Whig press.

[4] French conscripts who served in Spain were good soldiers; those inducted in the winter of 1812-13 did their duty well.

and the French border, was the largest, and numbered 60,000 to 70,000 men. The Army of the North under Clausel was about 30,000 strong. Three French armies now occupied central Spain; the Army of the South commanded by Gazan, the Army of the Centre under D'Erlon, and Reille's Army of Portugal. If these three concentrated, they would have a total strength of over 100,000 sabres and bayonets; all were within six days' march of Arevalo.

Wellington planned to prevent such concentrations. As in 1812, he endeavoured to hold Suchet on the east coast by threats of seaborne landings. The Anglo-Sicilian force at Alicante now commanded by Sir John Murray was supposed to be under Wellington's general direction; he had given Murray detailed instructions.[1]

Murray fought a creditable action at Castalla in March. On 28th May, his force of over 18,000 men of four nationalities was carried in transports 300 miles up the coast and put ashore near French-held Tarragona. Wellington stressed in his instructions to Murray and the co-operating Spanish commanders that they should avoid general actions except under the most favourable circumstances. The C-in-C expected nothing brilliant from Murray.

Clausel's army in the north was to be kept occupied as Caffarelli's had been the year before. Wellington had to do little more than encourage the guerrillas and supply *matériel*. The struggle between Popham, Mina, Longa, and other guerrillas, and the French garrisons was still going on. The French concentration in central Spain during the previous October and November had allowed serious insurrection to break out along the Biscay coast; the great road into Spain from France was more often closed than open. Napoleon himself had ordered that two-thirds of Reille's Army of Portugal should be loaned to Clausel to restore French control of the eastern half of this area, but progress was slow. Spanish leaders were now carrying out a form of warfare which Wellington had long been suggesting to them.[2] They all sensed victory; Mina now had two fine 24-pounder ship's guns and was using them efficiently for small sieges.

[1] Sir John Murray had commanded the reinforced brigade that crossed the Duero east of Oporto on 12th May 1809. He should not be confused with Sir George Murray, Wellington's Q.M.G. Bentinck retained the right to withdraw troops for use in Sicily.

[2] Wellington had finally accepted the supreme command of all Spanish armies; Mina, Longa, Sanchez, and most other guerrilla chiefs now held regular commissions and did their best to obey orders. Wellington's eternal admonition was that they should not risk formal battles, but rather to continue with their irregular operations. Some of them had grown so powerful, however, that they could seize quite large fortified places.

The French still had in central Spain about 80,000 men, but they were scattered to enable them to live on the country. The remaining third of Reille's force lay at Palencia; Gazan, with the still powerful Army of the South remained between Madrid and the Portuguese border. D'Erlon and the reconstituted Army of the Centre was in the vicinity of Segovia. These three appeared to be expecting Wellington to attack from the west; they would then concentrate just north of the Guadarramas.

But Wellington intended to bypass central Spain entirely, and to move so fast that by the time his opponents had concentrated, the Allied army would have thrust far to the north. This plan had taken definite shape by 10th February 1813 when Wellington took the first step in transferring his communications from Portugal to the Biscay coast.[1] To disguise his intention, however, he advanced Hill well into Spain as if to march on Madrid by the Tagus valley.[2]

The commencement of Wellington's operations was originally scheduled for the first week in May, but the spring rains were delayed. Fresh forage which depended on these, could not be obtained for almost three weeks. The pontoons which were being brought up from the Tagus, travelled more slowly than had been anticipated.[3] But Wellington had the largest and most experienced section of his army, 81,000 Anglo-Portuguese with 17 batteries of artillery, ready to march soon after the middle of the month.

On 20th May, Wellington advanced on Salamanca from Ciudad Rodrigo with the Light Division, three British cavalry brigades, and

[1] On this date, Wellington wrote to Bathurst, *Dispatches*, X, 104–5,
'As it is possible that the events of the next campaign may render it necessary for the army to undertake one or more sieges in the north of Spain, I beg leave to recommend that the ordnance and stores contained in the enclosed lists should be embarked in transports and sent to Coruna, to be at my disposal as soon as may be convenient; and that twice the quantity of each article may be in a state of preparation in England, to be shipped when I shall report that they are necessary.'

[2] *Fortescue*, IX, 132, says, 'Above all, the advanced position of Hill at Coria and the constant movement of his Spanish troops served, as Wellington had intended, to attract the attention of the French staff to the wrong quarter.' Allied troops were cantoned as far east as Bejar.

[3] These heavy, clumsy boats were placed on horse-drawn carriages which utilized wheels and axles taken from the artillery. Their journey over bad roads at comparatively high speed and in complete secrecy was possibly the greatest feat of transportation during the whole war. They were shifted from the Tagus to the Duero in less than a month; oxen and the old wagons would have taken twice as long.

Spaniards under Sanchez and de España. They would meet on the way Hill's 'corps' which now included Morillo's Spaniards. Salamanca was captured on the morning of the 26th after a running fight with a division of French infantry and two brigades of cavalry who lost 500 casualties in addition to their baggage, ammunition, and accumulated supplies. By evening, Wellington was in his San Christobal-Arapiles position with his right extending to Alba; he was hoping to give the impression that the entire Allied army was there, but in fact only 30 per cent of his field army was with him.

The other 70 per cent under Graham had crossed the Duero well inside Portugal by the pontoon bridge, had halted near the border for three days, and had then marched east into Spain in three columns on the morning of the 25th. Graham had six of the eight Allied infantry divisions with him as well as other troops, almost 60,000 men in all. This army was held up on the 29th by the rain-swollen Esla which flows south into the Duero. Normally, there were several fords. But just as the difficulty was encountered, Wellington appeared. He had left Hill at Salamanca at dawn on the 28th, ridden fifty miles before dark to the Duero opposite Miranda, crossed high above the swirling currents in a basket suspended by ropes, and then ridden the rest of the way to Carvagales, Graham's headquarters, on the 29th.

Wellington pushed a force of cavalry and infantry across the Esla at daybreak next morning, an infantryman hanging to the downstream stirrup of each trooper.[1] A French picket observing the river here was captured in its entirety. Once a foothold was gained on the far bank, the pontoons were placed in position. Three infantry divisions together with cavalry and artillery were across before dark. The French gave up Zamora without a fight.

The beauty of this whole manoeuvre was that Wellington had passed the Duero—a great military obstacle if defended in spring—before the French had any reason to suspect that the entire Allied army was not at Salamanca.[2] Hill was now ordered to move on Toro. Wellington and Graham pushed back the French along the north bank of the Duero beyond that town. Enemy cavalry and infantry delayed too long here on 2nd June and suffered seriously in their retreat.

By the evening of the 3rd, Wellington had his entire force united north of the Duero. The French were streaming north, but in disorder;

[1] This crossing was achieved at some cost; several horses and men were drowned in the deep, swiftly flowing river.

[2] The Allied southern command was disproportionately strong in cavalry so that a heavy screen could be thrown forward to prevent French reconnaissance at close quarters.

Joseph and Jourdan ordered a concentration at Valladolid; Madrid had been given up for the last time on 27th May. Wellington realized that if Joseph and Jourdan could unite with Clausel, the Allied army would be at a serious numerical disadvantage; but he had no intention of giving them time to concentrate.

Joseph and Jourdan retired towards Burgos. For the next nine days, the Allied army followed in three columns. Hill advanced along or close to the great road; Wellington and Graham were moving along parallel routes about ten and twenty miles west respectively. Giron, with a considerable Spanish army was still further to the west.[1] If Wellington had followed the enemy in a single column, there would have been many extensive rearguard actions, for the French needed time not only to bring in their outlying units, but to send on in advance their vast baggage and plunder trains. The presence of these Allied flanking forces further west made such delaying tactics impossible. The French fell back 100 miles without offering any serious resistance. On 12th June they occupied a strong position just west of Burgos and appeared to offer battle. Wellington attacked in front with Hill's 'corps' and at the same time brought down the Light Division on their flank and rear. The French retreated so fast that no infantry contact was made.

At 7 a.m. on the 13th, the French blew up the castle at Burgos; it was now obvious that they were not going to hold the town as they had done the previous autumn.[2] In twenty-one days, Wellington had cleared the French from central Spain; Joseph could only continue his retreat toward France. But from Burgos to the Ebro and beyond, the great road ran through mountainous country abounding in strong defensive positions which could not be easily flanked. If the Allies followed the French through such territory, Clausel's army would inevitably join Joseph's before Wellington could bring on a battle with either of them alone.

Within an hour of hearing the explosions, Wellington ordered his columns to swing away from Burgos to the northwest and north.[3] The

[1] It should not be inferred that these separate forces marched across country, nor that they rigidly maintained their positions. Their routes conformed to roads, but in general followed this pattern. See the excellent folding map at the back of *Oman*, VI, for exact details.

[2] This was badly mismanaged by the French, who killed hundreds of their own soldiers and many Spanish civilians, but did not completely destroy the fortifications. These explosions were both seen and heard in the Allied camps twelve miles away.

[3] *Oman*, VI, 359–60, discusses Wellington's strategic planning at this time and quotes Croker to prove a spontaneous decision. I consider that the entire pattern of outflanking

French were to be followed on the great road by Sanchez's Spanish lancers only. During the next week, the Allied army accomplished prodigies. The roads in this territory were so bad that the French who knew them well considered it impossible for an army accompanied by artillery to pass through the area at all. But Wellington had discovered that in early summer an active, well-conditioned army could negotiate these mountains, even with artillery, baggage and supplies (Plate 38).[1]

The Allied army marched north until it reached Villarcayo and Medina de Pomar on the 15th and 16th before turning east again. For four days there was no contact with the French. On the evening of the 17th, however, the cavalry of the two armies was again skirmishing. The French had 'taken up the line of the Ebro' as Wellington had expected, but the Allies were already north and east of that line.

On the 18th, Graham's column was advancing east and nearing a good road running south from Bilbao to Miranda de Ebro. A French column was retiring north along this road; the two collided in a short, bloody skirmish followed by a prolonged cannonade a mile south of Osma. The Light Division was marching approximately parallel with Graham, but three or four miles further south on twisting mountain tracks through rugged country. The head of the Light Division suddenly ran into the middle of a French division at the village of San Millan. Wellington was with them in person; he handled the Light Division and some cavalry flawlessly. He ordered forward the riflemen and followed with the line battalions of both brigades. There was some confusion, but the Light Division was at its best.[2] The French suffered

to the left, preparations for crossing the mountains near the headwaters of the Ebro, and reaching Santander, were all so well organized that the decision could *not* have been made on the spur of the moment.

[1] This advance across country made necessary the dismantling of field guns, carrying the pieces over precipitous heights, and reassembling them on the other side. The feat is even more remarkable to one following these same routes today. *Harry Smith*, I, 97, says, 'Our Division halted the next day (20th), but the army never did, from the day of breaking up its cantonments until they fought the battle of Vitoria. It was a most wonderful march, the army in great fighting order, and every man in better wind than a trained pugilist.'

[2] *Oman*, VI, 375–6, states that after the first French brigade was broken and 'had been driven through the village, and was making off along the road, with the Rifle battalions in hot pursuit, the second brigade, with the baggage in its rear, came on the scene most unexpected by the British, for the track by which it emerged issued out between two perpendicular rocks and had not been noticed. Perceiving the trap into which they had fallen, the belated French turned off the road, and made for the hillside to their right, while Kempt's brigade started in pursuit, scrambling over the rocky slopes to catch them up. The line of flight of the French took them past the ground over which Vandaleur's men were chasing their comrades of the leading brigade, and the odd result followed that they came in upon the rear of the 52nd, which performed the extraordinary feat of bringing up its left shoulder, forming line facing to the rear at a run, and charging backward.'

400 casualties, and lost all their baggage, knapsacks, and quantities of muskets; partially unarmed survivors were scattered among the mountains.

Wellington now left the Light Division and rode across country to Graham. As soon as he arrived, the Allies south of Osma delivered a crushing attack which forced the French back the way they had come. The defeat of Joseph's belated effort to prevent the French northern flank from being turned had failed; the entire French army had to abandon the line of the Ebro and fall back further along the 'great road'.

Prisoners taken at San Millan and Osma were immediately interrogated. They were from the three divisions of Reille's Army of Portugal which formed a part of Joseph's army as recently concentrated; the rest of Reille's force was still in the north. This was reassuring; the Allies had still a numerical superiority over the French forces in their front. The French prisoners had no idea of the whereabouts of Clausel. The sudden advance of the Allies had turned an already bad communications system into chaos. French armies were completely cut off from each other; the guerrillas were more active than ever. Three squadrons were required to carry a message twenty miles over a good road.[1]

Wellington's 'correspondents' were able to advise him of Clausel's position, even if Joseph and Jourdan remained in ignorance of it. Clausel's army had been at Pamplona on the morning of the 16th; it was unlikely that it would be able to join Joseph's until the 22nd. The French must be brought to battle before then. Graham was sent ahead to the north before turning east, while Hill and Wellington marched south from Osma. The British and Portuguese losses in the fighting and from straggling had been small; the 6th Division remained at Medina de Pomar with some cavalry to protect the lines of communications. The Allied army now numbered a little over 70,000; Giron's Spanish army was detached, and in movement even further north.

Wellington's forces were engaged before 7 a.m. on the 19th. After advancing south as far as Espijar on the Bilbao–Miranda road, the C-in-C turned east and ordered into line the 4th and Light Divisions supported by Hill's entire 'corps'. At least three French divisions with several batteries were in strong positions running roughly north and south in the valley of the Bayas. The remaining French army had

---

[1] When on 9th June Joseph finally sent orders from Burgos to Clausel to join him, he sent 1,500 men to protect the courier. This force reached Clausel near Pamplona after six days, but answering dispatches never got through at all: *Oman*, VI, 356.

retired north and was within supporting distance on the great road near Puebla de Arganzon.

By the early afternoon Wellington had decided that a serious action on the 19th was undesirable. The French army was resting and concentrated; his own was considerably dispersed and tired.[1] Graham's force was not as far advanced to the east as Wellington wished. The weather was unseasonably cold; it rained throughout the entire area. The French were allowed to retreat undisturbed into the valley of the Zadorra west of Vitoria.

'Correspondents' came in during the evening with the intelligence that French convoys had collected in Vitoria to such an extent that several days would elapse before they could be dispatched to the east. Joseph must fight with or without Clausel's help, or abandon a large part of the spoil taken from Spain by himself and his officers. The French were reported to be taking up positions in the western valley.

The valley of the Zadorra is roughly rectangular, about six miles wide by ten long, but is a valley only in comparison to the mountains which hem it in. The only flat land lies around the town of Vitoria at the eastern end of this amphitheatre. The western two-thirds is composed of rolling country broken by some steep hills. The river enters this valley through a defile in the northeast corner, flows from east to west in a fairly straight line on the northern side of the valley for about four-fifths of its length, and then bends sharply to the south around a rugged eminence. The Zadorra then makes a series of loops, before flowing out through a defile in the mountains to the southwest. The great road from Burgos to Bayonne entered and passed out of the valley through these same defiles, but ran south of the Zadorra through the middle of the valley.

There were secondary roads into the valley of minor importance; the one leading directly east from Vitoria to Pamplona was at that time only just practicable for wheeled traffic in good weather.[2] There was a fair road running directly west through the village of Nanclares into the valley of the Bayas, and another which ran through a pass in the southern range of mountains (Plate 40). Finally, there were two fair

[1] Wellington must have had a good knowledge of the country to the east; he was surely already considering the complicated movements to be undertaken thirty-six hours later.

[2] The present main road follows this old track for some miles before turning north toward San Sebastian; the old 'great road', passing out of the valley to the northeast through the defile of Sallinas, is now only a secondary road.

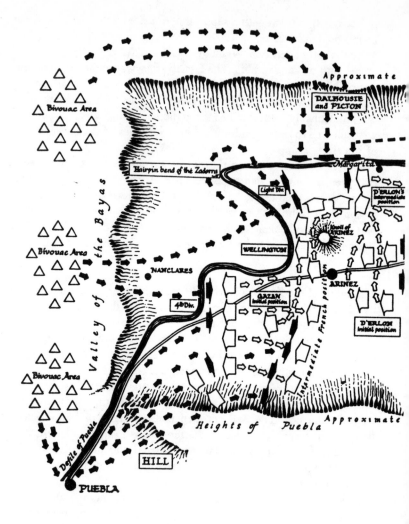

XII.

(1) Hill with 2nd Division, Silveira's Portuguese Division, and Morillo's Spanish Division —20,000.

(2) Wellington: North (Dalhousie) 7th and 3rd Divisions.
South (C-in-C personally) 4th and Light Divisions—30,000 altogether.

256

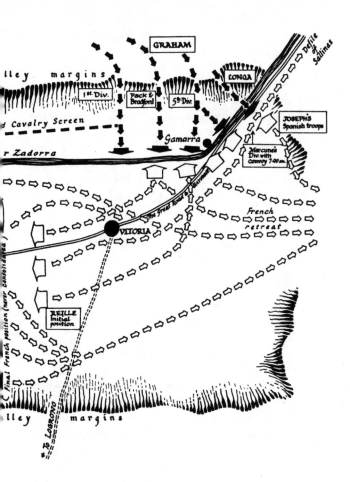

VITORIA

(3) Graham with 1st and 5th Divisions, Pack's and Bradford's Portuguese, and Longa's Spaniards—25,000.

roads to the north from Vitoria which crossed the Zadorra before entering the mountains between the valley and the Biscay coast.

By the evening of the 20th, Wellington knew the French dispositions. Gazan's four and a half infantry divisions formed a first line facing directly west just behind the Zadorra. There were several hills in their immediate rear which provided good positions for numerous artillery. Gazan's left rested on the heights forming the southern rim of the valley and his right on a hairpin loop of the Zadorra.

Their second line was composed of the two full divisions of D'Erlon's Army of the Centre bivouacked on either side of the great road about midway between Gazans' forces and Vitoria. Some other units of D'Erlon's army were either far to the northeast defending the defile of Sallinas, or guarding Joseph in person. Reille's three infantry divisions formed a third line immediately west of Vitoria. There was a considerable amount of artillery and cavalry supporting both the second and third lines.

Apparently, the French expected Wellington to attack from the west after crossing the Zadorra.[1] Such an operation was sure to be costly and could easily be defeated by forces posted in three strong lines.

But Wellington had no intention of attacking head on, and divided his army into four columns. Hill's 'corps' entered the valley from the southwest both over the mountains and through the defile. A little further north, Wellington was personally in command of two columns. That on the right was composed of the 4th and Light Divisions together with four brigades of cavalry which would advance through Nanclares just as the French expected the entire Allied army to do. But this force was not to attack until Gazan's line was already hard hit on both flanks.

The left centre column was composed of the 3rd and 7th Divisions with a proper proportion of cavalry and artillery; it was to enter the valley at its northwestern corner and attack Gazan's line from the northern flank and rear. Gazan's army of about 35,000 would be overwhelmed by 50,000 men.[2]

Swinging north *behind* the mountains, Graham, with the 1st and 5th Divisions, Pack's and Bradford's Independent Portuguese Brigades, Longa's Spaniards, cavalry, and artillery, was to enter the valley at its northeastern corner, after first cutting the great Vitoria-Bayonne road.

---

[1] In June this stream is fordable in many places and was crossed by a dozen bridges within the valley, none of which had been destroyed.

[2] Including Morillo's fine Spanish Division which had long been associated with Hill's veterans.

Graham had over 20,000 men, but would be operating initially at least eight miles from his nearest support.

During the night of the 20th, Wellington received positive intelligence concerning Clausel. He had moved from Pamplona with the intention of joining Joseph on the Ebro and had marched southwest to Logrono. Joseph's retreat to Vitoria would cause Clausel to march northwest again. Even assuming he knew Joseph's position exactly, which was doubtful, Clausel could not reach Vitoria before the 22nd.

At daylight on the 21st, Wellington advanced with the right centre column, halted it under appropriate cover, and awaited developments in a position on top of a hill west of the Zadorra. He could see Joseph, Jourdan, and Gazan with their large and colourful staffs on the round hill of Arinez (Plate 42).[1] He could see also much of the western valley, and the mountains over which Hill was advancing, but was prevented from observing Graham's operations by the Arinez knoll.

Hill moved from his bivouac area in the Bayas valley, crossed the Zadorra at Puebla, and followed the great road toward the defile, sending Morillo's Spaniards diagonally over the mountains to the east. He supported Morillo with Cadogan's Brigade and some additional light companies. This flanking column was able to climb right up to the crest of the mountains, but once there was soon engaged in a spirited action with the southernmost section of Gazan's first line which had ascended from the valley. This contest started before 8.30 a.m.; there were heavy casualties on both sides. The 1/71st was particularly hard hit; the Scots mistook French for Spanish infantry and allowed them to approach too close and even open fire. The 1/50th and the 1/92nd restored the situation; the heights at least were firmly in Allied hands.

His flank protected, Hill pushed up the defile with a heavy force and sent O'Callaghan's Brigade along the lower foot-hills to the right (Plate 39). This force soon joined the Anglo-Spanish units further up the mountainside in a combat with the French that raged intermittently and savagely until about noon. The French skirmished well, but were repulsed with heavy loss whenever they attacked frontally to recover the crests

Graham was skirmishing before 9 a.m. at the northern end of the Allied line, fully twelve miles from Hill. But, in accordance with specific orders, he proceeded cautiously. He was not to commit himself

[1] *Fortescue*, IX, 163, points out that this was the place where Sir Thomas Felton and his 100 Englishmen sold their lives so dearly in battle in 1397.

to heavy fighting until actually in contact with the other Allied columns to the west, except that he was to cut the great road. He carried out his orders to the letter; Longa's Spaniards were thrown forward towards the Zadorra on his left flank. They had the road under musketry fire by 10 a.m. and cut before noon. The rest of Graham's force advanced more warily and was lightly engaged along a wide front just north of the Zadorra by 1 p.m. Oswald's 5th Division was involved in more serious and bloody fighting around the Gamarras.

During the morning, Wellington noticed a curious movement by the French army when two divisions of cavalry and one of infantry proceeded south in the direction of Logrono. He considered the possibility of Joseph moving to meet Clausel; this would have meant the sacrifice of the numerous trains parked around Vitoria, but within an hour the cavalry came trotting back.[1]

Shortly before noon, a Spanish peasant approached the Light Division and was immediately taken to Wellington. The bridge across the Zadorra at Tres Puentes was neither defended nor observed by the French. Wellington at once ordered Kempt's Brigade of the Light Division to pass around the hairpin bend of the river and across this bridge. The execution of this manoeuvre secretly was dependent on the unusual topography of this area. The river curves around the base of a U-shaped precipice more than 300 feet in height and only 300 yards wide. This high ground slopes down to the east to the general level of the valley before rising again at the knoll of Arinez. The entire march of Kempt's Brigade was concealed from the French, except for perhaps the actual crossing of the bridge.[2] Kempt took up a position to the east on a hill lower than either the knoll of Arinez or that within the hairpin bend (Plate 41).

Three of the four Allied columns were up; two were engaged, but Dalhousie and Picton were delayed temporarily in the mountains. Dalhousie was still in the broken country to the west, but Picton, advancing by a more southerly path, was in position shortly before noon with the 3rd Division.

' "Damn it! Lord Wellington must have forgotten us," Picton said. It was near noon, and the men were getting discontented, for

[1] This strange manoeuvre was explained later; Joseph believed that the Allied movements in the north were feints, and that Wellington's main attack would come from the south.

[2] Two round shot were fired at Kempt's men, one of which killed this unfortunate peasant.

the centre had not yet been engaged; Picton's blood was boiling, and his stick fell with rapid strokes upon the mane of his horse; he was riding backwards and forwards, looking in every direction for the arrival of an aide-de-camp, until at length a staff officer galloped up from Lord Wellington. He was looking for the seventh division, under Lord Dalhousie, which had still not arrived at its post, having had to move over some difficult ground. The aide-de-camp, riding up at speed, suddenly checked his horse and demanded of the general whether he had seen Lord Dalhousie. Picton was disappointed; he expected now at last that he might move, and, in a voice which did not gain softness from his feelings, he answered in a sharp tone, "No, sir! I have not seen his lordship: but have you any orders for me, sir?"—"None," replied the aide-de-camp.—"Then pray, sir," continued the irritated general, "what are the orders you do bring?"—"Why," answered the officer, "that as soon as Lord Dalhousie, with the seventh division, shall commence an attack upon that bridge" (pointing to one on the left), "the fourth and sixth are to support him." Picton could not understand the idea of any other division fighting in his front; and, drawing himself up to his full height, he said to the astonished aide-de-camp with some passion, "You may tell Lord Wellington from me, sir, that the third division under my command shall in less than ten minutes attack the bridge and carry it, and the fourth and sixth divisions may support if they choose," Having thus expressed his intention, he turned from the aide-de-camp, and put himself at the head of his soldiers, who were quickly in motion towards the bridge; encouraging them with the bland appellation of "Come on, ye rascals!—Come on, ye fighting villains!" [1]

Picton had only a country bridge and a narrow ford by which to cross the Zadorra. French artillery were placed so as to sweep the entire area over which he would advance; two infantry divisions were drawn up awaiting his attack. But on Wellington's orders, Kempt's Brigade was attacking this formation from the west; the rest of the Light Division and the 4th were pouring across the Zadorra against Gazan's original first line, now greatly weakened. D'Urban's Portuguese dragoons crossed the river to the southeast of Nanclares. Hill was now moving forward against Gazan's southern flank; Graham's guns were thundering far to the northeast.

[1] H. B. Robinson, *Memoirs of Lieutenant-General Sir Thomas Picton*, II, 208-10.

Kempt's Rifles in skirmish order took the French artillery opposite Picton in the flank. After one, two, or three salvos delivered at long range, these guns limbered up and abandoned their position. Picton stormed across the stream toward the knoll and village of Arinez, smashing all opposition and rolling up the French flank. But Gazan managed to form a line of defence facing north across the knoll. Wellington took personal command of the 3rd Division, Kempt's Brigade, and a brigade of Dalhousie's 7th Division which had just come up. With these forces, he carried the knoll and the village behind it on the great road. This occurred shortly after 3 p.m.

Even as Wellington entered Arinez, the French second line had moved north to the Zadorra to fill the rent caused by Picton's attack (Plate 42). Two French divisions here were engaged with Colville's Brigade of Picton's Division when the rest of Dalhousie's 7th Division finally entered the fight.[1] The anchor of the French position, the village of Margarita, was taken by Vandeleur's Brigade of the Light Division.

The French forces in the western valley were still strong and comparatively undamaged. Gazan's divisions from the first line took up an intermediate position facing west on the southern side of the great road; D'Erlon's fell back into line to the north of it. At first, there was a small gap between the two forces. The entire French line was supported by artillery whose fire was heavier than in any battle yet fought in the Peninsula.[2] But artillery could not stop veteran infantry in two-deep lines advancing through broken country. The French were never able to consolidate their position, even though they were numerically equal to their immediate adversaries.

Hill's entire Corps was now deployed at the southern end of the Allied front; Picton, the Light Division, and Dalhousie were forcing D'Erlon back. Wellington launched Cole's 4th Division, still comparatively fresh, into the gap between D'Erlon and Gazan. Both French armies in this sector retreated diagonally away from the great road. Gazan's veterans, some of whom had now been in action for more than eight hours, were forced to the south where they had to cross mountain spurs. Their cannon sunk up to the hubs in marshy streams and were abandoned. D'Erlon's men retreated northeast following the Zadorra, with the 3rd, Light, and 7th Divisions in pursuit.

[1] Fortescue states that all three brigades of the 7th Division were now up, but Oman maintains that only Grant's Brigade had reached the field. Neither Barnes's nor LeCor's Brigades had a man killed or wounded, so Oman is probably right.

[2] The French had about 80 guns, but Dickson, Wellington's chief of artillery, was able to bring 70 Allied pieces against them.

In the course of a few minutes, the French units in the centre of the valley disintegrated. Generals and drummer-boys alike realized that they were beaten and looked to their personal safety.[1] They threw away their packs, and in some cases their muskets and ammunition; they fled back to the east, not by battalions or companies, but in small, irregular groups. The French had suffered moderate casualties only, but realized that they had been both outfought and outmanoeuvred. Graham's thrust had been a fatal blow to their morale.

Graham had been involved in actions along the Zadorra northeast of Vitoria. Both Reille's divisions, originally in a third line just west of Vitoria, had been ordered back to engage him.[2] For more than three hours there was bloody fighting for the villages on the north bank of the river and their bridges.[3] Once Wellington had broken through the French centre, Graham threw his entire command into an all-out attack. The men of Reille's two divisions were strongly posted and well supported by artillery, but they were beaten back. Most of them mingled with the disorderly mob which was all that remained of Gazan's and D'Erlon's forces. A part of Reille's command and some cavalry did manage to retain some sort of formation and covered the French retreat as their broken armies streamed back along the poor roads and across country out of the eastern end of the valley.

Joseph's army was also 'protected' by an even more effective rear-guard, the great mass of valuable personal property contained in thousands of carriages and wagons parked east of Vitoria. There was an abundance of money, food, wine, spirits, and women. Wellington's army was never able to withstand such temptations.

'As L. and I rode out of Vitoria, we came to the camp in less than a mile. On the left-hand side of the road was a heap of ran-sacked waggons already broken up and dismantled. There arose a shout from a number of persons among the waggons, and we found that they had discovered one yet unopened. We cantered

[1] At about 5 p.m. Joseph issued orders for a general retreat east through Vitoria toward Salvatierra, but this would be after Gazan's force had shown signs of disintegration: Fortescue, IX, 182.

[2] Reille's third division under Maucune had been ordered back towards France at 7 a.m. to protect an enormous convoy travelling by the great road. This was the French division so roughly handled by Wellington and the Light Division at San Millan.

[3] Graham has been criticized for not attacking with more abandon, but it would appear that from 9 a.m. until late afternoon he did exactly what Wellington expected of him. He cut the great road and fully engaged Reille's corps. His critics overlook his isolation and Wellington's specific orders to be cautious.

up and found some men using all possible force to break open three iron clasps secured with padlocks. On the side of the fourgon was painted "Le Lieutenant-General Villate". The hasps gave way, and a shout followed. The whole surface of the waggon was packed with church plate, mixed with bags of dollars. A man who thrust his arm down said that the bottom was full of loose dollars and boxes. L. and I were the only ones on horseback and pushed close to the waggon. He swung out a large chalice, and buckling it to his holster-strap cantered off. As the people were crowding to lay hold of the plate, I noted a mahogany box about eighteen inches by two feet, with brass clasps. I picked out four men, told them that the box was the real thing, and if they would fetch it out we would see what it held. They caught the idea: the box was very heavy. I led the way through the standing corn, six or seven feet high, to a small shed, where we put it down and tried to get it open. After several devices had failed, two men found a large stone, and, lifting it as high as they could, dropped it on the box. It withstood several blows, but at length gave way. Gold doubloons and smaller pieces filled the whole box, in which were mixed some bags with trinkets. Just then an Ordnance storekeeper came up, and said there was no time to count shares: he would go round and give a handfull in turn to each. He first poured a double handfull into my holster. The second round was a smaller handfull. By this time I was reflecting that I was the only officer present, and in rather an awkward position. I said they might have the rest of my share—there was first a look of surprise, and then a burst of laughter, and I trotted away. I rode eight or ten miles to the bivouack and found the officers in an ancient church—housed à la Cromwell. On the 23rd, before we left our quarters, I and —— went up into the belfry, and counted out the gold—the doubloons alone made nearly £400. I remitted £250 to my father, and purchased another horse with part of the balance.'[1]

Never previously in the history of European war did a victorious army capture so much booty. Never had so many guns been taken in a battle.

[1] *Oman*, VI, 443-4, quoting from an officer. Oman adds,
'Oddly enough, two contemporary diaries mention Mr D's luck. He got by no means the biggest haul. Sergeant Costello of the 1/95th says that he got over £1,000. A private of the 23rd carried off 1,000 dollars in silver—a vast load! Green of the 68th records that two of his comrades got respectively 180 doubloons, and nearly 1,000 dollars.'

The French dragged away only two field pieces, and not a single carriage or wagon. Joseph's army was larger at Vitoria than Marmont's at Salamanca and suffered fewer casualties, but it was even less able to fight again without complete reorganization and re-arming. Most of the men who escaped lacked equipment and weapons. The actual French loss exceeded 8,000; the Allies lost 5,100.

The misbehaviour of both infantry and cavalry at the termination of the battle cannot detract from the importance of the victory itself. The majority of the French who had fought at Vitoria reached France before the end of the month; the 'propaganda value' of the battle was immense. Napoleon had begun the campaign of 1813 with two remarkable victories over the combined armies of Prussia and Russia. Following Lutzen and Bautzen, he had concluded an armistice with his immediate opponents; this might have been the prelude to further imperial triumphs at the negotiation table. But the news of Vitoria hardened the coalition against him; the war was renewed. Neutral Austria, who wanted to be on the winning side, entered the struggle as one of the Allied Powers.

Tactically, Vitoria produced little that was new. The British cavalry did not pursue well. Individual brigades trotted around in a haphazard fashion and accomplished little; superb opportunities were wasted. Their commanding officers were partly at fault, but the vast quantity of plunder easily accessible to mounted soldiers was the main factor. Hill's light troops, who saw action early among the mountains east of the defile, were not particularly efficient.[1] Picton's magnificent charge in line was equal to anything that this fine division ever did; Cole's thrust into the French centre late in the battle was also well conceived and executed. The Allied artillery concentration against the French in their final position was remarkable for its great power. But Allied tactics were modified by the terrain and enemy dispositions, and were less typically Wellingtonian than usual.

Strategically, Vitoria was Wellington's greatest accomplishment. The complete victory, coming as it did at the end of a month's superb manoeuvring and one day before the arrival of Clausel, is a military achievement of the first magnitude. Wellington had beaten a more numerous and homogeneous enemy by careful planning, speed of manoeuvre, and the continuous application of his powers of command.

---

[1] There appear to have been but two companies of Rifles here (5/60th). The 71st and 92nd were magnificent in compact fighting, but not so good out of formation. The Light Division would have done this job better.

Sending Graham far to the northeast with instructions that prevented this force from coming to harm even if the French had been more enterprising, was a master stroke. The Allied C-in-C denied the French the only road by which they could have retreated as an army. The breaking of the French first line in the western valley by rolling up both flanks before attacking hard in front was typical of Wellington. The proper handling of four widely separated forces, finally consolidated on the battlefield, required great professional ability. In less than a month, the Allies had thrust the French from central Spain, beaten their major army decisively, and sent them packing towards France.

THE CONTENDING FORCES AND LOSSES AT VITORIA

ALLIED ARMY UNDER WELLINGTON   TOTAL = 79,062[1]

INFANTRY

    27,372 British   6,800 Spanish   27,569 Portuguese = 61,741

    1st Division, Kenneth Alexander Howard   = 4,854

        Edward Stopford's Brigade   1,728
            1/Coldstreamers, 1/Scots, 1 Co. 5/60th

        Halkett's Brigade   3,126
            1st, 2nd, 5th Line K.G.L., 1st, 2nd, Light K.G.L.

    2nd Division, William Stewart   = 10,834

        Cadogan's Brigade   2,777
            1/50th, 1/71st, 1/92nd, 1 Co. 5/60th

        Byng's or Walker's Brigade   2,465
            1/3rd, 1/57th, 1st Prov. Batt., 1 Co. 5/60th

        O'Callaghan's Brigade   2,530
            1/28th, 2/34th, 1/39th, 1 Co. 5/60th

        Ashworth's Portuguese Brigade   3,062
            6th Line, 18th Line, 6th Cacadores

---

[1] This is the total of the units listed below on 25th May 1813 as given by *Oman*, VI, 750-3. Losses after that time, caused by fighting, straggling, and sickness, reduce this total.

3rd Division, Thomas Picton = 7,459
    Brisbane's Brigade 2,723
      1/45th, 74th, 1/88th, 3 Cos. 5/60th
    Colville's Brigade 2,276
      1/5th, 2/83rd, 2/87th, 94th
    Power's Portuguese Brigade 2,460
      9th Line, 21st Line, 11th Cacadores

4th Division, Lowry Cole = 7,826
    Anson's Brigade 2,935
      2nd Prov. Batt., 3/27th, 1/40th,
      1/48th, 1 Co. 5/60th
    Skerrett's Brigade 2,049
      1/7th, 20th, 1/23rd, 1 Co. Bruns-
      wick Oels
    Stubbs's Portuguese Brigade 2,842
      11th Line, 23rd Line, 7th Cacadores

5th Division, John Oswald = 6,725
    Hay's Brigade 2,292
      3/1st, 1/9th, 1/38th, 1 Co. Bruns-
      wick Oels
    Robinson's Brigade 2,061
      1/4th, 2/47th, 2/59th, 1 Co. Bruns-
      wick Oels
    Spry's Portuguese Brigade 2,372
      3rd Line, 15th Line, 8th Cacadores

7th Division, Lord Dalhousie = 7,287
    Barnes's Brigade 2,322
      1/6th, 3rd Prov. Batt., 1 Co.
      Brunswick Oels
    Grant's Brigade 2,528
      51st, 68th, 1/82nd, Chasseurs Britan-
      niques
    Le Cor's Portuguese Brigade 2,437
      7th Line, 19th Line, 2nd Cacadores

Light Division, Charles Alten   = 5,484
  Kempt's Brigade   Not available[1]
    1/43rd, 1/95th, 3/95th, 1st Cacadores
  Vandeleur's Brigade   Not available[1]
    1/52nd, 17th Port. Line, 2/95th,
      3rd Cacadores
Pack's Independent Portuguese Brigade   = 2,297
  1st Line, 16th Line, 4th Cacadores
Bradford's Independent Portuguese Brigade   = 2,392
  13th Line, 24th Line, 5th Cacadores
Silveira's Portuguese Division   = 5,287
  Da Costa's Brigade   2,492
    2nd Line, 14th Line
  A. Campbell's Brigade   2,795
    4th Line, 10th Line, 10th Cacadores

CAVALRY   7,424 British   893 Portuguese   = 8,317
  Eight British and Two Portuguese Brigades

ARTILLERY   = 3,300
  3,000 British (78 Guns)   300 Portuguese (12 Guns)

SPANISH FORCES   = 7,000
  Morillo's Infantry Division   4,000
  Longa's Brigade (5 Batts.)   2,800
  Artillery, etc.   200

FRENCH ARMY UNDER JOSEPH   TOTAL = 66,000[2]

ARMY OF	INFANTRY				CAVALRY	ARTILLERY	
	Divisions	Brigades	Regiments	Personnel	Personnel	Personnel	Guns
South	4½	9	18	26,000	6,000	1,500	60
Centre	2	4	9	9,500	1,500	700	30
Portugal	2	4	8	9,500	2,800	1,700	12
Spanish Guard, Reserve, etc.				4,000	1,000	1,800	36
				49,000	11,300	5,700	138

[1] The new 17th Portuguese Line (2 Batts.) was assigned to one brigade or the other. Logically, it would seem that one battalion should be placed in each brigade.

[2] *Fortescue*, IX, 166, says, '43,000 infantry, 6,000 or 7,000 cavalry, and 150 guns.' Oman, who was at this time collaborating with Fortescue gives the incomplete 'morning states' shown here and concludes, 'the French had 63,000 at Vitoria . . .': *Oman*, VI, 754.

CASUALTIES [1]				
	KILLED	WOUNDED	MISSING	TOTAL
British	509	2,941	225	3,675
Portuguese	242	636	43	921
Spanish	89	463	—	552
Allies				5,148
French	756	4,414	2,829	7,999

TOPOGRAPHICAL OBSERVATIONS

The valley of the Zadorra containing Vitoria is considerably changed to the east around the town itself, but not in the western half where most of the fighting took place. Some of the bridges have been widened for modern traffic, but not all. The gorge through which the Great Road and the Zadorra passed out of the valley still serves this purpose and cannot be mistaken. One can climb the heights of Puebla along the same cart tracks followed by Hill's force. The knoll of Arinez, north of the village of the same name, commands a fine view.

In the main, it is possible to follow the lines of march of the various corps of the Allied army prior to Vitoria through mountainous, well-watered country, but not all the roads originally used are passable for motor vehicles.

---

[1] Much uncertainty exists as regards the official French totals set out here, which are manifestly incomplete.

Attention is again called to the difference in the 'killed to wounded' ratio, for the British and Portuguese.

XVI

BATTLES IN THE PYRENEES:
SORAUREN

PHASE ONE: DRIVING THE FRENCH ACROSS
THE BORDER

WELLINGTON lost more men through temporary desertion in search of plunder after Vitoria than the French lost both in the battle and in the succeeding retreat. Even those soldiers who did not plunder spent the night in celebration and were in no condition to march at dawn. Wellington was beside himself with indignation.

'We started with the army in the highest order, and up to the day of the battle nothing could get on better; but that event has, as usual, totally annihilated all order and discipline. The soldiers of the army have got among them about a million sterling in money, with the exception of about 100,000 dollars, which were got for the military chest. The night of the battle, instead of being passed in getting rest and food to prepare them for the pursuit of the following day, was passed by the soldiers in looking for plunder. The consequence was, that they were incapable of marching in pursuit of the enemy, and were totally knocked up. The rain came on and increased their fatigue, and I am quite convinced that we have now out of the ranks double the amount of our loss in the battle; and that we have lost more men in the pursuit than the enemy have; and have never in any one day made more than an ordinary march.

'This is the consequence of the state of discipline of the British army. We may gain the greatest victories; but we shall do no good until we shall so far alter our system, as to force all ranks to perform their duty. The new regiments are, as usual, the worst of all. The —th — — are a disgrace to the name of a soldier, in action as well as elsewhere; and I propose to draft their horses from them, and to send the men to England, if I cannot get the better of them in any other manner.' [1]

Wellington appreciated the superb fighting qualities of his men, but deplored their lack of discipline. As always, he managed to carry on, after loosing a few verbal broadsides.[2] There were still French in the area. Joseph was retreating at speed towards Salvatierra, but Clausel was known to have had a powerful force at Logrono on the night of the 20th. Foy with his own reinforced division and several garrisons was moving southeast from Bilbao. Maucune's Division and some cavalry had left Vitoria on the morning of the battle to escort a convoy along the great road to France.

The Allied wounded had to be cared for and proper hospitals established. The spoils of victory not already in private hands had to be preserved. The town was a valuable base which required protection; the civilian population had to be re-established.

Longa's Spaniards were ordered to follow Maucune, while Giron's Galicians would join Longa *en route*. The Allied 5th Division remained at Vitoria; the 6th would be up from Medina de Pomar early in the afternoon. At about 10 a.m. the rest of the army stumbled east towards Salvatierra in three columns, but the narrowing valley forced them together into a single wide mass. The Allied army reached Salvatierra in the late afternoon and bivouacked there.

Wellington received various intelligence reports during the day. Giron would not be able to support Longa until the 23rd; Foy and Maucune were almost certainly joining forces. Wellington sent Graham with the 1st Division, Pack's and Bradford's Portuguese, and some

---

[1] *Dispatches*, X, 473.

[2] Wellington, ibid., 496,

    'We have in the service the scum of the earth as common soldiers; and of late years we have been doing everything in our power, both by law and by publications, to relax the discipline by which alone such men can be kept in order. The officers of the lower ranks will not perform the duty required from them for the purpose of keeping their soldiers in order; and it is next to impossible to punish any officer for neglects of this description. As to the non-commissioned officers, as I have repeatedly stated, they are as bad as the men, and too near them, in point of pay and situation, by the regulations of late years, for us to expect them to do anything to keep the men in order. It is really a disgrace to have anything to say to such men as some of our soldiers are.'

I disagree with *Oman*, VI, 454, in this connexion. Wellington did not say that *all* his soldiers were 'the scum of the earth', but referred specifically in this quotation to 'some of our soldiers'. Who would know these men better, Wellington who commanded them for years in the field or Oman?

artillery and cavalry, north by a rough road from Salvatierra which intercepts the great road east of Mondragon.[1] If Foy turned to fight Longa anywhere further to the west, he might be cut off. Graham would command any Spanish troops in his immediate area.

On the afternoon the 22nd, Clausel's cavalry entered the valley of Vitoria by the Logrono road and found Allied infantry in force there. Clausel knew nothing of the French defeat of the previous day and was marching hard to join Joseph. But even from the southern rim of the valley, he could see signs of the disaster; he learned some of the details from stragglers and pro-French Spaniards picked up in the hills. He retired the way he had come.

Longa and Giron united on the morning of the 23rd, but found themselves face to face with Foy and his accumulated garrisons, a force too strong for them to attack. The French retreated along the great road, with the Spaniards hanging on their rear. This same procession continued next morning.

Meanwhile Graham was approaching the great road and was within sight of it before noon on the 24th. Two French forces were seen converging. The westernmost, of about 5,000 men, turned south a short distance along the Salvatierra road to meet Graham. In the combat that followed, Graham inflicted 200 casualties on the enemy which he discovered to be Maucune's infantry division supported by cavalry and artillery. The larger force which was approaching from the west was Foy's army. These two French forces, now combined, held off Graham and retreated on Tolosa. Foy as senior to Maucune took command of over 16,000 men. Graham pursued with his own command and those of Longa and Giron, a total of some 26,000 men.

On the 25th, Graham and Foy fought a minor action at Tolosa. This town was one of the original French fortifications along the great road. Its masonry works were strong, but were commanded by the surrounding hills. Foy had no intention of holding the place, or even leaving a garrison there, but he did want to gain time for the retreat of Maucune's convoy. For a short while it appeared that the Allies were about to surround the enemy, but the French escaped from the trap. The action was indecisive, with casualties of about 400 on each side.

As Foy retired from Tolosa towards France, he regarrisoned San Sebastian. With unusually good judgement, he collected all French

[1] The idea of sending Graham north by this road may have originated in the mind of George Murray, Wellington's trusted Q.M.G. Due to a temporary disorganization of Murray's staff, however, neither Graham nor his units received their orders until the morning of the 23rd: *Oman*, VI, 455–6.

detachments and minor garrisons in the area, but left an efficient force in the one place where it could be of value. He then pulled his main army back across the border. Graham blockaded San Sebastian on the 28th and reached the river Bidassoa on the 30th.

Meanwhile Wellington's army had advanced on Pamplona from Salvatierra. On the 23rd, cavalry contact was regained with the retreating French at Yrurzun. There was a running fight the next afternoon west of Pamplona between the French rearguard and the Light Division with their usual auxiliaries, Ross's Horse Artillery and the Hussars of the K.G.L. The French lost one of the two artillery pieces they saved from Vitoria, but suffered no crippling losses in personnel.[1] While this was going on, the main French army passed around Pamplona and retreated to the border, only a day's march away.[2] Even though Pamplona was garrisoned, Joseph had no intention of trying to rally his shattered army for another battle beneath its walls.

Wellington had surrounded Pamplona by the evening of the 25th; the town was extremely strong and said to be well provisioned. Clausel's army might present a more rewarding objective. Wellington knew that Clausel had been near Vitoria on the 22nd, but assumed that the French general would countermarch to Logrono and continue down the Ebro valley to safety. However, Mina reported that from Logrono Clausel had turned northeast toward Pamplona and not southeast toward Zaragoza. The 4th and Light Divisions from Pamplona, the 6th Division from Vitoria, and several cavalry brigades were set in motion in an effort to trap Clausel on the north side of the Ebro. The Allied attempt failed; only a few stragglers and six abandoned field pieces were taken. Clausel crossed the Ebro and was free to join Suchet on the east coast, or move north through Jaca and across the Pyrenees.

By the evening of the 26th, Wellington knew that Reille's Army of Portugal had taken a by-road northeast from Yrurzun through the Baztan, the upper valley of the Bidassoa, and was now in France. The rest of Joseph's army had divided at Pamplona, Gazan's Army of the

---

[1] *Surtees*, 216, writes,

'We now moved forward in close pursuit of the enemy for about two miles farther, when a shot from Colonel Ross's guns having struck one of the leaders in their gun, and our people at this time pressing them so closely as not to give time to disentangle the dead horse, they unwillingly were compelled to throw their only gun into the ditch, and there abandon it.'

Presumably, the French piece that did survive was a howitzer.

[2] These hungry troops were not allowed to enter the town where they might have plundered the garrison's stores.

South marching toward Roncesvalles and St Jean Pied-de-Port while D'Erlon's moved north in the direction of the Baztan, Maya, and Bayonne.

As soon as the Allied troops returned from their strenuous but unproductive pursuit of Clausel, Wellington set out to complete his task of 'throwing the French back into France'. He knew that Reille was now on the north bank of the Bidassoa and had taken command of Foy's force in addition to his own. Only D'Erlon remained in Spain, keeping a precarious grip on the Baztan.[1]

On 4th July, Hill advanced on D'Erlon by the main road from Pamplona and was engaged soon after entering the Baztan valley. Wellington took personal command at about noon next day and proceeded to push back the French, even though he was using four weak brigades against at least four divisions. Three days of confused manoeuvring in rugged mountains ended with D'Erlon crossing the border. The total combined losses—French and Allied—were under 500.

The French now held but a single Spanish town in the western Pyrenees, Vera, which lay between the Baztan and Irun. Wellington cleared it of French units on the 15th. Graham had already begun the siege of San Sebastian; Pamplona was blockaded, and an encircling system of earthworks begun; French 12-pounder field pieces taken at Vitoria were used to arm them. Spanish units only would invest Pamplona.

Wellington now consolidated his position after having forced back the French nearly 400 miles in less than forty days. His port of communication with Britain was now shifted from Lisbon to Santander; Passages, a superb small harbour a few miles east of San Sebastian, was also used. The supplies and siege *matériel* abroad transports in Corunna harbour were ordered to Santander on 10th June.[2] Further supplies, described as 'twice the quantity of each article', were ordered from

---

[1] D'Erlon with three incomplete divisions was withdrawn on 3rd July and replaced by Gazan with four and a half.

[2] Wellington to Col. Bourke, in charge of British depots in Galicia, *Dispatches*, X, 429,
'There are at Coruna certain ships loaded with biscuit and flour, and certain others loaded with a heavy train of artillery and ammunition, and some musket ammunition; and I shall be very much obliged to you if you will request any officer of the navy who may be at Coruna when you receive this letter to take under his convoy all the vessels loaded as above mentioned, and to proceed with them to Santander. If he should find Santander occupied by the enemy, I beg him to remain off the port till the operations of this army have obliged the enemy to abandon it.'
This was eleven days *before* Vitoria!

England to the Biscay ports on 26th June.[1] The siege ordnance began to arrive at Passages early in July; it was soon emplaced to batter San Sebastian.

Wellington has been criticized for not following up his victory at Vitoria by an immediate advance into France. The Allied army recovered rapidly from its partial disciplinary breakdown; it was well supplied with everything necessary for fighting. The French army was, disorganized, destitute of artillery, and low in ammunition, food, and muskets. Its morale was also badly shaken. A pursuit like that which Napoleon launched against the Prussians after Jena would have taken Wellington at least to Bayonne, had he been willing to cross the border.

The principal reason for his refusal to do this was the situation in northern Europe. Napoleon had returned to Paris from Russia in the winter of 1812–13 and had managed to raise and take into the field in the spring an army of more than 200,000 men. He had beaten the Russians and Prussians on 2nd May and again on 20th–21st May; he demanded an armistice which was signed on 4th June. Wellington knew that this was to run at least until 1st August.

If Napoleon made peace in the north, or extended the armistice six months, he could send south sufficient reinforcements; the Allies would then have little chance in southwestern France. On the other hand, Wellington believed that if he stayed in Spain and took both Pamplona and San Sebastian, should strengthen and regarrison them, and settle his field army in the Pyrenees, he could hold the French at bay regardless of the position in northern Europe.[2]

PHASE TWO: SOULT'S COUNTER-OFFENSIVE TO SORAUREN

On 15th July, Wellington received confirmation of rumours of a change in French commanders. Soult had replaced Joseph and Jourdan on the 12th and was reorganizing all French forces in the area. Soult was at his very best in such duties; defeated, ill-armed, scattered units were bound into a cohesive whole. Artillery was replaced, ranks filled, and

---

[1] Wellington to Bathurst, 26th June 1813, ibid., 464, 'I now therefore beg your Lordship to order to Santander the other trains requested to be in readiness for this service.'

[2] Wellington to Bathurst, 12th July 1813, ibid., 523-4,
    'I hope we shall soon have San Sebastian; and if we get well settled in the Pyrenees, it will take a good reinforcement to the French army to drive us from thence. I think I can hold the Pyrenees as easily as I can Portugal. I am quite certain I can hold the position which I have got more easily than the Ebro, or any other position in Spain.'

morale restored. Reports came in of an imminent French offensive, the logical objectives of which would be the relief of Pamplona or San Sebastian, or perhaps both.

Four fortresses, San Sebastian, Pamplona, Bayonne, and St Jean Pied-de-Port, bound the area of the coming campaign. Bayonne was the main French supply base and the bastion of their right. St Jean protected their left deep in the mountains. San Sebastian and Pamplona were in front of the French right and left respectively, blockaded, but still extremely strong. The terrain within this quadrilateral consisted of roughly 1,000 square miles of rugged mountains, steep hills, and deep valleys; it is forty miles as the crow flies from Pamplona to San Sebastian and thirty miles from San Sebastian to Bayonne. The actual marching distances are, of course, much greater.

One is inclined to think of the western Pyrenees as a range of almost impenetrable mountains running east and west broken by ravine-type passes at intervals. They are in fact old, rounded mountains; a light infantryman could walk almost anywhere. There are few slopes so steep that they cannot be climbed by using just hands and feet; the passes are rarely clearly defined and are always flankable by light troops. The mountains and the serpentine border run approximately northwest to southeast in this area. The border does not always follow the line of the highest peaks; the river Bidassoa divided the two countries for the first ten miles in from the sea.

In the early nineteenth century the Pyrenees were crossed by roads suitable for wheeled traffic and large armies at only four places; three

---

[1] Soult's new organization is detailed in the Appendix; his address to the army was brilliant. *Oman*, VI, 587-8, quotes,

' "Soldiers! with well-equipped fortresses in front and in rear, a capable general possessing the confidence of his troops could by the choice of good positions have faced and defeated the motley levies opposed to you. Unhappily at the critical moment timid and downhearted counsels prevailed. The fortresses were abandoned or blown up; a hasty and disorderly retreat gave confidence to the enemy; and a veteran army, weak in numbers (it is true) but great in everything that constitutes military character, that army which had fought, bled, and conquered in every province of Spain, saw with indignation its laurels blighted, and was forced to abandon its conquests, the trophies of many sanguinary days of battle. When at last the cries of an indignant army stopped the dishonourable flight, and its chief, touched by a feeling of shame, and yielding to the general desire, gave battle in front of Vitoria, who can doubt that a general worthy of his troops could have won the success merited by their generous enthusiasm, and their splendid sense of honour? Did he make the arrangements and direct the movements which should have assured to one part of his army the help and support of the rest? ... Soldiers! I sympathise with your disappointment, your grievances, your indignation. I know that the blame for the present situation must be imputed to others. It is your task to repair the disaster." '

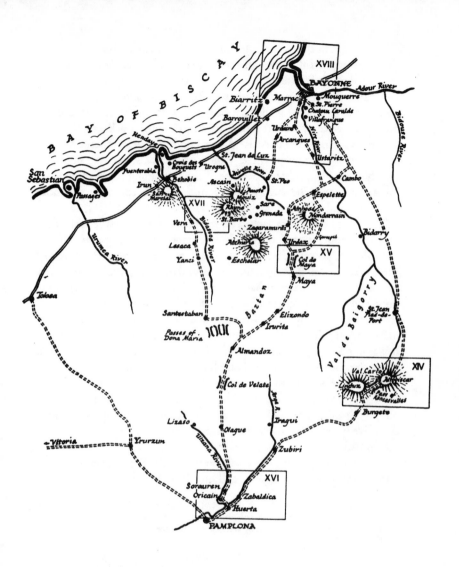

XIII. THE PYRENEES QUADRILATERAL

of these were in this western sector.[1] The great road through Irun was the most important, although the Roman road from Pamplona to St Jean Pied-de-Port was still in good condition. Another road from Pamplona into France through the Baztan was also acceptable; this crossed the Pyrenees by the pass of Maya. But, as Wellington pointed out, there were at least seventy 'passes', or mule tracks, in the area, which also crossed the border.[2] A few hundred unencumbered soldiers could pass along any of these. Guides might be necessary, but were readily available, probably because of the smuggling that had gone on for generations. The Basque population of both countries was both numerous and prosperous.

The Pyrenees are approached on the French side by fertile table land; transverse spurs extend only a short distance from the peaks. On the Spanish side, however, is a belt of broken country furrowed by rugged valleys; ridges run in various directions, and the wild terrain, dissected by irregular streams, extends back thirty miles. In France the roads were good and fairly straight; in Spain they were tortuous and poor.

Wellington occupied an irregular and discontinuous line from Irun to beyond the Roman road which crossed the border at Roncesvalles. It was unnecessary to hold any specific territory, but he had to prevent a French penetration to either Pamplona or San Sebastian. He had fewer than 60,000 Anglo-Portuguese to hold more than forty miles of front.[3] He distributed these in depth with particular regard to the road system on the Spanish side. Wellington was again setting up a dynamic defensive system in which lateral communications were more important than fortifications.

He could not prevent a breakthrough, for the French could concentrate at any point they desired and attack without warning. But once

[1] *Fortescue*, Maps for VIII, No. 19, shows twelve other roads crossing the border, but none was practical for artillery. A contemporary Map of the Pyrenees by Roussel and Blottierre shows many more, but they were obviously poor.

[2] *Dispatches*, X, 568,

'I do not think we could successfully apply to this frontier of Spain the system on which we fortified the country between the Tagus and the sea. That line is a very short one, and the communication easiest and shortest on our side. The Pyrenees are a very long line; there are not fewer than seventy passes through the mountains, and the communication, as far as I have been able to learn hitherto, is on the side of the enemy. We may facilitate the defence by fortifying some of the passes; but we can never make the Pyrenees what we made between the Tagus and the sea.'

[3] Casualties were not so important in this reduction as the fact that most of the Allied cavalry was left in the valley of the Ebro. Wellington could now use nearly 30,000 Spaniards for tasks within their capacity such as holding strong static positions on the Bidassoa, blockading Pamplona, and covering distant border crossings.

they pushed across the border, they would be met with ever-increasing force. Irun, Maya, and Roncesvalles were the principal avenues of approach for French heavy columns, but field fortifications had a limited use; each could be out-flanked. The Allies built none.

Graham commanded the coastal sector. The siege operations at San Sebastian were conducted by Oswald's 5th Division and Bradford's Independent Portuguese Brigade. At Irun and to the south along the Bidassoa there was a numerous Spanish army including Longa's Division. Between the Bidassoa and San Sebastian, Graham had the British 1st Division.

Hill commanded in the Baztan with three-quarters of the 2nd Division, Pack's Independent Portuguese Brigade, and Silveira's Portuguese Divisions previously commanded by Hamilton. In the area between Hill and Graham—Wellington had his headquarters at Lesaca immediately to the rear—there were the Allied 7th Division at Eschelar and the Light Division at Vera (Plate 43). The line from the Baztan to the sea, about half the entire front, was defended by the equivalent of almost seven of Wellington's ten Anglo-Portuguese divisions.

The southeastern half of the front included territory on both sides of the pass of Roncesvalles. Wellington placed Morillo's Spaniards in the front line and supported them with Byng's Brigade of the 2nd Division. Cole's 4th Division was distributed along the road south toward Pamplona for about ten miles. Picton's 3rd Division was in support of this whole flank at Olague. The 6th Division waited at Sanesteban just to the rear of the Baztan, and could support either the northern or southern sector of the Allied line as required.

After the 15th, Wellington was hearing every day of Soult's movements. The reorganized French army was more numerous than the Allies; it included not only Joseph's troops which had fought at Vitoria, but also Clausel's, Foy's, and some new units.

What were Soult's intentions? Pamplona was well supplied with all necessaries and was not being actively attacked. San Sebastian was in danger of being taken by assault: its walls were crumbling under Allied fire already. Wellington, in Soult's place, would have feinted to the south through Maya and Roncesvalles, and delivered his main attack along the coast where a penetration was most likely to be profitable.

The news from across the border seemed to confirm such a plan. On the 23rd, heavy infantry concentrations were reported on the roads toward St Jean Pied-de-Port, but there was unusual activity on the lower Bidassoa as well, where flying bridges and pontoons were being prepared. There were infantry concentrations also in the area just east of Irun. Wellington sent specific instructions to Cole, Byng, and Morillo to 'maintain the passes in front of Roncesvalles to the utmost but to disregard any wider turning movement to the Allied right.'

An assault on San Sebastian was scheduled for the morning of the 24th; it was postponed, but failed when delivered the following day. When Wellington received this unwelcome news at about 11.30 a.m., he rode from Lesaca to San Sebastian to see for himself what had happened. He left believing that all was quiet between Irun and Roncesvalles.

But soon after dawn on the morning of 25th July Soult attacked the Allies at Maya with 21,000 men, and sent an additional 40,000 against Roncesvalles. Wellington received no intelligence of these movements before he left, nor would the sound of battle carry so far under normal conditions. Although the two French forces joined later, their initial thrusts were separated by nearly twenty miles of rugged mountains.

Soult personally accompanied the larger left flank force which consisted of two Corps. Clausel's three divisions to the east marched by the Roman road from St Jean Pied-de-Port over the Pyrenees towards Pamplona.[1] The pass of Roncesvalles is nearly a mile broad and consists of a rounded plateau between higher mountains which is approached from the north by a U-shaped valley, the Val Carlos. Two long narrow spurs project into France, but rise to their greatest height on both sides of the pass itself; these peaks are known as the Linduz to the west and the Altobiscar to the east. The Roman road climbs the eastern spur on the side away from Val Carlos, doubles around the Altobiscar, and descends to the pass. The tracks in Val Carlos itself were so bad as to

---

[1] The Roman road has not been used for heavy vehicles for many years, although fought over during the Spanish Civil War. It can still be traced and is in many places in fair condition; in the early nineteenth century it was well maintained, but is much too narrow for modern traffic. Below the pass on the Spanish side is the monastery at which the bones of Roland were exhibited until recently.

Forces present:—French: Six Infantry division and auxiliaries—40,000.

Allies: Cole's 4th Division, Byng's Brigade (2nd Div.), Campbell's Portuguese Brigade, Morillo's Spaniards—13,500.

To St. Jean Pied-de-Port The Roman Road

CLAUSEL'S 3 DIVISIONS

BYNG'S 1st position

The Altobiscar Mountain

BYNG'S 2nd position

Val Carlos

The Pass

1/57th

✝ Chapel

✝ Monastery & Village of Roncesvalle

ANSON'S Brigade

National Guards + One Regular Battalion

Regiment of LEON

ORBAICETA

STUBB'S Brigade

← To PAMPLONA

BURGUETE

REILLE 3 Divisions

ROSS 1st position

ROSS 2nd position

Linduz Mountain

National Guards

Val de Baigorry

CAMPBELL'S Portuguese

XIV. RONCESVALLES

be militarily useless.[1] There was however a roadway which climbed the western spur of Val Carlos to the Linduz; it was narrow and steep, but thought to be militarily passable. Soult ordered Reille's three divisions to advance by it.

The French were attacking on each side of Val Carlos with 20,000 men, and hoped to gain the full altitude of the pass before having to fight. To defend the pass, Cole had Byng's Brigade of the 2nd Division (2,000 men) on the Roman road with outposts well down the French side. Part of Morillo's Spanish Division (3,500 men) was further east and some lay across the head of Val Carlos. To the west in the valley of Baigorry was A. Campbell's Portuguese Brigade (2,000 men) of Silveira's Division, but this force was under Hill's command from the Baztan. Initially the French had a numerical advantage of about seven to one, but the terrain greatly favoured the Allies.

Clausel attacked before dawn, but the Allied picket on the Roman road was not surprised. It gave the alarm and retired on its supports. At 6 a.m., the French were endeavouring to push back the Allied security line here; it was composed of the three light companies of the British brigade, a company of the 5/60th Rifles, and about the same number of Spanish light infantry. This force, which did not exceed 500 men, was deployed on a front of 300 yards with deep valleys on either flank. Almost every man was able to find shelter behind rocks, or in the rear of small ridges, where he could load comfortably and fire from a rest. For four hours, the *voltigeur* companies from three infantry divisions tried to drive in this line, but failed. The Allies inflicted casualties out of all proportion to those which they suffered themselves. They delayed the advance of Clausel's entire corps.

There was a lull in the fighting between 10 a.m. and noon. The French then attacked again, this time using infantry in columns. These made little headway at first, but finally succeeded at about 3 p.m. in driving Byng back to an even stronger position on the side of the Altobiscar. The only disadvantage in this retirement was that it left a way open for the French to move south through Orbaiceta and turn the Allied right flank. The main pass was still securely held.

During the morning, Cole had brought up Ross's Brigade from Burgete into the pass, and was able to obtain a fair idea of the French pattern of attack. Clausel was trying to force his way up the main road, but the progress made by Reille and his three divisions on the mule

[1] The modern main road approaches the pass through the Val Carlos.

path toward the Linduz was also apparent. Ross was dispatched along the crest of the western ridge to meet the latter. Cole's other two brigades were now within supporting distance about Roncesvalles, having used roads widened on Wellington's orders.

During the morning, French National Guard units (semi-trained militia) attacked in the Baigorry Valley where they ran into Campbell's Portuguese and were routed with considerable loss in an unequal fight. In a somewhat similar action north of Orbaiceta, National Guards supported by one regular battalion fought Morillo's Regiment of Leon stationed in a foundry, but made no progress. It was quiet in the Val Carlos itself where one British (1/57th) and three Spanish battalions waited in line just north of the pass.

Reille's troops were still working their way, sometimes in single file, along the narrow crest toward the Linduz. The head of this column collided with Ross's advance guard, his company of the 60th Rifles, at about 2 p.m. This contact took place in an area which was then partially wooded, and no more than 60 yards wide.[1] There followed some confused fighting in which the 20th distinguished itself; at least one company used their bayonets. The Allies were greatly inferior numerically, but neither side could use more than one battalion at a time on this narrow front. When the 20th had exhausted its ammunition, the 1/7th took its place; the 1/23rd remained in reserve throughout the afternoon, but was never in action.

Between 4 and 5 p.m., the entire Roncesvalles position was enveloped in fog, or more properly, a low cloud.[2] These fogs descend surprisingly quickly and are so thick that visibility is less than 20 yards. At once the Linduz fighting ceased; the opposing infantry bivouacked within hearing of each other. Byng on the Altobiscar was not again engaged; both sides remained stationary in the thick fog. Neither French corps was yet within a mile of the pass itself.

Sir Lowry Cole was in a difficult situation. His battlefield courage is unquestioned; at Albuera, he had delivered his attack without orders and won the day. He had fought well at Salamanca and Vitoria, but could he remain calmly on the defensive with a greatly inferior force as Wellington had so often done? He had only 13,000 men to hold an unfortified position against 40,000. Cole imagined the French army just

---

[1] Veteran soldiers, both Allied and French, often avoided descending steep slopes to flank opponents.
[2] I was on the Linduz one afternoon in bright sunlight when one of these thick fogs came in from the Bay of Biscay, forcing me to return to the pass by compass.

walking forward in the fog and enveloping him. In spite of Wellington's specific orders to hold on at all costs and ignore any turning movement to the east, Cole took counsel of his fears and ordered a retreat along the road to Pamplona (Plate 44).

Meanwhile, also on the 25th, the pass of Maya was attacked by D'Erlon's corps. As already observed, the carriage road from Pamplona to Bayonne crosses the Pyrenees here; this pass is also flat-topped and nearly as wide as that at Roncesvalles. The road here ascends from France by the valley of Urdax immediately in front of the pass; it then travels laterally west along the pass itself for almost a mile before descending into Spain.[1]

There is a secondary road running roughly parallel to the main road, but a mile and a half further east, and beyond a mountain spur.[2] Near the watershed this swings to the west between two peaks and then joins the main road for a short distance before breaking away to the west. This secondary road was blocked to the north, near the watershed, by a strong British picket on the Gorospil peak, but could not be observed by the picket except in their immediate neighbourhood. This country is singularly blind; numerous lower peaks and ridges obstruct the view in almost every direction (Plate 45).

Hill had assigned the defence of Maya to Stewart and the two remaining British brigades of the 2nd Division. Cameron's Brigade was camped south of the Gorospil between the watershed and the village of Maya. Dawn observations on the 25th revealed no French columns advancing on the pass, although there were some enemy units moving about near Urdax. After the early morning stand to arms, the British troops, except for a picket on the Gorospil, were dismissed. It should be mentioned that Pringle had just taken command of his brigade; he had arrived from Britain only twenty-four hours before. He knew little of his position and not much more of his troops, but was senior to

[1] The actual border here is well to the French side of the watershed. The pass itself, and the village of Urdax, are in Spanish territory.

[2] *Beatson*, 109, says, 'This track . . . is known as the "English road"; but why so-called I do not know, as it was already in existence in 1813, though probably much improved then.' A section of this track north of the watershed was also known as the Gorospil Path.

Forces Present—French: D'Erlon's three divisions and auxiliaries—20,000.
           Allies: Cameron's Brigade, Pringle's Brigade, Three batts 7th Div.—6,000.

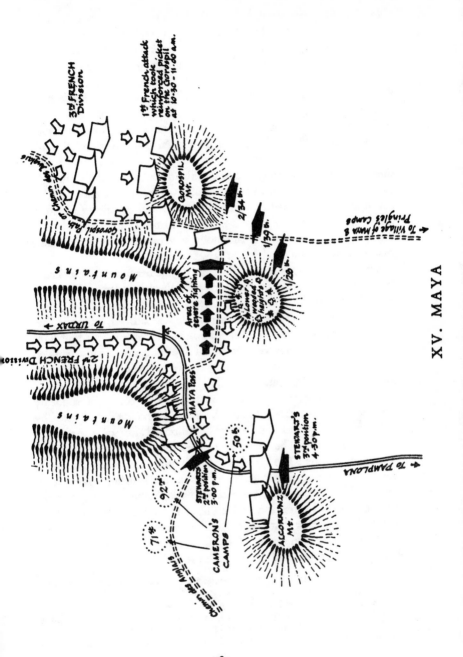

XV. MAYA

Text labels within the figure:

3rd FRENCH Division

1st French attack which took reinforced picket on the Gorospil at 10·30-11·00 a.m.

Gorospil Mt.

Gorospil Pass

6th Chemin des Anelos

2/34 th

1/9 th

1/28 th

Mountains

Area of severe fighting

The Lower Aldudes Heights

To URDAX →

2nd FRENCH Division

Mountains

MAYA Pass

STEWART'S 2nd position 3·00 p.m.

92nd

71st

Chemin des Anelos

Camp

CAMERON'S CAMPS

50 th

STEWART'S 3rd position 4·30 p.m.

ALCORRUNZ Mt.

← To PAMPLONA

→ To Village of MAYA & Pringles Camps

285

Cameron who commanded the other brigade. Stewart should, under such circumstances have been present personally, but was not there.[1]

Cameron's previous arrangements for protecting the main road were adequate; he had a battery of artillery under his command and had posted his whole force in accordance with Wellington's theory of a flexible defence. But the dispositions made for Pringle's Brigade were curious. One company was kept continuously alert on the Gorospil peak. Behind them, but some 800 yards to the south of the watershed on the road to Maya village, the three light companies and the rifle company of the brigade were in an 'alert' camp. Still further south, there was another camp which one of the three battalions, less its light company, occupied in turn for a week at a time. It was expected that the light companies and one line battalion would be able to ascend to the Gorospil in time to prevent the French from taking this section of the pass. The other two line battalions were camped near Maya, some two miles away, and much lower down the valley.

Between 6 and 7 a.m. an observer on Cameron's peak noticed a French force advancing by the Gorospil path toward Pringle's men. A staff officer from divisional headquarters rode over to the Gorospil peak but could see nothing from its summit. He was satisfied, however, that the French were moving on this position and ordered up the four light companies from the advance camp. All five companies were assembled in an extremely strong position, but were possibly disgruntled at leaving their breakfast uneaten, and did not keep a good watch.

These five companies, approximately 350 men, were suddenly attacked at approximately 10 a.m. by a line of 700 *tirailleurs* backed by strong French columns. The Gorospil position fell after some 40 minutes of severe fighting. The majority of the defending force was killed, wounded, or taken. The 2/34th, the active support battalion that week, now came up and endeavoured to restore the situation against very heavy odds. It failed and was driven back. Some minutes later the 1/39th, after a longer and stiffer climb from the village of Maya, attacked to the west, but was equally unsuccessful. Finally, the 1/28th reached the pass even further west and was able to take and hold some high ground just south of the secondary road.[2]

[1] No one knows exactly what took place at Stewart's headquarters at Maya on the morning of the 25th. Both the Gorospil pickets and Cameron's reported enemy activity, but Stewart had heard firing between Campbells' Portuguese and the National Guards in the Val de Baigorry. He left his post to investigate something not his primary responsibility.
[2] *Fortescue*, IX, 258, who was writing and publishing before Oman by this time, states that the 2/34th arrived before the Gorospil fell and that at least some companies of it

Cameron was still not engaged; he saw that Pringle was in trouble and sent east one of his battalions, the 1/50th.[1] This fresh force joined that part of Pringle's Brigade not driven south down the Maya road, and attacked in line, moving west to east. At first they were successful and brought the French to a standstill, but were opposed to greatly superior numbers. The 1/50th was finally driven back west in some disorder.

Pringle, who had now taken command of both brigades, sent forward against the advancing French mass a wing of the 1/92nd (Gordon Highlanders). This half battalion formed on an open heather-covered crest hardly 50 yards wide; their two-deep line extended slightly down slopes on both flanks (Plate 46). In one of the most magnificent exhibitions of courage and weapons efficiency in military history, less than 400 men fought an entire division for twenty minutes. The Scots poured in volley after volley, inflicting heavy casualties in the tightly-packed mass before them; but, because of the configuration of the ground, it was possible for many more French soldiers than usual to return their fire.

'They stood there like a stone wall overmatched by twenty to one, until half their blue bonnets lay beside those brave northern warriors. When they retired, their dead bodies lay as a barrier to

---

joined in the latter stages of this fight. *Oman*, VI, 630, states that they did not, pointing out in a note his disagreement with Fortescue. Oman based his opinion on *Bell*, I, 103, who says,

'the pass up was narrow, steep, and tiresome, the loads heavy, and the men blown. We laboured on, but all too late—a forlorn hope; our comrades were all killed, wounded, or prisoners. The enemy had full possession of the ground; some ten thousand men were there, nearly all with their arms piles, enough of them arranged along the brow to keep us back.'

However, Fortescue followed *Sherer*, 258, who commanded the original picquet company of the 2/34th and wrote,

'These fellows fought with ardour, but we disputed our ground with them handsomely, and caused them severe loss; nor had we lost the position itself, though driven from the advances of it, when joined by the hastily arriving groups of the right corps of our brigade (my own regiment). The enemy's numbers now, however, increased every moment; they covered the country immediately in front of, and around us. The sinuosities of the mountains, the ravines, the water-courses were filled with their advancing and overwhelming force. The contest now, if contest it could be called was very unequal; and, of course, short and bloody. I saw two-thirds of my picquet, and numbers, both of the light companies and my own regiment, destroyed. Among other brave victims, our captain of grenadiers nobly fell, covered with wounds; our colonel desperately wounded, and many others; and surviving this carnage, was myself made prisoner.'

[1] Pringle may have ordered the 1/50th forward himself, for he took over command of both brigades at about this time.

287

the advancing foe. Oh, but they did fight well that day; I can see the line now of the killed and wounded stretched upon the heather, as the living retired, closing to the centre.' [1]

Pringle continued to feed in soldiers piecemeal against fearful odds; his two brigades were slowly forced back. Another French division had come up the main road from Urdax and a third behind the first up the Gorospil path. Four British battalions were opposed to three divisions. It was of course impossible in this restricted area for the French to make their numerical superiority completely effective, but by 4.30 p.m. the French had over-run Cameron's camps and forced their way well down into the valley. Stewart eventually reached the field and took up a position east of the Alcorrunz peak. A stray battalion, the 1/82nd from Grant's Brigade of the 7th Division, had joined the British force a little earlier. There was more severe fighting, but with no great advantage to either side.

Suddenly, at approximately 6 p.m., the whole complexion of the action was altered when Barnes and two battalions of his brigade coming from the west along the *Chemin des Anglais* reached the field. These fresh troops charged forward, together with the surviving Gordons, into the flank of the far more numerous but exhausted French force.

'General Stewart, having regard to the extraordinary loss and fatigue sustained by them, desired that the 92nd should not join in the charge of Barnes' troops. But this time the pipe-major was not to be denied. He struck up the charging tune of "The Haughs of Cromdale", his comrades, seized with what in the Highlands is called "mire chath"—the Frenzy of battle—without either asking or obtaining permission, not only charged, but led the charge, and rushed down on the enemy with irresistible force, driving back their opponents in the most splendid style. The power of the national music over the minds of Scottish soldiers was never more conspicuous.' [2]

The French were thrust completely from the valley below and back into the pass itself. The firing continued until darkness obscured all targets. The fighting at Maya had lasted ten hours and had been exceptionally bloody. British casualties were over 1,500 of 6,000

[1] *Bell*, I, 103-4.   [2] *Gardyne*, I, 297.

engaged, including the three battalions from the 7th Division which arrived late in the day. The French loss, due mainly to more efficient musketry on the part of the 'thin red lines', was greater by about 500, but was distributed among 20,000 men. The pass itself remained in enemy hands, but Stewart's force still occupied strong positions within 400 yards of it. Four Portuguese field pieces were lost, the first and only guns ever taken from Wellington in any action.[1]

British soldiers have rarely fought so courageously, but have not often been worse commanded. The initial dispositions and security measures were poor in the face of heavy concentrations of French infantry. The handling of units in battle was worthy of the Duke of York or Dalrymple. Two fine battalions were slaughtered piecemeal to no purpose; four more were badly cut up.

Hill reached Maya after the fighting was over; he ordered Stewart to retreat on Elizondo in the middle of the Baztan Valley. Wellington had not instructed Hill to hold any one section specifically; so long as he blocked the main road through the Baztan, the French were contained. The retreat from Maya was entirely successful; the French under D'Erlon were ignorant of it until next morning.

Wellington rode back from San Sebastian to Lesaca on the afternoon of the 25th and heard rumours of a fight. At nightfall, Dalhousie gave him a second-hand, verbal, and erroneous account of Maya. The C-in-C received a dispatch from Cole at about 10 p.m., but this report had been written at 1 p.m. Wellington understood from these accounts that both passes were still being held. He also realized that Soult was launching a major offensive against the Allied right. He received at about 4 a.m. on the 26th a dispatch from Hill informing him of the retirement of Stewart and Barnes to Elizondo, but no further news came in from Cole. Wellington ordered the 7th and Light Divisions to retire to the southeast and be ready to support Hill. Graham was directed to embark the siege *matériel* at Passages and prepare to meet an advance over the Bidassoa. Instructions were sent to O'Donnell who commanded the Spanish force blockading Pamplona which freed one

---

[1] Stewart came up just in time to countermand Pringle's order for the battery to retire; the guns were lost soon after. Beresford and Stewart lost a howitzer at Albuera. Colborne considered Stewart the bravest man he ever saw, *Harry Smith*, I, 170-1, but in view of Albuera, his disobedience during the November retreat from Salamanca, and Maya, Stewart's military ability appears not to have equalled his courage. Pringle certainly did not cover himself with glory, but was new to his command and the entire situation.

full division for use by Picton in the field. The 6th Division, now under Pack, was sent south.

Wellington rode towards Elizondo to see for himself what was happening in the Baztan and met Hill before noon. Hill was establishing a strong defensive position in front of Irurita in the central valley and had everything under control. Wellington proceeded south, still without news from Cole. His headquarters that evening was at Almandoz, half way between Irurita and the Col de Velate, the southern pass from the Baztan. At 8 p.m., he finally received a dispatch from Cole announcing his retreat from Roncesvalles. Immediately, Wellington sent orders to both Picton and Cole to hold the French east of Zubiri.

Wellington rode south at dawn on the 27th, reaching Olague before 10 a.m. where he heard rumours of a further retreat by Picton's command during the night. This was infuriating, for Wellington knew the strength of the country. Cole and Picton were giving up territory in which the French, no matter how numerous and energetic, could not mount a powerful and sustained offensive; there was but the single valley road and no serviceable parallel routes.[1] Picton and Cole were obviously taking counsel of their fears and behaving 'like children' in not sending frequent reports because the intelligence they had to communicate was disagreeable.[2]

Wellington left Q.M.G. Murray at Olague, and continued south accompanied only by Fitzroy Somerset, his military secretary, both magnificently mounted. As they entered the village of Sorauren, Wellington saw his troops on a ridge to the southeast; the French were

[1] Soult did try to advance with his two corps on parallel routes, but found it impossible Clausel kept to the main road, one ox cart width, but Reille used mule tracks along the crests of hills; 17,000 men were sent up steep ridges, down dangerous slopes, and single-file through the woods. This lost Reille so much time that he returned to the main road behind Clausel.

[2] *Fortescue*, IX, 255–6, quotes Wellington, 'All the beatings we have given the French have not given our generals confidence in themselves and in the exertions of their troops. They are really heroes when I am on the spot to direct them, but when I am obliged to quit them they are children.'

Forces contending: French—Six Infantry and two Cavalry divisions; about 30,000 actually engaged.

Allies—Pack's 6th Division, Cole's 4th Division, Picton's 3rd Division. Morillo's and O'Donnell's Spaniards, Byng's Brigade (2nd Div), Campbell's Brigade (Hill's Corps); about 18,000 actually engaged.

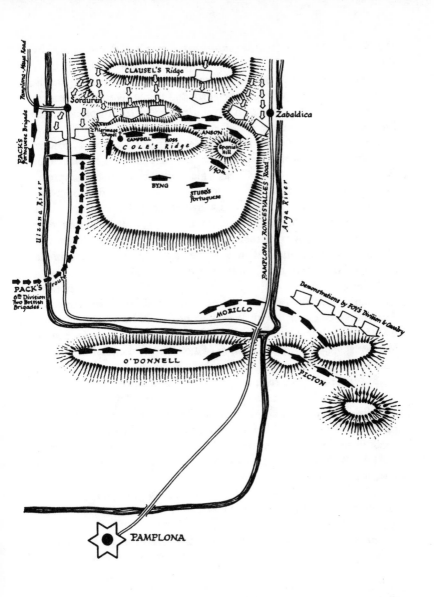

XVI. SORAUREN

already moving over the ridge immediately north of that occupied by the Allies (Plate 48). The C-in-C scribbled thirteen lines to Murray ordering the rerouting of Allied forces marching south and gave the dispatch to Somerset who galloped back to Olague. Wellington turned toward the Allied position; as he spurred away from Sorauren, the French entered it from the east.

Wellington galloped up the ridge, later known as 'Cole's', toward the pilgrimage chapel, a single horseman in a low hat, a plain blue jacket, and a short white cloak. He approached first Campbell's Portuguese Brigade; suddenly, they recognizing the rider. Spontaneously a shout went up: 'Douro! Douro! Douro!' The Portuguese had called Wellington this since he had taken Oporto, more than four years previously. He was with them again; their confidence was restored. Within seconds, British infantry further along the line joined in the cheering. Nosey had come! Nosey was in command.[1]

Wellington rode to a prominence in the front of the Allied position and calmly examined the entire area. The Allied 'southern' army was drawn up facing north with Pamplona behind it. Its left, under Cole, was thrust well forward and occupied the east-west ridge up which he had just ridden. It had an elevation of 2,000 feet and a total length of a mile and a half. This ridge rose steeply at either end from deep troughs (Plate 47). The Ulzana river and the Maya/Pamplona road ran through the western valley; that to the east contained the Arga river and the road from Roncesvalles to Pamplona. These two narrow valleys run parallel for several miles before converging just north of Pamplona. A break in the high land between them occurs on the level of Sorauren; Zabaldica lies in the Arga valley in a somewhat similar position. The French occupied the ridge north of the cleft, or transverse valley, and the Allied that to the south. A bridge of land joins the two ridges slightly east of centre, but it was lower than either ridge, and no more than 300 yards wide.

After Cole had abandoned the pass of Roncesvalles on the night of 25th–26th July, he took up a position no less strong next morning east

---

[1] Memoirs and diaries from the ranks often contain the same general statement that Wellington was 'worth 10,000 bayonets'. Their confidence in him, and themselves under his command, was unbounded. *Wheeler*, 196, says,

'If England should require the service of her army again, and I should be with it, let me have "Old Nosey" to command. Our interests would be sure to be looked into, we should never have occasion to fear an enemy. There are two things we should be certain of. First, we should always be as well supplied with rations as the nature of the service would admit. The second is we should be sure to give the enemy a d——d good thrashing. What can a soldier desire more.'

of Zubiri. Picton came up from Olague that afternoon, but he and Cole let their imaginations dwell on the dangers of confronting Soult's 40,000 men with only 19,000 of their own and decided to retire further in spite of the orders they had received.[1]

This retreat continued until the Allied 'southern' army was practically free of the mountains and was about to take a position chosen by Picton partly within range of the French guns on the walls of Pamplona. Cole noticed about a mile in his front the Sorauren-Zabaldica ridge and received permission to occupy it with his entire division, Byng's Brigade, Campbell's Portuguese Brigade, and some of Morillo's Spaniards. To the rear of Cole, in the position originally selected by Picton, was O'Donnell's Spanish Division behind the river Ulzana, now turned at 90 degrees to the Sorauren valley. To the east and in line with O'Donnell there were the rest of Morillo's Spaniards, Picton's 3rd Division, and some British cavalry. The Allied left was pushed well forward, and the right refused.

Wellington now studied the French dispositions; through his telescope, he could pick out Soult and the French staff. The enemy did not seem ready to attack; they were still moving about in columns and certainly did not yet have 40,000 men in the area. Wellington concluded that there would be no major French attack that day.[2] He then re-examined the Allied disposition in detail and made only one change. A round hill southwest of Zabaldica, rising high above the Arga, was defended by Spanish troops only. If this were lost, Cole and Picton would be separated. The 1/40th of Anson's Brigade was placed in support of the Spaniards.

Late in the afternoon, a thunderstorm broke, which can be compared in severity only to that before Salamanca. Even though welcomed by some in the Allied army as an omen of victory, it caused a considerable delay in the arrival of reinforcements from the north. Pack and his 6th Division, now re-routed by Murray in accordance with Wellington's hurried but precise instructions, would have been up by dawn on the

---

[1] The road crosses a spur of the Pyrenees even more rugged and precipitous than the main range; Picton's lame excuse was that the position could be flanked. Picton was magnificent in battle under Wellington, but certainly overcautious here.

[2] This was based in part on the fact that Soult also was naturally cautious and would know of Wellington's arrival not only on account of the cheering, but also because Wellington was in plain sight. *Napier*, V, 226, says, 'Suddenly he (Wellington) stopped at a conspicuous point, for he desired both armies should know he was there, and a double spy who was present point out Soult, who was so near that his features could be distinguished.' Fortescue suggests that Soult did not know of Wellington's arrival because he did not mention it in his report to Napoleon!

28th had it not been for the storm. Hill, who was moving south along the Maya-Pamplona road, was held up for hours.

PHASE THREE: THE BATTLE OF SORAUREN AND THE FRENCH RETREAT

The Allies were under arms before dawn, but daylight revealed no immediate French offensive. Two divisions of cavalry, and one of infantry, were demonstrating in front of Picton, but did not attempt to attack. As the morning wore on, the French were observed to be regrouping as if for an advance against the Allied left. Cole's ridge was held by five brigades; Campbell's, Ross's, and Anson's in the first line, with Stubbs's and Byng's in reserve. Pack's 6th Division would be in the valley of the Ulzana behind Cole's left flank before noon. Wellington had been in continuous communication with this force since daylight; he made certain that Pack understood the importance of his joining the main army, even if he had to break through a screen of French light troops which might conceivably be sent from Sorauren to impede him. The head of Pack's column could be seen from Wellington's position by 10 a.m.; it entered the Ulzana valley before 11 a.m. The division was advancing according to Wellington's orders up the valley with one brigade to the west of the Ulzana and two to the east, when the French finally attacked.

A French reinforced division passed down the Ulzana valley to attack Pack, but soon came under fire at medium range from both flanks. The Portuguese brigade of the 6th Division had been west of the stream and met little opposition. It was nearly level with Sorauren when it opened fire across the Ulzana. Some of Cole's skirmishers came down from beside the chapel and delivered a closer and more effective fire. The French here were somewhat inferior in numbers and lost heart before they came to grips with Pack's two British brigades. When close fighting commenced, they broke and fled into the village.

But this French movement in the Ulzana valley was only the first part of a general attack. Soult sent five more French divisions against the Allied positions on Cole's ridge. For a few minutes, the situation was serious. Although the Allies occupied extremely favourable ground, they were outnumbered by about two to one.

A brigade of French infantry ascended the slope towards the chapel, the same path up which Wellington had ridden the previous day. Four more brigades traversed the cleft west of the land bridge, while one division attacked directly across it, one brigade behind the other. In the Arga valley to the east, another division was assaulting the round hill held by the Spaniards.

The Allied skirmish line was not so numerous as that of the French and was pushed back with comparative ease. On Cole's left, the slope to the chapel from Sorauren was steep, but open and regular. Near his centre the ground was more broken. The ascent was steeper; scrub and rock ledges impeded the enemy advance. The French attacking across the land bridge were the first to close, as they had little climbing to do. Here were four battalions formed one behind the other in columns of double companies. Even though they had the advantage of not having to descend into the steep defile and climb the other side, they were still some 200 feet below Cole's crest. As they moved towards it, two of Anson's battalions, the 3/27th and 1/48th, formed in the familiar two-deep line, appeared on the skyline, and moved forward to meet the head of this column. The musketry advantage of line over column was about 1,200 against 300; the French battalions were overthrown one after another. The second brigade of this division was too far behind to support the first.

The French onslaught to the west was more successful initially. The 7th *Cacadores* were cleared from the chapel in hard fighting on the extreme Allied left. Four French brigades with their battalion columns in line were forcing back Ross and Campbell; the odds here were about three to one in favour of the French. But Wellington was present, and sent the two victorious battalions of Anson's Brigade in a diagonal charge downhill against their flank. Anson's third battalion would be able to hold the land bridge, at least temporarily.

Never in the Peninsular War did two battalions accomplish so much, so quickly. The 3/27th and 1/48th smashed each successive enemy battalion, apparently by charging each after a short period of fire.[1] With remarkable tactical skill, Wellington contrived to gain a two to one numerical advantage at each encounter, although he was out-numbered in the general area by more than two to one. Ross and Campbell returned to the fray with new vigour while Wellington committed the physically fresh brigades of Byng and Stubbs. The entire French attack between Sorauren and the land bridge was defeated and

---

[1] Reference has already been made to the tendency of British officers to describe as 'bayonet charges' attacks in which only a few casualties were inflicted by bayonets. These two battalions had their bayonets ready, but the French avoided hand to hand combat at the last moment.

cast down into the transverse valley, but the Allied infantry were ordered not to press their advantage too far.

Meanwhile, a bloody struggle was going on in the Arga valley. The Spanish-held hill had been assaulted by an entire French infantry division in three separate charges. Morillo's Spaniards behaved well at the first attack and drove the French back into the valley. The second attack, however, was made before the Spanish infantry had reformed after their too lengthy pursuit; in a short sharp action, the Spaniards were broken. The French rushed forward believing themselves to be victorious, but were met just at the crest of the hill by the 1/40th in line. A battalion volley at close range brought the disordered French masses to a halt; the thin red line began to deliver its characteristic rolling fire. The fight went on for several minutes; the single British battalion would have been lost, had it shown the slightest irresolution. But the 1/40th remained firm, even though losing heavily. Suddenly, the French mass disintegrated and was driven down into the valley near Zabaldica. A third French assault was delivered a few minutes later, mostly by infantry which had failed earlier, but they never reached the hilltop.

The battle terminated with four hours of daylight left. Soult's general attack was completely beaten, but at heavy cost. The Allies lost 2,652 men of whom 1,358 were British, 1,102 Portuguese, and 192 Spaniards. It is almost impossible to determine precisely French losses for any given day of Soult's offensive; a total of 4,000 at the battle of Sorauren on the 28th may be reasonably assumed.

Wellington had finally stopped the French advance on Pamplona; and Soult himself was now in a dangerous situation. His systems of transportation and supply could not maintain his army where it was, nor were supplies to be found locally. An immediate retreat through Roncesvalles and Maya would probably have been sensible from a purely military standpoint, but Soult and Napoleon had also to consider the propaganda value of remaining in Spain in the political struggle to keep Austria neutral and Russia and Prussia discouraged.[1]

On the 29th the contending armies remained quiet above the villages of Sorauren and Zabaldica. Far to the north, Wellington had withdrawn Hill and Dalhousie from the Baztan by the Maya-Pamplona road as far as Olague where they turned off to the west to take up a position roughly in continuation of the Picton-Cole line. Alten's Light Division

---

[1] *Oman*, VI, 640-1, gives a complete account of the need for good news and the deliberate falsification of facts in the French press.

was marching toward Yrurzun; it was not in direct contact with the Hill-Dalhousie force, but close enough to support it. By dawn on the 30th, Wellington was sufficiently concentrated to take the offensive. He realized, however, that Soult would soon have D'Erlon's three infantry divisions from Maya in addition to his own force, a total of over 50,000 men. But the news from the Bidassoa was encouraging; the enemy had made a half-hearted effort to cross the river, but had failed.

During the 29th, Wellington had ordered artillery and ammunition to be taken to the top of Cole's ridge.[1] These pieces were positioned behind the land bridge and to the rear of the chapel. The 6th Division, now under Pakenham, for Pack had been wounded the day before, outflanked the village of Sorauren to the west across the river. Dalhousie's 7th Division was in position to extend Pakenham's line. Hill was ready to fight D'Erlon. Picton's force was alerted for a forward movement. Wellington was determined to take the offensive at the first sign of Soult retreating.

Long before dawn on the 30th, Allied pickets heard sounds of movement in the French army. At daybreak, masses of men could be seen hurrying north along the Arga valley. Lookouts reported the French to be in motion toward Maya in the Ulzana valley also. But at the same time other troops were moving into Sorauren. The Allied artillery opened fire against the village, the columns on the Maya road, and the infantry on the enemy ridge before them.

Wellington followed up this short, vigorous bombardment with a co-ordinated attack. Picton stormed up the Arga valley; Cole hurtled down from his position and assaulted the opposite ridge. Sorauren was the objective of three columns under Pakenham's direction. One descended from the chapel, the second pushed north through the Ulzana valley, while the third thrust east from the steep hills across the river. Dalhousie, northwest of the village, was in position to support them.

All these attacks were delivered with the precision and impetuosity of Salamanca. If the French had fought as well as they had done on that field, the Allies might have been repulsed. Wellington's army was less

---

[1] *Beatson*, 177, writing of battle on the 28th,

  'It was almost entirely an infantry fight, for there was little artillery up on the allied side and the French made little use of theirs. On both sides the ground was beyond the capability of movement of the artillery of that day—modern field artillery would now make light of the Oricain hill ground—so that the allied infantry was deprived of that support which had been so splendidly given by the British gunners on the field of Vitoria.'

numerous than the enemy and was attacking extremely strong positions. The French ridge was as strong as Cole's, while Sorauren had been barricaded and protected with earthworks. But Wellington had correctly judged French morale. It had risen high after Soult's artful stimulation, but five days of frustration in the mountains and the bloody repulse of the 28th had caused it to collapse.

In the Arga valley, on the French ridge, and in the vicinity of Sorauren, the Allies were victorious. French divisions on or near the Maya road were able to get away more or less intact, but Maucune's Division in Sorauren itself was practically wiped out. Foy's Division at Zabaldica was all but surrounded. Picton had cut the Pamplona-Roncesvalles road; Cole lay between Foy and the Maya road. Foy was forced to retreat by goat paths over the hills to the northeast without vehicles or baggage. His division was still in fair order, but disorganized forces from other units lacking officers, weapons, and the will to fight, joined him. With dubious loyalty to Soult, but with considerable tactical skill, Foy shepherded his motley flock of over 10,000 men across country into France.

The second battle of Sorauren was over by noon, the result of which was most satisfying to Wellington. His losses had been slight; the enemy casualties were much greater and included large numbers of prisoners. But the French force in the Ulzana valley was still intact and powerful. Furthermore, reports from Hill indicated that he was being forced back on the extreme Allied left by D'Erlon's three divisions.

This secondary struggle between D'Erlon and Hill near Lizaso was inexplicable to Wellington at the time. The results amply bore out his judgement; Hill, at first with only four brigades, fought two stubborn actions against great odds and escaped without more serious consequences than the loss of ground. Soult won a technical victory and broke through to the Pamplona-San Sebastian road.[1] He was with D'Erlon in person during this clash with Hill while miles away the greater part of his army under Reille and Clausel was being destroyed as an organized force by Wellington's co-ordinated blows.

During the evening of the 30th, Wellington reviewed the situation in the light of intelligence available at headquarters. Soult's army was

---

[1] Napier gives this credit to Soult, but even if the French army were still intact, which it certainly was not, would Soult have marched across the front of an army commanded by the victor of Salamanca?

no longer an offensive threat, except perhaps for D'Erlon's corps still numerous and comparatively fresh. But an effective pursuit depended upon determining exactly where the various enemy units were and guessing their intentions. Wellington knew that the French artillery and cavalry had been ordered back by way of Roncesvalles on the 29th; Picton had possession of this road early on the 30th, but reported that the cavalry and artillery were already in France. D'Erlon's three divisions were still in the neighbourhood of Lizaso. There was a force of French infantry in movement near Olague on the Maya road, and another, mostly Foy's command, in the vicinity of Iragui, some ten miles east toward the Roncesvalles road. Wellington was erroneously informed that the Iragui force was larger than that near Olague.

Wellington's plans for the 31st called for Picton to prevent the French from retiring by the Roncesvalles road and for Cole to cut the Maya road in their rear. Both were accomplished. The Allies took Elizondo in the Baztan and dispersed a French force awaiting a convoy of supplies from Bayonne. The convoy itself was taken in its entirety that evening. If Soult had endeavoured to retreat by Roncesvalles or through the Baztan, his army would have been destroyed.

In part by good management, and partly on account of the remarkable recuperative powers of French troops, Soult was able to avoid any fatal contact with the Allied army. He concentrated not on the Maya road, but to the west of it, and north of Lizaso. His subsequent retreat was north rather than east. The main French force of 35,000 was pursued by about 18,000 under Hill and Dalhousie. Picton, Cole, and Pakenham were further east, but Foy was already nearing the border and out of danger.

Hill pressed after Soult doggedly; there was bloody rearguard fighting. But the French were using mountain tracks; there was no way round either flank.[1] Soult avoided the Baztan entirely, passed along the western bank of the Bidassoa, and crossed the river at Yanci. He lost considerable numbers in killed, wounded, and prisoners, but no guns or wagons, because he had none.

There was a time during the afternoon of 1st August when a more energetic attention to Wellington's orders by Graham and Longa would have closed the bridge at Yanci and cut off the French retreat. The Light Division, after much marching and countermarching, came down on the French column from the side to inflict heavy

---

[1] The Dona Maria passes used by the French are still without roads.

casualties, but just too late to seal off their road.[1] Soult managed to take up a defensive position during the evening between Vera and Eschelar with his rear in contact with France, but Wellington pushed him over the border on the 2nd.

Soult's nine-day offensive failed to relieve either San Sebastian or Pamplona. He lost at least 13,500 of his original 60,000 men. Those who did recross the border resembled in their destitution the remnants of the army he pulled out of northern Portugal in June 1809. Only Foy, because he was not engaged on the 28th and because of his rather unusual decision to leave Soult in the lurch, was able to bring back a nearly full division in any kind of order. The French army was more disorganized and defeated after the Battles of the Pyrenees than they had been after Vitoria.

Allied losses had also been heavy, a total of 7,100 of about 40,000 actually in action during the whole nine days.[2] Four guns had been lost at Maya; beasts, baggage, and artillery had broken down and been destroyed or abandoned, particularly by Hill and Dalhousie, during the thunderstorm on the night of the 27th, although no enemy had been within miles.

The Allied army was in a critical situation on the 27th. Wellington had advised Hill that it might be necessary to swing back on Tolosa which would have given up the Pamplona blockade. Graham had been ordered to load his siege *matériel*, but it is probable that the situation was never so serious as these precautions might indicate; Wellington was ever the most cautious of commanders.

Cole's early retirement during the night of the 25th and Picton's similar action the following night contrary to definite orders put Wellington at a great disadvantage. His system of defence in this area was based on the assumption that he would have twenty-four hours more time for bringing reinforcements into position. Except for O'Donnell's Spanish Division, there were no additional Allied troops close enough to Pamplona to be of use on the 27th. Wellington sent the fastest moving 'reinforcement' in his whole army, himself; from the moment of his arrival at Sorauren on the 27th, Soult's good luck deserted him.

---

[1] The Light Division accomplished prodigies in marching: *Surtees*, 228, writing of this last day, 'We travelled at least thirty-two miles over mountains ... where you were sometimes nearly obliged to scramble upon your hands and knees.'

[2] See computation in the Appendix to this chapter.

The two battles of Sorauren demonstrate yet again the efficiency of Wellington's line formations when opposed to columns. These conflicts show clearly, however, the importance of flexibility, concealment, support, and tactical surprise. The position of the 1/40th behind the Spanish hill was perfect for its task. Allied artillery on the summit of Cole's ridge gave the attack early on the 30th just the boost it required to succeed where a more numerous French assault had failed two days before under much the same circumstances.

Wellington's ability to make an immediate and vital change in his dispositions is again apparent. Had he not ordered the 3/27th and the 1/48th after their first action to move obliquely against the French columns to the west, Soult's attack, if not his entire offensive, could have succeeded. If a commander is incapable of making these vital re-adjustments, any planning of strategy, logistics, and tactics, however excellent, is rendered valueless.

Because of the time and distances involved, more Allied generals had independent commands than previously. Hill was adequate; Pringle, Stewart, Cole, and Picton handled their responsibilities poorly. Graham, Longa, and Alten missed great opportunities. Wellington himself, and the entire Allied army, learned much about fighting in some of the most difficult campaigning country in the world. Once firmly established here in positions of Wellington's choosing, and with San Sebastian and Pamplona in their hands, they would be proof even against Napoleon in person at the head of large French reinforcements.

THE CONTENDING FORCES IN THE BATTLES OF THE PYRENEES

ALLIED ARMY UNDER WELLINGTON   TOTAL = 80,000 approx.
   30,000 British   30,000 Portuguese   20,000 Spanish

The Anglo-Portuguese organization remains as shown in the Appendix to Chapter XV, but individual units were weaker. Allied cavalry was mainly in the Ebro valley and did not see action.

'CORPS' LIEUTEN- ANCIES	Divisions	INFANTRY Brigades	Personnel	CAVALRY Personnel	ARTILLERY Guns	Personnel
Reille	3	6	17,235 ⎫		18 ⎫	
D'Erlon	3	6	20,957 ⎬	808	18 ⎬	9,000
Clausel	3	6	17,218 ⎭		18 ⎪	
Villate		5	17,254	6,339	86 ⎭	
		23	72,664	7,147	140	9,000

FORCES ACTUALLY ENGAGED

·FRENCH   TOTAL = 53,000 approx.

  Nine infantry divisions

ALLIES   TOTAL = 40,000 approx.

  Hill's entire 'corps' including Morillo's 14,000 approx.
   Spaniards

  Picton's 3rd Division, Cole's 4th   26,000 approx.
   Division, Pack's (later Pakenham's)
   6th Division, and Dalhousie's 7th
   Division (averaging 6,500 each)

TOPOGRAPHICAL OBSERVATIONS

Today, much of the main road between San Sebastian and Madrid differs from the Great Road of Napoleonic times, but the old road is still in existence and can be followed if one has an old map and a good sense of direction. Between Vitoria and the border it passes through Mondragon, Vergara, Villafranca, Tolosa, Hernani and Oyarzun. Pamplona and San Sebastian have grown greatly with the passage of years, but the campaign area in the Spanish Pyrenees has changed hardly at all. The bridge and Hermitage Chapel at Sorauren, the Roman road across the Altobiscar, the Chemin des Anglais at Maya, the Hog's Back above Vera, Cadoux's bridge, and many other remaining landmarks make this among the most interesting of Peninsular territory to explore. The weather is unpredictable and often bad, but the mountain scenery is magnificent.

[1] Taken from *Oman*, VI, 768, who also lists, but does not include in this total, the garrison of Santona, San Sebastian, Pamplona, conscripts at Bayonne, sick, and detached. The new divisions were more uniform than previously; each consisting of two brigades of about 3,000 men each.

XVII

SAN SEBASTIAN FALLS:
THE BORDER IS BREACHED

WELLINGTON was tempted to pursue Soult's disorganized and defeated army across the border on 2nd August. He gave orders to Hill the previous day which prepared the way for a push through Maya to attack the French in flank and rear when they came streaming back from Eschelar and Vera. But reconsideration of the larger issues caused Wellington to give up the attempt. It would be better to take San Sebastian and starve Pamplona into submission before crossing the Bidassoa.

Foy had regarrisoned San Sebastian as he retreated into France after Vitoria; it had been blockaded by land since 28th June. Graham began actual siege operations early the next month with Oswald's 5th Division and Bradford's Independent Portuguese Brigade. The Allies used guns brought from Portugal, and those shipped from Corunna and Santander; these latter were unloaded in the safe harbour of Passages.[1]

In 1813, San Sebastian was a small compact town located on an isthmus which was bounded on one side by a tidal river, the Urumea, and on the other by a landlocked bay. The town was square, some 400 yards on a side, and situated 600 yards from the mainland. It had a population of almost 10,000. The isthmus to the south was low and sandy, but immediately north and above the town there was a fortified rock mountain crowned by an old castle. A waterborne landing at the base of the town walls, or around the periphery of the rock, would be almost impossible. An attack along the isthmus was practical, but

---

[1] *Napier*, V, 184, says,

'... one hundred regular sappers and miners, now for the first time used in the sieges of the Peninsula. There was also a new battering train, originally prepared to besiege Burgos, consisting of fourteen iron twenty-four pounders, six eight-inch brass howitzers, four sixty-eight-pound iron carronades, and four iron ten-inch mortars. To these were added six twenty-four pounders lent by the ships of war, and six eighteen pounders which had moved with the army from Portugal, making altogether forty pieces commanded by Colonel Dickson.'

would require an assault on the most powerful part of the fortification. The south face of the town was covered by Vauban-type masonry and earth outworks of more recent construction than the main walls. An approach from the east might be less time-consuming; artillery could easily fire across the Urumea and smash down the massive but old and perpendicular town wall. Even though this rose sheer from the sea for 20 hours each day, at low tide men could walk between the wall and the estuary, and even ford the river from its eastern bank right at its mouth.[1]

The French governor, General Rey, was a courageous and able soldier. His garrison was adequate and of good quality; he could be supplied by sea at night with both men and munitions from France.[2] He built and occupied outworks along the isthmus, after destroying outlying buildings. His internal preparations for the siege were efficient and carried out apparently with the voluntary co-operation of the civilian population.[3]

Wellington reconnoitred the place in person on 12th July and approved the general plan of attacking the east side of the town with batteries placed on the isthmus and in the sand hills east of the Urumea.[4] The French were pushed back to their permanent fortifications by the 17th. Batteries were established and breaches made; a mine was placed in the already severed water main leading into the town, and exploded. The 5th Division and Bradford's Portuguese assaulted the place unsuccessfully on the 25th.

After Soult had been defeated in the battles of the Pyrenees and thrust back into France, Wellington decided that time was no longer pressing; haste in earlier sieges had contributed to high casualty rates. After 2nd August the Allied army awaited the arrival of further siege *matériel* and ammunition. On the 19th, the first of three convoys sailed into Passages direct from Britain; the other two soon followed.

---

[1] There is an average tide of 16 feet in this area.

[2] The Royal Navy was handicapped by a lack of light vessels due to the American war; French sailors were at home in these waters. Coasting vessels from Bayonne and St Jean-de-Luz were protected by the castle guns, which had a range of fully 2,000 yards in daylight.

[3] *Fortescue*, IX, 226, stresses the pro-French attitude within San Sebastian. *Schaumann*, 389 and 396-7 remarks on the aid received by the French from the inhabitants in both building and defending new fortifications. The place had been under French control for more than five years; many there believed that it would be annexed to France permanently.

[4] For a technical criticism of these operations see *Jones*, II, 92-7.

For the first time Wellington had plenty of siege artillery and ammunition of every type, including 68-pounder carronades.[1] Old batteries were again armed; new ones were constructed. Wellington returned to the border to watch Soult and left Graham again in command at San Sebastian. Fire was opened on 26th August; French artillery on the walls and even in the castle was silenced. Damage to the east wall was extensive, and consisted of a main breach almost 100 yards wide with a lesser breach to the north. The demibastion at the southeast corner of the town was completely smashed; it appeared unlikely that the garrison could resist an assault. In the earlier attack, the French had beaten off their assailants primarily because they had constructed a new ditch and wall behind the first. Wellington and Graham were informed of what was going on inside San Sebastian. Rey had kept both his garrison and Spanish civilians hard at work deepening and widening this defensive ditch, strengthening the secondary wall, and raising fortifications in the streets. Positions into which field guns could be moved when required had been prepared on the walls. The French were known to have dug mines in front of the breaches. In order to get these exploded prematurely, Graham delivered a false attack on the night of the 29th, but the enemy was not deceived.

The real attack was scheduled for 31st August at low tide, which came at noon. The heavy Allied bombardment ceased, or shifted to the castle, as the storming columns moved out at 11 a.m. along the exposed left bank of the Urumea. The 5th Division and Bradford's Portuguese Brigade had been reinforced by 700 volunteers from the 1st and Light Divisions. The first assault was against the main breach; 35 minutes later Portuguese volunteers were to ford the Urumea at its mouth and attack the lesser breach.

With the lifting of the Allied bombardment, the French appeared from their cover with their light artillery. They manned the high curtain on the south side of the town by which the assailants had to pass, and the secondary wall behind the inner ditch which ran the entire length of the breaches in the east wall. Their musketry was heavy and effective; their artillery fire was slow, but both accurate and destructive. When the Allies started to climb the breaches, showers of shells with it fuses and other combustibles were rolled down on them. The ditch

[1] These short large bore pieces were lighter than guns of the same rating and did not fire solid shot, but were effective firing common shell and shrapnel. Jones, II, 51 and 63. Together with other pieces, they had been ordered from Portugal by Wellington on 10th February.

beyond the first wall was 20 feet deep with no way across, except where two or three house walls had been cut not quite cleanly.

The first assault failed in spite of the great courage of both officers and men. Graham and the 5th Division commanders fed in new units as required.[1] The British and Portuguese were striving against conditions as bad as those at Badajoz. The French guns, which had only appeared after the bombardments lifted, were taking a continuous toll with grape and canister; severe musketry fire continued.

When the attack on the main breach was at its height, 800 Portuguese volunteers commenced to ford the 900 yard wide estuary. This crossing was executed at the double, often in three feet of water. They were fired at from the castle and lost heavily; any seriously wounded man drowned immediately. They were unable to enter the town through the lesser breach, but did achieve a lodgement in it.

Fighting at both breaches continued; the defenders seemed as strong as ever. The breaches themselves had been swept clean of small debris by waves at high tide; even when ascended there was still the infernal ditch. Then some volunteers of the Light Division found a precarious lodgement in the ruins of certain houses just inside the eastern wall. The Portuguese further north were able to place a few men in position to enfilade the French behind the main breach. But the Allied attack slowly lost impetus.

Graham was watching from a forward battery and could communicate with other batteries by semaphore. After more than an hour of bloody fighting, he made a most unusual decision for that time. He ordered all his batteries to reopen on the French defences in spite of the Allies beneath the walls. Some pieces were as much as 1,200 yards from the fortifications; the margin for error cannot have been more than 40 feet vertically (about ten mils in modern terms). But the artillery was new and of British manufacture.[2] The crews knew their ranges precisely and were experienced. Not a single projectile was misdirected; few Allied casualties were caused by ricochets and flying fragments.

The French out in the open on top of their walls were surprised by the sudden return of the bombardment. Solid shot ploughed along the high curtain from end to end. Bursts of 8-inch shrapnel shells—from

---

[1] Oswald, long in command of the division, was superseded by Leith, who returned to the front only a few hours before the assault. They held joint command on the 31st, and both were seriously wounded. The entire division fought like devils, for their honour had been questioned after their previous failure.

[2] These pieces had fired over 60,000 rounds between them, and were somewhat enlarged at the vents, but their practice was still predictable.

the 68-pounder carronades—showered the inner French defences with small balls. Heavy grape from the 24-pounders in the closer batteries was also effective. The French light artillery pieces were smashed before they could fire another round. The whole complexion of the fight changed.

When the bombardment lifted for the second time, the 5th Division, the Light and 1st Division volunteers, and the Portuguese surged up the breaches. Just as they were reaching the top they were aided by the explosion of several ready magazines within the French fortification. The inner wall was scaled at half a dozen places. The street barricades and other internal defences were carried. The street fighting was bloody, but did not last long. Rey, and about a third of his garrison retreated to the castle.

San Sebastian was soon in flames; drink was found. Although the British and Portuguese had more excuse for mistreating the civilian population here than at Badajoz, they behaved somewhat better. Spaniards fought alongside the French behind their fortifications, yet little or no physical harm was done to Spanish civilians not taking an active part in the fighting.[1]

There was a good deal of anti-British feeling in Spain at this time. Wellington was accused in Spanish newspapers of having ordered San Sebastian to be set on fire and the inhabitants to be treated in the most barbarous manner because the town had traded principally with France before the war and not with Britain. If Wellington had wanted to burn the place, he could have done so easily by ordering Dickson, his chief of artillery, to go ahead with a mortar bombardment which was planned but not carried out.[2] The burning out of the town by mortar shells before the assaults were commenced would have saved a considerable proportion of the total Allied casualties suffered during the siege, approximately 3,700.

[1] After carefully sifting all available evidence, *Oman*, VII, 35, says, 'as to personal injury to inhabitants, if any really occurred, it was probably during the street fighting, when French and English balls were flying about in all directions.' Yet *Napier*, V, 283–4, indicates greater disorders.

[2] Wellington writes on 9th October, *Dispatches*, 172,
'Every thing was done that was in my power to suggest to save the town. Several persons urged me, in the strongest manner, to allow it to be bombarded, as the most certain mode of forcing the enemy to give it up. This I positively would not allow for the same reason as I did not allow Ciudad Rodrigo or Badajoz to be bombarded; and yet if I had harboured so infamous a wish as to destroy this town from motives of commercial revenge, or any other, I could not have adopted a more certain method than to allow it to be bombarded.'
Britain paid for the complete repair of the defences of San Sebastian at a cost of £12,000.

The castle was an exclusively military objective. It was overwhelmed by mortar fire in two hours on 5th September, and surrendered. The French lost during the siege about 2,500 men; an additional 1,000 prisoners were taken when the castle fell. Strong fortifications defended by brave men ably directed can never be taken easily, unless they can be isolated and starved into submission. Even during the five days in which the French held only the castle, French coasting vessels were able to unload ammunition and supplies and take out wounded during the hours of darkness. Wellington had little alternative but to take San Sebastian by storm, and did so reasonably effectively. His artillery was well chosen and well handled.

Wellington was not personally at San Sebastian on the 31st. He had received intelligence from several sources towards the end of August indicating that Soult, in spite of the poor condition of his army, was going to launch at least a token attack towards the town. This happened to coincide with the final Allied storm; at dawn on the 31st, the French crossed the border in two areas some distance apart. For the first three miles inland the Bidassoa is a sluggish tidal estuary with sand flats on either side. Further upstream, the river flows for five miles at the bottom of a deep cleft through mountains, known as the gorge of the Bidassoa. On reaching Vera, the country becomes less rugged. Soult attacked on the 31st both above and below this gorge; the actions which resulted were completely separate and dissimilar; although originally conceived in the expectation that they would converge, they never did.[1]

The bridge by which the great road passed from France into Spain at Behobie had been burned, but there were four or five good infantry fords in the vicinity which might be used at low tide.[2] Terrain favoured the French near the bridge, where they had several batteries of artillery in prepared positions on the north bank of the river; the Allies could

[1] Soult's plan was probably based on that which brought victory to the French when fighting over the same territory in August 1794; one army had crossed the river near the coast, while the other had swept round from Vera to take the Spaniards further west in the flank and rear.

[2] The main road still crosses the border at this point; the fords can be seen from the modern bridge.

not actually hold their side of the stream. Wellington took advantage of the long hill of San Marcial which runs parallel to, but a mile south of the river here; this strong position was occupied by Spanish troops in a line of field fortifications. There were three divisions under General Freire in line from Irun to beyond Behobie; Longa's Division extended this line to the right into the gorge. The 1st Division and Aylmer's Independent British Brigade were in the rear as support. The San Marcial position overlooks the great road which turns seaward towards Irun from the Behobie bridgehead (Plate 49).

Soult sent what appeared to be three infantry divisions across the Bidassoa near the destroyed bridge and covered them with the fire of 36 field pieces and some larger guns. The crossing was made in dense early morning fog. French *tirailleurs* and columns pushed back the Spanish skirmishers lining the river and advanced toward the heights of San Marcial. The attack was expected to develop according to the normal French pattern; *tirailleurs*, infantry columns, and close support artillery. But Soult's execution was seldom up to his planning; the final advance was begun when only two divisions were across, and the field artillery were not yet ready. The main Spanish positions were out of effective range of the French heavy guns. Both the French *tirailleurs* and their columns broke formation in ascending the slopes of the San Marcial hill; the Spanish were strongly placed and well supported. General Freire followed Wellington's tactics in advancing to meet the enemy rather than remaining in his field works. The disordered French mass was halted when only half way up the hill. The Spaniards were in short columns; at a range of 100 yards they delivered a volley and charged. In individual combat, a Spaniard was at least the equal of a Frenchman; the fighting was bloody, but the enemy were rolled back downhill. This was at about 10 a.m.

The tide continued to fall in the Bidassoa; the fords closer to Irun were soon practical. Another French division was seen to cross; at noon Soult sent this forward over the same ground. It was met in the same way. The two divisions already repulsed were beaten completely, but the Spanish yielded a foothold on the western end of the San Marcial ridge, where this fresh division attacked. Freire sent a message asking for assistance from Wellington, who was on a hill further south observing the fight. Wellington declined to send it, pointing out to the Spanish A.D.C. that General Freire had been successful on his own, and that the French could not possibly hold 300 yards of crest without close supports, and to send unnecessary British reinforcements would detract from the honours which could be won by the Spaniards alone. Even as the C-in-C explained his point, the French were seen to retire.[1]

San Marcial was a Spanish victory in every sense of the word. No other forces were closely engaged. The French retreated so rapidly and in such disorder after their second repulse that they sank one of their own pontoon bridges just thrown across the Bidassoa. Their casualties were about 2,500, compared to 1,700 Spaniards.

Soult's second thrust, above the gorge of the Bidassoa at Vera, had also begun at dawn on the 31st. Wellington had guessed that Soult would try to repeat the strategic movement which had been successful in 1794, when French Republican armies had entered Spain. The strength of the French force at Vera was not known precisely, but Wellington had no intention of allowing it to envelop his left. He conceived an unusual way of accomplishing his purpose without too much fighting. On the 30th, he had instructed Dalhousie to demonstrate at dawn the following day against the French flank and rear from the direction of Maya.[2] He had placed the Light Division high up in the hills south of Vera to the east of any French force which might try to cross the Bidassoa south of the gorge and turn northwest. The firing at Maya was clearly audible; the French had noticed the Light Division.

Four French divisions under Clausel advanced cautiously at Vera. One division never even left the north bank of the Bidassoa; another, immediately after crossing, turned south to 'contain' the Light Division. The two divisions which actually sought action were engaged in a day long fire fight with a British brigade of the 7th Division under

[1] *Stanhope*, 22, reports a conversation with Wellington;
'I asked him about the Spanish troops. "Oh, poor devils, they never won a battle. I made them win one though at San Marcial. They were standing an attack, and sent to me pressingly for succour. Meanwhile the French finding my troops at hand on their side were beginning of their own accord to withdraw. This the officer who came to me did not see with his naked eye, but I could through my glass. Look, I told him. Why he said, they do seem to be retiring. Well, I said, if I send you the English troops you ask for, they will win the battle; but as the French are already in retreat you may as well win it for yourselves. So they accordingly did; and now I see that in their accounts this is represented as one of their greatest battles—as a feat that does them the highest honour." '

[2] Wellington's orders to Dalhousie were for light demonstrations, but the latter either instructed or permitted Le Cor with his Portuguese of the 7th Division to seize Zagaramurdi. This brigade and Madden's Portuguese of the 6th Division who had moved through Urdax, then attacked in earnest the French around Ainhoa, but were repulsed. In this series of actions, Wellington's orders were exceeded, but French reactions more than satisfied his calculations. D'Erlon who commanded in front of Maya, reported the threat to Soult, who then sent back Foy's Division of D'Erlon's Corps to Maya from the lower Bidassoa.

Inglis and the Portuguese Brigade of the 4th Division under Miller. Wellington had additional forces in readiness for a counterattack but none were needed. The threat to the French flank and rear was enough; Clausel, on Soult's orders, retired after dark under cover of drenching rain.

This storm caused the Bidassoa to rise; for several hours there was more than six feet of water over the fords used by the French during the morning. In a rather confused action, Captain Cadoux and 80 Rifles (the 95th) held the only bridge in the area for two hours against enormous odds and inflicted 200 casualties (Plate 52). The French divisional General Vandermaesen was killed leading his troops against this post. It is possible that if Cadoux had been supported, the French might have been cut off; however, his gallant action ended in his death and the rout of his small command. The French recrossed the Bidassoa. The casualties in the fighting at Vera appear to have been approximately 1,300 to 850 in favour of the Allies.

Regretfully, Wellington had to forego another good opportunity to enter France on the heels of a broken French force, for there was still no positive news from the north. He did not hear until the 3rd of September of the end of the armistice and of the Austrian declaration of war against Napoleon. Besides, the castle at San Sebastian, and Pamplona, were still holding out at that time.

The month of September was a period of comparative rest for the Allied army. Wellington, personally, never had more problems, the majority of which were in connexion with the Spanish. Even though nominal C-in-C of the Spanish army and receiving the wholehearted co-operation of Spanish commanders in the field, his troubles with their government were out of all reason.

The Liberals in the Cortes had a majority and were predominantly anti-British. Wellington found himself unable to promote, nor even retain with him, generals of ability. He was not informed of orders issued directly to subordinate Spanish commanders. The Spanish government, through inefficiency or worse, was not supplying food or munitions to its own forces. The British commissariat had to feed not only the British and Portuguese, but often the Spaniards also, with supplies transported hundreds of miles by sea. Pay was virtually unknown in the Spanish service; their staff departments were incompetent. Individual soldiers were brave and skilful fighters, particularly under such veteran leaders as Longa, Mina, and Morillo.

Wellington had a continuous struggle against petty inconveniences. Only four months earlier, the Spanish government was still in Andalusia, for the northern half of the country was held by the French, but already Spanish custom inspectors were delaying British supply ships entering Passages in order to determine whether powder barrels and flour sacks contained contraband. A hospital requisitioned for the use of Allied wounded was stripped of every internal convenience before being turned over to them. British wounded were allowed to starve in a ropewalk at Bilbao.

Conditions in Portugal, although not nearly so bad, were far from satisfactory. The shift of war from the Portuguese border had removed the threat of French occupation; the Regency now demanded a larger subsidy and more latitude in spending it. They wanted their own soldiers to be formed into a separate organization, rather than incorporated in essentially British formations. They also wanted their battle-seasoned veterans to be returned home to protect Portugal against a possible *Spanish* invasion. Beresford could handle most of these problems, and was sent back to Lisbon temporarily.

Operations on the east coast against Suchet had gone badly. Murray proved himself an extremely poor commander. Within a fortnight of Vitoria, the French here had pulled back across the Ebro, except for isolated garrisons.[1] Murray had undertaken the siege of Tarragona, aided by the Catalan army under Copons.[2] He then disobeyed Wellington's orders, raised the siege needlessly, and retreated aboard his transports, leaving Copons in a serious predicament. Murray was replaced by Sir William Bentinck and sent before a court-martial. Bentinck forced Suchet to abandon Tarragona, but was himself brought to a halt at Ordal, not far from Barcelona.

On the brighter side, Wellington received the full support of the Tory government after Vitoria. Even the Duke of York allowed him to form and keep provisional battalions.[3] The army was in fine spirit even if somewhat low in numbers. Its equipment was worn, but could

[1] News of Vitoria reached Suchet at Valencia in five days; he retired immediately, for Wellington could have marched down the Ebro valley and cut him off from France.

[2] The Catalan army, although capably led, was in reality a guerrilla organization; even after six years of experience, it was most effective when fighting in the mountains of Catalonia.

[3] This had long been a bone of contention; Wellington wished to retain veteran infantry, even after battalions were reduced by casualties and sickness to less than 400 men, by combining two into a single 'Provisional' battalion. The Duke of York and the 'Horse Guards' preferred them to be sent home, to be replaced eventually by new units. Much correspondence, *Dispatches, passim,* and elsewhere.

be replaced. Its staff departments had reached maturity and required a minimum of supervision from Wellington.

As September wore on, news from the north improved. Russia, Prussia, and Austria were now fighting Napoleon in earnest. Early reports of battles at Dresden, Kulm, and Katzbach indicated that Napoleon was in general being beaten. Now was the time to invade France. Wellington believed erroneously that Soult's army was no larger than his Anglo-Portuguese force of about 60,000, but was justifiably worried when contemplating the probable misbehaviour of the Spaniards he took across the border.[1] At one time Wellington considered entering Catalonia instead of invading France, but discarded the idea when Copons and William Clinton, another stand-in for Bentinck who had again returned to Sicily, had reached a stalemate with Suchet.

Pamplona had not yet fallen, but was now close to starvation. The Allied army might as well move forward, and anticipate its imminent surrender. Wellington had accurate information concerning the French dispositions between Roncesvalles and the sea, not only from his 'correspondents', but also by his own observation from the Spanish peaks with a good glass in clear weather. The French appeared to have been greatly influenced by the Allied thrust at Maya on 31st August and had a large part of their troops well inland. Wellington planned therefore to attack nearer the coast, in fact in almost exactly the two areas used by Soult on the 31st, the lower Bidassoa and Vera.

Wellington discovered that the Bidassoa was fordable at low tide far nearer the sea than was generally realized. These fords, used normally by shrimpers, were attempted at low tide at night and found to be no more than mid-thigh deep, in spite of the great breadth of the estuary here. Once the opposite shore was taken, the old pontoon train from the Tagus, which was with the army, could be thrown across. A particularly low tide coming about an hour after dawn was required, and this would occur on 7th October. There was plenty of time to make all necessary preparations.

[1] Wellington to Bathurst, 19th September, *Dispatches*, XI, 124,

'I acknowledge that I feel a great disinclination to enter the French territory under the existing circumstances. The superiority of numbers which I can take into France will consist in about 25,000 Spaniards, neither paid nor fed, and who must plunder, and will set the whole country against us.'

The Allied attack from Vera was to be made on a front of about three miles, towards the great spine of the Pyrenees. The French had been erecting field fortifications and installing guns here on both the main ridge and on spurs running down into Spain. Wellington believed that a sudden, vigorous thrust would succeed, and for such work, the Light Division was best; Longa's Spaniards would support their left flank, while Giron's divisions would be on their right. They would have as their objective the majestic Great Rhune, the bald summit of which dominates the whole border area.

Long before dawn on 7th October three brigades of the 5th Division were guided along the south bank of the Bidassoa estuary and concealed behind the counterscarp of the fortifications of Fuenterrabia and a bank to the south of it. The shrimpers were ready to lead them at daybreak across three separate fords. Meanwhile the 1st Division was waiting within striking distance of the fords which Soult had used more than a month before; Wilson's Portuguese Brigade (formerly Pack's) and Lord Aylmer's British Brigade were in support with Freire's Spanish divisions and Bradford's Portuguese on the right. At exactly 7.25 a.m., three batteries of artillery at Irun opened just as the morning fog was lifting; the Allied line waded towards the French shore.

The 5th Division had already forded the Bidassoa before pickets noticed them; the 1st Division was half way across the river before any shots were fired in their direction. The Spaniards incurred stiff opposition on their left, but their right encountered only pickets near the mouth of the gorge. The 5th Division stormed into the French village of Hendaye without serious fighting; the three brigades then took slightly divergent routes. That under Robinson advanced along the shore, taking a coastal battery of heavy guns and finally occupying some ruined fortifications half way between the Bidassoa and St Jean-de-Luz. The other two brigades pushed further inland and seized some new earthworks together with their garrisons near the Croix des Bouquets.

The 1st Division thrust back those forces opposite them with ease, but the French holding Behobie resisted for an hour. They retired also when the left flank of the 1st Division threatened to envelop their rear, and retreated to their fortified camp at Urrugne, about four miles away. Fighting ceased here at 11.30 a.m.; Wellington ordered that the pursuit should be carried no further.

Considering the numbers engaged, casualties were not great. The Allies lost 400 and the French 450. But the latter lost in addition all

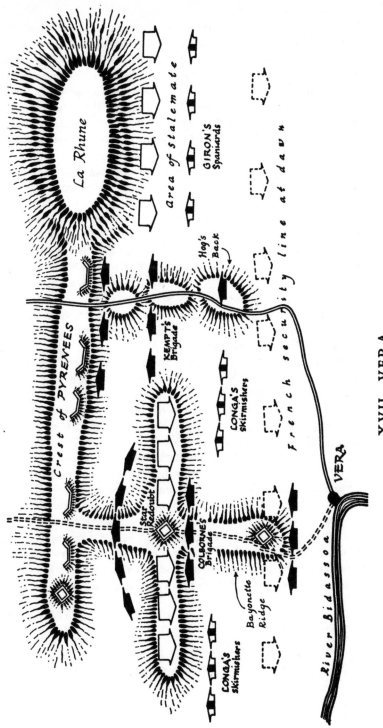

La Rhune

Crest of PYRENEES

area of stalemate

GIRON'S
Spaniards

Hog's
Back

KEMPT'S
Brigade

LONGA'S
Skirmishers

French security line at dawn

Star
Redoubt

COLBORNE'S
Brigade

LONGA'S
Skirmishers

Bayonette
Ridge

VERA

River Bidassoa

XVII. VERA

their artillery, huts, most of their baggage, and their self-confidence.

The fighting at Vera was more serious, although there were fewer engaged. Wellington had ordered a false attack by the 6th Division in the vicinity of Maya to ensure that French forces around Vera would remain unsupported. Soon after dawn the two brigades of the Light Division, Colborne's on the left and Kempt's on the right, advanced north about a mile and a half apart. Half of Longa's men were in skirmishing order to the west of Colborne's Brigade; the other half in the same formation connected Colborne with Kempt.

Both brigades of the Light Division moved forward along roughly parallel tracks over successively rising heights, crowned by French fieldworks. Colborne had to climb a long straight spur of the Pyrenees extending two miles south into Spain which was named the Bayonette, and pointed directly at Vera.[1] About half way along this spur a ridge intersects it at right angles; the French had an extensive closed work here named the Star redoubt. Colborne's Rifles and *Cacadores* cleared the French from other field works on the Bayonette south of the Star, but the entire brigade had to deploy to take the latter place. The 52nd, attacking in line, very quickly negotiated a ten foot ditch and an earth and stone parapet on the other side. The French lost a number of prisoners in their precipitate retreat.

The fighting at the Star had been bitter, but Colborne's men kept up the pressure and pushed back the French without giving them a chance to rally, until they reached the main crest. The fieldworks here were manned by fresh troops; the French were as numerous as their immediate opponents, protected by breastworks, and supported by artillery. But the audacity of Colborne's immediate attack and the success that the brigade had already achieved carried the main crest in several places; its defenders slid down the northern slopes into France.

Meanwhile Kempt's Brigade had similar success to the east. The road here was better, but was protected by a strong, bold hill known as the 'Hog's Back'. This was taken by the 3/95th. Kempt then moved north on a broader front. Behind his skirmish line, he had, from right to left, the rest of his two Rifle battalions, two battalions of the 43rd, and two battalions of the 17th Portuguese Line. After some preliminary skirmishing, Kempt's Brigade broke into a complete line of earthworks on

---

[1] The circuitous cart track from Vera along the Bayonette ridge can be followed easily on foot; it climbs the western side of the spur by stages. The direct ascent made by the Rifles under fire must have been particularly gruelling. Ruins of the defensive earthworks along the Bayonette are still recognizable.

the main crest. After a brief struggle they seized the position from end to end, and were uniting with Colborne on their left flank.

The advance of Kempt and Colborne had been so fast that Longa's battalions of skirmishers had been unable to keep up. They had been heavily engaged in the wooded valley between the two ridges along which the Light Division brigades had thrust. The French who opposed Longa were partially cut off on either flank by Kempt and Colborne; about 300 unwounded Frenchmen surrendered to Colborne personally. The French division which opposed Colborne and Kempt on this ridge was routed long before midday.

Giron, in addition to supporting Kempt on his eastern flank was also attacking the southern underfeatures of the Great Rhune, an extremely difficult task because of the climbing involved, although this area was not at first strongly held. Later in the morning French troops defending the mountain were reinforced. For hours the Spaniards were heavily engaged in rough country. The struggle went on well into the night, but the Great Rhune remained in French hands.

Wellington's offensive from Vera was successful; the Great Rhune fell next day after being outflanked. A shallow penetration had been made into France and the line of the Pyrenees was broken at surprisingly little cost. French casualties in the fighting at Vera and Maya were about 1,250; the Allies lost approximately 800.[1]

Wellington's success owed much to the element of strategic surprise. The sudden appearance of the 5th Division on the French flank and rear after crossing the secret fords at Fuenterrabia made a complete victory possible. This was gained quickly and at little cost. Wellington's forethought in providing a threat to the enemy at Maya helped Alten and Longa to defeat the single division at Vera isolated from the French masses further east.

The fighting on 7th October exhibited a new development in Wellington's offensive tactics. Above Vera, the French had made use of long lines of earthworks for the first time; these should have given them a great advantage, but the flexible Light Division probed for weak points in the enemy fortifications, swept round their flanks, and when necessary took a part of a line by direct assault. Once a penetration was made, the rest of the line soon fell. The French were pinned down by

[1] *Oman*, VII, 534–6, gives precise details of British, Portuguese, and French casualties; the Spaniards probably lost 450.

their own field fortifications; they were demoralized by watching other units overwhelmed piecemeal. Soult's static defences were tested for the first time and found wanting, but continued to be used. His system was diametrically opposed to Wellington's idea of a flexible defensive position. Wellington spent time and money in providing lateral communications, but nothing on field fortifications.[1]

Pamplona was at last approaching the limits of its powers of resistance. The city had been reported to be short of supplies in June; a complete blockade had been maintained since that time.[2] Starvation faced both the garrison and civilian population; there was little food inside the town during September and less in October. Dogs, cats, and rats brought high prices. On 25th October, the French governor commenced negotiations for capitulation with Carlos de España. The French threatened to blow up the fortifications, if they were not allowed to return to France. Wellington instructed de España to state categorically that the entire garrison would be punished severely should the Pamplona defences be damaged in any way; the French surrender must be unconditional. The Allies finally made some concessions in connexion with French non-combatants, but the garrison marched out, piled their arms, received their first full meal in weeks, and were on their way to Passages and prison camps in Britain before the end of the month.

TOPOGRAPHICAL OBSERVATIONS

The town of Fuenterrabia retains much of its old fortifications; the dike to the south which sheltered Allied troops before their crossing of the Bidassoa can still be made out. The shrimpers' fords are gone forever, for a deep channel has been dredged, and an airfield has been constructed in the estuary.

---

[1] *Schaumann*, 389–90, a remarkable observer of things of basic military importance, makes an interesting and pertinent comment in his diary concerning the keeping open of communications in the Allied sector of the Pyrenees; 'Higher up we came upon a number of peasants employed and paid by Lord Wellington's general staff, who were levelling some of the more dangerous portions of the road with bundles of wood and logs and making them practicable for artillery.'

[2] During the summer the garrison had been able to obtain food from gardens in the vicinity of the town walls.

XVIII

BATTLES NEAR BAYONNE

FIRST PHASE: THE BATTLE OF THE NIVELLE

THE surrender of Pamplona released not only the Spanish troops who were blockading the place, but Hill's veteran 'corps' covering them. With Spanish garrisons in Pamplona and San Sebastian, Wellington would not need to hold Roncesvalles or any other specific border position, and could use his entire field army offensively.

Soult still had a numerically formidable army recently reinforced by thousands of recruits and supported by National Guard units. His positions were naturally strong and had been heavily fortified; many field works contained artillery. An attack on the extreme right was considered and partially planned, but abandoned. Its success would have been uncertain; the Roncesvalles passes were often choked with snow during the winter.

There remained the area between the coast and Maya, a front of about sixteen miles as the crow flies. The French positions followed roughly the line of the Nivelle, but the river itself was not a serious military obstacle except at high tide near the coast. Wellington had time to gather information and make observations from the summit of the Great Rhune. On a clear day he could see with a telescope details of French fortifications between the sea and the Mondarrain mountain; these were seven and ten miles away respectively.

The first third of the French front, extending from the shore to the village of Ascain, was the most heavily fortified. It was defended by three full divisions, with a reserve equal in number to at least a fourth division. The rest of this position, reaching to the Mondarrain, although twice as long, was not so well fortified, and held by five divisions only. The anchor of this defence system was the Lesser Rhune, a lower peak only 700 yards from the Great Rhune, but separated from it by a ravine. If it could be taken, the two parallel lines of trenches and enclosed works below it and to the east could be assaulted with advantage at various points. But the French position on the naturally strong Lesser Rhune had been strengthened by earth and masonry works.

Wellington was examining these one day with senior officers of the Light Division. Colborne, a brigade commander, pointed out some of the difficulties of attacking the Lesser Rhune and the other enclosed redoubts situated on the surrounding hills (Plate 51).

'Ah, Colborne, with your local knowledge only, you are perfectly right,' observed Wellington; 'It appears difficult, but the enemy have not men to man the works and lines they occupy. They dare not concentrate a sufficient body to resist the attacks I shall make upon them. I can pour a greater force on certain points than they can concentrate to resist me.'

After the C-in-C had conversed for some time with Sir George Murray, his QMG, the latter took writing materials from his sabretache and began to formalize a plan of attack for the whole army. He then read this back, while Wellington directed his telescope to specific positions. When Murray had finished, Wellington relaxed.

'Murray, that will do nicely. We will soon be in possession of the fellows' lines. Shall we be ready tomorrow?'

'I fear not, my Lord, but the next day.' [1]

The general plan decided upon called for a false attack between the coast and Ascain to pin down some 23,000 French soldiers in that area with an equal quantity of Allies. Sir John Hope, who had taken the place of Graham, whose eyes had temporarily failed, was ordered to drive in outposts, demonstrate, and cannonade, but not to commit himself to serious fighting. Hope had the 5th and 1st Divisions, Aylmer's, Wilson's, and Bradford's Independent Brigades, and Freire's two weak Spanish divisions ranged in this order from the coast.

Meanwhile, Beresford and Hill were to launch their two specially constituted corps, totalling 55,000 men, between Ascain and the Mondarrain against about 40,000 Frenchmen.[2] Hill with his usual units, and the 6th Division under Clinton in addition, about 26,000 in all, were to attack on the right, east of the upper Nivelle.

Beresford was in theoretical command of Longa's Spanish Division, the Light Division, Giron's Spanish Divisions, and the 4th, 7th, and

[1] *Harry Smith*, I, 142–3, was present and describes this scene vividly.

[2] This dividing of the Allied army into corps for a particular task is typical of Wellington after 1812. It should be borne in mind that these assignments were temporary. The divisions remained autonomous units for administrative and logistical purposes.

3rd Divisions (from left to right), but Wellington remained throughout the action with Beresford. Wellington's force in the field numbered about 80,000; 63,000 French opposed them, but the numerical advantage to the Allies was caused by the inclusion of unproven Spanish units. Hope and Beresford each had two divisions of these.[1]

Wellington finally ordered this attack for 10th November.[2] The Light Division would take the Lesser Rhune, a task of great difficulty. The whole area is so rugged that even Wellington could move up only three small, or 'mountain', guns to support this thrust.[3]

The crest of the Lesser Rhune is long, narrow, and practically unassailable directly across the ravine separating the two mountains. But Wellington had detected a route by which the Light Division could descend into the ravine, work round to its head, and assault from the flank. In this manner, the positions along the ridge might be taken one after the other; there were three successive enclosed works. About half way along this ridge, a ditch and parapet at right angles to the line of the crest connected the Lesser Rhune with the next height towards the coast, known as the Mouiz, on which the French had built and garrisoned a powerful star redoubt.

Long before dawn on the 10th, experienced officers and NCO's, who had already practiced following their routes during previous nights, led the Light Division forward into the ravine and there ordered their men to lie down in formation until daylight.

'Day broke with great splendour, and as the first ray of light played on the summit of the lofty Atchubia the signal guns were fired in rapid succession. Then the British leaped up, and the French, beholding with astonishment their columns rushing forward from the flank of the great Rhune, ran to the defences with much tumult. They opened a few pieces which were answered from the top of the greater Rhune by the mountain artillery, and at the same moment two companies of the forty-third were detached to cross the marsh if possible and keep down the fire from the lower part of the hog's-back; the remainder of the regiment, partly in line partly in a column of reserve advanced

[1] Morillo's men and Longa's were veterans, but Freire's and Giron's could not be relied on.

[2] This attack was originally ordered ahead of time to take place the day after Pamplona fell, Harry Smith's account notwithstanding. However, Hill was delayed by snow when moving from the Roncesvalles area into a position from which he could advance.

[3] These were 3-pounder field guns, no longer regularly used by the Allied artillery.

against the high rocks. From these crags the French shot fast, but the quick even movement of the British line deceived their aim, and the soldiers, running forward very swiftly though the ground was rough, turned suddenly between the rocks and the marsh, and were immediately joined by the two companies which had passed that obstacle notwithstanding its depth.'

'Then all together jumped into the lower works; but the men, exhausted by their exertions, for they had passed over half a mile of very difficult ground with a wonderful speed, remained for a few minutes inactive within half pistol-shot of the first stone castle, from whence came a sharp and biting musketry. When they recovered breath they arose and with a stern shout commenced the assault. The French as numerous as their assailants had for six weeks been labouring on their well-contrived castles; but strong and valiant in arms must the soldiers have been who stood in that hour before the veterans of the forty-third. One French grenadier officer only dared to sustain the rush. Standing alone on the high wall of the first castle and flinging large stones with both his hands, a noble figure, he fought to the last and fell, while his men, shrinking on each side, sought safety among the rocks on his flanks.'

'Close and confused then was the action, man met man at every turn, but with a rattling musketry, sometimes struggling in the intricate narrow paths, sometimes climbing the loose stone walls, the British soldiers won their desperate way until they had carried the second castle, called by the French the place of arms and the magpie's nest, because of a lofty pillar of rock which rose about it and on which a few marksmen were perched. From these points the defenders were driven into their last castle, which being higher and larger than the others and covered by a natural ditch or cleft in the rocks, fifteen feet deep, was called the Donjon.' [1]

Further to the northwest, the 1/95th and 3/95th moved forward as a heavy line of skirmishers. Behind them the 1/52nd turned to the left and then attacked in line. The Rifles thrust the French from three ravelins in front of their main works. When the 1/52nd came up, supported by the 1st and 3rd *Cacadores* and the 17th Portuguese Line, both the Mouiz redoubt and the strong trench connecting it with the Lesser Rhune fortifications were taken by assault.

[1] *Napier*, V, 368-9, at his superb best. He personally commanded the 43rd in this action.

With the fall of the Mouiz redoubt and this trench, Napier and his gallant battalion stormed forward again. Scaling ladders were used to ascend the Donjon in many places, but certain 'light bobs' scrambled up wherever rock crevices gave any foothold. Once a section of the rampart was won, the men aided each other to mount the natural scarp. The garrison was driven out after a stubborn fight and retired into the valley of St Ignace to the northeast, leaving the Lesser Rhune in Allied hands before 8 a.m.

Once the Lesser Rhune was taken, the way was open for the advance of nine Allied divisions on a front of about five miles directly east of the Great Rhune (Plate 50). West of the Nivelle, Beresford's alignment was, from left to right, Giron's two Spanish divisions, and the 4th, 7th, and 3rd Anglo-Portuguese Divisions. East of the river, Hill continued the line with the 6th, Hamilton's Portuguese, the 2nd, and Morillo's Spanish Division. Morillo was ordered to threaten, but not to attack enemy works on the Mondarrain. Each division had precise orders as to the routes by which they were to move. Hill's units had started forward before dawn, but Beresford's struck first because they were nearer the enemy. The 4th Division seized the fortified village of Sare before 9 a.m.; the 7th, commanded by the Portuguese General LeCor, was equally far advanced, having taken by storm the Granada redoubt. The 3rd Division managed to get possession of the bridge of Amots by 11 a.m., cutting the only good lateral communication the French had between their left and right (Plate 54).

The 6th Division on Hill's extreme left soon caught up with the 3rd Division on the other side of the Nivelle; Hamilton's Portuguese took the village of Ainhoa before noon. The French were tied to their parallel lines of fortifications and had not sufficient reserves. A single point was attacked in overwhelming strength, and a breach made. French units to either side of the penetrations had either to retreat, or risk being cut off.

The Light Division, after its initial success early in the morning, waited for approximately two hours until other divisions on their right had occupied the redoubts of St Barbe and Granada and the village of Sare. Then Alten sent forward both his brigades through the St Ignace valley and up the far side, capturing two redoubts and a number of entrenchments on extremely strong ground. Beyond these there lay another valley and then a solitary hill crowned by a particularly well constructed closed work known as the Signals Redoubt. The Light Division surged over this area, isolating this redoubt which withstood two bloody assaults by the 1/52nd. Colborne then harangued the French commander under the protection of a flag of truce; he pointed out that the French were cut off and threatened to turn any survivors over to the Spaniards, if further fighting were necessary to take the fortification. The French battalion surrendered at once; they had little food or water, and realized the hopelessness of their situation.

By the middle of the afternoon, both Beresford and Hill had reached and taken their objectives. All day long Hope's corps had appeared to be on the point of delivering an attack between Ascain and the sea. There was enough fighting here to deter the French from weakening their position by sending reinforcements east. Lord Aylmer's Brigade entered and held the fortified village of Urrugne; Freire's Spaniards had almost reached the village of Ascain. The 23,000 Frenchmen opposing Hope suffered no serious loss and for the most part still lay in their original fortifications.

Wellington's original plan also took in the possibility of Beresford and Hill sweeping northwest from St Pee to the sea, isolating the French right. This thrust was not carried out for three reasons. There was not sufficient time left in the short November day, and Wellington never fought offensively in the field at night if he could help it.[1] Some units had been unaccountably slow in reaching their final objectives, even though the French had already retired.[2] A sweep north by Beresford and Hill would have left the French an opportunity for an unlikely but possibly effective counterstroke from Ascain against the pivot of the Allied line. This critical area was held by Freire's and Longa's three Spanish divisions. To risk a reverse in order to gain a more complete victory may have been a standard procedure for Napoleon, but was unthinkable for Wellington.[3]

The French beyond the Mondarrain were commanded by Foy, who had his headquarters at Bidarray. When he heard the sound of battle further west, he advanced toward Maya in Hill's rear.[4] At first, he was successful and captured some British baggage, but was brought to a

[1] This aversion to night attacks may have originated from a petty affair in India outside Seringapatam; Wellington personally led an attack which was at first unsuccessful.

[2] The 6th Division in particular: Beatson, Bidassoa and Nivelle, 176.

[3] Neither Fortescue nor Oman emphasizes this point, but Beatson, Bidassoa and Nivelle, 175, quotes Wellington as saying to Col. Bunbury at dinner, 'If I could have trusted the Spaniards for two hours—if they could have been brought only to hold their ground—I would have obliged the whole of Soult's right wing to lay down their arms.'

[4] Soon after dawn Foy received an order from his immediate superior D'Erlon, to march north and join the French centre, but Foy ignored this and moved southwest on his own responsibility.

stand by three Spanish battalions fighting in the area defended by Pringle on 25th July, the Gorospil peak and the territory between it and Maya village. Foy then retreated right back to Cambo.

The French lost during the day approximately 4,300 men and 59 pieces of artillery. The Allied casualties were about 2,700. These penetrations by Beresford and Hill caused the French opposing Hope to fall back hurriedly. Soult retired to the vicinity of Bayonne, west of the Nive, but held the line of that river to the southeast as well as a bridgehead on the west bank at Cambo.

SECOND PHASE: THE BATTLES OF THE NIVE

Bayonne was now uncovered, but was difficult to attack on account of the river system around it. The Adour flows west into the Atlantic; the Nive flows north into the Adour at Bayonne. The town straddles the Nive and had a strong subordinate fortification north of the Adour. The whole place was powerfully defended, had a numerous and skilful garrison, and was well supplied. It was at this time both a manufacturing and storage arsenal and had been for years the principal base on which French armies in Spain had depended. Supplies were brought into Bayonne from the north and east by river boats on the Adour.

Bayonne was politically important, and unusually loyal to Napoleon. He had conducted his none too savoury political manoeuvres which originally placed Joseph precariously on the Spanish throne from the Palace of Marrac just to the south of the town. The great road from Spain enters Bayonne from the southwest; an Allied advance along it would pass through a narrowing triangle between the Nive and the sea. Since the French held the right bank of the Nive, as well as the Cambo bridgehead, Soult could attack in the flank an Allied advance to the west of the river. Soult's effective military strength was growing, in spite of casualties, as he was driven closer to his base.

The Nive was the key to the strategic situation; this river is larger than the Nivelle, and its flow most unpredictable. It was fordable in certain places in normal weather, but would rise several feet in a few hours after heavy rains or melting snow in the Pyrenees.

Wellington pushed the French from their bridgehead on the left side of the Nive at Cambo on the 16th, but the Allied army made no further offensive moves for three weeks. Wellington was forced to slow up on account of conditions beyond his control. News from the north of Europe was not entirely satisfactory, but the local political situation had deteriorated also. The possibility of the overthrow of Napoleon's regime had caused several factions to spring up. Wellington was careful not to encourage the supporters of the Bourbons until the intentions of the Allied governments became clear. If Napoleon was to be shorn of international power but left on the French throne, French Royalists should not be encouraged to rise against him. On the other hand, if a Bourbon restoration was the Allied objective, a revolution in France against Napoleon would be of great value.

Longa's Spaniards, on the night after the battle of Nivelle, had entered the French village of Ascain in the wake of Soult's retreating forces, had plundered the place and committed atrocities. Wellington could understand the reasons which drove individual Spanish soldiers to these actions; they were hungry, and only behaving as the French had in Spain for six years. But from a military standpoint, such acts of revenge could lead only to disaster. In France, almost every man had been trained as a soldier; there were sufficient veteran officers to direct military operations, and plenty of weapons. If the civilian population should act toward the Allies as the Spaniards had towards the French, Wellington's offensive into southern France was sure to fail.[1] The Forces under Longa, Freire, and Giron were sent back across the Pyrenees immediately; only Morillo's better disciplined battalion remained with the army.

The behaviour of the Spanish government was even worse than that of the troops. Wellington resigned as Spanish C-in-C because of their bad faith. The Cortes indulged in all forms of anti-British conduct unworthy of an ally in time of war, and were utterly incapable of keeping any promise. The Spanish armies not under Wellington's control—he continued to exercise partial command until his resignation was accepted—were now more interested in politics than in fighting the French. Wellington knew of Napoleon's scheme of restoring Ferdinand to the Spanish throne in return for what would amount to

---

[1] Wellington in his long letter to Bathurst, 21st November 1813, from St Jean-de-Luz discusses both the political problem with regard to the future French government, and the state of the Spanish army: *Dispatches*, XI, 306–7,

'I must tell your Lordship, however, that our success, and everything, depends upon our moderation and justice, and upon the good conduct and discipline of our troops. I despair of the Spaniards. They are in so miserable a state, that it is really hardly fair to expect that they will refrain from plundering a beautiful country, into which they enter as conquerors; particularly adverting to the miseries which their own country has suffered from its invaders. Without any pay and food, they must plunder, and if they plunder, they will ruin us all.'

military alliance against Britain, but heard nothing of it from the Spaniards themselves.[1]

Wellington had with him in France at this time, exclusive of cavalry, 36,000 British, 23,000 Portuguese, and Morillo's 4,000 Spanish troops, a total of 63,000 men. Soult had a few hundred more, also exclusive of cavalry, National Guards, conscripts not yet assigned to units, and the sedentary garrison of Bayonne. Wellington had the common sense and moral courage to sacrifice a numerical superiority of 40,000 Spanish soldiers, even though he realized that if Suchet and Soult should unite they would have a total force between them of considerably over 100,000 French infantry. But he discounted such a combination because of the time it would take, and the fact that, if Suchet moved north, southeastern France would be open to Spanish invasion.

Heavy rains fell late in November, but offensive operations were again possible in December. Wellington chose to advance on both sides of the Nive, although his army was divided by this unpredictable river. But he had first to cross it. Soult was defending the line of the Nive between Cambo and Bayonne with three divisions of infantry as well as cavalry and artillery. On their southern flank, below Cambo, there was a powerful mixed force, equal to another division at least, commanded by General Paris.

A beacon was fired before dawn on 9th December; it was the signal for an Allied crossing of the Nive. Hill's 'corps' of three nationalities plus cavalry and artillery waded across the river at three fords in the vicinity of Cambo. Morillo's division, a regiment of cavalry, and a battery then moved southeast against General Paris, forming a flank guard. Hill's remaining divisions, the Allied 2nd and the Portuguese division previously under Howard, but now commanded by Le Cor, turned north and advanced towards the Adour.

Beresford had also crossed the Nive further north, with the 3rd and 6th Divisions, over pontoon bridges laid during the night.[2] The whole advance across the river was on a front of about five miles; four Allied

---

[1] This almost unbelievable burlesque of hypocritical diplomacy, known as the Treaty of Valençay, is a study in itself. However, the Spaniards eventually behaved well in this connexion. Ferdinand promised much to Napoleon until he was safe in his own country, and then repudiated everything. There was a period, however, when Wellington considered the possibility of sudden hostility from the Spanish army.

[2] Engineers had already passed a bridge from the left bank to an island in the centre; from this the far bank could be reached by fording, but other bridges were also laid.

divisions were opposed by three French. Soult offered little serious resistance, and retreated toward Bayonne.

In accordance with his usual procedure of using his entire force in a single consolidated offensive, Wellington sent Hope north in the area between the Nive and the sea. Hope's command consisted for this thrust of the 1st, 5th, and Light Divisions, and Wilson's, Bradford's, and Aylmer's Independent Brigades. The whole operation was more of a reconnaissance in force than an attack, for Wellington realized that the French held nothing in strength on this side of the river further south than their fortified camps around Bayonne. However, Soult would not be able to risk withdrawing troops from the left bank to fight on the right.

Wellington required a complete survey of the ground immediately south of the Adour between Bayonne and the sea. He was considering an idea for bridging the river there with vessels far larger and stronger than pontoons. He would have to provide booms and land batteries to protect it against French waterborne attacks.

Hope fully accomplished his reconnaissance and did some skirmishing. After spending several hours just out of range of the Bayonne artillery, he retired, leaving a line of outposts. The Independent Portuguese Brigades on the left and the Light Division on the right remained to support this picket line. The 5th Division was in immediate reserve, but Hope pulled back the 1st Division and Aylmer's Brigade to St Jean-de-Luz. These latter troops marched over 25 miles during the day.

Soon after 9 a.m. on the 10th, Soult attacked Hope's line of pickets. The French were using the two roads leading south from Bayonne. One of these passes directly south to Ustaritz and is never far from the Nive. The other, the great road, crosses the peninsula diagonally and then hugs the coast as far as St Jean-de-Luz. Because of the wooded, marshy, and water-logged condition of the country, the day's fighting took place on or near these roads.

The Light Division appears to have been engaged first and was pressed back along the Ustaritz road by four full French divisions. After a retreat of two miles, the division came to rest in a strong position between the Chateau and Church of Arcangues (Plate 53). There was a hill 1,200 yards long here, protected at each end by marshy ravines. The forward slope was open, but hedges and stone walls protected the summit; both the chateau and church were hastily converted into forts.[1] A further advantage of the position was that the French

[1] Both buildings are now in good repair, but still show their battle scars.

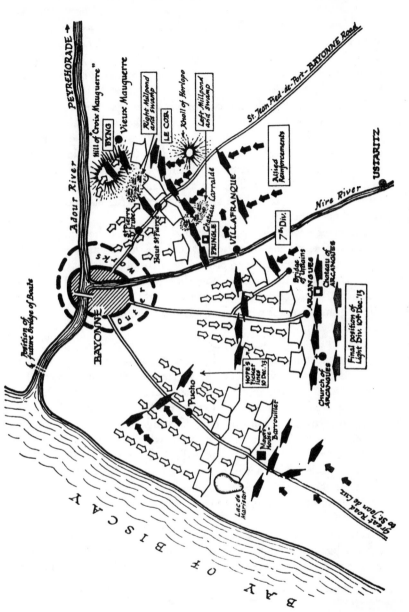

XVIII. NIVE AND ST PIERRE

were unable to see the reverse slope of the ridge. Under such circumstances, they would be unlikely to attack with vigour.

There was a great deal of skirmishing at Arcangues, but no concentrated French attack. An unusual duel developed between their artillery and the muskets of the 1/43rd at a distance of 400 yards, far beyond the normal range of the Brown Bess. The 1/43rd had taken up a position in and around the church, a strong building constructed in the Basque fashion with two balconies above the nave. Windows lit all three levels. The wall surrounding the churchyard was lower than the nave, giving the 43rd four protected firing levels. Due to the conformation of the land in front, the French artillery, if it wished to fire on the church at all, had to expose itself on a crest 400 yards to the north. No infantryman could hope to hit a single opponent at such a range, but a target as large as a battery of artillery was a different matter. The 43rd, firing four-tiered volleys, caused the French gunners to fire inaccurately, and later abandon their pieces.

The French force that was stopped at Arcangues also endeavoured to advance nearer the Nive, but ran into the 7th Division, posted by Wellington the day before to protect the pivot of his line at the bridge of Urdains. The Allies suffered only slightly in bringing the French to a stand.[1] Reinforcements sent from the right bank of the Nive by Wellington were not engaged at all; the fighting here was over by early afternoon.

Meanwhile, the French advance down the great road drove back the Allied picket line three miles between 9 and 10 a.m. The French attacked the two Independent Portuguese brigades posted where the great road passes between a freshwater lake and a rounded hill; a dwelling and outbuildings belonging to the Mayor of the small nearby village of Biarritz were situated here. This large farmhouse, also known as the Chateau Barrouillet, was occupied the previous night by A. Campbell's Portuguese. Bradford's Brigade was at first a few hundred yards further north, but was soon forced back on Campbell. Together they held a line on either side of the great road using the hastily loop-holed buildings, hedges, and a sunken crossroad, to reinforce their position.

Later in the morning, a full division of French infantry attacked in earnest, but was brought to a stand by the well-disciplined fire of the Portuguese. A second French division attacked in echelon half a mile to

[1] A tributary of the Nive was spanned by this bridge, but the stream was hardly a military obstacle. A middle-aged sportsman can clear it.

the east and made some headway, for it was partly beyond the Portuguese flank. By this time the 5th Division was coming up; it turned to the right and countered this French thrust. Sir John Hope also reached the field. The fighting continued to go badly for the Allies, for there was no real strength in their position and the French had a numerical superiority of at least three to two.

A third French division endeavoured to turn the Allied right, and the mayor's house was about to fall. At the last moment, Aylmer's Brigade, hurrying from St Jean-de-Luz, formed line without halting, and moved to the east against this latest thrust. The fighting was confused, for it took place largely in woods, but the French were finally pushed back.

The fighting on the 10th, actually two separate actions, is generally called the Battle of the Nive. The eastern attack delivered by the French against the Light Division was never close to achieving a breakthrough, nor was it pressed after midday. The fighting in the vicinity of Barrouillet, however, might easily have developed into a serious defeat for the Allies. If this had happened, Hope's poor dispositions and the fact that he ordered the return of almost half his corps to St Jean-de-Luz for the night would have been responsible.

Allied casualties at Arcangues were 225. The French lost over 400. Those lost around Barrouillet were about even, between 1,500 and 1,600 on each side. Soult suffered a more serious loss on the evening of the 10th when three whole German battalions in the French service deserted, with their officers, colours, and baggage.[1]

Wellington saw nothing of the fighting to the west of the Nive on the 10th, but reached Barrouillet by 10 a.m. the next morning. After a personal reconnaissance, he ordered that the French pickets should be pushed back. They retired to Pucho, a hamlet some two miles up the road towards Bayonne, offering only token resistance. When the field seemed quiet, Wellington left the district. Early in the afternoon the French counterattacked and recovered most of the area they lost in the late morning. The fighting which took place on the 11th was in moderate strength only; neither side brought anything like their maximum available force into action. The French attacked in earnest the next day. For a few minutes they held at least a part of the mayor's

[1] After Napoleon had lost Germany, Col. Krause of the 2nd Nassau Regiment received secret orders from his Duke to escape from the French when possible. Krause arranged this in detail with a close friend in the K.G.L. A fourth German battalion missed their opportunity and was disarmed by Soult, who until then had confidence in the loyalty of such troops.

house, but were driven out. Again the fighting was indecisive, but there were about 800 casualties on each side.

Wellington was with Hill on the 12th, east of the Nive; when he heard firing to the west, he sent the 3rd, 4th, and 6th Divisions towards the sound of the guns. A hurried reconnaissance disclosed the fact that there was only a screen of French pickets between Hill and the outworks of Bayonne. Hill's 'corps', less Morillo who was still facing Paris's force much further south, was ordered to move forward and take up a position extending in a semicircle from the Nive to the Adour at a distance of a little over two miles from the Bayonne defences. Wellington realized that Soult could now take advantage of his central position, and the Bayonne bridges, to attack on either side of the Nive with a superior force while holding the Allies at bay on the other, as indeed he had done when fighting Hope on the 10th and 12th. But Wellington was not greatly worried, for he also could move his divisions backward and forward across the Nive.

THIRD PHASE: ST PIERRE

Wellington warned Hill that he should be prepared for a concentration of a high proportion of the French army to attack him. Under normal circumstances, there was little danger of serious consequences unless the French could win a complete victory in less than four hours, the time required for reinforcements to cross the Nive at Ustaritz and reach Hill in his naturally strong position. To reduce this time factor, Wellington ordered a pontoon bridge to be thrown across the Nive near Villafranque, much closer to Hill than Ustaritz. The new bridge was in use by the afternoon of the 11th; the 3rd Division was encamped nearby to defend it, and was also ready to cross by it. Some artillery were placed by the Nive to beat off any possible attack on the pontoons by shallow draught gunboats. The 6th Division was in a very similar position about Ustaritz. Beresford's other two divisions, the 4th and 7th, were west of the Nive, for Soult had at least six of his divisions on this side until early evening.

On the night of the 12th, Hill's 'corps' could hear Soult transferring men and guns across the bridges at Bayonne. The rumbling of wheels was clearly audible in the Allied camp, only three and a half miles from the town centre. The night was clear and the moon bright; some diarists claim to have seen French troops crossing the southernmost bridge which lay outside the walls. The movement was so obvious that it could be a feint. No action was taken other than to prepare every man in Hill's, Beresford's and Hope's commands for battle long before daylight.

Late in the afternoon of the 12th, the Nive rose swiftly, although there was little rain locally, and the pontoon bridge at Villafranque was broken during the night. The recently repaired permanent bridge at Ustaritz was in danger, but held; it could be used if necessary.

Hill's position extended from the Adour to the Nive; it ran across low hills and behind two long, narrow millponds. The latter lay approximately at right angles to the front and divided it into three equal parts. The Bayonne-St Jean Pied-de-Port road ran through Hill's centre, the most open sector, after passing through the village of St Pierre, which was destined to give its name to the battle about to be fought.[1] This main road, which was in good condition, climbs a long, somewhat irregular hill between the two millpond swamps. After passing beside the knoll of Horlopo, it descends to the south.

On Hill's right, between the eastern millpond and the Adour, there was open high ground on which stood the 'Croix de Mouguerre'; the village of Vieux Mouguerre lay behind this hill.[2] A secondary road from Bayonne ascends to the 'croix' and then leads down into the village.

On Hill's left, between that western millpond and the Nive, the area open to a French attack was limited by sodden low ground and thick woods. A secondary road from Bayonne to Villafranque climbs a defensible hill on which there was a strong stone building, Chateau Larralde.[3]

Hill's whole front from the Nive to the Adour measured about three miles; he could be attacked to advantage only on three limited sectors of no more than 400, 900, and 500 yards wide respectively, from left to right. He had 14,000 men and twelve guns with which to defend these corridors. Pringle's British Brigade of the 2nd Division protected the left, in front of the Chateau Larralde, which they also occupied. In accordance with Wellington's orders, Byng's British Brigade of the

[1] The hamlet of Marichorry in the middle of Hill's centre was then known as Haut-St-Pierre; the modern St Pierre or St Pierre d'Irube is situated much closer to Bayonne.

[2] At the time of Oman's visits to the St Pierre area, *circa* 1926, the two mills were still in use, but neither is now in operation and the dams controlling the millponds have been cut. The original extent of the ponds and swamps is still fairly clear. Oman praises the view from the high, bare hill of Croix de Mouguerre; I concur heartily, even though the monument erected there by Soult's worshippers is disconcerting.

[3] Externally, this large and gracious dwelling appears to be virtually unchanged.

same division was placed in part at the very front of the Croix de Mouguerre hill close to the Adour; the rest lay further to the rear in front of Vieux Mouguerre. The remainder of the 2nd Division, Barnes's British Brigade and Ashworth's Portuguese, together with Hill's artillery, occupied the central sector in depth. Le Cor's Portuguese Division was in reserve behind the centre at the knoll of Horlopo.

At about 8 a.m., dense masses of French infantry and artillery could be seen advancing against all three sectors. The leading division marching along the main road in the centre made a particularly fine show.[1] The brigades were full and appeared to be composed of veterans. Calmly Hill counted other brigades and divisions before sending a dispatch to Wellington. One full division had turned toward Pringle's sector; a brigade was heading for Byng. Two and a half divisions were already beyond the Bayonne works supporting the French centre and left. Other troops could be seen still crossing the outermost Nive bridge. Hill knew of the loss of the Villafranque bridge and realized he would have to face odds of three to one, or greater, for at least four hours.

The French advance against his left was undertaken by a full division of 5,000 infantry against Pringle's Brigade of 1,800, but made practically no headway at all. In four hours of fighting, they accomplished little apart from driving in the British skirmishers. The Chateau Larralde was attacked once but was never in danger. The heavily wooded countryside broke up their columns; their reinforced skirmish lines were severely mauled by the British infantry who took full advantage of their superior fire discipline. Pringle's casualties were 130; the French lost about 450.

The fighting on the right did not go so well. The original dispositions were probably faulty; Byng had placed the Buffs (1/3rd) at the northern end of the Croix de Mouguerre hill with no support within 800 yards.[2] Their commander, Colonel Bunbury, panicked when attacked by the *tirailleurs* of a full French brigade and ordered the Buffs to retire faster than was necessary.[3] The enemy columns were hardly engaged. Even if Bunbury had stood his ground, it is unlikely that he could have remained long where he was; the odds against him were great.

Byng's entire brigade was soon engaged with not only the brigade

[1] Abbe's Division of over 6,000 men, which had suffered least of all Soult's forces in recent battles.

[2] *Oman*, VII, 265, points out that the other two battalions were placed further back, so that they could more easily reinforce the centre.

[3] The entire French brigade lost no more than 160 men during the day. Fortescue is harder on Col. Bunbury than Oman, condemning him as a coward.

that had pushed back Bunbury, but also with advance units of Foy's Division in an action that lacked both resolution on the part of the French, and deft tactical control from Byng. During the course of three hours, three British battalions were forced down from their hill and from around the marsh at the head of the eastern millpond.

Meanwhile, the main French attack occurred in the centre. Their first assault by a division and a half led to bloody fighting. The Allied skirmish line was heavy, consisting of three British light companies from Barnes's Brigade, four Portuguese light companies from Ashworth's line battalions, a company of the 5/60th, and the entire 6th *Cacadores*, but they were met by an even more numerous line of *tirailleurs*. Artillery in considerable quantities was brought into action early in this centre sector by both sides; Hill's two batteries made the French advance along the main road a costly undertaking; the whole front was open, although the hill was fairly steep.

The *tirailleurs*, closely followed by the heads of two columns, came on with courage and efficiency, although their formation was thrown into disorder by low walls, hedges, and cottages. Stewart was in local command; Ashworth's four line battalions waited behind his skirmish line. The Allied light troops were driven back slowly and to some extent intermingled with Ashworth line battalions; together they brought the French columns to a halt and then sent them reeling downhill again. But the pressure continued, and the French made headway in some places. Stewart resorted to the procedure he and Pringle had followed at Maya of feeding his front line piecemeal from Barnes's Brigade in his second line; several local counterattacks by fresh companies were successful. For three hours the French were held well below the crest.

During this long struggle, the 1/71st suffered a humiliation. Colonel Cadogan, the hero of a dozen actions, had gone home recently, and been replaced by a Colonel Peacock, not a Peninsular veteran. Stewart sent the 1/71st forward to the west of the road, but Peacock found his courage not equal to the situation and ordered his command to retire. He then made his way to the rear where Hill found him beating forward Portuguese ammunition bearers.[1] Stewart personally reformed the 1/71st and led it forward again.

The Allied centre was gradually being pushed back. Stewart committed his last reserve, seven companies of the 1/92nd. The French were nearing the crest of the hill and were now so close to the Allied artillery

[1] Hill is said to have sworn for the second time during the war here.

335

that gunners were being hit by sharpshooters. Byng's line on the right was in a similar condition and was withdrawn to a position adjoining Stewart's, above the right millpond. Hill now took personal charge of the battle in the centre and brought forward Le Cor's fresh Portuguese division. He also ordered Byng to leave the Buffs to hold back the French on the right and to bring over the 1st Provisional Battalion and the 1/57th to join Le Cor's counterattack in the centre.

The seizing of the initiative by a single strong force across the centre at the critical moment improved Allied morale and correspondingly deflated the French. As at Maya, the surviving Gordons charged behind their colonel, hereditary chieftain of the clan, and a single piper skirling 'Cogag na shee'. The guns were saved, and the French were thrown back after a few volleys at close range.

Hill's counterattack was delivered with every spare man he had. A commander as capable and reliable as Hill would not have risked the consequences of the failure in such a situation had he not known that his ordeal was nearly over. Word had reached him that the pontoon bridge at Villafranque was again in operation and the 3rd Division was coming across. The 6th Division from Ustaritz had been seen approaching and was now only half a mile from the Horlopo knoll. Wellington himself arrived on the field at the Allied artillery position on the crest of the Haut-St Pierre hill, but refused to take command and told Hill to finish his battle himself.

Hill did this easily, using only some artillery and a single *Caçadore* battalion in addition to his own troops. Pringle pursued the French on the left to within 800 yards of the Bayonne defences. The enemy in the centre were similarly pushed back, but on the right serious fighting continued. Hill brought back what remained of Byng's Brigade, reinforced it with one of Le Cor's, and attacked around Vieux Mouguerre. At first the enemy gave ground slowly and continued to thrust columns forward against the Allied lines. But Allied artillery fire, and the sight of the French retreat in the centre, caused the troops here to lose heart. Soult's left wing, with surprisingly little further resistance, was driven back to the hill of Croix de Mouguerre where Foy held strong positions with a division and a half of infantry. But this force was also thrust back in long-range fighting.

Soult had attacked with a potential three to one advantage, fought for four hours, and finally found himself where he began. He lost 3,300 men; the Allies suffered only 1,775 casualties. Hill had won the battle almost unaided; but the arrival, or impending arrival, of the 6th, 3rd,

4th, and 7th Divisions, and Wellington's own presence, cannot have failed to have had an influence on both sides.

The four days of fighting since the crossing of the Nive on the 9th had accomplished the close investment of Bayonne south of the Adour. The river was wide, however, and continued to be used by river boats from inland and coasting vessels from the sea, at least at night. Wellington had planned to bridge the river west of Bayonne, and Sturgeon of the Engineers had designed a structure based on his observations of the 9th. Because of the heavy tides and strong currents in the lower Adour, larger pontoons than normal, ships' cables, and special tightening devices would have to be used. Coasting vessels would be secured in the usual manner with anchors at each end, but with five large cables held rigidly in place on each vessel running across them to capstans on either shore. A gangway across these would be constructed by lashing three-inch oak planks to the outer cables.[1] Batteries, armed vessels, and booms were to protect the bridge from attack. Inland from Bayonne, the Adour would become impractical for French river-boats as soon as any stretch of the southern bank was in Allied hands and held by field artillery.

Wellington could not hope to throw a bridge across the Adour while Soult's entire army remained concentrated around Bayonne. The Allies therefore began a series of manoeuvres to the east, but still south of the Adour, which gave Soult the alternative of moving east to counter them or risk having his field army cut off in Bayonne.

By this time Wellington understood Soult's logistical problems per-haps as well as the French marshal did himself. Although the strong fortifications at Bayonne enclosed much ground on both sides of the Nive and Adour, food for 60,000 men in their field army in addition to the garrison and civilian population could not possibly be brought into the town once any considerable portion of the Adour's south bank was lost to them. If Soult remained there even a week with his whole command, he would reduce by almost two months the length of time the garrison might hold out. The Allied C-in-C moved artillery east along the south bank of the Adour, which stopped all river traffic by day. He was not surprised to hear on 14th December that Soult was

---

[1] Conflicting accounts exist as to how this was constructed; Sir Howard Douglas, *On Military Bridges*, 108–11 and Plate 3, describes this carefully as an engineer, and was personally present.

móving his divisions further inland. On the 20th, Soult's personal headquarters was reported to be at Peyrehorade, still on the Adour, but twenty miles east of Bayonne.

Wellington's strategy on the Nivelle and the Nive combined power with surprise; simple movements were well executed. There was little new tactically. There remains a baffling question in regard to command. Why was Wellington not personally with Hope during the serious fighting west of the Nive on the 10th, 11th, and 12th, except for part of a single day? Why was he not with Hill on the 13th?

There appears to be no definite answer. Wellington realized the importance of his presence.[1] Could his absence from both battles have been in part intentional? Wellington was always thinking ahead; he realized better than any of his critics, contemporary or later, that his subordinates lacked experience of independent command. Soon, he would be forced to appoint someone to such a position. Because of rigid seniority rules in the British army, it could only be Hope, Beresford, or Hill. Beresford had been given his chance at Albuera. At the Nive and St Pierre, Wellington tried out the other two as independent commanders without taking too serious a risk.

THE CONTENDING FORCES, THE NIVELLE

ALLIED ARMY UNDER WELLINGTON		TOTAL = 88,816[2]
63,143 British and Portuguese	25,673 Spanish	

INFANTRY

1st Division, Kenneth Alexander Howard		= 6,898
Maitland's Brigade	1,680	
1/1st Guards, 3/1st Guards		
Stopford's Brigade	2,042	
1/Coldstreamers, 1/3rd Guards		
Hinuber's Brigade	3,176	
1st, 2nd and 5th Line, 1st and 2nd Light Batts., K.G.L.		

---

[1] *Beatson, Bidassoa and Nivelle*, 174, quotes Wellington as saying,

'When I come myself the soldiers think that what they have to do is the most important since I am there, and that all depends on their exertions. Of course these are increased in proportion, and they will do for me what, perhaps, no one else can make them do.'

[2] These figures are based on *Oman*, VII, 537–40.

2nd Division, William Stewart   = 8,480
   Walker's or Barnes's Brigade   1,646
     1/50th, 1/71st, 1/92nd
   Byng's Brigade   2,184
     1/3rd, 1/57th, 1st Prov. Batt.[1]
   Pringle's Brigade   1,937
     1/28th, 2/34th, 1/39th
   Ashworth's Brigade   2,713
     6th Line (2 Batts.), 18th Line (2
     Batts.), 6th Cacadores

3rd Division, Charles Colville   = 7,334
   Brisbane's Brigade   2,684
     1/45th, 74th, 1/88th, 5/60th
   Keane's Brigade   2,347
     1/5th, 2/83rd, 2/87th, 94th
   Powers's Brigade   2,303
     9th Line (2 Batts.), 21st Line (2
     Batts.), 11th Cacadores

4th Division, Lowry Cole   = 6,585
   W. Anson's Brigade   2,367
     3/27th, 1/40th, 1/48th, 2nd Prov.
     Batt.[1]
   Ross's Brigade   1,799
     1/7th, 20th, 1/23rd
   Vasconcellos's Brigade   2,419
     11th Line (2 Batts.), 23rd Line (2
     Batts.), 7th Cacadores

5th Division, James Hay   = 4,553
   Greville's Brigade   1,456
     3/1st, 1/9th, 1/38th
   Robinson's Brigade   1,332
     1/4th, 2/47th, 2/59th
   De Regoa's Brigade   1,765
     3rd Line (2 Batts.), 15th Line (2
     Batts.), 8th Cacadores

[1] The British Provisional Battalions were as detailed below:
   1st composed of 2/31st and 2/66th
   2nd composed of 2nd and 2/57th
   3rd composed of 2/24th and 2/58th

6th Division, Henry Clinton		= 6,729
Pack's Brigade	2,767	
1/42nd, 1/79th, 1/91st		
Lambert's Brigade	1,895	
1/32nd, 1/39th, 1/61st		
Douglas's Brigade	2,067	
8th Line (2 Batts.), 12th Line (2 Batts.), 9th Cacadores		
7th Division, Carlos Le Cor		= 6,068
Barnes's Brigade	1,915	
1/6th, 3rd Prov. Batt.,[1] Brunswick Oels		
Inglis's Brigade	1,827	
51st, 68th, 1/82nd, Chasseurs Britanniques		
Doyle's Brigade	2,326	
7th Line (2 Batts.), 19th Line (2 Batts.), 2nd Cacadores		
Light Division, C. Alten		= 4,970
Kempt's Brigade		
1/43rd, 1/95th, 3/95th, 17th Line		
Colborne's Brigade		
1/52nd, 2/95th, 1st and 3rd Cacadores		
Hamilton's Portuguese Division		= 4,949
Da Costa's Brigade	2,558	
4th Line (2 Batts.), 10th Line (2 Batts.), 10th Cacadores		
Buchan's Brigade	2,391	
2nd Line (2 Batts.), 14th Line (2 Batts.)		
Independent Brigades		= 5,729
Aylmer's British Brigade	1,930	
76th, 2/84th, 85th		
Wilson's Portuguese Brigade	2,185	
1st Line (2 Batts.), 16th Line (2 Batts.), 4th Cacadores		
Bradford's Portuguese Brigade	1,614	
13th Line (2 Batts.), 24th Line (2 Batts.), 5th Cacadores		

[1] See previous note.

ARTILLERY		=	848
Five British Batteries			
Three Portuguese Batteries			

SPANISH UNITS EMPLOYED BY WELLINGTON		= 25,673
Freire's two Divisions	10,284	
Giron's two Divisions	7,653	
Longa's Division	2,607	
Morillo's Division	5,129	

FRENCH ARMY UNDER SOULT		TOTAL = 86,264[1]
Infantry; ten divisions	57,243	
Artillery, etc., 97 guns	4,200	
	_____	
FIELD FORCE	61,443	
Cavalry	6,788	
Garrison of Bayonne	8,033	
Forces to Southeast under Paris and others	10,000	
	_____	
OTHER FORCES	24,821	

TOPOGRAPHICAL OBSERVATIONS

The fighting areas around the Nive and Nivelle are clearly defined. Soult's fortifications can be discerned easily from any higher mountain. The summit of the Rhune can be reached by cogwheel railway. The church at Arcangues, and many of the other structures in this area which served as fortifications are in perfect condition today; the old defences of Bayonne have changed little.

---

[1] These figures are based on *Oman*, VII, 537–40.

XIX
ORTHEZ AND TOULOUSE

FIRST PHASE: THE ISOLATION OF BAYONNE
AND THE BATTLE OF ORTHEZ

THERE was no serious fighting during the first six weeks of 1814. Soult remained at Peyrehorade with half his force north of the Adour and the other half deployed east of the Joyeuse, a river running parallel to the Nive, but eight miles inland. Wellington had divided the Allied army into a siege force under Hope around Bayonne and a field force commanded by Hill, Beresford, and himself.

Hope had the 1st and 5th Divisions, the Independent Brigades of Aylmer, Bradford, and Wilson, and a British light cavalry brigade, a total of 18,000. In addition he also controlled Spanish units totalling 16,000 men, all fed and supplied with military essentials by the British government. The Allied field force numbered about 48,000 including Morillo's units, the only Spanish troops in France apart from those under Hope's command.

Early in February Soult commanded 62,500 men including the Bayonne and St Jean Pied-de-Port garrisons. Napoleon had taken 14,000 men from him as recently as 20th January for use on the Rhine.[1] Wellington was informed of this withdrawal, but realized that Soult could have a field army as numerous as his own if he had left only 10,000 in Bayonne, presumably an ample garrison.

During January Wellington was reassured as to the intentions of his Spanish allies. Even if Ferdinand wished to keep promises made to his captors, it was unlikely that he would be allowed to do so. The Spanish

---

[1] Napoleon told Soult that he, Soult, would not need these three divisions because Ferdinand had promised to cause Spain to change sides. Napoleon never kept any inconvenient promise himself; he can hardly have hoped that Ferdinand would do so when he had the valid excuse of duress.

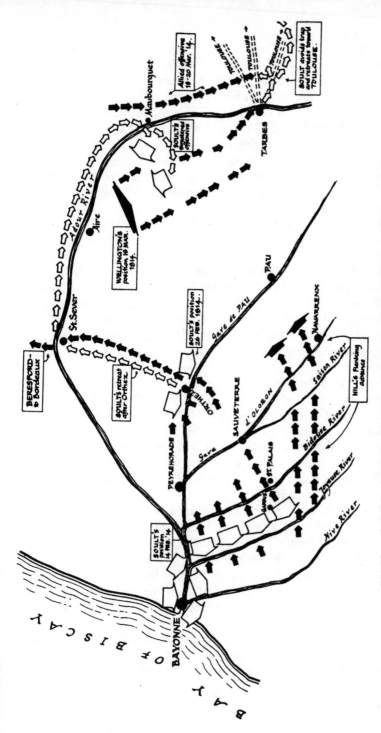

XIX. OPERATIONS IN SOUTHWESTERN FRANCE

Cortes was neither reliable nor efficient, but their hatred for the French was real. Even the anti-British faction was far more anti-French.

The weather cleared up early in February. Wellington could now attempt to lay the bridge of boats over the Adour between Bayonne and the sea. But Soult had to be manoeuvred further east. The Allied offensive began on 14th February with their field army moving east from the valley of the Nive across the plateau stretching from the Pyrenees to the Adour-Gave de Pau. This area is roughly a parallelo-gram, thirty miles east and west by eighteen miles north and south. It is divided by four rivers all flowing parallel to the Nive, not including the most easterly, the Gave de Pau.

Hill's 'corps', Picton's 3rd Division and some cavalry advanced at dawn on the Allied right flank close to the Pyrenees. Wellington's plan was to roll back the entire French line by outflanking it to the south. The reduced French field army could stretch only so far; Wellington did not believe that it could keep contact with Bayonne and still resist Hill thirty miles to the southeast. Wellington maintained four veteran divisions in the angle between the investing force at Bayonne and the swinging Allied right flank, to prevent Soult from carrying out any Napoleonic inclination he might have to break through the Allied centre.

Hill crossed the first river, the Joyeuse, easily, and then ran into stiff resistance in front of the second, the Bidouse. He seized both Garris and St Palais, isolating St Jean Pied-de-Port, which was invested by Mina's Spanish guerrilla army. The bridge at St Palais over the Bidouse was repaired by noon on the 16th. Hill continued his advance east toward the Saison. A slight action was fought around the village of Rivareyte on this stream on the 17th. Hill was already twenty miles due east of his starting point.

Wellington learnt with pleasure that Soult had finally withdrawn two field divisions from the north bank of the Adour, leaving a third within the defences of Bayonne, with which he had given up direct contact. On the 19th Wellington left his field army, which was advancing on the Saison, to visit the Bayonne force, intending to super-vise the construction of the bridge across the Adour. But the bad weather made this impossible, and after two days Wellington returned to his forces thrusting inland.

Before dawn on the 23rd, Hill's 'corps' pressed forward again, still close to the Pyrenees; the Allied centre and left were advancing more slowly. Hill crossed the Saison and before dark reached the ancient

French border fortress of Navarrenx on the Gave d'Oloron. It was too strong to be taken by escalade, but Morillo masked it nicely with his division; Hill pushed on, as did Picton further north. The French had now been driven back across four supposedly defensible rivers and were concentrating behind the last, the Gave de Pau, near the town of Orthez. By the evening of the 25th, Wellington had received detailed intelligence concerning Soult's latest position. Near Orthez there were six French infantry divisions, a cavalry division, and eight batteries of artillery with a total of 48 guns; the whole force probably consisted of 36,000 men.[1]

Meanwhile the weather had moderated on the coast. Hope had advanced on the 23rd into the area in which he had conducted his reconnaissance in force on 9th December. This time, he had both heavy and field artillery, pontoons and other boats, and miscellaneous equipment. In an operation worthy of comparison to Wellington's seizure of Oporto in 1809, Hope ferried a force across the Adour. It was soon attacked, but managed to hold its bridgehead (Plate 58). It included a battery using a new form of weapon, Congreve's rockets. It was also vigorously supported by artillery from the southern bank.

On the 24th, the navy brought sufficient vessels across the bar into the Adour to enable the bridge to be constructed. This whole operation went astonishingly well, although there were some losses of men and *matériel*; guns were moving across by the afternoon of the 26th. On the 27th, Hope fought and won a minor action at the village of St Etienne just north of Bayonne. Bayonne itself was completely surrounded, and the siege proper commenced. Its garrison numbered about 17,000 men including one field division.[2]

On the 26th, Hill's powerful 'corps', which had been thrusting far in advance on Wellington's right, was slowed down while Beresford on his extreme left was ordered to cross the Gave de Pau with the 4th and 7th Divisions in the vicinity of Peyrehorade. The latter then marched along the right bank of the river towards Soult at Orthez. The Allied pontoon train was moving just behind this force, so that the two halves of the Allied field army could reinforce each other across the river as required. Picton managed to cross the Gave de Pau only four miles below Orthez and seized a permanent bridge, which was repaired

---

[1] *Oman*, VII, 355, gives this figure, but omits his usual breakdown. Another 'division' of conscripts was known to be on the way to join Soult, but is not included.

[2] This was really more of a blockade. Hope never tried to breach the walls, although trenches and batteries were constructed.

quickly. Early on the 27th Wellington transferred his main striking force to the right bank; only Hill with the 2nd and Le Cor's Divisions and some light cavalry remained south of the Gave de Pau, 13,000 in all. Wellington had five divisions and cavalry north of the river, a total of 31,000. He had reconnoitred the enemy position from the southern bank the previous day.

Soult had deployed his army along an L-shaped ridge extending a mile north from Orthez at right-angles to the Gave de Pau before running west for three miles parallel to it. There were three subordinate ridges reaching out towards the river from the French position. The valleys between them were water-logged and almost impassable for artillery at the time of the battle. Soult had four and a half divisions of infantry posted to defend the main crest, half a division in Orthez, and one in reserve. The village of St Boes stood at the western end of the ridge; the main Bayonne-Orthez road ran between the river and the French position.

Wellington ordered Hill to skirmish, demonstrate, and threaten to cross the Gave at Orthez, but not to attack in earnest. If things went well north of the river, where the main Allied attack was to be delivered, he could cross at a point further east. The westernmost subordinate ridge, on which lie the ruins of a Roman Camp, does not connect directly with the French crest, as do the other two. The 4th Division was to attack St Boes from the west, with the support of the 7th, while the Light, 3rd, and 6th Divisions were to ascend the subordinate ridges. Wellington planned to direct the expected battle from the Roman Camp which the Light Division would seize. This lay three-quarters of a mile southeast of St Boes (Plate 56).

Ross's Brigade of the 4th Division cleared a French battalion from St Boes church and churchyard, which stands apart from the village itself (Plate 57). He was unable to take and hold the village which lay further east across a narrow tongue of land between two swampy hollows. The French had set up their defences so as to bring a concentration of artillery, firing over the heads of their own infantry, to bear on this spur and the village itself.[1]

---

[1] During the battle, the village was damaged to such an extent that it was rebuilt in a different place; this complicates on-the-spot research until the change is firmly in mind. The church and churchyard remain much as they were at the time of the battle.

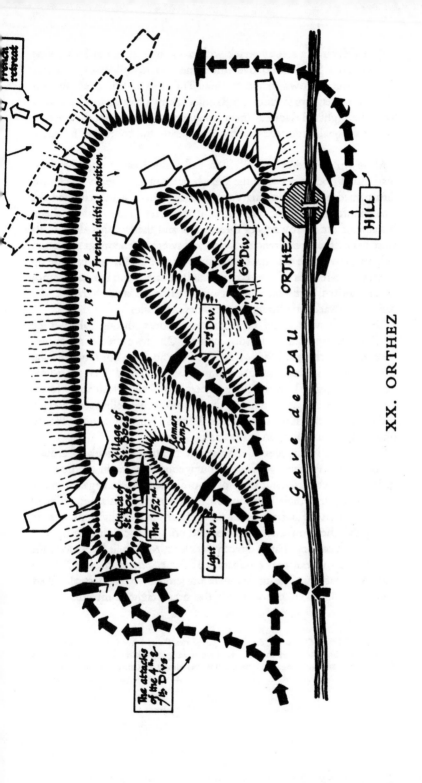

XX. ORTHEZ

Ross delivered a second attack with the assistance of the Portuguese brigade from his division over the same narrow saddle of land and through the hollows to either side. This also failed, even though Wellington sent north from the Roman Camp a battalion of *Cacadores* from the Light Division. A French counterattack towards the church-yard was equally unsuccessful, but a bickering fire continued for some time.

Meanwhile Picton's 3rd Division had pushed east along the main road into a pocket between the French position and the river. He had then turned north, following two secondary roads which climbed the two subordinate ridges, and drove in the French skirmishers there. Because of the narrowness of these ridges and the fact that their crests were below the main French position and swept by enemy guns, Picton did not press home his attack until supported. He sent one brigade up the ridge nearer Orthez and two up that just east of the Roman Camp; he then halted both columns just out of effective artillery range, and ordered forward only his light companies and Rifles.

There was now a lull of almost two hours, during which time Wellington reorganized his dispositions. On the extreme Allied left near St Boes, the 7th Division replaced the 4th; the 6th Division was sent forward to take its place immediately behind Picton's single brigade (Brisbane's) on the ridge adjacent to Orthez.[1] All three forces moved forward at 11.30 a.m. At the last moment Wellington directed the 1/52nd to thrust north from the Roman Camp to take the French opposing the 7th Division in the flank.

Each attack was successful after severe fighting, particularly around St Boes. The French had fought courageously earlier in the day, but once Wellington's second series of co-ordinated attacks began to make headway against their positions on the main ridge in three different places, they broke in panic. At least three of their six divisions were so cut up that they could not be rallied and brought back into the fight.

A French cavalry charge directly down the road to St Boes along the main ridge overran two companies of the 1/88th protecting Picton's divisional battery. The unfortunate horsemen were almost all killed, wounded, or taken prisoners by the other eight companies of the

---

[1] I have followed *Oman*, VII, diagram opposite 370. Some other accounts place the 3rd Division on the centre and the 6th on the eastern spur, which may have been how Wellington intended to fight the battle, but was almost certainly not the way it was fought.

battalion which closed in on either side of the defile through which the enemy endeavoured to press.[1]

On the south side of the river, Hill continued to demonstrate against Orthez. The old bridge had not been destroyed, but was so constructed that a successful assault would have been extremely costly (Plate 55). When Hill could see the Allied attacks on the north bank making headway, he left one brigade in the transpontine suburb of the town and moved two miles upstream with the rest of his force to the ford of Souars. In a well-managed attack led by the 1/92nd, the ford was taken, although defended by a French brigade.

By this time, Soult had obviously lost the battle, but his reserve division moved forward slightly and served as a pivot on which two others formed a line which they maintained for a time, although giving ground rapidly. As the French retreated northeast, they were joined by a division of conscripts from their depot at Toulouse. These ill-trained boys recently thrust into uniform all had muskets, but some lacked ammunition. They fought as well as could be expected until infected by the general panic; they then made off, discarding everything that reduced their speed. The whole French army had crossed the river Luy, eight miles from the battlefield, soon after dark.

The natural facility for retreating successfully after losing a battle, which the French showed throughout the Peninsular War, was exaggerated by an incident which could have been extremely serious. Wellington was disabled; a projectile hit his sword hilt, driving it against his thigh and hip. Bleeding was slight, but the injury incapacitated him. The British cavalry was more numerous than the French now and could have caused them much damage, but lacked central direction; it was hampered also by the water-logged condition of the valleys, and the many enclosures thereabout.

The French losses at Orthez were slightly above 4,000, not counting deserters, particularly numerous in the conscript division.[2] Soult also left guns and baggage on the field. The total Allied loss was 2,164.

Orthez was remarkable in that the Allies with numerically inferior forces drove the French from strong positions. All three thrusts north of the Gave de Pau ran into a defence that was at least numerically

---

[1] There is no large defile in this area. The sandy soil does exhibit unusual properties of retaining almost vertical sides in man-made cuts, of which there are several along this road, some topped with hedges.

[2] This force practically disintegrated; French civilian morale was now low: *Oman*, VII, 555–6.

equal to those attacking. Wellington would never have fought a battle in this manner prior to the decline of French morale, but appreciating the ascendency which his army had gained by its unbroken series of victories, he took full advantage of it.

SECOND PHASE: BORDEAUX, TARBES, AND THE GARONNE

Wellington was physically incapacitated on the morning of the 28th for the first and only time in the Peninsular War. He could barely walk, and was not able to ride with his usual facility for many days. Naturally, the Allied army was slow in following up its success; contact was lost with the fast retreating French. Before midday, Soult's army had crossed the Adour over thirty miles from Orthez. The Allies advanced slowly and reached St Sever twenty-four to forty-eight hours later. Soult had by that time retreated even further east; his contact with Bayonne was completely broken.

At St Sever, Wellington received a communication from Lynch, Mayor of Bordeaux. The mayor, a man of experience, ability, and integrity, was a descendant of an Irishman driven from his country by William III in 1688. He was one of the many secret Bourbon Royalists of Bordeaux and even though he had held high offices under Napoleon, promised to deliver the city to the British.

The Coalition of Allies against Napoleon had not yet decided whether in the event of victory to depose or to make peace with him on terms that would prevent him making war again. Wellington continued to warn all Frenchmen who considered declaring themselves against the Emperor that the British government could take no responsibility in the matter. Wellington was unwilling to take Bordeaux in the name of Louis XVIII, but Lynch would deliver it nevertheless. Beresford, with the 4th and 7th Divisions marched north from St Sever, and entered the city amid general acclaim on 12th March. Beresford and the 4th Division returned to the main army a few days later, but Lord Dalhousie and the 7th Division remained in Bordeaux until the end of hostilities.[1]

Meanwhile British cavalry made contact with Soult's army, which had marched southeast along the right bank of the Adour and had recrossed the river at Maubourguet. Wellington, with five divisions

[1] Dalhousie fought an action at Etauliers on 7th April which terminated to the Allied advantage.

only, held a position in front of Aire facing the French; Soult was superior numerically, but did not attack. Wellington received intelligence of reinforcements reaching Soult that more than made up his losses at Orthez and desertions incurred during the disorganized retreat. To counter these, and the permanent loss of the 7th Division, Wellington ordered up Morillo with half his division from the siege of Navarrenx, and Freire's force from Bayonne.[1] When the 4th Division rejoined the army on the 18th, the Allies moved forward again.

Wellington's immediate intention was to pin Soult against the Pyrenees at Tarbes; the Allied army marched south in three corps. Beresford on the extreme left was ordered to advance more quickly than either Hill on the right or Wellington in the centre. There were three main roads by which Soult could make his escape to the east. On the 19th, Beresford cut one of these and threatened the others; on the following morning, the second was severed. The trap was closing on at least part of Soult's army, but in a confused fight during the afternoon of the 20th two French divisions held back part of the Light and 6th Divisions long enough for the rest of Soult's army to make their way east along the southernmost road towards Toulouse. For a short while and on a limited front the fighting was extremely severe, but the French suffered only minor losses.[2]

Wellington had driven Soult half-way across southwestern France, but was faced by two serious problems. Firstly, if Suchet and Soult should combine forces, they would have a considerable numerical superiority in veteran soldiers alone, apart from newly raised conscripts. Suchet, in the northeastern corner of Spain, could reach Toulouse in a week, arriving perhaps before Wellington would be informed of his move.[3] Secondly, Wellington's system of intelligence had broken down. His maps were inaccurate and did not take into account winter conditions. He was no longer in an area covered by his 'correspondents'.

To complicate matters even further, news concerning Napoleon was conflicting. He was known to have been defeated by Blucher at Laon,

[1] Freire was replaced in Hope's command by the 'Army of the Reserve of Andalusia'; each force consisted of about 8,000 men.

[2] Surtees, 287, says,
'At length, after much smart skirmishing we gained the height, but found the whole of their infantry drawn up on a steep acclivity, near the windmill, which allowed them to have line behind line, all of which could fire at the same time over each other's heads, like the tiers of guns in a three decker. We continued, however, to advance upon them, till we got within a hundred paces of this formidable body, the firing from which was the hottest I had ever been in, except perhaps Barossa.'

[3] Rumours of this move came in several times, although the junction never took place.

but there was a rumour that he had turned on a Russian force at Reims and destroyed it.[1] The Northern Allies were not making the most of their great numerical and material advantages.

Wellington decided to direct his forces towards Toulouse, another city said to be strongly Royalist in sentiment. The most direct road was almost impassable; Wellington's modest coach, which he almost never used, required, in addition to its normal four mules, four large horses and two oxen to drag it through deep clay reaching almost to its axles. The difficulty of transporting two pontoon trains and 18-pounder siege guns can be imagined. But contact was made with Soult's army again on the 26th.

Local Royalists suggested that Soult might hold Toulouse, even if this meant standing a siege there. The city was situated on the right bank of the Garonne, a river larger than any that the Allied army had crossed apart from the Duero; it was strongly fortified and contained a large arsenal and numerous magazines. Both the old city and the suburb of St Cyprien west of the Garonne were surrounded by masonry walls so thick that cannon of the heaviest type could be mounted on their summits, and would still be protected by battlements. But these old walls were not strengthened by Vauban-type outworks, and could be breached by Wellington even with his limited siege train, if he could get his guns into position close enough for effective fire.

Toulouse was then surrounded at a distance of from 400 to 700 yards beyond the walls by a barge canal.[2] This man-made waterway approaches the city from the southeast, passes around it in a gentle curve, and then proceeds west into the Garonne. About seven-eighths of the total periphery of Toulouse was protected by either the river or the canal. Directly to the east, the Calvinet ridge overlooked both the canal and the city wall, and lay at a distance of less than half a mile from the latter. The area between these heights and the wall contained many strong stone buildings on both sides of the canal. Once a besieger had possession of the Calvinet, he could without difficulty and with little additional effort, press his formal investment by using these buildings instead of trenches, saps, and batteries.[3]

[1] The town did change hands twice, but no considerable action was fought there.
[2] This canal, called Midi or Languedoc, is still in operation; barges can travel by it from the Mediterranean to the Atlantic. Modern Toulouse has expanded far beyond the canal.
[3] This was common knowledge in the Allied camp. Some information was received from Royalists, but some British officers, including Wellington, had visited Toulouse before the war. Forty years ago, Oman found the whole of the Calvinet built over; it is now even more so.

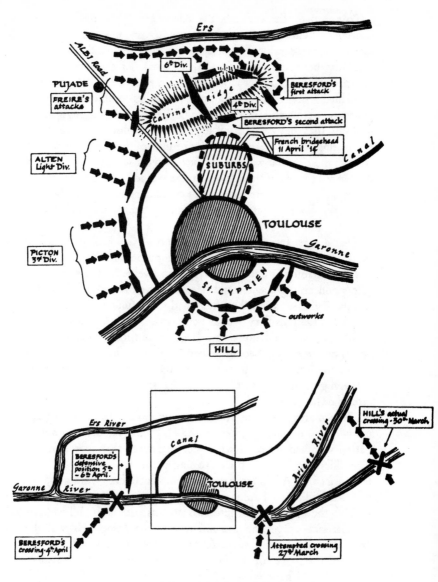

XXI. TOULOUSE

To approach the Calvinet the Allied army had first to cross the Garonne. Wellington decided initially to try upstream; from this direction, there was a chance that the Allies could advance on Toulouse between the river and the canal. At the very least, their approach to the Calvinet would be easier. Soon after dark on the 27th, the Allied army marched to a point five miles south of the city where pontoons were being formed into a bridge. By now the engineers were so skilful that they could lay it in darkness; a column of infantry could be crossing three abreast within four hours of the pontoons reaching a river in their special wagons. At first all went well, until the engineers discovered that even though the bridge was long enough to be broken down into two separate sections for crossing rivers such as the Nive, it lacked by about 80 feet the length required to cross the Garonne at this point.

Even a man so ready with expedients as Colonel Sturgeon could think of nothing that would answer the purpose in the time available. Trestle extensions might be provided in twelve hours; some form of suspension arrangement could be constructed in twenty-four. But in this particular situation the bridge had to be functioning by daylight, or Soult's field artillery would be in action against it before 10 a.m. If Wellington could not pass a large proportion of the Allied army across before then, it would be best to give up the operation entirely. He was understandably put out, but gave orders to retire immediately. By daylight, there was no evidence that the Allied army had tried to cross the Garonne here.

Three nights later, the bridge was successfully laid over the river a considerable distance further south; Hill with 13,000 men and three batteries pushed across in what was little more than a reconnaissance. The difference between these crossing points was that the first would have placed the Allied army in an area in which there was a good system of roads leading to Toulouse. Between this point and the second used by Hill, the Garonne split into two streams; although Hill had crossed the Garonne proper, he was still west of the Ariege. He was able to cross this also with a small force, but found no roads suitable for wheeled transport converging on Toulouse from here. Cavalry and infantry could have advanced across country, but artillery could not have followed without considerable delay. Upon receiving Hill's report, Wellington visited the area himself. A sweep on Toulouse from the south did not appear practical. He ordered Hill to recross both rivers; the pontoon bridge was taken up and transported north again.

By this time the engineers had found a spot some fifteen miles north of Toulouse where the Garonne was narrow enough to be crossed by their bridge. There was some danger, however, that the equipment was being stretched beyond its limit of safety; in order to reach the full length required, the pontoons themselves had to be spaced further apart than usual.

Wellington decided to try a crossing here and ordered the bridge to be laid early in the evening of 4th April. Beresford and 19,000 men, including cavalry and artillery, crossed over before and soon after dawn. Then the bridge was broken; for the second time in four months, heavy rain in the Pyrenees interfered with the course of Allied operations. A flood sweeping down the Garonne isolated Beresford even more completely than Hill had been at St Pierre on 13th December.

Beresford's force was larger, however, and had a shorter front; Wellington himself placed the army in position facing south with the river Ers protecting their left. This stream runs parallel to the Garonne, approximately two miles further east. Artillery was ordered up to the left bank of the Garonne to enfilade any advance that Soult might make against Beresford, but no French infantry moved out from Toulouse. By the afternoon of the 7th the river had fallen; the pontoon bridge was soon back in service.[1]

THIRD PHASE: THE BATTLE OF TOULOUSE

Wellington brought over his entire force except for Hill's 'corps' on the 8th; he personally reconnoitred the area between the Garonne and the Ers and the city itself. The Calvinet heights appeared assailable, although the area of approach was cramped by its proximity to the Ers. Soult had covered the whole ridge with his inevitable field fortifications, and from the arsenal had mounted numerous heavy cannon on the city walls and smaller pieces in the earthworks. But the Allies no longer feared such things. Nevertheless Wellington realized already that the forthcoming struggle for Toulouse would be more of a siege operation than a battle in the field.

The Allied army spent the 9th moving into position; the pontoon bridge was placed even nearer the city, so that Hill could be reinforced without delay should it be necessary. A concentric attack on Toulouse began before 7 a.m. on the 10th; Hill's 'corps' advanced against the

[1] One pontoon was swept downstream, but was recovered undamaged from a sand bar about five miles north.

suburb west of the river driving the French from their outer defences to the greater safety of their main walls. Hill's veterans now put on a superb show of manoeuvring; they engaged in bickering fire and artillery duels. They threatened to attack in earnest, but never did.[1]

East of the river, Picton and Alten were to drive in skirmishers and menace the area between the Garonne and the Albi road. The 3rd and Light Divisions were each extended over about a mile of front. Picton disobeyed his orders early and tried to take the French bridgehead across the canal near the point at which it entered the Garonne. He lost men to no advantage, and was forced to retire.

Wellington's main attack was to be delivered by two separate forces on the north end of the Calvinet, east of the Albi road. Freire with his two Spanish divisions supported by Portuguese artillery was to advance from the northeast and seize the village and knoll of Pujade. Meanwhile, Beresford would advance on their left with the 4th and 6th Divisions. He was to assault the Calvinet from the east from a position a mile and a half further south. Since Beresford had a greater distance to cover, Freire was instructed to wait at Pujade until Beresford began his attack before commencing his own assault.

After reaching the Ers and turning south along its left bank, Beresford's column was held up by the condition of the ground. The soil was mostly clay, and was saturated with water; roads were soon churned into deep mud. As both divisions had their regular batteries with them, these pieces had to be man-handled forward. Beresford saw that his artillery was slowing his advance to a snail's pace. He ordered his batteries to turn west, ascend a low ridge, and open fire on the French positions; enemy artillery had begun to cause casualties in the Allied columns, although the range was over-long for accuracy.

Beresford was still about a mile short of where he had intended to turn on the French, while Freire had been in position with his two Spanish divisions for some time. The Portuguese artillery around Pujade had almost silenced the French light guns in their earthworks on the northern end of the ridge. The Spanish general, for reasons never fully explained, now ordered his force to commence their assault. Two full brigades pressed forward in line, with a third in direct support and a fourth in reserve.[2]

Freire led the advance himself; most of his field officers were mounted

[1] Soult was not deceived by this demonstration against St Cyprien, and shifted some of its garrison to the Calvinet.

[2] The least illogical reason for this premature attack is that the Spanish staff mistook the opening of fire by Beresford's marooned artillery for the commencement of his

and rode ahead. Bravely they moved forward in the face of some artillery fire from the Calvinet and a good deal from the walls of Toulouse. When the range shortened sufficiently for musketry fire the greater part of three French divisions opened from behind breastworks. Because of the contour of the northern end of the ridge, the French field batteries could continue to fire over the heads of their infantry. The Spaniards held their formation until they were within less than 60 yards of their objective. Here they had to descend into a sunken road and climb the other side.

When the disordered ranks tried to reform on the far bank, hardly 40 yards from the French firing line, they failed and staggered back into the false security of the road. Two heavy guns from the city walls sent charges of grape along the trough, while French infantry left their breastworks, rushed forward to the embankment and fired volleys down into the confused mass in the road. Another French force from behind the Calvinet moved round and attacked their right flank and rear. The Spaniards finally broke and fled back in disorder. Their officers had demanded too much; they had attacked veteran infantry more numerous than themselves, protected by fortifications, and supported by exceptionally powerful artillery.

When Wellington saw the Spanish divisions surge forward in their premature attack, he could not tell how soon they would be defeated. He sent instructions immediately to Beresford to wheel right and ascend the Calvinet ridge, wherever he might be. But by the time Beresford had received the message, Freire's fight was over. Such an assault on Beresford's part on the strong central section of the ridge would no longer help Freire. With commendable judgement, he disobeyed the order and continued south for another half mile before he swung to attack as originally planned.

The Calvinet ridge does not extend due north and south, but makes an angle to the southeast; the southern sector was not only further from the guns on the city walls, but was neither so' well fortified nor so strongly held. The 4th and 6th Divisions deployed and formed for the attack; Allied cavalry faced French cavalry on their left flank.[1] The

---

infantry attack. But Beresford's whole force was in plain sight from the Pujade knoll. Could national pride have caused this gallant, but isolated and inefficient, demonstration of courage? Freire had asked for and received this position of primary importance at Toulouse because of the minor parts previously played by Spanish troops in Allied victories.

[1] There was some French cavalry on Beresford's right also, but this was kept at bay by a British battalion forming square when the horsemen approached.

three brigades of each division advanced in a single two-deep line one behind the other; the 4th Division on the left and the 6th on their right. All then moved forward on a front of a mile and a half. Before they reached the crest two French brigade columns burst over the ridge from the west, each heading for the centre of one of the leading Allied brigades. Again French columns opposed British lines. General Taupin, who should have known better, lost his division and his life without delaying the progress of Beresford's attack. The 4th and 6th Divisions were soon in possession of the lower half of the Calvinet ridge; their casualties had been comparatively light.

Beresford now turned the 4th Division to face the canal opposite the centre of Toulouse, for the French troops driven off the ridge had taken shelter in a large entrenched redoubt between the Calvinet and the canal. Meanwhile the 6th Division was deployed across the crest facing northwest. A further advance would clear the ridge entirely, including that section already assaulted by the Spaniards. There was now a lull in the fighting; Beresford was waiting for his batteries to come up and support him further. By 4 p.m., all was ready.

The 4th Division advanced east to the canal, cleared the French from some intermediate works, consolidated its position, and prepared for the expected counterattack. The 6th Division attacked the northern half of the Calvinet ridge both from the south and southeast; it suffered heavy casualties from artillery firing over the heads of entrenched infantry and from the infantry itself. The 1/42nd was mishandled and disorganized before the main assault commenced; its colonel had the two halves of his battalion in the wrong relationship to each other and insisted on forming them properly, while under fire, before advancing.[1] The main French work in this sector, the redoubt of the Augustins, changed hands five times, but finally remained with the Allies.

Meanwhile, Freire's Spaniards had been rallied, and attacked again gallantly; they were actually in possession of the French trenches at isolated points. After hand-to-hand fighting, they were driven out, but assisted Beresford greatly in occupying a large number of French infantry and artillery which would otherwise have been used exclusively against the 6th Division.

During the action just described, Picton made another costly attack with Brisbane's Brigade against the French canal defences near the

[1] Col. Macara wanted his theoretical right wing units on his right, but paid for this useless adjustment with lives. The Scots particularly used to consider such things of great importance.

Garonne. He had observed Freire's first defeat; when he had noticed the firing die down after Beresford's initial assaults, Picton assumed that Beresford also had failed. Remembering his attacks on the castle at Badajoz which finally took the place, he stormed ahead again. Some of Brisbane's men stood exchanging volleys at close range with enemy infantry protected by breastworks, while others tried to pull down heavy palisades with their bare hands and a few tools. The unequal contest was stubbornly maintained for some time; Brisbane and many of his command fell before the survivors drew back.

There was another lull in the battle; Wellington reformed his forces. Freire's men were then ordered forward again, this time supported by the Light Divisions. Soult now gave up all territory beyond the canal except for a small area in front of the 4th Division. The French would be forced to abandon this also as soon as the Allied artillery moved into position and received more ammunition. The summit of the Calvinet commanded this area and the lower French positions were well within artillery range.

If Soult allowed himself to be shut up in Toulouse, his army could resist for no more than a month on the supplies available there. Apart from the remarkably ill-advised attack of Taupin's French Division in columns on Beresford's two divisions in line, the fighting had all been of the type normal to siege operations, and the numbers of casualties also followed the same pattern. The British, Portuguese, and Spanish losses totalled 4,568; 1,900 of these were suffered by Freire's two weak divisions. The French lost 3,236, and most of their abundant artillery which had been beyond the canal.

Wellington's position on the morning of the 11th was not pleasant. Since he realized the importance of the ridge, he assumed that Soult would appreciate this also and counterattack. Beresford's divisions were weak from fatigue and were short of ammunition. A major realignment was necessary; supplies must be brought across the river. Siegeworks facing the town would have to be erected. No further Allied attack on Toulouse was possible that day, but British cavalry advanced south along both banks of the Ers. By darkness, they had almost reached the Toulouse-Carcassonne road and the Garonne. Four more hours of daylight would have enabled them to cut Soult's escape routes.[1] By

---

[1] Since Soult's force was nearly equal to the Allies numerically, he might have cut his way out, but such operations, after containing works have been completed, are inevitably costly and sometimes fail.

midnight the Allied camps were invaded by French Royalists. Soult had abandoned Toulouse already and moved southeast.

Only a few hours later, on the 12th, Wellington received trustworthy information from Paris that Napoleon had abdicated; the Bourbons were being restored.[1] Toulouse, always a Royalist stronghold, was the scene of wild rejoicing and fittingly welcomed as deliverers both Wellington and the Allied army.

Soult at Carcassonne at first refused to capitulate, but finally agreed to do so on receipt of positive orders from the new French government and from Berthier, Napoleon's Chief of Staff. All sieges in Spain and southwestern France came to peaceful conclusions with two exceptions, one of which was a sortie from Barcelona before official news had been received, which led to needless casualties.

A more serious action occurred on 14th April at Bayonne, still loyal to Napoleon. The governor, General Thouvenot, may not have been brilliant, but he was steadfast to extreme obstinacy. He still had a powerful garrison of 15,000 men which he set in motion in an all-out attack on the village of St Etienne soon after darkness. The Allies had been informed of the sortie by a deserter. They were not surprised by the attack itself, but by its great strength. The French took almost the whole village, together with many prisoners.

But the Allied recovery was speedy and complete; the French lost in bloody fighting all the territory they had taken. Casualties totalled 843 for the Allies including 236 prisoners soon released; the French lost 891 in killed and wounded. There appears to be no excuse for this action, in which Hope was wounded and General Hay killed. The governor had been informed on the 12th of Napoleon's abdication and of the Allied occupation of France. He may not have been officially notified by the 14th of what had happened in Paris on the 6th, but he had little reason to doubt the news in view of what had taken place during recent weeks.

After almost six years, the fighting was over. To the army as a whole, the spring of 1814 was the most pleasant of their lives. The French people treated Wellington's men more as deliverers than conquerors. Food and wine were plentiful, of fine quality, and cheap. The British

[1] This official news was brought by well-known French and British officers travelling together; Wellington sent them both on to Soult.

cavalry and some artillery proceeded in leisurely fashion across France to Calais before sailing for home. Spanish units repassed the Pyrenees, while Anglo-Portuguese divisions marched to Bordeaux.

Some British units had the bad luck to be sent to America, even though the causes of the war, if not the war itself, had ceased to exist. Others embarked for Britain. Within every division except the 1st, there was a trying period of leave-taking. The British and Portuguese had to part company, both as units and as individuals.[1] At one time the latter had been treated as auxiliaries of inferior fighting quality. They had won full partnership in the welter of battle.

Wellington himself, now only 45 years of age and with a reputation second only to Napoleon among the military men of his time, returned to Spain to prevent Ferdinand from bringing about a civil war. Later, he entered Paris as British Ambassador. Eventually he reached London to receive a hero's welcome. He took his place in the House of Lords as Baron, Viscount, Earl, Marquis, and Duke. The House of Commons voted him £400,000 to buy an estate. Little did he realize that only nine months were to pass before he would be called into the field again to fight Napoleon himself at Waterloo.

THE CONTENDING FORCES; FEBRUARY, MARCH, AND APRIL, 1814

ALLIED ARMY UNDER WELLINGTON[2]

Bayonne Corps under Hope 1st and 5th Infantry Divisions, Aylmer's, Wilson's, and Bradford's Infantry Brigades, and Vandeleur's Cavalry Brigade, Freire's and de España's Spanish Infantry Divisions	TOTAL = 18,000 British and Portuguese 16,000 Spanish

[1] Another parting was even more disagreeable and in some cases pathetic. British soldiers had taken Portuguese and Spanish wives. Many of these 'marriages' were broken up by official orders and the women were sent back to their own country. Diarists do not agree as to how this separation was carried out. If an actual marriage had taken place beforehand, the soldier and his wife were surely safe. But formal marriage was rare; occasionally soldiers were allowed to marry their women at Bordeaux and take them home, but in most battalions this was not permitted. It is hard for us today to understand the position of women in the British armies of 150 years ago. Legal wives and others endured with their men all the trials, dangers, and privations of military life. These Portuguese and Spanish women were loyal, faithful, and courageous.

[2] The Allied organization remained substantially as shown in the Appendix to Chapter XVIII.

Field Army under Wellington, Hill, and Beresford at Orthez, 27th February   TOTAL = 44,042

2nd Division	7,780
3rd Division	6,626
4th Division	5,592
6th Division	5,571
7th Division	5,643
Light Division (part)[1]	3,480
Le Cor's Portuguese Division	4,465
Fane's, Vivian's, and Somerset's Cavalry Brigades	3,373
Artillery (42 guns), Staff, Train, etc.	1,512

Field Army under Wellington, Hill, and Beresford at Toulouse, 10th April   TOTAL = 46,573

2nd Division	6,940
3rd Division	4,566
4th Division	5,363
6th Division	5,693
Light Division	4,275
Le Cor's Division	3,952
Freire's Spanish Divisions	7,916
Morillo's Spanish Division (half)	2,001
Cavalry (actually across the Garonne)	3,617
Artillery (46 guns), Staff, Train, etc.	2,250

[1] The Light Division at Orthez lacked the 1/43rd and 1/95th.

Bayonne Garrison   = 17,000
   Regular Garrison plus the 3rd
     French Division
St Jean Pied-de-Port and Navarenx   = 3,500
Garrisons, not including National Guards
Field Army (at Toulouse particu-   TOTAL = 42,000
   larly)
   Six Divisions, Cavalry, Artillery

TOPOGRAPHICAL OBSERVATIONS

Orthez remains very much as it was in 1814. The original bridge is in limited use; even in France it is considered to be an historic monument. The Roman camp is well-preserved. The church of St Boes appears to have been little damaged, even though the village itself was hard hit. Every action in this area can be followed with ease.

Toulouse has changed completely. The old walls were pulled down long ago, except for some surrounding the suburb across the Garonne. A tremendous increase in population has pushed the town far beyond the old canal and has completely covered the Calvinet ridge with a maze of blind streets.

XX

EPILOGUE

THE British, after fighting in the Peninsula between August 1808 and April 1814, finally achieved their objective, the complete defeat of Napoleonic France. Few students of military history believe that if Napoleon had taken into Russia in 1812 the veteran French troops that he was then using in Spain, instead of an army more than half of which was composed of fair-weather allies, he would have been defeated. Even if forced to retire, his masterful campaign of 1813 would have restored him to dominance in Europe; only the news of Vitoria prevented this.

The final Allied victory in the Peninsula was achieved by a British army which at no time exceeded 60,000 men supported by Portuguese and Spaniards of varying quality and quantity against French armies usually totalling over 300,000. Napoleon sent more than 600,000 men across the Pyrenees, some of whom were veterans accustomed to almost uninterrupted military success elsewhere. The French operated under a system which had beaten Continental Europe. The British army of 1808 had a reputation based on a few successes in minor actions, mostly outside Europe, a number of similar failures, and no major land campaign since Marlborough's time.

On the basis of bare facts, it would have seemed highly unlikely that what was essentially a British victory in the Peninsula would have been possible. Battles, and ultimately wars, are decided on the quality and quantity of force applied by the contending armies, and the direction of that force. In 1808, few disinterested people would have considered Britain's land forces to be superior to those of France in any of these three categories, yet Britain and her Allies won. How did this happen? There were many reasons; some involved Wellington; but first we will discuss those that had little to do with him.

The direct assistance of Spanish and Portuguese civilians should never be under-rated. The common country people were altogether hostile to the French and usually well-disposed to the British, although the urban population and the upper classes were not always similarly inclined. The guerrillas were a constant threat to and drain on the invaders' forces.

The organized armies of the two Peninsular nations also aided the common cause considerably. The Spanish regular army could never be ignored by the French; Wellington could not have remained six months in the Peninsula if the French had been able to concentrate on his army alone. Occasionally Spanish armies may have appeared in an unfavourable light, but they were no more incompetent than most of Napoleon's other Continental opponents.

The British economy was able to provide a never-ending flow of men, money, supplies, and munitions to support not only its own forces, but also those of its Allies. All had to be transported to the Peninsula by the British navy and merchant marine. Ships converged on Portuguese and Spanish ports not only from the British Isles but from North and South America, the eastern Mediterranean, and the Indies. A large subsidy was paid regularly to Portugal to keep her economy functioning. Spain also received much material and monetary assistance.

The British army sent out to the Peninsula was on the whole well-trained, well-armed, and well-equipped; the men themselves appear to have been physically superior to the French, Portuguese, and Spanish.[1] British soldiers were noted for their courage, but were too fond of drink. They were quick to get out of hand and did not stand adversity well.

The regimental organization of the British infantry was partly responsible for its indomitable spirit. In theory, and usually in practice, the officers came from the county families, while the men were of more humble origin.[2] Even before the Peninsular War the bravery of British officers was proverbial, but their professional efficiency was rarely up to French or Prussian standards. The aristocratic system was more satisfactory in the infantry battalions, where it was somewhat modified,

[1] Napier and others observed that the British troops stationed in Paris after Waterloo were taller and stronger than those of any other nation.
[2] Some officers rose from the ranks, and gentlemen sometimes served in them. But ranker officers were often paymasters, commissaries, and the like. Sometimes the temptation to drink was irresistible for enlisted men who had received commissions; after the iron discipline imposed on them in the ranks, they could not adjust themselves to the comparative freedom of the officers' mess.

than in cavalry regiments where the pretensions of the young officers were equalled only by their lack of interest in routine military matters. Wellington was frequently tried by the foolhardy bravery of his horsemen and their subsequent loss of discipline. In actions requiring professional skill, the best cavalry in the British army were the K.G.L. units.

There were, of course, other perhaps less important contributory factors for the Allied victory in which Wellington had little or no part. He did nothing to create the patriotism of Portugal and Spain, though he did channel it into more effective forms. His former political experience made it possible for him to superintend the government of Portugal and take on much responsibility for Spain. Wellington had little to do with Britain's material contribution, but he made sure that the money and goods supplied to them were used wisely. He was more conscious of economic factors than most military commanders. After 1811, his advice was often sought by the Tory government at home on matters not concerning his theatre of operations, nor even of a military nature. His suggestions were never ignored.

The contributions to Allied success made by Wellington personally fall into three classes: his military system, his grand strategy, and his combat manoeuvres and tactics. In all three, the changes he made in previous British standards and procedures were startling. The final results confirmed his wisdom.

The Headquarters that came to the Peninsula was not dissimilar to others which had accompanied previous British expeditionary forces. But soon it ceased to be a British Headquarters, and became Wellington's Headquarters.[1] Individual assignments were broadened; responsibilities to superiors at home were relaxed to an unprecedented degree. The whole group worked as a team and accomplished what was necessary in any field without strict regard to the old departmental boundaries. Wellington was a good teacher, but an even better executive; his ability to delegate was unique at that time, once he was confident that his staff required no further supervision.[2]

[1] *Ward, passim.*

[2] It appears likely that once Wellington assigned a task to someone and had given him a few basic instructions, he expected him to get on with it, on the assumption that men who have the capacity to do a job could learn it best for themselves. Wellington gave them a clear idea of the result to be achieved and let them work out the details with just enough supervision to prevent damage to the public good. Once the system was in operation, new men were instructed by other members of the staff. All assisted each other, and bothered the C-in-C only in dire emergencies.

In August 1808, British transport and supply, apart from harbour areas, was primitive in the extreme. During the five years after the unfortunate Talavera campaign, the Allied army seldom lacked essentials. Troops could be assembled at any time, kept concentrated as long as necessary, and moved in any direction with the certainty that their supplies and equipment would keep up with them. The privations described by diarists only confirm the not unusual capacity of British soldiers for complaining. Because of a new man's blunder, food was short for four days during the retreat from Salamanca in November 1812. The troops had tents, but lacked greatcoats, in the Autumn of 1813. Officers had to pay high prices for butter, cheese, fine wines, and pepper. Compared to actual starvation suffered by other contemporary armies, some of them British, Wellington's soldiers were most fortunate. Their worst hardships would have been considered relatively minor in French armies in the Peninsula.

The commissaries were soon able to handle efficiently all supplies arriving from overseas. They had learnt also to buy stuff locally, and to deliver it wherever required on time. As in India, Wellington had in Portugal and Spain almost as many men to supply his forces as there were in the army itself. For years, tens of thousands of mules and oxen were maintained by the British Commissariat. Always, and without fail, Wellington paid for goods and services.[1]

Wellington did more than just instruct his commissaries and their hordes of assistants. He was always carrying out special projects, such as clearing the Tagus and Duero for navigation, restoring bridges at Alcantara, Almaraz, and elsewhere, and improving roads just in case they might be used. His forethought in connexion with the transfer of supply lines from Lisbon to Passages made it possible for him to exert continual pressure on the French army during an average advance of ten miles per day for over six weeks. The men supplied hardly realized that their rations were no longer being sent up from Portugal, but had reached them by way of Biscay.

Military intelligence under Wellington was essentially common sense, attention to detail, and a great deal of accumulated experience. He wanted to know personally everything that could possibly be of value

[1] Wages were sometimes in arrears, but never so much that confidence in ultimate payment was shaken in the minds of the Portuguese and Spanish civilian employees who showed, on the whole, an honesty, ability, and courage of a high order.

not only concerning Spain and Portugal, but also the rest of Europe. His primary means of obtaining general and political information was by the drudgery of interminable correspondence with friends, colleagues, and others, and the reading of newspapers. He supplemented this with personal conversation whenever possible.

The military situation in the Peninsula was susceptible to a better organized system of intelligence. Wellington required information concerning the actual movements of French forces and precise details of their dispositions. He accomplished this in part by direct reconnaissance. Wherever possible, Wellington preferred to see for himself. To gather information at greater distances, cavalry could be sent, but was not always successful. Small reconnaissance parties were superior for this duty. Young staff officers operating independently, or with a small group of men, all superbly mounted, could go anywhere. Their thoroughbreds were expensive and required much attention, but were a tremendous advantage. Individual scouts could ride around enemy camps, and formations on the march, determining not only their numbers, but also the composition of each unit. They might be chased a dozen times a day, but could outdistance French dragoons with such ease that they were often allowed to do their reconnaissance undisturbed.

Other fruitful sources of direct intelligence were the guerrilla bands. Their observations were occasionally inaccurate, but could be checked by other means. The guerrillas also provided the most reliable of all information concerning enemy dispositions, movements, and future intentions, by intercepting dispatches. Wellington always paid hard money for these; Scovell could break any French code.

The C-in-C used a system of monetary reward for a high proportion of his numerous 'correspondents' throughout the Peninsula. In some cases, civilians gave or sent information from purely patriotic motives; a professor at the University of Salamanca, or prelates of the Spanish church, might have been insulted if offered money. But almost all these 'correspondents' incurred the risks involved in obtaining information partly, at least, for money.

Prompt and proper interrogation of prisoners and deserters was always considered of primary importance. An appreciation of this extended throughout the entire army; many individuals acquired skill in conducting these examinations.[1]

[1] Wellington himself questioned General Brennier at Vimiero; *Schaumann*, 180–1, recalls how he, a commissary officer, undertook some interrogation near Talavera.

Even though Wellington had an ample staff of able men, he preferred to act as his own chief of intelligence. The Adjutant General had been given this responsibility in the past, but this post in the Peninsula was often filled by men incapable of doing this type of work.[1] By sifting all intelligence himself, Wellington knew everything, and did not have to rely on what a subordinate considered important enough to put in his *resumé*. His abnormal capacity of knowing what was happening 'upon the other side of the hill' may have resulted from this personal attention to detail.[2]

Wellington's system of military management depended to a considerable extent on a new organization instituted by him in 1809, the autonomous division. Prior to the Peninsular War, the basic British military unit had been the battalion or regiment. Brigades, when formed, had been temporary only; they were primarily for command purposes and were not completely autonomous. The new divisions were self-sufficient and could be detached from the main force; they made possible extended and complicated manoeuvring, greatly aided the proficiency of the army in battle, and were the basis of an internal economy which enabled them to provide for themselves for months at a time under any conditions. These independent units each had their own staff, artillery, and often cavalry.[3]

Of even more importance than the new divisional concept itself was the incorporation into them of Portuguese troops. Wellington soon appreciated that if the army was to have any chance of success against the French, its numbers would have to be increased. Additional manpower was not available in Britain. The use of Portuguese troops was essential, but Portuguese units alone might prove incapable of holding a position. Wellington solved this problem by combining British and Portuguese units in the new divisions. The normal ratio was one

[1] Charles Stewart was AG for a long period early in the war and resented this infringement of his 'rights', but was not the man for such duties: *Londonderry, passim*.

[2] *Oman*, VII, 96, says,
'The Duke of Wellington being once asked what was the special faculty which had brought him through so many difficulties, and led him to so many victories, replied that he thought that he could guess what was going on "upon the other side of the hill" better than most men . . . he knew precisely what amount of credence should be given to information volunteered by a trusted intelligence officer like Colquhoun Grant, a nervous brigadier, a French deserter, or a Spanish alcalde of an optimistic frame of mind.'

[3] The divisions were little armies within themselves; the longest infantry-cavalry association was between the Light Division and the 1st Hussars, K.G.L.

Portuguese brigade, which always included some British field and company officers, to two British brigades.[1] There were also two independent Portuguese brigades and one wholly Portuguese division.

Wellington occasionally divided his army into 'corps', but this was a temporary procedure. Only Hill's familiar force of three nationalities was so constituted for any length of time. The division continued to be the basic unit except for purposes of command, but even the division was not so inflexible that it could not be itself divided when necessary.

The organization of Wellington's Army has been precisely detailed in many places; the training that he gave his men is much harder to appreciate. Diaries make occasional mention of schools attended by all soldiers. The proficiency of the Allied divisions can only have resulted from intensive and efficient training which British armies before that time sometimes lacked. We do not have precise details of what took place, but the results were apparent.

No part of Wellington's system was so vital to him as the care of his men. Throughout the eighteenth century and the first half of the nineteenth, both nations and commanders were astonishingly lax and thoughtless in this regard, hardly appreciating that a man lost through sickness weakened an army as much as one lost in battle. Napoleon was one of the most wasteful of generals. But Britain just did not have the men; Wellington had to avoid heavy casualty lists, and took pains to expose his men as rarely as possible both to the enemy, and to the hazards of sickness. He imposed rigid discipline in order to curb excesses bad for their health. At the same time he was acutely conscious of their need for clothing, cooking utensils, tents, blankets, shoes, and regular pay. Under Wellington, uniforms varied widely, even in battalions, but were the most comfortable and serviceable that the British army had ever known. In spite of the enormous distances covered, the infantry was seldom poorly shod. Wellington recognized in McGrigor an able surgeon-general and supported fully any innovations which improved health and reduced mortality among casualties.

Wellington insisted that officers and NCO's took a real interest in the health and well-being of their men. He lectured his officers repeatedly in this connexion; even battalion commanders had to stand trial before courts-martial for neglecting their men.

Wellington's system of military discipline protected the inhabitants of Portugal, Spain, and France. If troops plunder, rape, and murder

[1] This ratio was not rigid; the 1st and 2nd Divisions did not at first contain Portuguese brigades; the Light Division had Portuguese troops included in each of its two brigades.

civilians, they must expect retaliation. The Allied armies under Wellington always paid in hard money for their requirements and treated the local population reasonably well. After a few weeks, even the people of southern France were more willing to help the Allies than Soult's French forces.

Wellington suggested and had approved the first corps of sappers and miners, and the first military police in the British army. The post of judge advocate general was established after his recommendations in connexion with prompt punishment for disciplinary infractions. Wellington's broad experience and fertile imagination were a constant help to his engineers, whether concerned with such tasks as bridging, pontoon transportation, or the clearing of rivers.

In his early campaigns, Wellington outlined in his dispatches to his superiors in London exactly what he was planning, and why; later, he was more secretive in regard to his intentions, and would only report the results of his operations. His strategic planning was always simple, practical, and based on the very latest intelligence. Having considered his problems, he then put his decisions into action without worrying unduly about matters beyond his control. He realized the value of speed and strategic surprise, whilst understanding fully what could and could not normally be accomplished.[1] He was equally conscious of the limitations in manpower under which he fought and the consequences of even a single defeat. The loss of a brigade prior to 1810 would probably have precipitated the recall of the British army.

After defeating Junot's armies twice, in offensive and defensive battles, Wellington returned to the Peninsula in the spring of 1809; and his plan for ejecting Soult from North Portugal was simply conceived, courageously carried out, and completely successful. The Talavera campaign was based on what proved to be an erroneous assumption, that Cuesta and the Spanish government would behave reasonably and according to their own best interest. Wellington fought the battle and won, but days too late for the decisive result he had every reason to hope he would achieve. The advance so far into Spain would have

---

[1] Wellington disapproved wholeheartedly of actions of extreme gallantry in which a few men defeated hundreds. These were dear to the hearts of British officers and were often successful in the colonies, but rarely against French veterans.

been hazardous, but for the presence of the Tagus and the rough terrain to the south of it.[1]

Wellington staked his military reputation and even his future employment on his ability to hold Portugal. Sir John Moore and almost every other general officer in the British army had stated that Portugal was militarily indefensible. It may have been indefensible by any force that Britain could put in the field, even if aided by the Portuguese regular army, but Wellington was counting on considerable additional help. The Spanish guerrillas were to limit the French to employing a force of no more than 100,000 men in their attack on Portugal.[2] The Portuguese nation was to defend itself in accordance with Wellington's broadly conceived co-ordinated plan. The Allied regular army was to fight only where it could do so at an advantage, as it did at Busaco. It then retired behind the Lines of Torres Vedras, thereby foiling Massena, the most capable of the French marshals. Wellington finally defeated him completely.

In the period between Massena's retreat in March 1811 and Wellington's advance on Salamanca in May 1812, the Allies defeated the French in two defensive battles, and outfaced them in two further campaigns. They finally opened both corridors from Portugal into Spain by taking Badajoz and Ciudad Rodrigo. Marmont's error of judgement near the Arapiles on 22nd July 1812 gave Wellington his finest opportunity of fighting offensively. His victory at Salamanca delivered southern Spain from French domination. Wellington's 'gamble' to force the French beyond Burgos failed, but was not disastrous.

The final offensive, which pushed the enemy back into France, was projected months before the army advanced. Supplies were then ordered to Galician harbours, and 'twice this amount of each item' was already prepared in Britain to be shipped when required.[3] When all was ready, Wellington's army hurtled forward swiftly; its great enveloping movements, so skilfully co-ordinated, quite confounded Joseph. Wellington won at Vitoria when neither Clausel nor Foy were present.

Wellington's strategic defence against Soult's counter-offensive led to

[1] Apparently the only French commander to appreciate how this river could be used by the Allies to protect themselves against superior forces before Wellington actually did so was Napoleon, then hundreds of miles away.

[2] Massena commanded over 125,000, but only took across the border between 75,000 and 80,000 men.

[3] This *matériel*, to the last cannon ball and bag of flour, was ready and waiting to be shipped, a remarkable example of the fine support Wellington received from home.

a bloody repulse of the French in the Battles of the Pyrenees. Wellington then crossed into France, but he first isolated and blockaded Bayonne, before forcing Soult to retire on Toulouse; all this was the result of carefully co-ordinated manoeuvres of the entire Allied army. Wellington achieved strategic surprise often by varying the emphasis of his attack, but never by taking chances. He could bluff successfully when required to do so by a situation which developed during a campaign, but never counted on it in his plans. He appreciated, after the Pyrenees were crossed, that his was the more powerful army, but he did not risk it unnecessarily.

Wellington's combat tactics and manoeuvres were, of course, finally responsible for his victories on the battlefield. A number of commanders have been capable of organizing a good army, and conceiving grand strategy. Only a few have been able to fight well on the field of battle.

The army would take up a defensive position on a reverse slope with protected flanks, with a powerful security line of skirmishers in front, and artillery dispersed, but well forward. If the French attacked, their *tirailleurs* were neutralized and their columns destroyed by musketry from the thin red lines. French cavalry, supposedly the finest of battlefield horsemen, had to their credit during six long years struggle with Wellington only the temporary disorganization of two new battalions on the third day at Fuentes, which were immediately protected. French artillery, the Emperor's pride, influenced the final result of battles not at all.[1]

Offensive tactics are more subject to variation than defensive, for they depend to a great extent on the formation and position of the enemy. Wellington employed his skirmishers to drive in French *tirailleurs*, and his lines to shatter their columns. Opposing artillery was taken, or driven off by the speed of the Allied infantry attack, before it could do decisive damage. Terrain and other factors prevented Wellington from employing his own cavalry as shock troops in battle, except at Salamanca where Le Marchant's dragoons were extremely effective. At the same battle, the C-in-C broke a French division in line by enfilading artillery fire from two massed batteries, but the massing of Allied artillery was unusual.

[1] Cavalry and artillery were both of real value to the French at Albuera, but Wellington was not there.

In driving Massena from Portugal and Soult through southwestern France, Wellington showed a remarkable facility for co-ordinating several separated units, each fighting isolated actions. He overwhelmed one or more sectors while holding others inactive; he was inevitably flanking any point or points which he was attacking frontally. Wellington's movements were governed by shrewd common sense. If his opponent reacted in some other way, or took up other positions, he would have continued the attack with appropriate combinations.

Although Wellington preferred to be attacked, he had no use for field fortifications. He took up defensive positions primarily to shield his infantry from artillery, and then attacked the enemy as they were nearing their objective. Both offensive and defensive battles were fought by the Allied army unprotected by fieldworks. Those few that were constructed were never used. On the other hand, Wellington made liberal use of the spade in improving his lateral communications; his form of defence was strong on account of its lack of rigidity. Reinforcements could reach any point in a defensive line quicker than from a corresponding position in the original offensive formation.

The intellect which can master intricate organizational problems, including diverse and detailed military and political factors, frequently cannot handle troops in action. Wellington could move a battalion, a brigade, a division, a corps, or entire armies as if they were limbs of his own body. Had Arthur Wellesley been killed at any time before 22nd June 1813, Napoleon would have remained on the throne of France. In no other activity of men is one man so important as he who directs an army in battle, and the responsibility was even greater 150 years ago.

But this battlefield genius went further than mere direction and articulation. Wellington had great powers of anticipation. So often in reviewing an individual battle one comes upon a sudden decision made by him which eventually proved to be decisive to the Allied victory. At Rolica, when Lake attacked prematurely, Wellington threw forward other brigades to cover the 28th and took advantage of the disarrangement of the French line. At Vimiero, Wellington shifted three-fifths of his force immediately he saw the direction in which the French army was moving. At Talavera, he anticipated that his centre would pursue too far and be broken by the French support; he formed a second line. This capacity of making an immediate and correct decision won Busaco, Fuentes de Onoro, Salamanca and Sorauren; even Orthez, when Colborne and his 52nd were sent forward. So frequently throughout the war, Wellington was in exactly the right place to make the essential

decision instantly; He was a counter-punching fighter, a master of his
art who was at his best under the pressure of battle.

Wellington has been frequently criticized over the years. Some ludicrous
statements have been made by French historians, who endeavouring to
glorify either Soult or Napoleon, attack almost every disposition
that Wellington ever made. They accuse him of being either overcautious or rash in every action. Occasionally, he is accused of being
both at the same time, by different writers, or even by the same writer.

At the other extreme, Fortescue and Oman had a critical approach
to military history. They were extremely competent, but felt it necessary to offer alternative solutions to Wellington's problems. They had
complete knowledge, unlimited time, and no other responsibilities.
Their opinions certainly appear sound, yet one wonders if their alternative suggestions would have worked out in practice. Soult had no
trouble in making fine plans, but never won a battle against the Duke.
Criticism of this type may obscure what actually happened, and lessen
the worth of what is written. To fault Wellington on his strategy or
tactics is ill-advised. To venture an opinion contrary to his concerning
the British army appears to me to be ridiculous. How can a writer
living a century later know more of the army from studying diaries
and memoirs, than Wellington knew from daily contact over many
years?

Wellington has been criticized for not producing good subordinate
generals. Is this true? Hill was uniformly successful in independent
command; Graham and Beresford were above average. Few commanders have been more fortunate. Even if this criticism were true, is
it valid? Should a C-in-C endeavour to win battles, or set himself up
to be a kind of military schoolmaster?

Wellington has also been condemned for not remaining faithful to
his wife throughout his seven years away from home. He was scrupu-
lously honest and lived precisely in accordance with his personal code
of gentlemanly behaviour. Wellington was a powerful man at the
peak of his physical strength. His health and well-being were matters
of extreme importance. His actions were never in any way flagrant nor
inappropriate, but could not be concealed entirely because of his

position.[1] Life at headquarters could hardly have been more simple and decorous.

> 'Everything was strikingly quiet and unostentatious ... no one would have suspected that he was quartered in the town. There was no throng of scented staff officers with plumed hats, orders and stars, no main guards, no crowd of contractors, actors, valets, cooks, mistresses, equipages, horses, dogs, forage and baggage wagons, as there is at French or Russian headquarters! Just a few aides-de-camp, who went about the streets alone and in their overcoats, a few guides, and a small staff guard; that was all! About a dozen bullock carts were to be seen in the large square of Fuente Guinaldo, which were used for bringing up straw to headquarters: but apart from these no equipages or baggage trains were visible.' [2]

Wellington was not idolized by his soldiers as some successful generals have been. He cared little for personal popularity, sometimes even appearing to go out of his way to avoid it. He was captain of a team; when it performed badly, he did not administer criticism with proportionate severity, but blasted everybody, innocent and guilty alike. They all did better the next time. Wellington was a driver; he was at his best that way.

Wellington has been called undemocratic. This was natural to a man who spent his military career fighting against the greatest spontaneous democratic upheaval of all time, the French Revolution and the various evolutions in French political power which followed. Wellington was no hypocrite; his personal experience with democracy had emphasized its weaknesses. Neither the Irish House of Commons nor the Spanish Cortes inspired confidence in the system. Councils of War are notoriously poor at running military operations; why should the same basic principle work any better in the governing of a nation?

Wellington was an aristocrat and a gentleman; he was coldly efficient, confident of his own ability, and sure of the army he created. He

[1] His criticism of his oldest brother for flaunting his amours was very sharp, *Wellington at War*, 137 and 189. His condemnation of certain unseemly conduct of junior officers is also strong, ibid., 173,

> 'I believe that there is no officer upon the General Court Martial who wishes to connect the term Honour with the act of going to a Brothel; the common practice forbids it; and there is no man who unfortunately commits this act who does not endeavour to conceal it from the world and his friend.'

[2] *Schaumann*, 317.

might not be greatly loved by his men, but when it came to fighting, they wanted him to lead them, and no one else. His greatest vote of confidence came that morning above Sorauren, and was first cast by the Portuguese *Cacadores*. 'Douro! Douro! Douro!' they shouted. The British, from Picton to the youngest drummer-boy, understood, and caught up the cry. Both disorganized retreat and the danger of defeat were over. 'Arty' would set things right; he never failed them, nor asked them to do anything beyond their strength on any field.

BIBLIOGRAPHY

THE works of three men have been of major importance in my research. Wellington himself comes first; most of his writings appear in Gurwood's edition of his *Dispatches*, and the *Supplementary Dispatches* edited by the 2nd Duke, but many other volumes contain certain letters from him, and orders not found elsewhere. There are extensive reports of conversations with him. The other two were historians, writing about a century after the events which they describe. Oman's *A History of the Peninsular War*, and Fortescue's *A History of the British Army* are together perhaps the best secondary sources available for any single period in military history.

Guedalla's magnificent short biography, *The Duke*, and Napier's *History of the War in the Peninsula* are of hardly less value. Diaries, reminiscences, and memoirs of men who were themselves present at actions which they describe accurately are also of considerable importance.[1] A few specialized studies are of great merit. Oman's *Wellington's Army* is particularly rewarding, but his *Studies in the Napoleonic Wars* is uneven. Muriel Wellesley's *The Man Wellington*, compiled from contemporary sources, gives a good likeness of the Duke. Ward's *Wellington's Headquarters* is a superb modern study of great value in a specialized field.

A vast mass of material, both primary and secondary, is of somewhat lesser importance, but almost every book published has some interest or merit. Many are superior from a historical point of view to volumes which outsold them. Southey's *History of the Late War in Spain and Portugal* was completely eclipsed by Napier, but was carefully written and far less influenced by personal prejudice.

---

[1] The most interesting from a historical point of view are those written in the form of diaries and journals and committed to paper immediately, or within a few days. Reminiscences written late in life, particularly after reading *Napier*, are often of far less value. *Harry Smith* is an exception.

I pretend to no all-inclusive knowledge in this wide field, nor have I consulted manuscript sources. The bibliography is reasonably complete in regard to military operations. Neither Oman nor Fortescue ever compiled any.[1] There are two separate lists below; those in the first are works which have been referred to two or more times in the Notes and References and are prefixed by their *short titles*. The second lists all other works which I have consulted, even if briefly. I am sure that there are others which I have overlooked. Some books in the second list are more important and of greater historical value than some in the first.

SHORT TITLES USED IN NOTES AND REFERENCES

All books were published in London, unless otherwise stated

Beatson: Beatson, Brig. Gen. F. C., WITH WELLINGTON IN THE PYRENEES, BEING AN ACCOUNT OF THE OPERATIONS BETWEEN THE ALLIED ARMY AND THE FRENCH FROM JULY 25TH TO AUGUST 2ND, 1813. 1914.

Beatson: Bidassoa and Nivelle: Beatson, Major Gen. F. C., WELLINGTON: THE BIDASSOA AND NIVELLE. 1931.

Bell: Bell, Douglas, WELLINGTON'S OFFICERS. 1938.

Blackmore: Blackmore, Howard L., BRITISH MILITARY FIREARMS 1650–1850. 1961.

De Rocca: De Rocca, M. (Translated by Maria Graham), MEMOIRS OF THE WAR OF THE FRENCH IN SPAIN. 1816.

Dispatches: Gurwood, Lt. Col., THE DISPATCHES OF THE FIELD MARSHAL THE DUKE OF WELLINGTON DURING HIS VARIOUS CAMPAIGNS IN INDIA, DENMARK, PORTUGAL, SPAIN, THE LOW COUNTRIES, AND FRANCE, FROM 1799 to 1818. 1837–8.

Duncan: Duncan, Capt. Francis, HISTORY OF THE ROYAL REGIMENT OF ARTILLERY. 1872.

Dundas: Dundas, Col. David, PRINCIPLES OF MILITARY · MOVEMENTS, CHIEFLY APPLIED TO INFANTRY. 1788.

D'Urban: D'Urban, Major Gen. Sir Benjamin (Edited by I. J.Rousseau), THE PENINSULAR JOURNAL OF MAJOR GENERAL SIR BENJAMIN D'URBAN 1808–17. 1930.

[1] I have a collation of every reference used by Fortescue in that part of his work referring to the Peninsular War, and by Oman. There is an unfortunate lack of consistency, even by the same author in different volumes. Neither gives details of an edition, or even the exact title. In *Wellington's Army*, 375–83, Oman does give a list of books, mainly 'autobiographies, diaries, journals, and series of letters' of this period.

Fortescue: Fortescue, Hon. J. W., HISTORY OF THE BRITISH ARMY. 1899–1930.

Gardyne: Gardyne, Lt. Col. C. Greenhill, THE LIFE OF A REGIMENT. THE HISTORY OF THE GORDON HIGHLANDERS FROM 1794 TO 1898 INCLUDING AN ACCOUNT OF THE 75TH REGIMENT FROM 1787 TO 1881. 1903.

Grattan: Grattan, Lt. Gen. William, ADVENTURES WITH THE CONNAUGHT RANGERS, 1804–14. 1847.

Guedalla: Guedalla, Philip, THE DUKE. 1931.

Harry Smith: Smith, Sir Harry, THE AUTOBIOGRAPHY OF LIEUTENANT-GENERAL SIR HARRY SMITH. 1901.

Hawker: Hawker, Col. P., JOURNAL OF A REGIMENTAL OFFICER DURING THE RECENT CAMPAIGN IN PORTUGAL AND SPAIN UNDER LORD VISCOUNT WELLINGTON, WITH A CORRECT PLAN OF THE BATTLE OF TALAVERA. 1811.

Hay: Hay, Major Leith, NARRATIVE OF THE PENINSULAR WAR. Edinburgh, 1831.

Jones: Jones, Col. John T., JOURNAL OF SIEGES CARRIED ON BY THE ARMY UNDER THE DUKE OF WELLINGTON IN SPAIN BETWEEN THE YEARS 1811 AND 1814. 1827.

Leach: Leach, Lt. Col. J., ROUGH SKETCHES OF THE LIFE OF AN OLD SOLDIER, DURING HIS SERVICE IN THE WEST INDIES: AT THE SIEGE OF COPENHAGEN 1807; IN THE PENINSULA AND THE SOUTH OF FRANCE IN THE CAMPAIGNS FROM 1808 TO 1814 WITH THE LIGHT DIVISION; IN THE NETHERLANDS 1815: INCLUDING THE BATTLES OF QUATRE BRAS AND WATERLOO. 1831.

Leslie: Leslie, Col. T., MILITARY JOURNAL. Aberdeen, 1887.

Londonderry: Londonderry, The Marquess of, NARRATIVE OF THE PENINSULAR WAR FROM 1808 TO 1813. 1828.

Man Wellington: Wellesley, Muriel, THE MAN WELLINGTON, THROUGH THE EYES OF THOSE WHO KNEW HIM. 1937.

Marbot: Marbot, Baron de, THE MEMOIRS OF BARON DE MARBOT. (Translated by Arthur John Butler.) 1893.

Maxwell's Peninsular Sketches: Maxwell, W. H. (Edited by), PENINSULAR SKETCHES: BY ACTORS ON THE SCENE. 1844.

Moore's Diary: Moore, Sir John, DIARY OF SIR JOHN MOORE (Edited by Gen. Sir T. F. Maurice). 1904.

Napier: Napier, Major Gen. Sir W. F. P., HISTORY OF THE WAR IN THE PENINSULA AND IN THE SOUTH OF FRANCE FROM THE YEAR 1807 TO THE YEAR 1814. (1832–40.) 1850.

Napier Autobiography: Napier, Gen. Sir George Thomas, PASSAGES IN THE EARLY MILITARY LIFE OF SIR G. T. NAPIER, WRITTEN BY HIMSELF. (Edited by W. C. E. Napier.) 1884.

National Biography: Stephen, Sir Leslie and Lee, Sir Sidney (Edited by), DICTIONARY OF NATIONAL BIOGRAPHY. Oxford, 1917.

Nineteen Movements: Anon, NINETEEN MOVEMENTS AS ORDERED FOR THE BRITISH ARMY. Calcutta, 1809.

Oman: Oman, C. W. C., A HISTORY OF THE PENINSULAR WAR. Oxford, 1903–30.

Oman's Moore: Oman, Carola, SIR JOHN MOORE. 1953.

Oman's Studies: Oman, Sir Charles (C. W. C.), STUDIES IN THE NAPO-LEONIC WARS. 1929.

Rifleman Harris: Harris, John (Edited by Henry Curling), RECOLLEC-TIONS OF RIFLEMAN HARRIS (1848). New York, 1929.

Schaumann: Schaumann, A. L. F. (Edited and translated by Anthony M. Ludovici), ON THE ROAD WITH WELLINGTON. THE DIARY OF A WAR COMMISSARY IN THE PENINSULAR CAMPAIGNS. 1924.

Sherer: Sherer, Col. Joseph Moyle, RECOLLECTIONS OF THE PENINSULA. 1824.

Stanhope: Stanhope, Philip Henry (5th Earl), NOTES OF CONVERSA-TIONS WITH THE DUKE OF WELLINGTON. (The World's Classics) 1947.

Supplementary Dispatches: Wellesley, Arthur, Duke of Wellington, (Edited by his Son, the Duke of Wellington), SUPPLEMENTARY DISPATCHES AND MEMORANDA OF FIELD MARSHAL ARTHUR DUKE OF WELLINGTON. 1858.

Surtees: Surtees, William, TWENTY-FIVE YEARS IN THE RIFLE BRIGADE. 1833.

Tomkinson: Tomkinson, Lt. Col. William, DIARY OF A CAVALRY OFFICER IN THE PENINSULAR AND WATERLOO CAMPAIGNS 1809 TO 1815. 1894.

T.S.: Anon., JOURNAL OF T.S. OF THE 71ST HIGHLAND LIGHT INFANTRY, in 'Memorials of the Late Wars'. Edinburgh, 1828.

Ward: Ward, S. G. P., WELLINGTON HEADQUARTERS: A STUDY OF THE ADMINISTRATION PROBLEMS IN THE PENINSULA 1809 TO 1814. Oxford, 1957.

Wellington at War: Brett-James, Antony, WELLINGTON AT WAR. 1961.

Wellington's Army: Oman, C. W. C., WELLINGTON'S ARMY 1809–1814. 1903 and 1913.

Wheeler: Wheeler, W. (Edited by Capt. B. H. Liddell Hart), THE LETTERS OF PRIVATE WHEELER 1809–1828. 1951.

Wyld's Atlas: Wyld, James, ATLAS—MAPS AND PLANS SHOWING THE
PRINCIPLE MOVEMENTS, BATTLES, AND SIEGES, IN WHICH THE BRITISH
ARMY WAS ENGAGED DURING THE WAR FROM 1808 TO 1814 IN THE
SPANISH PENINSULA AND THE SOUTH OF FRANCE. 1840.

OTHER WORKS

Anon., CHARACTER OF THE ARMIES OF THE VARIOUS EUROPEAN POWERS.
1802.

Anon., PAPERS PRESENTED TO THE HOUSE OF COMMONS RELATING TO
SUPPLIES AND MONEY EMBARKED FOR SERVICES IN PORTUGAL AND
SPAIN. 1809.

Anon., RULES AND REGULATIONS FOR THE MANUAL AND PLATOON EXER-
CISE FORMATION, FIELD EXERCISE, AND MOVEMENT OF HIS MAJESTY'S
FORCES. 1807.

Anon., THE TRIAL OF LIEUTENANT GENERAL SIR JOHN MURRAY, BY A
GENERAL COURT MARTIAL, HELD AT WINCHESTER. 1815.

Aldington, Richard, THE DUKE, BEING AN ACCOUNT OF THE LIFE AND
ACHIEVEMENTS OF ARTHUR WELLESLEY, FIRST DUKE OF WELLINGTON.
1943.

Alexander, Sir James Edward, LIFE OF FIELD MARSHAL, HIS GRACE, THE
DUKE OF WELLINGTON, EMBRACING HIS CIVIL, MILITARY AND POLITI-
CAL CAREER TO THE PRESENT TIME. 1840.

Anderson, Lt. Col. Joseph, RECOLLECTIONS OF A PENINSULAR VETERAN.
1913.

Anglesey, The Marquess of, ONE-LEG, THE LIFE AND LETTERS OF HENRY
WILLIAM PAGET FIRST MARQUESS OF ANGLESEY. 1961.

Aubrey-Fletcher, Major H. L., A HISTORY OF THE FOOT GUARDS TO
1856. 1927.

Barnes, Major R. Money, A HISTORY OF THE REGIMENTS AND UNIFORMS
OF THE BRITISH ARMY. 1954.

Beamish, Major North Ludlow, HISTORY OF THE KING'S GERMAN
LEGION. 1832.

Beatson, Major Gen. F. C., WELLINGTON, THE CROSSING OF THE GAVES
AND THE BATTLE OF ORTHEZ. 1925.

Bell, Sir George, ROUGH NOTES BY AN OLD SOLDIER, DURING FIFTY YEARS
SERVICE. 1867.

Beresford, Lord, REFUTATION OF COL. NAPIER'S JUSTIFICATION OF HIS
THIRD VOLUME. 1834.

Blakeney, Robert. A BOY IN THE PENINSULAR WAR, THE SERVICES, ADVENTURES AND EXPERIENCES OF ROBERT BLAKENEY. 1899.

Blayney, Major Gen. Lord, NARRATIVE OF A FORCED JOURNEY THROUGH SPAIN AND FRANCE, AS A PRISONER OF WAR IN THE YEARS 1810 TO 1814. 1814.

Buckham, Rev. E. W., PERSONAL NARRATIVE OF ADVENTURE IN THE PENINSULA DURING THE WAR IN 1812–1813. 1827.

Bunbury, T., REMINISCENCES OF PORTUGAL, SPAIN, FRANCE, INDIA, ETC. 1861.

Cole, John William, MEMOIRS OF BRITISH GENERALS DISTINGUISHED DURING THE PENINSULAR WAR. 1856.

Cooke, Capt.; Munster, The Earl of; Moodie, Lt. T. W. D., MEMOIRS OF THE LATE WAR: COMPRISING THE PERSONAL NARRATIVE OF CAPTAIN COOKE; A HISTORY OF THE CAMPAIGN OF 1809 IN PORTUGAL OF THE EARL OF MUNSTER, AND A NARRATIVE OF THE CAMPAIGN IN 1814 IN HOLLAND BY LT. T. W. D. MOODIE. 1831.

Cope, Sir William H., THE HISTORY OF THE RIFLE BRIGADE (THE PRINCE CONSORT'S OWN) FORMERLY THE 95TH. 1877.

Costello, Edward, ADVENTURES OF A SOLIDER WRITTEN BY HIMSELF. 1852.

Costello, Edward, MEMOIRS OF EDWARD COSTELLO OF THE RIFLE BRIGADE, COMPRISING NARRATIVES OF WELLINGTON'S CAMPAIGNS IN THE PENINSULA, ETC. 1857.

Crauford, Rev. Alexander H., GENERAL CRAUFURD AND HIS LIGHT DIVISION. 1891.

Croker, John Wilson (Edited by Louis J. Jennings), THE CROKER PAPERS. THE CORRESPONDENCE AND DIARIES OF THE LATE RIGHT HONOURABLE JOHN WILSON CROKER. 1885.

Cuninghame, James, THE TACTIC OF THE BRITISH ARMY, REDUCED TO DETAIL: WITH REFLECTIONS ON THE SCIENCE AND PRINCIPLES OF WAR: UNITING IN ONE VIEW, THE EVOLUTIONS OF THE BATTALION, BRIGADE, AND LINE, AND POINTING OUT THEIR COMBINATIONS WITH EACH OTHER, AND USES ON ACTUAL SERVICE. 1804.

Dalrymple, Gen. Sir Hew, MEMOIR, WRITTEN BY GENERAL SIR HEW DALRYMPLE, OF HIS PROCEEDINGS AS CONNECTED WITH THE AFFAIRS OF SPAIN, AND THE COMMENCEMENT OF THE PENINSULAR WAR. 1830.

Dalrymple, Lt. Col. William, TACTICKS. Dublin, 1782.

Davies, Godfrey, WELLINGTON AND HIS ARMY. Oxford, 1954.

Diez, Don Juan Martin, THE MILITARY EXPLOITS OF DON JUAN MARTIN DIEZ, THE EMPECINADO WHO FIRST COMMENCED AND THEN ORGAN- IZED THE SYSTEM OF GUERRILLA WARFARE IN SPAIN. 1823.

Donaldson, Joseph, RECOLLECTIONS OF AN EVENTFUL LIFE CHIEFLY PASSED IN THE ARMY. Glasgow, 1825.

Donaldson, Joseph, THE WAR IN THE PENINSULA, A CONTINUATION OF THE RECOLLECTIONS OF AN EVENTFUL LIFE OF A SOLDIER. Glasgow, 1825.

Douglas, Gen. Sir Howard, AN ESSAY ON THE PRINCIPLES OF CONSTRUCTION OF MILITARY BRIDGES AND THE PASSAGE OF RIVERS IN MILITARY OPERATIONS. 1853.

Dumouriez, Charles Francois Duperire, AN ACCOUNT OF PORTUGAL, AS IT APPEARED IN 1766 TO DUMOURIEZ, SINCE A CELEBRATED GENERAL IN THE FRENCH ARMY. 1797.

Eliot, William Granville, A TREATISE ON THE DEFENCE OF PORTUGAL, WITH A MILITARY MAP OF THE COUNTRY: TO WHICH IS ADDED, A SKETCH OF THE MANNERS AND CUSTOMS OF THE INHABITANTS, AND PRINCIPAL EVENTS OF THE CAMPAIGNS UNDER LORD WELLINGTON IN 1808 AND 1809. 1810.

Fane, John, MEMOIR OF THE EARLY CAMPAIGNS OF THE DUKE OF WELLINGTON IN PORTUGAL AND SPAIN. 1820.

Fitchett, W. H., WELLINGTON'S MEN—SOME SOLDIER AUTOBIOGRAPHIES. 1900.

Forbes, Major Gen. A., A HISTORY OF THE ARMY ORDNANCE SERVICES. 1929.

Fortescue, Hon. J. W., WELLINGTON. 1925.

Foy, Maximilien, HISTORY OF THE WAR IN THE PENINSULA UNDER NAPOLEON. 1827.

Foy, Maximilien, VIE MILITAIRE DU GENERAL FOY, ETC. 1900.

Fraser, Edward, THE SOLDIERS WHOM WELLINGTON LED, DEEDS OF DARING, CHIVALRY AND RENOWN. 1913.

Gleig, George Robert, THE LIFE OF ARTHUR DUKE OF WELLINGTON. 1865.

Gleig, George Robert, PERSONAL REMINISCENCES OF THE FIRST DUKE OF WELLINGTON, WITH SKETCHES OF SOME OF HIS GUESTS AND CONTEMPORARIES. 1904.

Gleig, George Robert, THE SUBALTERN. 1825.

Graham, Brig. Gen. C. A. L., STORY OF THE ROYAL REGIMENT OF THE ARTILLERY. Woolwich, 1944.

Halliday, Andrew, M.D., THE PRESENT STATE OF PORTUGAL, AND OF THE PORTUGUESE ARMY: WITH AN EPITOME OF THE ANCIENT HISTORY OF THAT KINGDOM, A SKETCH OF THE CAMPAIGNS OF THE MARQUIS OF WELLINGTON FOR THE LAST FOUR YEARS: AND OBSERVATIONS OF THE MANNERS AND CUSTOMS OF THE PEOPLE, AGRICULTURE, COMMERCE, ARTS, SCIENCES, AND LITERATURE. 1812.

Hamilton, Thomas, ANNALS OF THE PENINSULAR CAMPAIGNS FROM 1808 TO 1814. Edinburgh, 1829.

Harley, Capt. John, THE VETERAN, OR FORTY YEARS IN THE BRITISH SERVICE: COMPRISING ADVENTURES IN EGYPT, SPAIN, PORTUGAL, BELGIUM, HOLLAND AND PRUSSIA. 1838.

Henderson, Col. G. F. R. (Edited by Capt. Neill Malcolm), THE SCIENCE OF WAR, A COLLECTION OF ESSAYS AND LECTURES 1892–1903. 1905.

Hicks, James Ernest, NOTES ON FRENCH ORDNANCE—1717 TO 1936. Mt. Vernon, New York, 1937.

Jarry, Gen. John, INSTRUCTIONS CONCERNING THE DUTY OF LIGHT INFANTRY. 1803.

Jones, John T., WAR IN SPAIN AND PORTUGAL, AND IN THE SOUTH OF FRANCE. 1818.

Kincaid, Capt. John, ADVENTURES IN THE RIFLE BRIGADE IN THE PENINSULA, FRANCE AND THE NETHERLANDS FROM 1809 TO 1815. 1830.

Kincaid, Capt. John, RANDOM SHOTS FROM A RIFLEMAN. 1835.

Larpent, F. S. (Edited by Sir George Larpent), THE PRIVATE JOURNAL OF JUDGE-ADVOCATE LARPENT. 1853.

Leslie, Major John H. (Edited by), THE DICKSON MANUSCRIPTS BEING DIARIES, LETTERS, MAPS, ACCOUNT BOOKS, WITH VARIOUS OTHER PAPERS OF THE LATE MAJOR-GENERAL SIR ALEXANDER DICKSON (Series 'C'—From 1809 to 1818). Woolwich, 1905.

Lewin, Ross, THE LIFE OF A SOLDIER, A NARRATIVE OF 27 YEARS SERVICE IN VARIOUS PARTS OF THE WORLD. 1834.

Long, Lt. Gen. Robert Ballard (Edited by T. H. McGuffie), PENINSULAR CAVALRY GENERAL 1811–1813. 1951.

McGrigor, Sir J., AUTOBIOGRAPHY AND SERVICES WITH NOTES, ETC. 1861.

MacKinnon, Col., ORIGIN AND SERVICES OF THE COLDSTREAM GUARDS. 1833.

MacKinnon, Major Gen. Henry, A JOURNAL OF THE CAMPAIGN IN PORTUGAL AND SPAIN, CONTAINING REMARKS ON THE INHABITANTS, CUSTOMS, TRADE, AND CULTIVATION OF THOSE COUNTRIES, FROM THE YEAR 1809 TO 1812. Bath, 1812.

Mampel, Johan Christian, THE YOUNG RIFLEMAN'S COMRADE, A NARRATIVE OF HIS MILITARY ADVENTURES, CAPTIVITY AND SHIPWRECK. 1826.

Maxwell, Sir Herbert, THE LIFE OF WELLINGTON, THE RESTORATION OF THE MARTIAL POWER OF GREAT BRITAIN. 1907.

Mercer, Gen. Cavalie, JOURNAL OF THE WATERLOO CAMPAIGN KEPT THROUGHOUT THE CAMPAIGN OF 1815. 1927.

Muller, William, THE ELEMENTS OF THE SCIENCE OF WAR: CONTAINING THE MODERN, ESTABLISHED, AND APPROVED PRINCIPLES OF THE THEORY AND PRACTICE OF THE MILITARY SCIENCES: VIZ. THE FORMATION AND ORGANISATION OF AN ARMY, AND THEIR ARMS, ETC., ETC. 1811.

Neale, Adam, M.D., LETTERS FROM PORTUGAL AND SPAIN: COMPRISING AN ACCOUNT OF THE OPERATIONS OF THE ARMIES UNDER THEIR EXCELLENCIES SIR ARTHUR WELLESLEY AND SIR JOHN MOORE FROM THE LANDING OF THE TROOPS IN MONDEGO BAY TO THE BATTLE AT CORUNNA. 1809.

Patterson, Capt. John, THE ADVENTURES OF CAPTAIN JOHN PATTERSON WITH NOTICES OF THE OFFICES, ETC., OF THE 50TH, OR QUEEN'S OWN REGIMENT, FROM 1807 to 1821. 1837.

Pearce, Robert Rouiere, MEMOIRS AND CORRESPONDENCE OF THE MOST NOBLE RICHARD MARQUESS WELLESLEY. 1846.

Petrie, Sir Charles, WELLINGTON: A REASSESSMENT. 1956.

Roberts, Gen. Frederick Sleigh, THE RISE OF WELLINGTON. 1895.

Robinson, Major Gen. C. W., WELLINGTON'S CAMPAIGNS: PENINSULA-WATERLOO 1808–1815; ALSO MOORE'S CAMPAIGN OF CORUNNA. 1914.

Robinson, H. B., MEMOIRS OF LIEUTENANT-GENERAL SIR THOMAS PICTON, INCLUDING HIS CORRESPONDENCE, FROM ORIGINALS IN POSSESSION OF HIS FAMILY, ETC. 1836.

Rottenburg, Col de, REGULATIONS FOR THE EXERCISE OF RIFLEMEN AND LIGHT INFANTRY, AND INSTRUCTIONS FOR THEIR CONDUCT IN THE FIELD. 1798

Sheppard, E W., COOTE BAHADUR, A LIFE OF LIEUTENANT-GENERAL SIR EYRE COOTE. 1956.

Shipp, John, THE MILITARY BIJOU, OR THE CONTENTS OF A SOLDIER'S KNAPSACK, BEING THE GLEANINGS OF 33 YEARS' ACTIVE SERVICE. 1831.

Sidney, Rev. Edwin A. M., THE LIFE OF LORD HILL, LATE COMMANDER OF THE FORCES. 1845.

Southey, Robert, HISTORY OF THE PENINSULAR WAR. 1823–32.

Stothert, Capt. William, A NARRATIVE OF THE PRINCIPAL EVENTS OF THE CAMPAIGNS OF 1809, 1810, 1811, IN SPAIN AND PORTUGAL. 1812.

Vauban, THE NEW METHOD OF FORTIFICATION. 1762.

Warre, Lt. Gen. Sir William, (Edited by the Rev. Edmond Warre), LETTERS FROM THE PENINSULA 1808–1812. 1909.

Wilson, Lt. A. W., THE STORY OF THE GUN. Woolwich, 1944.

Yonge, Charles Duke, LIFE OF FIELD MARSHAL ARTHUR, DUKE OF WELLINGTON. 1860.

INDEX

topography 124; use of artillery at 136